The Folklore of Shropshire

The Folklore of Shropshire

by

Roy Palmer

Logaston Press

LOGASTON PRESS
Little Logaston Woonton Almeley
Herefordshire HR3 6QH

First published by Logaston Press 2004
Reprinted 2007, 2010, 2013, 2017
Copyright © Roy Palmer 2004

ISBN 978 1 904396 16 1

Set in Times by Logaston Press
and printed in Great Britain by
Bell & Bain Ltd., Glasgow

Contents

		page
	Acknowledgements	*vii*
	Introduction	*ix*
	Map of Shropshire	*xii*
Chapter 1	Landmarks	1
Chapter 2	Local Lore	25
Chapter 3	Water	47
Chapter 4	Warriors	67
Chapter 5	Worshippers	85
Chapter 6	Witchery	123
Chapter 7	Life	149
Chapter 8	Labour	175
Chapter 9	Leisure	203
Chapter 10	Music and Song	229
Chapter 11	Dance and Drama	261
Chapter 12	Calendar Customs	291
	Bibliography	321
	Index	329

The legends of Shropshire may be reckoned in hundreds. I believe that almost every type is represented in the county, stories of devils and giants, ghosts, bogies and monster fishes, submerged forests, buried treasure, curses come true, bells ringing under water, phantom hordes, freezing wells, black dogs—they come crowding thickly one on top of another. (Lillian Hayward)

Acknowledgements

I am, as ever, particularly indebted to my wife, Pat, for accompanying me on excursions to Shropshire, taking photographs, transcribing, inscribing and (on occasions) composing tunes.

Mike Raven of Market Drayton kindly gave me a copy of his unpublished 'A Shropshire Garland. Songs and Carols collected in Shropshire'. I have also found his *Shropshire Gazetteer* particularly useful and informative. Gordon Ashman, who died in 2003, was helpful in many ways. I knew him over many years, and I shall greatly miss his astuteness, good humour and sanity, as well as his knowledge.

I am indebted to Bev Langton for information on the Shrewsbury Morris, and to Jon Hayward for the loan of a photocopy of the tune books of Edward Philpott. I should also like to thank C.R. Bird, Douglas Brooks, E.C. Cawte, Mary-Ann Constantine, Alan Dakers, Wilf Darlington, Brian Davies, Philip Donnellan, Trevor Hill, Roger Hoole, Lavender Jones, Peter Morgan, Ron Nurse, Charles Parker, Henry Peacock, Gerald Porter, Phyllis Ray, Geoff Ridyard, Mike Rust, Myfanwy Thomas, Sally Tonge, Stephen Tunnicliffe, Jocelyn Williams and Veronica Thackeray.

I am grateful for the help of these institutions: Birmingham Reference Library, Bodleian Library, Folklore Society, Hereford Library, Herefordshire Record Office, John Rylands Library of the University of Manchester, Llandrindod Wells Library, Royal Air Force Museum (Cosford), Shropshire Records and Research Centre, St. Bride Printing Library, Vaughan Williams Memorial Library (English Folk Dance and Song Society), Worcestershire History Centre, Worcestershire Libraries.

For illustrations I thank Gordon Ashman pp.107 (upper) and 256; Colin Bird pp.43 and 44; Dr. J.C. Burne p.*xii*; *Guardian* and *Observer* p.52; Philip Donnellan pp.178 and 179; Hereford Library (for a photograph by Alfred Watkins) p.2 (lower); Jon Hayward p.239; Ironbridge Gorge Museum Trust p.51; Annie Jones p.269 (both); Logaston Press pp.4/5 (upper); Pat Palmer pp.*xi*, *xiii* (lower), 2 (upper), 3, 6 (lower), 7, 9, 10 (both), 11, 15, 18 (both), 21, 22 (both), 23, 24, 30, 31 (both) 34, 38 (both), 48, 54, 55, 57, 59, 61 (both), 62 (lower), 63 (both), 64 (both), 65, 66, 67, 80, 84, 87 (both), 90 (upper), 91 (lower), 92 (both), 93 (both), 106, 107 (lower), 108, 110 (both), 111 (all), 112 (upper two), 113, 114 (all), 115 (all), 116, 117, 125 (both), 126, 130, 140 (upper), 143, 177, 201, 203, 204, 206, 208, 230, 252, 254 (lower), 255, 309 and 310; Ted Picken pp.185 and 188; Canon Derek W. Price pp.153 and 183; Mrs. B. Rhys (items from the Wight Collection in Herefordshire Record Office) pp.1, 100, 140 (lower) and 172; Graham Roberts p.131 (upper), *Shrewsbury Chronicle* p.267; *Shropshire Magazine* pp.164 and 170, Shropshire Records and Research Centre pp.277 and 301; *Titterstone Clee*, ISBN 0950927406 pp.196 (both), 197 (both), 198 and 238; Dave Trumper p.266; Welsh Folk Museum p.235 and Mike Yates p.247. Postcards are from the author's collection.

Pat Palmer wrote the tune for 'Welcome Yule' and adapted that for 'Souling Song'.

Introduction

Far to the west in the mental landscape of my Leicestershire childhood lay Shropshire's blue hills, unremembered, because unvisited. My father's much-loved, red-haired mother, Selina Statham, came from there (Bayston Hill), but to his enduring grief she had died when he was a child and been replaced by an archetypically harsh step-mother. As a homage to his Shropshire connection my father visited 'the Show' as often as he could, and I picked up from him the expression to characterise a circuitous route of 'Going all round the Wrekin'.

Despite its modest stature (1,335 feet) the Wrekin has shown an uncanny gift for attracting attention. For John Leland in the 16th century it stood 'as a Pharos', and a local adage confirms that 'a Shropshire mon is nivver lost if he con see the Wrekin'. John Masefield, on the heaving deck of a ship out in Cardigan Bay mused:

> There, somewhere, nor-nor-east from me,
> Was Shropshire, where I longed to be,
> Ercall and Mynd, Severn and Wrekin, you and me.

The Wrekin, seen from Berrington

For George Farquhar the Wrekin was a symbol of the warmth of Shropshire people: he dedicated his play, *The Recruiting Officer*, to 'All friends round the Wrekin' because, in his view, 'the kingdom cannot show better bodies of men, ... more generosity, more good understanding, nor more politeness than is to be found at the foot of the Wrekin'.

A landmark of such prominence inevitably stimulated the imagination of those who saw it. In Edward Thomas's poem, 'Lob', the cultural baggage of an English countryman includes this:

Charlotte Burne

And while he was a little cobbler's boy
He tricked the giant coming to destroy
Shrewsbury by flood. 'And how far is it yet?'
The giant asked in passing. 'I forget;
But see these shoes I've worn out on the road
And we're not there yet'. He emptied out his load
Of shoes for mending. The giant let fall from his spade
The earth for damming Severn, and thus made
The Wrekin hill; and little Ercall hill
Rose where the giant scraped his boots.

Stories of the Wrekin make up only a part of the rich variety of the folk-lore of Shropshire. Anyone setting out to explore this is necessarily indebted to the seminal book, *Shropshire Folk-lore*, by Charlotte Burne, which in turn is based on extensive material gathered over many years by Georgina Jackson (1824-95), who was prevented by ill-health from seeing her work through the press. Burne (1850-1923), though, was no mere editor: she became a formidable and distinguished folklorist in her own right. Among the many whom her work deeply influenced was the novelist, Mary Webb (1881-1927).

Important though their work was, the songs and stories, customs and beliefs of Shropshire, did not end with these women. To take traditional singers alone, yet to come were May Bradley of Ludlow, Arthur Lewis of Hope Bowdler, Arthur Lane and Fred Jordan of Corvedale.

There is no longer a workhouse at Oswestry where 'Red Moll' when ordered to keep silent by the overseer threw a basin of broth at his head and was

Mary Webb, c.1897

Teme Bridge, near Llanfair Waterdine,
where Radnorshire ends and Shropshire begins

punished by being put in the scold's bridle. The mine is gone from which a collier came to tell a workmate's wife that he had been killed, only to be greeted with: 'You needn't tell me he's dead. After he went through the gate this morning he came back and kissed me again. ... He never done that before'. Yet as long as the Wrekin stands Shropshire's lore will last, subject to change and decay but also rebirth and re-invention.

A map of Shropshire from the 1930s

CHAPTER 1

Landmarks

Boundaries matter. Anyone questioning the point should consider the long-running dispute over a yard-wide strip of land at Hopesay which led to thousands of pounds in legal expenses and, early in the 21st century, a term of imprisonment for one of the contending neighbours.

In the past a boundary or mere might have been marked by a long-lived tree such as an oak, a specially-placed stone, or a purpose-built structure. Offa's desire to delineate the frontier between England and Wales resulted in the famous dyke which Maisie Herring memorably characterised as 'a long green roller that never breaks'. Other liminal ditches are of even greater antiquity.

Stone circles and monoliths, further man-made features of the landscape, continue to grip the imagination. Many are sited on Shropshire's abundant hills, whose names are deeply evocative: the Breiddens, made up of Moel y Golfa and the Middleton, Bulthey, Bausley, Criggin and Rodney's Pillar Hills;

The Wrekin in winter

1

Brown Clee, whose first element derives perhaps from the Welsh, *bryn* (hill) or *bron* (breast), and its second from the Old English, *clifu* (cliffs); Titterstone Clee, called after a great rocking stone, long since gone; the Stretton Hills—the Lawley, Caer Caradoc, Helmeth, Hazler Hill, Hope Bowdler Hill and Ragleth; and the 'blue-topped' Wrekin itself. (The epithet is the poet, John Dyer's)

The profiles of such hills and even more modest mounds, ever-present yet ever-changing with the weather, become part of the mental landscape of all those that know Shropshire, and it is not in the least surprising that they inspired storytellers. Below-ground features, too, exerted an inexorable pull on memory and emotion.

Brown Clee from Clee St. Margaret

Markers

The name of Meeroak Farm below Great Hagley, near Bucknell, incorporates the word for boundary. Another Meer Oak stood near Church Preen where the parishes of Buckley and Langley meet. The Ale Oak at Mainstone preserves the Old English word, *hale*, meaning corner or nook. Some of the many Round Oaks reflect the round or circuit followed when people perambulated their parish bounds (see chapter 5).

Mark stone at English Bridge, Shrewsbury

Hoar (grey or ancient) was almost synonymous with boundary-marker, as in the Hoar Stones between Hawkstone and Moreton Say, on Clunbury Hill, and near the Castle Inn at Bishop's Castle. There are two more Hoar Stones near Oswestry, one of which is also known as Carreg-y-Big (see below). A Mere Stone stands on Hoar Edge near Wilmoor Pool, south of Titterstone Clee. Brynbeddin Wood on Hodre Hill above Chapel Lawn is (or was) collectively owned by villagers, whose strips of land were indicated by mere stones.

Marker stones pointed the way along a section of ancient track which ran from Onibury over Brand Hill to Clungunford, then to Hopton Castle, Black Hill, Pen-y-Cwm and Pen-y-Wern, on to Rock Hill, north to Whitcott, and finally to Fron Camp and Newcastle before going into Wales. Alfred Watkins photographed a former waymarking stone by the English Bridge at Shrewsbury. Near the Severn ferry crossing at Hampton Loade the Butter Cross can still be seen. It may have been a sort of signpost to the crossing or a meeting place for a market. Local tradition at nearby Alveley suggests that in times of plague farmers' wives from round about preferred to sell their wares at the cross rather

Butter Cross, Alveley

than go into the village. Markets were held at the Croeswylan Stone south of Oswestry during an outbreak of plague in 1559. Not far away is Carreg-y-Big (pointed stone), at Crown House, Selattyn, which may have marked both a boundary and a battle, since battles were often fought on boundaries.

The tower on Callow Hill at the south-western end of Wenlock Edge, constructed in 1838, may have been intended to mark where different landowners' holdings met. Its name, Flounder's Folly, comes from the builder, Benjamin Flounder of Ludlow. It is said that he wished to provide work during a slump, and that from the top of the tower he hoped to see his ships riding at anchor in Liverpool Bay.

Dykes and Ditches
Offa's Dyke was formerly known in Shropshire as Offa's or Awf's Ditch. According to Charlotte Burne, people

Offa's Dyke to the west of Oswestry, here running along the far edge of the field in the foreground

thought it 'a furrow turned up by the Devil in a single night with a plough drawn by a gander and a turkey'. Michael Drayton in 1613 characterised it as '... that Mound which *Mercian Offa* cast / To runne from Northe to South, athwart the Cambrian wast[e]'. The dyke and the modern long-distance path which takes its name follow sometimes diverging routes from the Bristol Channel to the Irish Sea. They enter Shropshire just above Knighton and leave near Selattyn. Most of Clun Forest and also the parish of Llanyblodwel are to the west of the dyke, despite being English. Contrariwise, Church Stoke, Hyssington and Mellington lie to the east of it, though they are in Wales.

Offa, king of the Mercians from 757 until 796, is claimed somewhat fancifully to have founded Shrewsbury on the site of the lost city of Pengwern (see chapter 4). He seized power during the civil war which followed the assassination of Aethelbald, his cousin. Aethelbald had his own dyke, 37 miles long, stretching from the Dee estuary to Old Oswestry hill fort, south-west of the present town. Roughly half of this runs some three miles to the east of Offa's Dyke, and is known as Wat's Dyke—from the Welsh, *gwaeth* (worse), said Hartshorne. The 15th-century record of the dyke as Clawdd Wade has led to a suggestion that a Mercian general called Wada supervised construction and left behind his name. The area in between the two dykes was once a sort of buffer-zone or no-man's-land between Welsh and English; or, as the poet, Thomas Churchyard had it, between Danes and Britons.

Wat (or Aethelbald) may have inspired Offa to build bigger and better. Another possibility is that Offa decided to emulate his ancestor and namesake, the 4th-century Offa of Angel, who according to tradition ordered a boundary dyke to be constructed across what is now Schleswig-Holstein. Stories of a bad but beautiful wife may also have migrated from one Offa to the other. For some

heinous crime the lady is cast adrift in a boat without sail, rudder or oars. She makes a landfall in Britain and is taken to Offa, who promptly marries her. She reverts to her habits of murderous scheming and plotting. Kyndrytha, for that is her name in the Mercian stories, orders Ethelbert of East Anglia to be killed in 794 at Sutton Walls, near Hereford, where she and Offa had invited him as a possible suitor for their daughter. Death turned Ethelbert into a martyr and miracle-worker, and one of his posthumous cures profoundly affected Lydbury North (see chapter 5).

Cantlin Stone

More Stones

Near Craignant, north-west of Selattyn, a 19th-century stone marks Offa's Dyke at that point. Other monoliths are associated with various individuals. An eight-foot block at Whitcot Keysett commemorates a prehistoric hero whose name unfortunately has not been recorded. Another anonymous victim of much more recent date was found, robbed and murdered, in a remote spot just off the Kerry Ridgeway in 1691. The pedlar's brass-bound box in which he would have carried cutlery and trinkets for sale turned up close by, broken and empty. The man was dubbed William Cantlin from the punning William Cantell, since only he can tell his name, people said. The parish of Mainstone declined to bury him, so Bettws-y-Crwyn did, and erected a small stone with his presumed initials where the body had been discovered. So things stayed until 1858, when Beriah Botfield of Hopton Wafers, MP for Ludlow, had an elaborate cross erected instead. Eventually this disintegrated, and in 1997 the fragments were removed to Bettws churchyard and placed on Cantlin's grave, where they can be still seen. A replica was installed where he had died. The original charitable action by the parishioners of Bettws received its recompense in 1875 when the Parliamentary act enclosing Clun Forest brought the murder site within the bounds of the village.

A more fortunate life is remembered near Melverley, where an obelisk on the Breidden Hills is dedicated to Admiral Lord Rodney (1718-92), who had no personal connection with the area but apparently remarked that in his opinion Montgomeryshire oak surpassed all others for shipbuilding. Local tradition, as expressed by Peter Davies of Little Ness, turned this into

The western side of Rodney's Pillar with its Welsh inscription

The Breidden Hills from the Severn

the belief that Rodney 'sighted from Liverpool the oaks on the foothills of the Breiddens which would provide timber for his ships'—a curious reversal of the notion that Benjamin Flounder looked from Wenlock Edge to see his ships at Liverpool.

A group of Montgomeryshire gentlemen, grateful for Rodney's fillip to their commerce, paid for the 57-foot pillar to be erected in 1781. Formal inauguration followed on 10 August 1782, a date subsequently unforgettable for at least one person, the labourer who fell asleep at Melverley on a haycock which was swept away by a sudden flood caused by a cloudburst on the Vyrnwy. He woke up only when the hospitable haycock, still intact, reached Montford Bridge, 11 miles down the Severn. The west face of the pillar bears an inscription in Welsh, with an English translation:

> Y colofnau uchaf a syrthiant
> ar tarrau cadarnaf a ammharant,
> on clôd Syr Sior Brydges Rodney,
> a gynnydda beunydd
> ai enw da ef ni ddilevir.

The boulder at Mainstone which is believed to have given the village its name

> The highest pillars will fall,
> the strongest towers will decay,
> but the fame of Sir George Brydges Rodney
> shall increase continually,
> and his good name shall never be obliterated.

A rather more modest relic is a rough boulder thought to have given the village of Mainstone its name, both elements of which—the first is the Welsh, *maen* (stone)—mean the same thing. The stone, which used to stand outside the west gate of the churchyard, is now kept by the pulpit inside the church. Village youths once demonstrated their strength by heaving up the two hundredweight stone and throwing it back over one shoulder. Another granite mass known as the Brading Stone had a part to play at Norton-in-Hales, where formerly anyone choosing to work after midday on a Shrove Tuesday would be seized and bumped (? bradled) against it.

Eccentric behaviour is attributed, tongue-in-cheek or otherwise, to certain stones. At the Beeches (formerly called the Beach), east of Montgomery, a massive stone called the Whirlstone stands in the brook, where it turns (hence the name) when it hears the cock crow. Surely, this means never, but in past times, cockcrow or no, people believed that it turned on Wake Sunday. The Lea Stone, two miles east of Bishop's Castle, girates only when the clock strikes 13, which cannot be very often. H.T. Timmins heard this explanation as to how the stone got there from 'an old fellow breaking stones by the wayside' in the 1890s:

> Oh, they 'ud used to tell us, when we was childern, as the Devil fell lame one day a-walkin' by here, and throwed that there old stwun out of's shoe, and then fled away up to Stiperstones yander.

Conversely, the devil is said to have taken the stone out of his shoe as he sat in his chair on the Stiperstones and flicked it with his finger to Lea, nine miles away.

The devil is associated with another boulder on a hill near Horderley, not far from Craven Arms. Local belief has it that the devil would appear if anyone ran round the stone 20 times. The *Shrewsbury Chronicle* reported in 1916 that children gathering wimberries on the hill put some of the fruit into holes in the stone so as to avoid offending the devil. On another hill, Whitsburn, south-west of Minsterley, is the Lord's Stone, a monolith on which the devil trod so hard as he rushed from the Stiperstones that his footprints sank into it.

Stone Circles

Strangely enough, no satanic associations are reported from Shropshire's stone circles, though Augustus Hare thought Mitchell's Fold to be 'universally regarded by the natives as the abode of "pooks"'. The word—English, puck, Welsh, *pwca*—means mischievous or malicious spirit. Of the four circles which were close to Corndon Hill near the Montgomery border, the last vestiges of Mitchell's Fold Tenement and the Whetstones were destroyed towards the end of the 19th century. The splendidly-named Waldegrave Brewster, vicar of Middleton-in-Chirbury from 1872 until 1901, wrote of the latter that 'A few years before I came here the last stone was blasted'. He added that according to local tradition the Whetstones marked the burial place of soldiers killed in battle.

Widow Preece of Rorrington told Brewster in 1881 that the Hoarstones were a fairies' ring, and that six 'fairesses' danced there on moonlit nights. This circle is on damp moorland—hence the alternative names of Marshpool and Black Marsh—at the foot of Stapeley Hill. Gaps in the ring to the north, east

Corndon Hill from Hyssington Churchyard

and south-west aligned respectively with Bromlow Callow, the Stiperstones and Corndon Hill. Two stones had small holes drilled, and local miners would fill these with black powder and set it on fire to celebrate a wedding. An older tradition from the days of clandestine open air catholic masses claims that the sacrament was given from these holes, and that the circle for this reason bore the name of the Roman Stones.

Edward Lhuyd, the illegitimate son of Edward Lloyd of Llanforda, was probably educated at Oswestry School. He went on to Jesus College, Oxford, and in 1691 became keeper of the Ashmolean Museum. Two years later he was invited to contribute additional notes on the antiquities of Wales to Edmund Gibson's translation from Latin to English of Camden's *Britannia* (published in 1695, the original having appeared in 1586). As a result of the request, Lhuyd visited Medgel's Fold, as he called it, on Stapeley Hill. However, according to W.T. Bryan, the sketch he made shows the circle known as Mitchell's Fold Tenement, some 300 yards from Mitchell's Fold itself.

The name, Mitchell, derives from the Old English, *micel*, meaning large. It seems that the first written mention of tales attaching to the circle came in a letter from a James Ducarel to his brother in 1752: 'I must tell you that the country people have many legends, fables, and traditions concerning Medgley's Fold, where they say a great personage, I believe a Giant, used to milk his cows'.

Some 40 years later the giant had become a witch who milked a bountiful cow into a sieve and caused her to disappear; and only in 1841 did Charles

Mitchell's Fold

Hartshorne add, in *Salopia Antiqua*, that the deranged cow wandered as far as Dunsmore Heath in Warwickshire, to be killed there by Sir Guy of Warwick. In 1862 Thomas Wright provided a full version of the whole story in his paper, 'On the Local Legends of Shropshire':

> The peasantry of the neighbourhood tell us that this district, without being more fertile, was once more populous than it is at present, and that the population was kept from starvation by a benevolent being which

The bountiful cow ...

came nightly, in the shape of a white cow, and abundantly supplied the inhabitants with milk. A condition, however, was attached to the comparative happiness of the people; and this was, that if the cow were milked dry, which, it appears, could not happen so long as each person took only a pailful at a time, she would disappear for ever, and the people would be reduced to extreme misery. Now, there lived at the same time a malevolent old witch, who was envious of the flourishing condition of the people of the neighbourhood, and meditated continually on the means of overthrowing it. Her name was Mitchel. One night she went with the others, apparently one of the peasantry of the neighbourhood, but carried a pail with a sieve for the bottom. The milk, of course, passed through this, and the cow, who always allowed herself to be milked by each person until the pail was full, let Mitchel go on milking until at last she became dry. The condition was immediately fulfilled, and the population of this now solitary district all died miserably for want of their usual food; but divine vengeance fell upon the wicked hag, who was turned into a stone on this lofty hill, and the circle of stones was raised to imprison her. Hence it is still called *Mitchel's Fold*. I asked a woman of the locality, who had just given me a rather imperfect version of the legend, if she knew what ultimately became of the cow, and she replied, 'Why, yes, sir; I have heard that it was turned into a dun cow, and that it went away a great distance from hence to the Earl of Warwick'.

Brewster gleaned a little more from his parishioners, who told him that there was once a horizontal stone across two of the uprights in the circle, and that one

... and malevolent milker on a capital at Middleton-in-Chirbury

Bowdler of Middleton Hall who blasted stones and brought them down to edge a horsepond never prospered afterwards. In addition, Widow Preece related:

> Rowlands of Priest Weston, when a servant at Hockleton, with some others went up to Mitchell's Fold one night to see what was to be seen. They saw a headless woman milking the cow into a can. They tried to enter the fold but could not. They went back to the hedge and saw an old woman with a head milk or drip the cow into a riddle. The cow then disappeared. They tried to enter the fold again and look for drippings on the grass but again failed to enter.

Brewster also noted this poem:

> Once through the land, the old folks say, a. mighty famine spread;
> Old age and tender infancy died out for want of bread,
> And brave strong men grew pale with want, and hollow-eyed with grief,
> To see their dear ones suffering when there was no relief.
> No more the labourer's happy song woke with the summer's morn,
> No more the farmer's wide-stretched fields stood thick with full-eared corn.
> For cruel famine ruled the land, and want's relentless ire
> Had long since hushed the children's laugh and damped the cottage fire.
> But there were fairies in those days (I wish there were some now),
> And one came through the country then, and brought with her a cow,
> A snow-white cow whose shape and size old people speak of still,
> And closed her in the circle of grey stones on Stapeley Hill,
> And bade the slaving peasant wives each night and morning go
> With one pail each, and milk, she said, should never cease to flow.
> What words can tell the joy with which this bounty was received,
> And how they blessed the fairy cow who had such ample store
> That e'en when crowds were satisfied would yield one pailful more.
> Now in the country dwelt a witch, an ill-disposed old crone,
> Who practised not the good advice of letting well alone.
> Besides, it grieved her that although she had in sorcery dealt
> The people had not sought her aid when this distress was felt.
> So for their harm she wrought her spells, but vainly tried them o'er,
> Till she recalled the fairy's words, 'One pailful each, no more'.
> Then with full glee she took her pail, the bottom broke away,
> And placed a sieve where it had been, and started off, they say,
> Before the sunlight lit the earth or anyone was near,
> To see that she so drew the milk that it might disappear.
> And by this means the spell was loosed; the white cow sank away
> Down through the ground, but in the stones the witch was forced to stay.
> And when the thronging people came and found the woman there
> With her false pail, the much-loved cow they saw not anywhere.
> They saw the wasted milk and then knew what the witch had done,

So walled her up and left her in that living tomb of stone.
The famine passed but still this tale is in the country told
Of how the witch was starved to death, walled up in Mitchell's Fold.

W.T. Bryan's considered view is that Mitchell's Fold, in view of the high density of burial mounds and cairns in the vicinity, 'was the scene of rituals and rites of passage concerning fertility and birth, death and the afterlife, for the people who lived hereabouts thousands of years ago'.

Hills

The Wrekin's presence as Shropshire's best-known landmark has inspired powerful stories. The name transferred to the hill from Wroxeter.

An anthropophagous (cannibal) giant, identified by some as Gwendol-Wrekin ap Shenkin ap Mynyddmawr, holds off from attacking Shrewsbury only as long as the townspeople send him regular supplies of young women. After giving the giant a herbal brew which sends him into a deep sleep, one intended victim escapes. Back in Shrewsbury she tells how she has seen the bones of her forerunners, and the citizens resolve to send no more sacrificial victims. Incensed at being defied, the giant fills a great shovel with earth and sets out to bury the town. He is unsure of the way, and asks directions of a cobbler he meets at Haygate, near Wellington. The man shows the bag of shoes he is carrying home to be mended, and says he has worn them all out on the long walk from Shrewsbury. The giant, taken aback, lowers his shovel. Part of the earth slides off and forms Ercall; most of the rest becomes the Wrekin. He shakes off the last of it, and makes the Little Wrekin. Still angry, he starts out

The Wrekin from Wellington

The Needle's Eye

again from Charlton Hill with a fresh shovelful, but as he fords the Severn, falls in and drowns.

Individual features of the Wrekin have their own associations. Hell Gate and Heaven Gate, earthworks near the top of the hill through which the track passes, are evocatively named, as is the Bladder Stone—called Balder Stone by some, after the Norse god—at the south-western end of the hilltop path. On the south face of the latter is a narrow cleft, the Needle's Eye, tradition-ally attributed to cleavage in the earth at the time of the crucifixion. There is another Needle's Eye at the Stiperstones but this seems to lack the beliefs which have clung to its namesake at the Wrekin, where, according to John Wood, 'Lovers who thread the needle without stumbling may hope for a smooth passage through their married life together'. Colin and Janet Bord have a more elaborate version:

> Traditionally every young woman who visited the area would scramble through the cleft and be met on the other side by her boyfriend or fiancé, who would receive a kiss or, if this was not forthcoming, could demand a forfeit of any coloured ribbon or handkerchief that she might have with her. A girl who looked back while she was negotiating the cleft would never be married.

On the south-eastern side of the Wrekin a depression is known as the Raven's Bowl or the Cuckoo's Cup. The water there is reputed never to dry up, and it is considered lucky to drop in a pin. The feeder spring miraculously appeared in order to slake the thirst of a hermit who lived in a nearby cave and accounted for the hill's being known for a time as Mount St. Gilbert.

Some of the features are further explained in a story told by Wood:

> Two of the race of giants were exiled, and for a stronghold piled up the Wrekin with soil dug from the bed of the Severn, making a trench through which the river still flows. Their footprints along the top caused bare patches that have never since become grassgrown. In a quarrel one threw at the other his spade, which, missing him, cleft the Bladder Stone and formed the Needle's eye. Whilst the fight was going on a raven pecked at the eye of one, and the ensuing tear scooped out the Raven's Bowl, where it has never since dried up. The other giant now got the better of him of the teardrop, and heaped on top of him the Ercall, under which the blind monster still moans at night.

Shropshire seems to have more than its share of giants. The 13th-century *Romance of the Fitzwarrens* claims that the city of *Viroconium* (Wroxeter) was taken over by giants. Sir Lancelot slew two giants, Tarquin and Taruinius, at the Red Castle in Hawkstone Park, where there is also a Giant's Well. A female of the species is buried on Llanymynech Hill (see below). A Giant's Chair (duly marked on O.S. maps) is on Titterstone Clee, but another feature of the same name on the Stiperstones has become known as the Devil's Chair.

The word, Stiperstones, comes, says Michael Raven, 'from "stripped-stone", an effect caused during the last Ice Age, ... a geological freak that is unique to Britain'. The mystery and even fear generated by that serrated skyline led to sinister associations. According to one narrative, the devil came from Ireland with a leather apron full of stones either to block Hell Gutter, a ravine on the side of the hill, or to dam the River Severn. He sat down to rest on what became the Devil's Chair but when he got up his apron strings broke. The great stones were scattered all round, and can still be seen.

The Devil's Chair on the Stiperstones

Whenever he can the devil flops into the chair so that his weight can help to push the Stiperstones down, since he believes that if they sink into the earth, England, a country which he supremely hates, will perish. If anyone else sits in the chair a thunderstorm will immediately erupt. Mary Webb wrote this atmospheric passage in *The Golden Arrow*:

Giant under attack

> Nothing ever altered its look. ... It remained inviolable, taciturn, evil. It glowered darkly on the dawn; it came through the snow like jagged bones through flesh; before its hardness even the venturesome cranberries were discouraged. For miles around, in the plains, the valleys, the mountain dwellings it was feared. It drew the thunder, people said. Storms broke round it suddenly out of a clear sky; it seemed almost as if it created a storm. No one cared to cross the range near it after dark—when the black grouse laughed sardonically and the cry of a passing curlew shivered like broken glass.

The golden arrow of Webb's novel was lost on Earl's Hill, one of the summits of Pontesford Hill, possibly during the battle of 661 between the West Saxons and the Mercians, after which Wulfhere, son of Penda of Mercia, laid waste the country round about. Until the late 19th century people believed that anyone who found the arrow would come into a fortune. Crowds once flocked to the hilltop on Palm Sunday to look for the arrow and to enjoy games, drinking and dancing at Pontesford Wake (see chapter 12).

Various tumuli—above Ratlinghope just off the Portway over the Long Mynd, and near Old Field at Bromfield, which serves as Ludlow racecourse—are known as Robin Hood's Butts. On the latter of these Robin Hood took aim at the weathercock on Ludlow Church steeple, almost two miles distant. His arrow fell a few feet short and stuck on the chancel roof, where it remained. In fact, though, the iron arrow was the emblem of the Fletchers' Guild of Ludlow.

Underground

A golden arrow would indeed have been a thrilling find, and any notion of buried treasure has a powerful appeal. At Little Ness a mound by the church is believed to be associated with the 7th-century king of Powys, Cynddylan, the last Welsh lord of Pengwern. According to a local story a man who dug into the mound in search of treasure found a huge chest. When he lifted the lid a great black cat sprang out and glared at him. Undeterred, he fetched horses and a thick chain which he fixed to the chest. As soon as the horses began to pull the chain broke into a hundred pieces and the cat disappeared. What happened to the chest and its contents does not seem to have been recorded.

In 1344 a serpent or dragon guarded treasure at Bromfield. A Saracen magician obtained Earl Warren's permission to kill the beast, and managed to do so. Then a gang of men from Herefordshire set about digging for the treasure one night, only to be arrested on the orders of the earl, who pocketed whatever was found. Charlotte Burne believed that the story applied to a Denbighshire village called Bromfield, but Thomas Wright insisted on its Shropshire pedigree. He pointed out a similar event of 1287 at Wroxeter when an enchanter by the power of his magic forced a friend to relinquish the treasure he was charged with guarding.

A rather more likely tale concerns the outwitting of a credulous miser at Bishop's Castle, thanks to the belief that somewhere in the neighbourhood was a place where buried money would quickly double. Wright wrote:

> I have heard that ... there was ... a miserly old man, who had saved, for him, the considerable sum of £40, and who had a great desire to purchase a small plot of land; but on enquiry the price demanded for it turned out to be more than double the money he had been able to save. He was returning home, in sorrowful mood, when he met an acquaintance, who, to console him, told him that a similar thing had happened to himself, but that he had sought and found relief in this plot of ground where the number of coins buried was doubled. The miser fell into the snare, and buried carefully in the ground his forty sovereigns, with all the formalities required by the legend. At the same minute of the next month, which was the time specified ..., the miser went to dig up his money, and he certainly found it doubled in number of pieces, for instead of forty sovereigns of gold, there lay eighty brass buttons. His treacherous friend had disappeared, and his only consolation was the assertion of his other acquaintances, who maintained that his loss was a judgement upon him for making use of 'witchcraft'.

Giants are also associated with treasure. One of the breed buried his dead wife on Llanymynech Hill with her golden necklace. The deaths of three brothers who went looking for it failed to frighten off other searchers. Two giant brothers, one who lived at Norton Camp on the southern tip of Wenlock Edge, the other across the Onny Valley at View Edge, kept their treasure in a great chest in the cellars at Stokesay Castle. When either needed something from the chest if he did not have the key he called across the valley for the other

Stokesay Castle

Bridgnorth Castle

to throw it over. One day the key fell short and dropped into the castle moat, where it remains. One giant died of chagrin; the other's fate is not told. The chest, still undiscovered, like the cellars in which it lies, is guarded by a raven.

Treasure is still waiting to be found at Bridgnorth in a passage running under the Severn from the Hermitage (see below) to the castle. Various other strongholds reputedly have underground links: for example, a tunnel from Shrewsbury Castle to Lyth Hill; and another from Holdgate Castle to Upton Cressett, six miles away. Clun Castle has similar (possibly imagined) passages to a quarry above the village; south-east to the Pulpit Rock, by Rock of Woolbury; and north-east to a house called the Villa. The latter had a cellar

Clun Castle

in which a door with five small holes led to the passage. Some brave—not to say foolhardy person managed to insert his fingers, whereupon they were cut off by a stroke from a heavy blade inside. Unfortunately, the whole tale collapsed when the passage turned out to be an old drain.

More convincing is the story of Paul Holmyard, a tenant of Sir Vincent Corbet at Moreton Corbet in the time of James I. When he was faced with arrest over his religious views Holmyard fled into passages beneath the old chapel of the castle and emerged two days later at Clive, having made his way through the disused workings of a Roman copper mine.

Various religious establishments, perhaps prudently, had underground links, though the distances involved often make the suggested routes fanciful, to say the least. By this means Lilleshall Abbey was linked to Longford Hall, some three or four miles away, near Newport; Buildwas Abbey to Wenlock Priory; Haughmond Abbey to High Ercall, passing beneath the River Roden, and also to

Lilleshall Abbey

19

Rock Cottage, Bridgnorth, which had rooms extending into the cliff face

Shrewsbury Abbey. The latter had further passages to St. Mary's Church and to the Austin Friary, both inside the town. In Ludlow the Bull Inn had a tunnel to the church, and Ludford House another to the Teme.

Richard Gough tells of a cave near Myddle called Goblin Hole, which was 'made into a habitation'. William Preece who lived there for a time 'had killed a monstrouse boar, of soe large a size that the bristles on his back were as big as pikeeavell grains' (pitchfork prongs). Workmen who built a bridge nearby in 1649 called it Bristle Bridge, in remembrance of the story.

Until well into the 20th century some people in Bridgnorth, Quatford, and as far south as Shrawley, lived in sandstone caves, fashioned into dwellings and furnished with doors, windows and chimneys. Caves at the Hermitage on a bluff across the Severn from Bridgnorth, were indeed used by a series of hermits, including Ethelward, brother of the 10th-century Saxon king, Athelstan. The tradition that a tunnel led from the Hermitage beneath the river to the cellars of the castle, or alternatively to the Franciscan Friary in Bridgnorth's Low Town,

The Hermitage at Bridgnorth, c.1920

Ogof's Hole

was exploded in 1878 when a careful excavation revealed nothing. In the same year 'a worthy couple of the labouring class' was still living in part of the Hermitage, and the last tenant left only in 1928.

An earlier occupant was a witch (see chapter 6). Giants were often associated with such places: on the east side of Stapeley Hill there is a Giant's Cave, and a nearby field is called Giant's Grave. Ogo's or Ogof's Hole, a cavern beneath Llanymynech Hill (the entrance is just off the footpath which runs through a golf course) may have been a Roman copper mine, and Roman coins have been found there. People once believed that the cave had served as a prison for British slaves of the Romans; alternatively, that it led to fairyland and the enchanted castle of Carregofa. According to Maisie Herring, 'Into the cave they say a blind fiddler once wandered, and to this day you will be lifting a glass at the inn and you will hear him fiddling softly under your feet where he wanders lost in the tunnels ... (Or is it the sound of the Vyrnwy waters?)'. More prosaically, in Welsh, *ogof* means merely cave, and carregofa could be *carreg ofer*, waste stone.

Humphrey Kynaston, known as Wild Humphrey, lived at Myddle Castle until 1491 when, according to some, he was outlawed for killing a man at Church Stretton. Gough favours the view that he fled accumulated debts:

> Hee had two wives, but both of soe meane birth, that they could not lay claime to any Coat of Armes ... I have not heard of any children which wild Humphrey had but I have heard of much debt that hee had contracted; and being outlawed in debt, he left Myddle Castle (which hee had suffered to grow ruinous, for want of repaire), and went and shel-

Myddle Castle

tered himself in a Cave neare to Nescliffe; which, to this day, is called Kinaston's Cave, and of him the people tell almost as many romantick storyes, as of the great outlawe Robin Whood. Yet one thing I must remember that on a time when hee was gott over Mon[t]ford's Bridge, and was on that side Severne which is next Shrewsbury, and must needs returne over that bridge, the under shiriffe came with a considerable company of men to the bridge, (which was then made with stone pillars and wooden planks,) and haveing taken up severall plankes, and made such a breadth as they thought noe horse was able to leape over, they laid themselves in ambush; and when wild Humphrey returned, and was about to enter upon the bridge, they rose up to apprehend him, which he perceiving, put spurrs to his horse, and rideing full speed, leaped clearely

Montford Bridge, successor to the wooden structure of earlier times

over the breadth. The measure of this leape was afterwards marked out upon Knockin Heath, upon a greene plott by the way-side that leads from Knockin towards Nescliffe, with an H and a K cut in the ground att the ends of the leape. The letters were about an elne [ell, 3 feet 9 inches] long, and were a spade graff broad and a spade graff deep.

'Whilst Kynaston lived in the cave', added Hare, 'it is said that his mother came over from R[u]yton every Sunday to bring his dinner. He had a horse shod backwards, so that no one could trace him'. On Beelzebub, for that was the horse's name, in order to escape from pursuers Kynaston once leaped from the top of Nesscliffe to Ellesmere, a distance of nine miles. No doubt this started smaller, and gradually increased in the telling. Another version of the feat takes horse and rider a mere five miles, to Loton, and then on to the Breidden Hills.

Kynaston called one day on the Lloyds at Aston Hall, near Oswestry (where the present building dates only from 1760), and asked for a draught of ale. As he drank, still seated on Beelzebub, they were closing the gates and preparing to seize him, but when he had finished the beer he calmly slipped the silver tankard into his pocket, clapped heels to his horse, and jumped over the gates to freedom. The preternaturally clever horse, adding to suspicions that Kynaston benefitted from diabolical assistance, would pick its was up the steep steps to his cave when he whistled.

'His every want was supplied', wrote Burne, 'by the rich who feared him and by the poor who loved him'. For centuries after his death his favourite seat in the Three Pigeons Inn at Nesscliffe was pointed out, and for some

Kynaston's Cave. The stone steps have been superseded by a wooden staircase, but the cave entrance is barred

The Breidden Hills, seen from Kynaston's Cave

reason the coracle men of the Severn held him in particular esteem. After receiving a pardon from Henry VIII in 1516/7 he retired to a modest estate near Welshpool, and died there in 1534. For many years, pardon and will were preserved at Hardwick Hall, Welsh Frankton.

The cave continued to be occupied. One of the last to live there was a quarryman. Now the entrance is barred and the only tenants are bats, but the associations with Kynaston are still strong, and the place remains very much a landmark.

CHAPTER 2

Local Lore

The sheer variety and character of place names provides never-failing interest. Shropshire boasts the famous neighbouring villages of Wigwig and Homer, not to mention the joys of 'Doddington and Hollywaste, Cleeton St. Mary and Clee St. Margaret, Neen Savage and Neen Sollars, Baggins Wood and Baveny Wood, Stoke St. Milborough and Burwarton', all admired by Simon Evans, the literary postman of Cleobury Mortimer. On occasions, unaware of the origin of certain intriguing names, people made their own attempts at explanation. Fanciful or far fetched though it might be, folk etymology became well loved and widely repeated.

In western Shropshire, where almost 30 parishes border Wales—and indeed, many of them were once part of Wales—the Welsh language has left a considerable legacy in the names of villages and hamlets, farms and fields. 'The language only survives as a ghost in the hedgerows, with the place names offering mute reminders of a dead beauty': Hywel Williams's poignant and poetic remark on 'whole swaths of Wales' clearly also applies to parts of Shropshire. Field names in both Welsh and English are a threatened species in those areas where boundaries have been swept away in the cause of agricultural improvement, though once they and the stories behind them were widely known to local people.

When, to quote Dennis Crowther's lines, 'They never went far from the place they were born in, / With people next parish remaining obscure', villagers' fierce pride in belonging sometimes combined with acute hostility to outsiders. For analagous attitudes today one would need to look at soccer fans whose teams were involved in a derby match. Generic nicknames, familiar sayings and traditional rhymes all served to express rival sentiments.

Belonging—or otherwise—might well be demonstrated or revealed by the way of pronouncing the name of a place. People are still instantly and intuitively aware of accent and dialect, which can differ sometimes over distances of a few miles. Expressions and vocabulary, too, can be significant. I remember as a Midlander in Yorkshire using the expression 'all round the Wrekin' and seeing a friend's face light up. She turned out to be Shrewsbury born.

Some dialect words have gone or are going, partly because so many were connected with ways of life and working now abandoned. Dialectal pronunciation lingers. It would be sad if we could no longer recognise Shropshire men and women, if not by 'sharpness of shins' (see below), then at least by flavour of speech.

Origins

After their defeat by the Romans at Caer Caradoc, close to Knighton (see also chapter 4), the Britons, it is suggested, lurked near Garn Gap in the hope of taking revenge on the enemy. That is how the place acquired the name of Lurkenhope. On the other side of the Caer streams ran red with the blood of the slain for three days after the battle, and thus gave the River Redlake its name.

Rather less fancifully, Oswestry, a form of 'Oswald's tree', commemorates the Northumbrian king, martyr and saint who was defeated nearby in 642 by Penda, the pagan king of Mercia, at the battle of Maserfield. Oswald's body was butchered by the victors as a sacrifice to Woden, and the head, arms and legs hung from stakes (see chapter 3). The Normans seem to have called the place Oswalstreu, the Welsh (as they still do), Croesoswallt (Oswald's cross). Another battle, another derivation; and Haughmond Hill—locally pronounced Haymond or Aymon—overlooks the field of conflict of 1403 near Shrewsbury. Over 500 years on, an Edgmond woman told this story:

Caer Caradoc, near Knighton

> The time as the battle was, down by theer, the queen was roidin' awee fro' the battle—I suppose it 'ud be Queen Mary. And her'd gotten her horse's shoes turned backerts, as folks shouldna know the wee as her'd gone. And she was goin' up the hill, and theer coom a mon, and he says to her, 'Well, missis', he says, 'and how's the battle gettin' on?' And she answered him nothin' but 'Eh, mon', her says, joost loike that, 'Eh, mon', and niver said no moor, because her was froightened loike, at him speakin' to her; and so the hill come to be called Aimun 'Ill. It was an owd labourin' mon as towd may. We wun three on us gooin' to Sosebry, and we said, 'What was that place?' so then he towd us.

In fact, Queen Mary died in 1394, and Henry IV was married at the time of the battle to his second wife, Joan of Navarre.

The wheeze of throwing off pursuers by reversing a horse's shoes enjoyed a huge vogue, not least with the American makers of cowboy films. In Shropshire, apart from the fugitive queen, Dick Turpin tried it at New Invention and Humphrey Kynaston (see chapter 1) round Nesscliffe. Yet both farriers and experienced riders assure me that it is impractical to the point of impossibility.

Another horsey story concerns Gobowen. A passing cockney asks the blacksmith to replace a lost shoe while he remains mounted. The smith, whose name happens to be Bowen, works away, bent over the horse's hoof, then straightens up and asks for a shilling in payment. The rider gallops off, shouting 'There's a cockney's trick for you'. In response, the smith holds up the shoe he has merely pretended to fasten, and calls out 'And here is Go-y-Bowen's trick for you'. Hence, Gobowen, with the first syllable coming from the Welsh, *gof*, meaning smith. Scholars' insistence that the Welsh expression could only have been *Bowen-y-gof* did not prevent the tale from circulating: after all, metropolitan discomfiture has perennial appeal for provincials. Gobowen, by the way, may derive from Cob Owen (Owen's Cop or Mound), an earthwork in the locality.

Credulity has to be suspended with Selattyn's claim to come from the boast of a village schoolmaster, 'I sell Latin', as it does with the hoary account of the naming of the Strettons. James II—Charles II in another version—on a journey to Shrewsbury asks the name of the small village he reaches. He is told 'Stretton', and remarks 'It's a very little Stretton'. At the next place he makes a similar enquiry. The reply is again 'Stretton', and, having noticed a church there, the king observes 'It must be Church Stretton'. At a third village, after again being informed that its name is Stretton he exclaims, 'Why, they're all Strettons here, it seems'. Hence, Little, Church and All Stretton. Insipid though the tale may be, it is repeated in every guide book. It is true that James II visited Church Stretton, in 1687, but Alured Stretton (which became All) was first recorded in 1262, Parva (Little) in 1327, and

All Stretton and Caradoc Hill

Chirchestretton in 1337. The original settlement on a Roman road appeared as *Stratun* in the Domesday Book.

Along with scores of other Shropshire names, Cressage, as *Cristesache*, is there too. The oak of the last syllable could be the tree under which missionaries—in one account, St. Augustine himself—preached the gospel. The original tree seems to have stood near the site occupied by the present war memorial. A cutting from it, planted in a field some distance away, survived for 700 years, and was known as the Lady Oak. When this failed another tree grew from its hollow centre.

Jonathan Swift, clergyman and author of *Gulliver's Travels*, took shelter there one day from a thunderstorm as he travelled to Shrewsbury. A young couple he met confided that they were eloping and needed a parson to marry them, so Swift readily conducted the appropriate ceremony. Later, he wrote:

The Lady Oak, Cressage

Under an oak in stormy weather
I joined this rogue and whore together.
Let none but God who makes the thunder
E'er put this whore and rogue asunder.

Welsh Roots

Under the provisions of Henry VIII's act of union of 1536 the lordships of Clun, Chirbury, Oswestry and Whittington transferred from Wales to England. For over 200 years afterwards the Welsh language remained strong, and not merely in the areas formerly in Wales. It has been suggested that Welsh was once spoken to the point three miles east of Shrewsbury marked by Upton Magna. However, at Stanton Long, some distance farther east, as well as south, the field name of *penybrin* (hilltop) was recorded. In addition, at Quatford, almost as far east in Shropshire as it is possible to go, a tithe apportionment listed Commer alias *Cwm Mawr* (big valley) Wood.

During the 18th century several Shrewsbury printers turned out considerable numbers of ballads in Welsh (see chapter 10). At the same time the Welsh language flourished in Oswestry, where three centuries earlier the poet, Guto'r Glyn, had been made a freeman in gratitude for writing in praise of the town. When Richard Gough's uncle left money in his will for a sermon to be preached in Oswestry on St. Stephen's Day, he took the trouble to specify that it should be in English, which implies that otherwise it might have been in Welsh. In 1873 the bishop of St. Asaph required the Oswestry rector to keep a Welsh-speaking curate. Welsh-language services are still held in the town's Hermon Chapel. At Llanyblodwel until 1900 Welsh and English alternated in the church on a weekly basis.

The old Welsh Bridge at Shrewsbury, by John Malchair, 1791

The Welsh had—as they still do—their own words for a number of places and topographical features of Shropshire. Ludlow is rendered as Llwydlo, but there was an earlier form, Lystwysoc, from *llystwysog*, the prince's palace (referring to the prince of Powys). Other towns include Trefesgob (Bishop's Castle), Croesoswallt (Oswestry), Y Dref Wen (Whittington), Y Cnycin (Knockin), Amwythig (Shrewsbury) and Yr Eglwys Wen (Whitchurch). Efyrnwy, Hafren and Tefeidiad are the rivers Vyrnwy, Severn and Teme respectively. The Stiperstones are the dark rocks (Y Carneddau Tuon) and the Wrekin, (Y Din Gwrygon).

Despite almost 500 years of assimilation Shropshire, at least in the west, is still studded with Welsh names. Simple words recur such as *cefn* (ridge), *coed* (wood), *craig* (rock), *cwm* (valley), *llyn* (lake), *rhos* (moor), *rhyd* (ford) and *tref* (homestead, town). The rivers Caebithra, Cynllaith, Onny (from *onn*, ash tree), and others, continue to bear their Welsh names, as do settlements such as Hengoed (old wood), Porth-y-Waen (moorgate), Rhyn (from *rhyn*, hill or promontory) and Tyn-ycoed (woodhouse). Bettws-y-Crwyn (chapel of the skins) is though to takes its name from the annual tribute of hides once delivered to Chirbury Priory.

The trademark Welsh *llan* occurs at Llanymynech (monks' church) and at Llanyblodwel. The origin of the latter causes some dispute. Some favour (St.) Blodwel's church; others see a reference to *blodau* (flowers). One story suggests that after a great battle nearby the bodies of the slain were thrown into a well which became known as Blood Well, and then gave its name to a house built close by, Blodwel Hall. Gwallter Mechain (1761-1849), who quotes this derivation, comments:

Bridge over the River Tanat at Llanyblodwel

The church at Llanfair Waterdine

There is scarce an inhabitant here who is not able with the greatest ease and indifference to speak both English and Welsh. The Welsh language being still spoken on the confines of Offa's Dyke is a proof of its permanency, however some of the mixed or bastard tribe may be for its total extinction.

Llanbrook near Hopton Castle is something of a mystery because there is no church there, and none can be traced. Llan, though, originally meant 'religious enclosure', and if this were abandoned after a change of heart it would not necessarily have left any mark. Welsh and English are yoked in a number of names, such as Llanfair (St. Mary's church) Waterdine and Weston Rhyn. The Long Mynd (*mynydd*, mountain) also combines the two languages, and the Welsh component recurs at Mynd, near Bucknell Hill.

English and Welsh names marking pews
in the church at Llanfair Waterdine

Farms and Fields

A notable example of a Welsh name is Tŷ Bwchan at Pentre, some nine miles north-west of Shrewsbury. It probably comes from *tŷ bwgan*, meaning bogey house. In the churches of Bettws-y-Crwyn and Llanfair Waterdine the bench ends are inscribed with the names of the farms whose owners and families used to sit there. At Llanfair the straightforward English of Black Hall, The Green, Redwood, Panpounton and Little Selly stands next to the pure Welsh of Bwlch (gap, pass) and Graig. Cwm for one farmstead crops up for others in a variety of spellings: Commawr (big valley), Cwmcole (*cwm collen*, hazel valley) and Cumbrain (*cwm brân*, crow, rook or raven valley). More or less garbled names include Bruinbeddow (*bryn bedw*, birch rise), Melan a grog (*melin y grog*, pebble mill), Rhunnis (*rhyn is*, under hill) and Tyncoed (*tŷ'n y coed*, wood house). Menachty (*mynachdy*, monks' grange) is now known as Monaughty Poeth, the second element, meaning burnt, having been added after a fire in Victorian times. Finally, two apparently exotic English names, Skyborry and Wordy, conceal the Welsh *ysgub-orau* (barns) and *wyr dŷ* (grandchild's house) respectively.

As with farms, so with fields. Among Welsh names is Cae Cam (crooked field) at Oswestry. The word *cae* becomes *ka* in several fields at Ellesmere, including Ka Kiln. Clun has the glorious hybrid, Cae Rabbits. Another Welsh word for field or ground, *maes*, gives Maes-y-Rook at Trewern. Maes Cymery (*cymer*, confluence) is at Melverley where the Vyrnwy joins the Severn. The Welsh *erw* (acre) gives Arrow Maes and Errow Gam (crooked) at Selattyn, where we also find Nant Kelyn Duon (black holly brook), The Vaughnog (West Felton) derives from *mawnog* (peat bog), and Gongle (Kinnerley) from *congl* (corner). Pentre Cloud (*clawdd*) at Prees—incidentally, well away from the Welsh border—means homestead with hedge, dyke or embankment.

Of English farms Simon Evans asked 'How would you like to live

Simon Evans, man of letters

at Nethercott? at Winterdyne or Gold Thorn? at Overwood or Shunesley? at Withypool or Norgrovesend?' He was referring to places on his postman's walk near Cleobury Mortimer but his list could be paralleled for interest all over Shropshire. Clun could offer, as well as a string of Welsh names, Bergam, Hobarris, Menutton, Purlogue, The Quern, Whitcott and Woodside.

Some field names are matter-of-fact, not to say dull, as the Four (Cressage), Five (Hinstock), Six (Alberbury), Eight (Westbury), Ten (Hinstock again) and Eleven Acres (Pontesbury). Flatt Piece (Neen Sollars) is equally lack-lustre, though Seven Rudges (ridges, Clee St. Margaret) seems more evocative. Others promise more than they deliver. Merry Field (Bishop's Castle) and Merry Hill (Worfield) may have been not so much merry as miry. The apparently sinister associations of Devil's Den (Montford, Wistanstow), Devil's Dream (Albrighton) and Devil's Nest (Stanton-upon-Hine-Heath) may be no more than an indication of intractable, unrewarding land (but see other devil names in chapter 6). Honey Meadow (Minsterley, Woolstaston) might be literal, refer-ring to a wealth of flowers, or metaphorical, implying richly productive soil. The name could also have been applied ironically. Even Paradise (Chelmarsh, Cheswardine) might be doubted, but Providence (Eaton-under-Haywood) seems reliable enough. Gaudy Ground (Pontesbury) and Gaudywood Park (Neen Sollars) seem to recall Shakespeare's 'Let's have one other gaudy night' from *Antony and Cleopatra*, but they merely signal sites where dyer's weed grew. This furnished a brilliant, fast yellow dye, and had the French name, *gaude*.

No room for doubt remained in the downright derogatory Awkward (Stoke-upon-Tern), Clay Puddings (Prees), Famish Croft (Sutton), Hard Bargain (Bitterley), Hunger Hill (Cound, Woolstaston), Sour Leasow (Stirchley) and Wilderness (Hinstock). Far-flung places were given such names as Barbadoes (Berrington) or Pennsylvania (Burford, Church Stretton, Prees). The fear or knowledge of penal transportation to Australia must be why at least ten parishes—Atcham, Dawley, Farlow, Ford, Hordley, Leighton, Neen Sollars, Pontesbury, Selattyn, Wrockwardine—had a field called Botany Bay.

Rather more primitive disquiet is reflected in field names such as Elve Leasow (Worfield) and Fairyland (West Felton), Giant's Garden (Stokesay) and Goblin's Meadow (Shifnal). Hob Croft (Sutton Maddock) and Hob Flat (Cheswardine) could incorporate *hob* (hobgoblin) or *hobbe* (tussocky grass). We shall never be sure which, but the mischievous sprite, Puck, almost certainly features in Poukhill (Wrockwardine), Powk Fields (Ditton Priors) and Powkhole (Worfield). A dragon rather than a duck inspires Drake Hill (Wem) and Drake Pits (Norton-in-Hales); a monstrous serpent rather than a humble earthworm is evoked at Worms Hill (Burford, Wrockwardine), and a myste-rious water spirit—from the Old English, *nicor*—in Nicha Park (Uffington) and Nicco Wood (Hodnet).

Although the stories behind them now seem to be lost, more tangible terrors once attended Bloody (Quatford, Cheswardine, Eaton-under-Haywood), Cutthroat (Claverley) and Murder (Chelmarsh) Fields, together with Bloody Breech (Chipnall). The Babes in the Wood of pantomime fame are said to have been murdered in Babbinswood, near Whittington, but it is more likely that the drama merely acquired a local home there, thanks to the name. Black Graves at Wentnor might be plausibly explained as the burial place of plague victims. Money Brook at Meole Brace, it is claimed, is where in times of pestilence Shrewsbury people placed payment for goods left on the bank of the stream to avoid the risk of infection. Dangerous Meadow at Myddle could indeed have been a perilous place, and Deadman's Hollow on the Long Mynd might be the spot where an unlucky traveller's body was discovered. The part played by Gallantree (gallowstree) Field at Adderley, two miles from Market Drayton, may have been to display the body of a criminal hanged for a crime committed in the vicinity.

Rather more pleasant activities are reflected in a wide range of names connected with recreation, though the Cockpit (Little Ness), Cockpit Croft (Newport), Cockpit Leasow (Ford, More), Cockings Ley (Westbury) and Cocking Meadow (Clunbury, Ellesmere), together with Bear Stake (Edgmond), Bear Leys (Meole Brace) and Bear Yard (Acton Scott) recall the cruel pursuits of the past. The sport of kings left its mark on the maps with Grandstand (Bridgnorth St. Leonard's), Race Field (Richard's Castle), Raceground (Morville, Shrewsbury St. Chad's), Races Croft (Ellesmere) and Starting Chair (Rodington). Popular recreations are remembered in Archery Meadow (Worfield), Boxing Patch (Melverley), Quoitings (Montford), Running Meadow (Kinnerley), Shooting Butts (Meole Brace, Whitchurch) and Skittle Croft (Clee St. Margaret). The Plasters (Bromfield, Caynham) and Plowsters (Culmington) could mean play place, though the latter, thanks to time's ambiguity, could simply be a muddy field.

Part of Crawl Meadow, Bromfield

Music and dancing show strongly, with Bagpipers' Hill (Worfield), Dancing Green (Worthen), Maypole Piece (Ashford Carbonel), Minstrel's Yard (Little Wenlock), Morris Meadow (Acton Scott) and Morris Leasow (Beckbury), Singers' (Condover) and Tabor Green (Bishop's Castle). A different pastime altogether inspired Cupid Field (Shifnal) and Cupid's Ramble (West Felton). Significantly, perhaps, three parishes have a Cuckold's Corner (Rushbury, Tugford, West Felton), and three more a Mount Flirt (Bitterley, Eaton-under-Haywood, Onibury). Another case of courtship is commemorated in the Crawl Meadow at Bromfield. The story seems to have been first printed by the antiquary, Thomas Wright, in 1862:

> In the parish of Bromfield ... they tell of a young lady, whose father would not permit her to marry a gallant knight, because the latter was only a younger brother, and unable to offer a sufficient marriage settlement. The young lady, however, persisted in her resolution to marry the knight; and at last one day she informed her father that the ceremony was to be performed the next morning at Bromfield church. The angry parent told his daughter she might follow her will, but of all his great estates, she should receive for her portion no more land than she could crawl over before morning. She went from his sight, apparently unaffected by the threat, but next day she appeared at the breakfast table covered in muck, and announced that she had secured a tract of meadow reaching about half-way to Downton, round which she had crawled on her hands and knees during the long winter night. The father was so pleased with the spirit displayed by his daughter that he made her the heiress of all his estates, and they remained in the possession of her descendants many years.

The Crawl Meadow still exists at Bromfield, south-west of the church, and roughly opposite the former priory gatehouse. The moated site in the field could be where the brave girl's home stood. However, the attractive tale (also told of Tichborne in Hampshire) is of course a fictional narrative rather than an echo of a real event.

Towns, too, have their intriguing names which sometimes reflect, as in glebe, orchard and leasow, the fields they have buried. Augustus Hare wrote—not always accurately—of Shrewsbury:

> No town retains, or retained till lately [1898], more curious and suggestive street names, such as *Wyle Cop*, from vill-coppa, the town of the hill; *Mardol*, formerly Mardole, the pond at the nearby pastures; *Dogpole*, originally Dokenpoll, from Ducken, to bend; the *Cornchepynge*, from the Saxon Ceupan, to buy, and Ceping, market, now the corn-market; *Baxters' Row* or *Bakers' Row*, as the High Street was called till recent times; *Frankwell*, Frankville, the Frank's town; *Murivance* or

Muryvance, now Swan Hill, before the walls, a name of French extraction; *The Sextry*, Sacristy, now King's Head Street; *Shete Place*, now Shop Latch; *Tomboldesham*, now Tanner's Street; *Corvisor's Row*, now Pride Hill; *Merival*, S. Mary's Ville, at the east end of the New Bridge; and *Cardellan*, now Kiln Lane.

Timmins had a rhyme about Wyle Cop:

> They hew and they hack and they chop,
> And to finish the whole they stick up a pole
> In the place that's called the Wylde Coppe,
> And they pop your grim, gory head on the top -

which recalled its role in the mutilatory executions of the past (see also chapter 4). Neither he nor Hare, though, mentioned what is perhaps Shrewsbury's most notorious street name, Grope Lane.

Grope Lane, Shrewsbury

Pride and Prejudice

'I am of Shropshire, my shins be sharp': so ran a saying picked up by the antiquarian, John Leland, during his travels of the mid-16th century. Its meaning may not immediately be clear, but becomes so when one learns that well over 300 years later the word 'sharpshins' remained current in Shropshire, and signified both quick-footed and quick-witted. The latter sense applied in another axiom, 'Whoever crosses Clun Bridge comes back sharper than he went', the allusion being to slow countryfolk who travelled to market in the village from remote farms in Clun Forest and returned home duly stimulated. A more matter-of-fact explanation is that because of the bridge's narrowness anyone crossing needed to keep a sharp lookout for hazards such as approaching carts.

Clun Bridge

If the people of Clun were considered lively, the inhabitants of certain other places attracted less flattering epithets. The 'proud Salopians' were so designated because they allegedly declined an offer by Henry VIII of city status for Shrewsbury because they wished to keep its title of the first of towns. As a result the proposed Shropshire bishopric also came to nought. The 'wise men' of Madeley owed their ironic fame to the tale that, loath to lose the visiting cuckoo, they tried to hedge the bird in by holding hands in a circle round it. The Dawley Oaves derived their reputation for stupidity from one of their number who built in his outhouse a wheelbarrow which proved too big to get out of the door. 'Melverley, God help us' comes from a village subject to flooding in the north-west of the county, close to the confluence of the Vyrnwy with the Severn. According to 'a centuries-old Salopian jape', wrote E.M. Darling,

> when you meet a Melverley man in the summer his hat is jauntily over one ear and if you ask him where he comes from he raises his head still higher and says in a ringing voice, 'Melverley', but if you meet him in February his answer is, 'Melverley, God help us'.

The Wem Ranters were so labelled (or libelled) thanks to a vociferous and perhaps over-enthusiastic band of Primitive Methodists who lived in the town in the early 19th century. Wem Church was rebuilt in 1811, save for the tower, and it is possible that the Ranters coined the comment:

> A new church, an old steeple,
> A drunken parson and a wicked people.

The 'drunken parson' was Dr. Henry Aldrich, incumbent 1689–1710 though often absent on his duties as vice-chancellor of Oxford University. He enjoyed writing jovial catches and drinking songs such as this:

If on my theme I rightly think
These are five reasons why men drink:
Good wine, a friend, because I'm dry,
Or else I should be by and by,
Or any other reason why.

More neutrally, people remarked, 'Amen, says the clock of Wem'; more affectionately, they said there were treacle mines in the town. The implication, shared with various other places up and down the country, is either that the inhabitants prosper, or that they are idle. Either way, they enjoy the joke, and take a pride in their reputation. Wem's nickname of 'The Treacle Mines' has been explained by two local industries: tanning, which caused a sticky substance to be exuded on some of the town's pavements, and brewing, which required a treacle-like ingredient. Alternatively, in the 1930s one chemist's shop was reputed to draw its treacle from a mine in the backyard.

Bitterley Church

'Blest is the eye [island] / 'Twixt Severn and Wye, / But thrice blessed he / 'Twixt Severn and Clee', runs one rhyme; but a village in the 'island', too far from the river and too high on the hill, fares less well:

Bitterley, Bitterley, under the Clee,
Devil take me if ever I come to thee.

It is perhaps unfortunate that one of Bitterley's nearest neighbours is Bedlam. Dudleston Heath, near Ellesmere, also fares badly, in 'Dilluson Yeth, where the devil ketch 'is dyeth'. On the whole, the enumeration of the Stanton villages is a memory aid, though I am not sure where Stanton Long fits in:

Doom-laden sign near Bitterley

> Stan' upon Trent,
> Stan' upon Wye,
> Clean Stan', dirty Stan',
> And Stanton Lacy.

Four resoundingly alliterative villages received favourable treatment in the couplet given wide currency when A.E. Housman placed it at the head of one of the poems in *A Shropshire Lad*:

> Clunton and Clunbury, Clungunford and Clun,
> Are the quietest places under the sun.

Yet in traditional usage the word 'quietest', depending on the speaker's standpoint, was varied to 'dirtiest' or 'drunkennest'. According to J.E. Auden the original rhyme was:

> Clydach, Clyro and Clun,
> Three largest parishes under the sun.

Arthur Jagger in his poem, 'A Land of Promise', prefers the more picturesque variant:

> We'd take the road from Stokesay
> By Clunbury and Clun
> (The sleepiest, as folk say,
> Of spots beneath the sun);
> Up Titterhill [near Hopton Castle] we'd wander,
> At Heartsease [by the Teme] rest a spell,
> Or walk to Wolfpits yonder,
> Or Wain or Shepherd's Well

A person's origin and allegiance clearly determined which version of this rhyme, current in Edgmond and neighbouring hamlets, would be adopted:

> Tibberton tawnies, Cherrington chats,
> Adeney dogs and Buttery rats.
> Four bulldogs fast in a pen
> Darna come out for Edgmond men.
>
> Tibberton tawnies, Cherrington chats,
> Edgmond bulldogs and Adeney cats.
> Edgmond bulldogs made up in a pen
> Darna come out for Tibberton men.

Chats are gossips, tawnies, people of swarthy complexion.

Another clutch of places is rehearsed in lines written, according to Georgina Jackson, by a local rhymester who flourished in the 1770s:

> Cothercot up o' the Hill,
> Wilderley down i' the dale;
> Churton for pretty girls,
> An' Powtherbitch for good ale.

Churton was the contracted local pronunciation for Church Pulverbatch, which could also be Powtherbith, Powtherbatch or Powderbatch. Of Huglith, near Pulverbatch, people said that it was 'the last place God made, and he never allowed the sun to shine on it'. In a similar vein is the rhyme recorded in the Bishop's Castle register of baptisms and burials for the years 1760 to 1790. This was originally written and and stuck beneath the doorknocker of John Wingfield, the curate, by a friend who had called on him but found him out:

> The Bishop I find had a Castle behind
>   but the Bishop and Castle are flown
> For the Bishop, I wot
>   Could not dwell in a spot
> Which Satan had marked as his own.
> Then fly, Wingfield, fly, ere the wrath from on high
>   This damnable place has o'er taken.
> What Curate of Grace
>   Would dwell in a place
> By God and the Bishop forsaken?

Ellesmere, too, was marked down in at least one rhyme: 'The devil was flying over Ellesmere, and he said, / "Sweet little Ellesmere, you are all my own"'. On the other hand, a song written in the late 19th century by a David Studley dwelt on Ellesmere's high reputation:

> Oh long life to the Myttons, the Hatchetts,
> The Mainwarings, Dymocks, my dear,
> While the mountains re-echo the catches
> We sing to the praise of Ellesmere.
> There's never a town in famed Salop
> Can match it for frolic and fun,
> If throughout all Shropshire you gallop
> From rising to setting of sun.

Shibboleths and Speech

There are many local variations on place names, some simply reflections of local pronunciation such as the famous Abbey Forret (Abbey Foregate) in

Shrewsbury, and also Arcall (Ercall), Brug (Bridgnorth), Clibbery (Cleobury) Mortimer, Elsmer (Ellesmere), Haymond (Haughmond), Ludler (Ludlow), Odgestry, Osentry, Osstry or Ozestry (Oswestry), Oosasson (Woolstaston), Soosbury (Shrewsbury) and Wukenyets (Oakengates). Two villages with the same name, Albrighton, are usefully distinguished as Aiberton (near Shrewsbury) and Auberton (near Shifnal). Clungunford has the alternative form of Clungunnas. Both are stressed on the second syllable, and have been, presumably, since the 13th century, when the place was recorded as Cloune Goneford. The origin of the personal name involved may be Gunward, who held the settlement in the time of Edward the Confessor, so the current pronunciation may go back to those days.

The middle syllable of Pontesbury is elided in speech, though Pontesford either has all three elements sounded or becomes Ponsert. The many contracted forms of place names include Corra (Calverhall), Delbury (Diddlebury), Linsel (Lilleshall), Ratchope (Ratlinghope), Shenton (Shavington) and Shrayden (Shrawardine). Another local peculiarity is that Salopians say (or said) the Breidden, the Clee and the Wrekin for the hills (possibly under the influence of Welsh), but their main river is never the Severn, always Severn.

It would be a gross over-simplification to refer to a single Shropshire dialect, since there are variations within the county in both pronunciation and vocabulary. Clee Hill—Clay 'Ill to the locals—is a case in point. According to A.E. Jenkins, who was born there in 1928, the dialect had a sort of heyday between 1890 and 1939, when children travelling to secondary schools at Ludlow or Cleobury Mortimer had to become bilingual to avoid the taunts and incomprehension of their classmates. As late as 1970 a survey showed that many Clee Hill words were not understood by people at Diddlebury, only eight miles away. In 1982, though, Jenkins wrote: 'It is now virtually impossible to find a family who converse in the dialect as we knew it'.

Jenkins remembers the speech of his childhood with great affection, and includes a glossary running to some 30 pages in his book on Clee Hill. He notes local similes such as 'dyud [dead] as a ommer [hammer]' and ''appy as a biddy [baby]', together with a long list of words such as 'ardn' (stubborn), 'choober' (football), 'cwoys' (wood pigeons), 'klet' (skint), 'mullock' (rubbish), 'sobbing' (soaking wet) and 'wisket' (basket enclosing stoneware jar). He also points out that nicknames were widely used, and quotes examples such as Oxo, Muggins, Bronco, Piert, Poonfire, Crack and Tarpig. Although these were meaningless to an outsider, each had an explanatory anecdote. Jenkins comments: 'Many people did not respond unless they were addressed by their nickname. ... Many others, however, were unaware that they possessed a nickname because it was never used in their presence'.

He adds that, as in Wales, people were characterised by appending to their names their trade or some reference to it. This also applied in other parts of the county. A contractor at Bucknell was known as Morris the Roof. Wyn the Coal and Jones the Brow (a farm) came from Welsh Frankton, and many more examples could be quoted.

Welsh influence probably accounted for abbreviating David to Dai. The phrase, 'Thank you for me', used in acknowledging hospitality received, comes straight from the Welsh, '*Diolch i chwi drosta i*'. In Oswestry a foolish person was known as a 'gwerian' (Welsh, *gwirion*); more generally, 'grig' (Welsh, *grug*) means heather, and 'keffel' (Welsh, *ceffyl*, horse), a worthless horse.

During the course of what she called 'dialecting tours', starting in the 1860s, the antiquarian, Georgina F. Jackson, amassed the huge amount of material which she published in her monumental *Shropshire Word-Book*. Perhaps inspired by this work, Rev. Waldegrave Brewster noted from his parishioners at Middleton-in-Chirbury words—some of them missed by Jackson—such as 'to bezzle' (go about drinking), 'to kiddle' (slobber), 'to orse' (begin), 'to potch' (make holes), 'to tind' (ignite), 'dosselly' (backward), 'draughty' (thirsty), 'frum' (early), 'sniving' (swarming), 'glat' (gap in hedge), 'grig' (heather), 'weather gall' (rainbow) and 'wuller' (alder). From a Martha Jones he took down these expressions:

> We never miss the water till the well runs dry.
> As safe as a church tied to a hollybush.
> A quiet bee gathers no honey.
> To jump like a parched pea.
> A blind man gets small good from a lantern.

Proverbial-style expressions of this kind, pithy in expression and full of wisdom, were widespread:

> I live too near the wood to be afeart of a oolert [owl].
> She knows what it is to scrat before she pecks.
> 'Everyone to his liking', as the old woman said when she kissed the cow.
> We don't go by size, or a cow would catch a hare.
> It takes two blows to make a battle (Edgmond).
> I'll have a lick of the mundle [stirring stick], if I burn my tongue (Wem).

Some dialect words are still widely known, held in affection, and even treated as a badge of belonging. An unnamed Bridgnorth man, speaking of the 1940s, recalled using many terms such as 'fittle' (food), 'cyack' (cake), 'cyat' (cat), 'such' (toffees), 'dyeth' (death), 'yaffle' (green woodpecker) and 'quite' (wood pigeon), and says that he ended most of his sentences with 'surree' (which some claim to be a relic of 'sirrah'). Colin Bird, born at Stow, near Knighton, in 1928, remembers the language of the Radnorshire-Shropshire border at much the same time:

Colin Bird in 1947

Larpin was a young lad; swardy was a pig; a pishty was also a dog; a ferret was often referred to as a weasel; meowkin was a scarecrow; pilk was a fish, usually a spawning salmon; prill was a brook or stream; sheep or cattle on the roadside were said to be grazing the long meadow; a pooner was a hammer; poon was to hit; puck was picked. (I puck a basket full of blackberries yesterday).

Dunna was don't (I dunna know); woona was won't (I wunna go); binna was am not (I binna going). To poon someone was to give someone a thrashing. (I pooned patch of him). Anunt was opposite (up anunt the church).

Dull as a pikel, a dull person; surry was a person. (A man would meet another and say, 'How bist thee, surry?' A man who had not seen someone for a long time would say, 'I anna sin thee since the age of a little pig'. Talking squit was talking rubbish ('dunna talk such squit, surry'). Bree was the warble fly, stampeding cattle were referred to as 'on the bree' or 'the cows have got the bree today'. Awernt was 'I expect'. ('Awernt thee bist going to the fair today, surry').

A member of a group waiting for someone to turn up had been known to say, 'He woona come now, sure to'. (He won't come now, for sure).

Mr. Bird also has a fund of anecdotes such as these:

It was the custom on a pheasant shoot for a beater to shout 'Cock over, sir' when the first pheasant to rise on a drive flew towards the guns. On this occasion an owl flew through the trees towards the guns, and one beater shouted 'Cock over, sir'. 'That binna no cock, sir', shouted one old character, 'that be an oolert'.

43

A man biking from his home in Radnorshire to the pub in Bucknell, Shropshire, travelled through parts of Radnorshire, Herefordshire and Shropshire, a distance of about one and a half miles. On arriving at the pub he met a lady, obviously a visitor. They passed the time of day, and he man said 'I'm going to enjoy this pint tonight'. 'Have you cycled far?' the lady asked. 'Well, madam, I've come through three counties', he replied. How is that for wit?

When the farmer asked the boy to fetch the horse from the bottom pasture he asked 'Which horse?' 'The old horse, of course', said the farmer. 'Wear the old ones out first'. 'In that case', said the boy, 'you'd better fetch him yourself'.

Mr. Bird takes up the last subject in one of several poems he has written:

The Farmer's Boy

Come on now, larpin, shek theeself
And get out of thy bed.
I binna calling thee agen,
So hearken to what is said.

Then come and eat thy breakfast
And dunna thee act the fool,
Then tak this wad a sandwiches
And get down the road to school.

Stow, where Colin Bird was born in the Almshouse Cottages that lie in the arc of trees just to the left of the centre of the photograph. The vicarage and church are to the right

Do what the teacher tells thee to do,
Take heed to what he do say,
And atter school is finished
Hurry home and help with the hay.

The larpin left school and hurried home
And went to help his ald man with the hay.
His fayther said, How did'st thee get on?
What did the teacher say?

The larpin said, He harped on about geography,
Some place away out yonder.
Was that the place you went last year
When you bought them giss and gonder?

The fayther said, It wanna there:
That were a place this side a Clun.
Now ketch ald a the pikel and shek some hay:
We dunna have time for fun.

I want to clear this fild today
Afore it starts to rain.
It'll be another month or two
Afore we starts on the grain.

They cleared the fild afore the rain,
They puck up the pikel and rake.
The larpin said, Man alive, I be hungry:
I could eat a big clout a cake.

His fayther said, Thank ee, larpin, for working hard,
Thee hast helped me quite a lot.
The missus has cooked we a rabbit,
And there be some taters in the pot.

When theese get back up to the house,
Tie the ald mare up in the stable,
Then wash thee hands and coom thee hair,
And get up to the table.

The larpin et some rabbit and taters;
He said, I be as full as a tick.
His ald man said, Get up the wooden hill and into bed,
Thee hast earnt a good night's kip.

Writing in a county council publication, *Aspects of Shropshire* (1994), Tim Williams wrote:

> There are many specifically Shropshire words that I use or hear regularly, 'Clemmed' is to be starved—either starving hungry or starving cold. If you are afraid of the cold then you are 'nesh' and if you are a real trencherman, then I would consider you to be 'a good cratcher', presumably from the stall or 'cratch' from which cattle eat. Only last year clear evidence of the continuing natural tradition of dialect was given me out in the country, when a farmer friend told me to make my way through 'that glat over by the oak'. No problem for a Shropshire lad, of course, for glat—should you not know—is a hole or gap in a hedge.

It will be interesting to see how long such words last into the 21st century, and whether speech continues as recognisably that of Shropshire.

CHAPTER 3

Water

With rivers, lakes and wells the watery world has a strong presence in Shropshire. The Severn, with a 50-mile course through the county, has a massive presence. The names of its tributaries make an exotic litany: Meol, Cound, Mor, Borle, Vyrnwy, Perry, Bell, Worf. The Teme, which also joins (though not until the Severn is well past Shropshire) has its own feeders: Clun, Onny and Corve. To the evocative list one could add the rivers Rea and Roden, Tanat and Tug, and the curiously-named Unk (near Mainstone). The greatest of them all, Sabrina to the Romans, Hafren to the Welsh, Saefern to the Saxons, was known to Salopians simply as Severn. Within living memory a mother would have said to her child: 'If yo dunna take care, yo'll fall into Severn'. The usage has some antiquity. A board dated 1795 on a wall near Shrewsbury Abbey stated: 'This plate is fixed to let you know / That Severn to this line did flow'.

The Severn at Bridgnorth

The Teme at Ludlow

Once the Severn flowed north into the Dee estuary. During the ice age which ended some 10,000 years ago the blocked outfall of the river resulted in a great lake which covered the land as far south as Wenlock Edge. Eventually the Severn broke out and assumed its present course. Conversely, as the ice retreated, marshes and meres were left in its wake. These generated their own tales of watery denizens, sunken cities and unplumbed depths.

From the times of Romans and Celts (and no doubt even earlier) wells and springs not only supplied drinking water but were perceived to have healing, and even holy, powers. They were long the focus for pious—and sometimes riotous—gatherings. Now some are debased into mere wishing wells, though certain people seek to revive what they see as the pagan power of such places.

Sailing the Severn

Burghley's map of Shrewsbury, dating from 1575, shows a group of men dragging a boat upriver by a line fastened to the mast. By then the technique was already ancient: as early as 1198 the sheriff of Shropshire paid half a mark to hire a barge to take wine from Bridgnorth to Gloucester. Barges, 50 foot long and single-masted, could carry 50 tons. Trows (the word is pronounced to rhyme with blows) were 60 feet long, had two masts which could be lowered at bridges, and carried up to 80 tons. When the sails of either vessel could not be used the bow-hauliers took over.

In the 19th century some 4,000 men were working on the Severn. The establishment of proper towing-paths along the river eventually led to the replace-

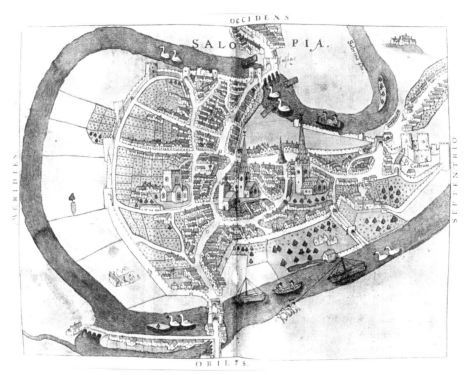

Burghley's Map of Shrewsbury, 1575

ment of the bow-hauliers by horses. The men fought a long rearguard action against being superseded. They laboured 'with loud contention and horrible imprecations', wrote one clergyman, John Fletcher of Madeley; another,

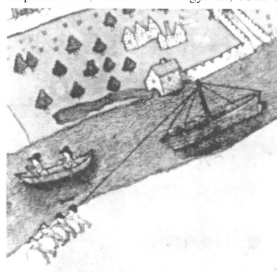

Detail of bow-hauliers from Burghley's map

J. Nightingale, complained in 1810 that they should already have given way to horses.

Hauliers were liable to three months' imprisonment if they failed to complete an assignment, and they sealed a contract by downing a mug of ale at their employer's expense in certain riverside inns known as mug houses. Several of these were close to Jackfield and Broseley. The bargmen and trowmen had a reputation only marginally less savoury than that of the hauliers. A typical waterman, wrote a 19th-century observer, 'has a broad back, legs which a flunkey may be jealous of—swelled like skittle pins at the calves, he is a hard drinker, a heavy swearer, given to gasconade and good living'. He frequented public houses with names like The Severn Trow, the Black Swan and the Tumbling Sailors (Jackfield), the Trow (Shrewsbury, near English Bridge), the Barge inn (now Barge Cottage, the Mount, Shrewsbury). Bridgnorth alone had 200 public houses, many of which catered for the river man. At the confluence of the Vyrnwy and the Severn stood the Come Merry, whose name, a corruption of the Welsh, *cymer fi* (take me) supposedly represented the last sigh of the tributary as it surrendered to the main stream. There, as well as drinking, bargemen set their gamecocks to fight in the pub's cockpit.

In a nearby public house, the Royal Hill, a novice had 'to pay his footing, a gallon or two of beer, and then made his mark with a poker [on the mantel-piece] to prove that he had done so, before he was admitted as a bargeman'. So Griff Philips, a former landlord of the Royal Hill, told Brian Waters in the 1940s. Bargemen were notorious as poachers and as pilferers from cargoes. Casks of wine and cider were particularly vulnerable to theft since quantities abstracted were readily replaced with Severn water.

Just as the bow-hauliers gave way to horses, so barges and trows declined in the face of competition successively from canals, railways and roads. In the 19th century the standard charge for river freight from Shropshire to Bristol was 10s. a ton downstream, 15 in the opposite direction. Pool Quay on the Welsh side of the Severn, west of the Breidden Hills, was the farthest port upstream, 180 miles from Portishead Point on the Bristol Channel. Craft of between 30 and 50 tons could sail from there—albeit only between October and May—for Bristol with bark, timber or lead, and return with grain. In the 1880s iron grates were carried from Coalbrookdale to Bristol for 6d. each.

Trows were built at Jackfield until the 1860s. The last such Shropshire vessel was the *William*, built at Shrewsbury. When in 1939 she was wrecked in the Bristol Channel, having sailed the Severn since 1801, she held the record of being the oldest vessel in the merchant navy then afloat. Barges disappeared from Shrewsbury, Ironbridge and Bridgnorth in the mid-1890s. The last left Ironbridge in 1895 with a cargo of fire-bricks. The last barge built at Pool Quay was launched in 1900 but undertook only local voyages, carrying Breidden stone.

Among other river craft, more for individual than for collective or commercial use, were rafts and punts, the last derived perhaps from the dugout canoes of prehistoric times. The coracle, with a similar pedigree, survives in the 21st century. Samuel Ireland (died 1800), the engraver, arrived one day at Buttington near Welshpool with a portfolio of his 'picturesque views of the Severn', and asked for a boat to Shrewsbury. It was summertime, and with low water in the river barges and trows were not sailing. Ireland declined the offered coracle, though this would have been quicker, especially if, at the loop in the Severn north of Shrewsbury enclosing the promontory known as the Isle, the waterman had taken advantage of the possible portage. One man claimed to have travelled by coracle from Pool Quay to the Bristol Channel in a fortnight.

The Rogers family of Ironbridge counted well over 300 years' continuity as users and makers of coracles. From the 19th century stories have survived of Tom Rogers, a man of 20 stones with a thirst to match his bulk. The vicar confronted him one day with the rebuke: 'Tom, you're drunk'. 'That's not possible, sir', came the polite reply. 'I've not had but 14 quarts'.

A policeman, suspecting him of poaching, stopped him in Buildwas with several dozen rabbits. 'It's a fair cop', said Tom, and meekly handed over his bag. When the pair arrived in Ironbridge, though, Tom said, 'I'm gwine home', and asked for the rabbits back. 'Oh, no, you're for the station'. Only then did Tom produce his permit to catch rabbits on the Leighton estate.

He was a keen swimmer, and as a young man swam with Matthew Webb, a doctor's son from Dawley, born in 1848. At the age of 27 in 1875 Webb became the first person to swim the English Channel, crossing from Dover to Calais in just under 22 hours. Seven years later he drowned while attempting to swim the rapids at Niagara. Many years later John Betjeman commemorated Webb in a poem which imagined that his ghost 'came swimming along the old canal that carried the bricks to Lawley'. This was set to music by Jim Parker, and recorded in 1976 by John Kirkpatrick, then of Aston-on-Clun.

Coracle Race on the Severn at Ironbridge,
from The Illustrated London News, *1880s*

Tom Rogers taught men to use the coracle, though in full view of Ironbridge his pupils had to be naked to avoid spoiling their clothes in the (very likely) possibility of an upset. He frequently won coracle races, including at the annual regatta at Shrewsbury over a 300-yard course from Porthill Bridge to Pengwern Boat Club.

Harry Rogers (died 1967) continued a long line of trout ticklers and game poachers. When his old home on the river bank at Ironbridge was condemned by health inspectors he simply pulled it down and in nine weeks built another, many of the materials supplied by the Severn in the form of flotsam. In time of flood he delivered the post, food and sometimes coal by coracle to those marooned in low-lying houses. If the river level kept on rising he would evacuate the people, drawing on his lengthy experience to negotiate the powerful and tricky currents.

The last of the Rogers dynasty was Eustace, who died in February 2003 at the age of 88. For many years he commuted by coracle from his home in Ironbridge to his work at Buildwas power station. On numerous occasions he rescued the living and retrieved the dead from the river. He made coracles for sale: they required 30 hours' work and a bullock hide. He had no children, so the long family tradition died with him, but he taught the skills of coracle making to members of the charitable Green Wood Trust at Coalbrookdale.

Eustace Rogers in 1976

Eel weirs on the Severn, 1890

Coracle racing has been revived at Ironbridge, Bewdley (Worcs.) and also (in 2003) at Leintwardine (Herefordshire), so the craft remains in demand.

As well as serving for transport coracles were used for fishing. Until 1890, when a byelaw prohibited the practice, two of them would row downstream with a net suspended between them to catch salmon. An alternative technique, favoured by poachers, consisted of stretching a net supported by corks from bank to bank. Both salmon and trout were taken in a trammel net, a sort of pouch, some 40 yards long and five feet wide.

The last fish weir on the Severn, at Preston Boats, downstream from Uffington, was swept away in a flood in 1910. Brian Waters describes how such structures functioned in catching eels:

> There were no fewer than twenty-eight weirs along the Salopian Severn, which served the double purpose of fishing and navigation; in the absence of locks, vessels were hauled past the weirs up a by-let, in many cases separated from the weir by a small island. As they descended the weir the eels were caught in a bag-like net, knit from thatching twine and fixed on long poles.

From Preston-on-the-Weald Moors, near Wellington, Georgina Jackson noted this rhyme, which indicated the migratory season for eels:

> When wollers [alders] han leaves as large as a mouse's ear,
> Then sniggles [eell] they'n run, they dunna car wheer.

The mere at Ellesmere

Meres and Pools

The word Ellesmere derives from Elli's mere, but many preferred to believe that the person involved was a Mrs. Ellis who, though she owned the only good well in the locality, would neither sell nor give away any of the water. To punish such meanness, the well overflowed one night, and kept on pouring out until it swamped not only Mrs. Ellis but the tract of over 100 acres which is now known as the mere.

A variation on the theme features an avaricious landowner who exacts a halfpenny for every bucketful drawn from his well until divine intervention makes the water gush so abundantly that it creates the mere, and provides plenty for all. According to a third twist in the tale:

> There was once a fine, fertile meadowland, having at its centre a well of crystal water, where all the neighbouring poor came to draw. This they had done from time immorial, but a new tenant came to the farm and declared that the water-seekers trampled down his grass. He shut out everyone except his own family, but when his wife came to draw water she found that the meadow had become one vast lake. It has always remained so. Yet the cruel farmer and all his successors were compelled to pay the same rent as before, as a punishment for his selfishness.

Running into the mere and disappearing into its depths is a mysterious causeway known as the Lady's (or Ladies') Walk. One wonders whether this was once associated with the mythical Mrs. Ellis. Local mothers warned their children not against Mrs. Ellis, though, but Jenny Greenteeth, whose long, bony arms would reach out and drag them down to their deaths in the water if they ventured too close. Jenny does not seem to be known elsewhere in Shropshire, though warnings of her threat were widespread in Lancashire.

Early in the 18th century Daniel Defoe described Ellesmere as being both 'remarkable for good fish' and 'famous for a great lake or mere, which the people pretend has in some places no bottom'. The latter belief—curiously common—was also held of two of Ellesmere's neighbours, Kettlemere and Blackmere. Of these, a local lad told a Victorian traveller that the one 'has no bottom to it, and the t'other's deeper than that, sir'.

Three pools—Llynclys, Berth and Bomere—were also considered to be bottomless. Llynclys is just off the A483 road south of Oswestry. The name may mean fair or holy lake (*llyn glwys*) or lake of the enclosure (*llyn y clys*). In its supposedly bottomless depths lie the five towers of a submerged city. Some say that these can be seen when the water is clear, but the exasperated writer of a guidebook complained that 'there never appears to have been a day when the water *was* clear enough'. Various traditions attempt to explain how the city came to be engulfed, one of them apparently dating back to the 9th century. Humphrey Llwyd (or Lhuyd) wrote in the early 1570s that a king (identified by others as Benlli Gawr) 'with his pallace and all his household was swallowed up into the bowelles of the earth' as a punishment for refusing to hear St. Germanus (Garmon) preach against the Pelagian heresy when he visited Britain in about 447.

Another story names a King Alaric who married a woodland spirit known as the Maid of the Green Forest. The wedding contract specified that the queen be allowed to absent herself every seventh night. After a time Alaric is unable

Llynclys

to contain his curiosity as to what the queen is doing when she is away, and he sends a man, Clerk Willin, to spy on her. Willin follows her to Ogo's Hole (for which, see chapter 1), and sees her come out the following morning radiant with renewed beauty. He immediately desires her for himself, and casts a spell to force her to meet him by the cross at White Minster (an old designation for Oswestry). She arrives as a wrinkled hag, since the spell has prevented the weekly renewal of her youth in fairyland. Alaric, his city and court (including Willin, presumably) are cast into the lake. Even the unhappy lady suffers the same fate, though she rises from time to time to the surface.

A further tale concerns a fiddler hired to play at a feast and dance held at a hall (*llys*) for the family and friends of the wealthy owner. For some reason the fiddler at one point had to go away from the hall; he found when he came back an expanse of water where it had stood, with his fiddle gently rocking on the waves in the middle.

Yet another twist is provided by Isaac Watkin, who explains:

> That the lord and lady of the hall (*llys*) were proverbial for their cruelty and want of charity to the poor. That on one occasion an old woman being refused alms, cursed the lady, adding with loud voice '*Daw dial, daw*' (vengeance will come, it will), and thrice was this woe repeated. The lady inquiring as to when this punishment should come upon her was answered by the beggar, '*Yn amser eich plant, eich wyrion, a'ch gorwyrion, eich seynydd a'ch gorseynydd*' (in the time of your descendants of the first, second, third, fourth and fifth degrees). The lady ridiculed this prognostication, saying she should not even see her descendants of the third degree, and therefore it was folly to speak of the fifth, but so it did happen for all that, for as the lord and lady, with their children, and children's children to the fifth generation, were all seated at a great feast, the earth opened its mouth, and the hall (*llys*) and all its occupants were swallowed up, and nothing remains to mark the spot saving the pool (*llyn*) called from that dire event Llync-[submerged]llys or the hall that was swallowed up.

Bomere Pool in the parish of Condover, just south of Shrewsbury, was taken by Mary Webb as the model for the sinister Sarn Mere in her novel, *Precious Bane*, though a film version made in 1988 chose to use Alkmund Pool, near Crossgreen on the other side of the town. Like Llynclys, Bomere has its drowned dwellings. The stories are rich in themes and variations, which shows that they must have been widely told. A village is drowned as a punishment for the irreligion either of a farmer who insists on cutting his corn on a Sunday, or of parishioners who fail to attend church on Christmas Eve. A Roman soldier tries to bring the people back to christianity, but in vain. After the cataclysm he rows again and again round the pool in search of the woman with whom he has fallen in love. In the end his boat sinks, he too drowns, and later haunts the pool.

Thomas Wright described another denizen of the place:

> There is also a monster in this 'mere', in the shape of a gigantic fish, who wears a short sword by his side, and employs himself, from time to time, in ringing a bell, which is heard more frequently than the bells of the [submerged] church. Once upon a time, it was determined to catch this fish, and a very large net was employed, but the fishers no sooner began to drag him towards the shore than he drew his sword, cut it to pieces, and made his escape. They next employed a net of iron, on which the weapon had no effect, and they thus succeeded in bringing him to land; but he escaped them again, and probably he frightened them too, for nobody seems ever to have repeated the attempt to catch him.

Wild Edric (see also chapter 4) was born at Condover, and owned it, according to an unfounded local belief. However, he did hold neighbouring Bayston. Nevertheless, tradition maintained that the Bomere sword belonged to Edric, who committed it to the fish's keeping when he vanished; only when his rightful heir appeared would the fish surrender it.

Hare offers, quoting a writer of 1874 in the periodical, *Shreds and Patches*, a different explanation of the sword:

> Some two centuries ago, or less, a party of gentlemen, including the squire of Condover, were fishing in the pool, when an enormous fish was captured and hauled into the boat. Some discussion arose as to the girth

Bomere Pool

of the fish, and a bet was made that he was bigger round than the squire, and that the sword-belt of the latter would not reach round his waist. To decide the bet the squire unbuckled his belt, which was then and there with some difficulty fastened round the body of the fish. The scaly knight (for so he no doubt felt himself to be) began to feel impatience at being kept so long out of his native element, and after divers struggles he succeeded in eluding his captors, and regaining at the same time his freedom and his watery home, carrying the squire's sword with him.

Wright in his turn added: 'I have heard that an attempt was once made to empty the lake by draining off the water through a channel, but that this attempt was defeated through some unknown agency, which filled up every night as much of the channel as had been dug the previous day'. Bomere Pool is privately owned, but a public bridleway passes close to it and affords views. On occasions noisy power sports shatter the peace of the place but on a quiet evening as shadows lengthen the smooth, dark water regains its air of ancient mystery.

A short distance away is Shomere. People used to believe that 'When Bomere meets Shomere the world will come to an end'. Of the latter it was said that on its shore was an old church pulled down on the orders of Oliver Cromwell, its bells cast into the water. In an attempt to recover the bells chains were attached, and 20 oxen began to pull. Among the bystanders one man triumphantly remarked to a doubter: 'We have them now in spite of God and the devil'. His voice broke the spell: the chains snapped and the bells sank back for ever into the depths. Similar stories are told both of Colemere and of Berth

The Boat House, Colemere

Pool, near Baschurch. In Crosemere there is said to be an ancient chapel whose bells can be heard ringing whenever a breeze ruffles the waters.

In a pool near Child's Ercall, two men going out to work one morning—runs a tale heard in 1879—see the figure of what they take to be the 'Old Lad'. Then they hear the voice of a woman, look more closely, and realise they have met a mermaid. She shows them a lump of gold, and offers them that and more if they will wade into the pool and take it from her hands. 'Christ', says one, 'if this inna a bit o' luck'. At this, the mermaid shrieks, and dives below the surface. Neither she nor the promised treasure is ever seen again.

Wells, Healing and Holy

In 642 Oswald, king of Northumberland, aged 38, was defeated in battle at Maserfield, near what is now Oswestry (see also chapter 2), by Penda of Mercia and Cynddylan of Powys. Penda ordered that as a sacrifice to Woden his dead opponent's head and limbs be cut off and hung on trees or stakes. An eagle snatched an arm and dropped it a little way from the battlefield at *cae nef* (heaven field), where a spring burst forth from the ground to create St. Oswald's Well.

Oswald's *disjecta membra*, carefully recovered by the pious, were sent all over Europe as holy relics, thus spreading his cult. His body was buried at Oswestry—so called from Oswald's Tree—but later moved to Bardsey Island in Wales, and then to Gloucester. Such items were highly prized by religious establishments because they attracted both pilgrims and revenue.

Oswald's Well, Oswestry

During his tour of England in the early 16th century the antiquarian, John Leland, heard the story of the eagle and the well. A chapel erected near or over the well still existed in the late 18th century; a nearby yew, known as the original Oswald's Tree, lingered until the mid-19th. Oswald's Well is still there, its masonry repaired by the civic authorities at either end of the 20th century. It seems gloomy and unfrequented, possibly because an iron gate bars access to the water. The neat suburban bungalows in the adjacent Oswald's Well Road are oddly incongruous, given the bloody history of the place.

A couple of miles to the south, the hamlet of Woolston also bears a form of Oswald's name: Domesday Book has it as *Osulvestone* (Oswald's Stone). The well there, though, belongs to Winifred, another 7th-century saint who lived at Holywell (Trefynnon) in Flintshire. She, too, was decapitated, in her case by a would-be seducer, furious at being rejected. Her head not only caused a well to emerge, but was miraculously restored to her body by St. Beuno, her uncle.

Her story was written at Shrewsbury when her remains were moved there in 1138. During this journey, at a pause at Woolston a further spring sprang, with marks like bloodstains on its pebbles. Pilgrims to Woolston believed that the well's water healed wounds, bruises and even broken bones. Another small spring nearby relieved sore eyes. After drinking the water some preferred stronger beverages, and by the 18th century alehouses had been established close by, though in 1755 the revels which had grown up there were banned. The well with the half-timbered building over it can still be seen.

St. Winifred

Like Winifred, the Shropshire saint, Milburga (or Milborough) had to repel attacks on her virtue. A cruel and lustful suitor pursuing her was thwarted at Stanton Lacy when the River Corve obligingly rose to bar the way as soon as she had crossed it. In gratitude she founded St. Peter's Church on the bank where she had found refuge. The chase, though, may have been resumed because a further incident is reported from

Stanton Lacy Church

Stoke St. Milborough, just four miles away. There, Milburga falls from her horse exhausted after lengthy flight. She is faint for lack of water but slakes her thirst when her horse paws the ground and a spring wells out. As Milburga prepares to ride on, men sowing barley ask what they are to say when pursuers arrive. 'Tell them Milburga passed this way when you were sowing barley', she replies, but adds that by evening the crop will be ready for harvesting. So it turns out. The labourers tell the truth, though their questioners must surely have wondered how barley came to be ripe in February.

The spring at Stoke St. Milborough still flows, and its water is considered good for sore

View from Stanton Lacy Church looking over the River Corve

eyes. Whether the saint's prohibition on geese continues to hold good is another matter: she banished them from her lands when some of them started to eat the barley seeds the men had sown. Her day is still 23 February. She has another well at Much Wenlock, where she was the second abbess of the establishment founded by her father, Merewald, king of Mercia, in 670. She died in 715. Knowledge of the site of her grave was lost when the abbey was sacked by marauding soldiers, possibly Vikings. Cluniac monks re-founded the priory in 1079, and some boys playing there fell 'by a miracle' into a tomb distinguished by the sweet smell of balsam which was identified as Milburga's resting place. After a solemn re-interment of the body pilgrims flocked to Much Wenlock. More miracles

An early 17th-century woodcut of St. Milburga, also depicting the miracles associated with her life

Stoke St. Milborough Church

62

St. Milburga's Well, Much Wenlock

were claimed at Milburga's tomb, included the curing of leprosy, blindness and scrofula. When the monasteries were dissolved under Henry VIII, Abbot Thomas Butler became parish priest of Much Wenlock and took with him the remains of Milburga, which he kept in the church. In 1547, though, they were removed and burned in a bonfire together with images of John the Baptist from Hope Bowdler and of St. Blaise from Stanton Long. However, Milburga's reputation for healing lived on. Her well at Much Wenlock cured eye diseases, and also—paradoxically, perhaps, for such a determined proponent of virginity—provided sweethearts for bereft young women who threw in a pin. For good measure, the Breton St. Owen also has a holy well in the town.

The Chapter House at Wenlock Priory

Holy Well in Hope Bagot churchyard

Another well at Hope Bagot

Many wells had their associated saint, such as St. Beuno's (Llany-mynech), St. Chad's (Chadwell, Newport), St. Hawthorn's (in fact St. Alkmund's, on the Wrekin), St. John's (Wem), St. Julian's (Ludford), St. Margaret's (Wellington, now gone, but once visited by Black Country people on Good Fridays). Others had to be content with an important personage: Lady Ida (Kinnerley), Fair Rosamund (near Diddlebury). Some merely had the vague reputation of being holy: Bettws-y-Crwyn, Chirbury, Hope Bagot, Rorrington. Efficacious in their own right were the Bill Well at Wem and the Pitch Well at Pitchford. Charlotte Burne heard this story of the Boiling Well at Ludlow:

Years ago, you know, there was what was called the Palmers' Guild at Ludlow. You may see the Palmers' Window in the church now: it is the east window in the north chancel, which was the chantry chapel of the Guild. The old stained glass gives the history of the Ludlow Palmers; how King Edward the Confessor gave a ring to a poor pilgrim, and how, years afterwards, two palmers from Ludlow, journeying homewards from the Holy Land, met with the blessed St. John the Evangelist, who gave them the same ring and bade them carry it to the king and tell him that he to whom he had given it was no other than the saint himself, and that after receiving it again the king should not live many days; which came to pass as he said. The Palmers' Guild founded many charities in Ludlow, and among them the Barnaby House, which was a hospice for poor travellers. Many used to pass through the town in those days, especially pilgrims going to St. Winifred's Well in Wales. And once upon a time an old palmer journeying thither was stayed some days at Barnaby House by sickness, and the little maid of the house waited on him. Now this little maid had very sore eyes. 'O master', said she, 'that my eyes might be healed'. Then he bade her come with him, and led her outside the town, till they stood beside the Boiling Well. And the old man blessed the well, and bade it have power to heal all manner of wounds and sores, to be a boon and a blessing to Ludlow as long as the sun shines and water runs. Then he went on his way, and the little maid saw him no more, but she washed her eyes in the water and they were healed, and she went home joyfully.

Well, Cleobury Mortimer

The well is still marked on the map, just off the Shropshire Way path near Burway Bridge, and close to the confluence of the Corve with the Teme.

Saltmoor Well at Ludford, said to have been revealed by the pigeons which gathered to drink from it, was recommended by practitioners in the early 19th century for both internal and external use to treat scorbutic and other disorders. The wells at Cleobury Mortimer were simply useful: they provided the village's water supply. The same applied to the Roman Well at Acton Burnell, though some potential users may have been put off by the local belief that frogs there were devilish imps who had chosen to assume that form. It is possible, though, that the story was invented to deter outsiders.

On set occasions wells attracted social gatherings. On Palm Sunday young people met at the Eas or East Well beside the River Perry, a mile west of the church at Baschurch, for what

St. Owen's Well, Much Wenlock

would now be regarded as the rather tame pastime of eating cakes and drinking sugared water. Small boys scrambled for lumps of sugar thrown into the stream which flows from the well. For men, there were jumping competitions, both long and high. Fights, seen by some as an essential element in having a good time, sometimes ensued, especially between the men of Little Ness and Ruyton-XI-Towns, who were divided by some ancient, half-forgotten rivalry.

Many places preferred Holy Thursday (Ascension Day). At St. Owen's Well in Much Wenlock girls threw pins into the water and afterwards paired up with boys for dancing. On the same day at Rorrington people also drank sugared water, but other attractions included a fair and a play (see chapter 11). The fairs were on Rorrington Green (now enclosed). The springs are a distance away, on Stapeley Ridge, and the stream flowing from them is called Holywell Brook. 'When Thomas Cleeton or Clayton died (who brewed the drink for the fair about a month before) the thing dropped': such was the recollection of Mary Preece, noted in 1884 but dating back to 50 years earlier. The well dressings, she remembered, came to an end at the same time.

Rorrington people had a curious belief that before the birth of Christ the water of wells was poisonous. One of the Druids of the Middleton Hills knelt to drink from a spring and found it bitter. With his fellow Druids he then walked in solemn procession from Mitchell's Fold to the well and held a ceremony there, after which the water became sweet.

CHAPTER 4

Warriors

Edmund Vale lists well over 30 castles in his book on Shropshire. The figure is by no means surprising, given the bloody history of the Marches. King Henry II gave Corfham Castle to Walter de Clifford, father of his mistress, the Fair (but unhappy) Rosamond. During the same king's reign (1154-89) Ludlow was held for a time by Joce de Dinan, who had occasion to imprison there two young knights, Walter de Lacy and Arnold de Lisle. One of the ladies of the castle, Marion de la Bruyère, fell in love with de Lisle, and helped him and his companion to escape by the classic means of a rope of knotted sheets. She seems to have been undetected, for she then arranged a return visit by her lover, up a rope ladder. Marion took him to her room, not knowing that a hundred of his men-at-arms were following him up the ladder with the intention of taking the castle. As soon as she realised that she had been duped, Marion slew

Ludlow Castle

de Lisle with his own sword, then leaped to her remorseful death from the Hanging Tower. The screams she made as she fell were said to have continued in ghostly echo for many years afterwards.

Historical traditions can be lighter. When Henry Tudor arrived at Shrewsbury in 1485 on his way to Bosworth, Thomas Mytton, chief bailiff of the town, barred the gate and swore that he would be 'slain to the ground and so run over' before he would open it. By the time Henry came back next morning wiser counsels prevailed but Mytton saved face by lying down on the Welsh Bridge and inviting Henry to step over him.

Violence and heartache predominate, though, with episodes in which Romans, Saxons, Normans, English against Welsh, English against each other, all left their marks on the collective memory, stimulated by features of the landscape, buildings and anniversaries. Latterly, re-enactments by knowledgeable and enthusiastic volunteers have attempted to provide something of the flavour of bygone combat.

After the Civil War certain battles and crimes continued to hold the popular imagination but were less and less transmitted through oral narrative. Occasionally, though, a case touches a collective nerve which continues to twitch for decades. In 1984 the 78-year-old Miss Hilda Murrell was found dead in a coppice on Haughmond Hill, six miles from her home in Shrewsbury. The police suggested a burglary gone wrong. Then it emerged that the gentle rose-grower was an anti-nuclear campaigner and that her nephew had served as an intelligence officer with the Royal Navy during the Falklands War. The theory was advanced that Murrell had been killed by MI5. Questions were asked in Parliament. Books, plays and television documentaries followed. No arrest ensued. In 2002 the police instituted a review of the 3,000 statements, 500 reports, 3,000 exhibits and 6,000 lines of enquiry associated with the case. In June the following year a 35-year-old Shrewsbury builder's labourer was charged with the crime. Murder will out, says the adage.

Hilda Murrell

Friends and Romans

Caratacus or Caradog (beloved one)—son of Cunobelinus, Shakespeare's Cymbeline—fought the Romans for several years, supported by the warlike Silures and Ordovices. In the year 51, imprudently for a guerrilla leader, he engaged in a pitched battle with a Roman army led by Publius Ostorius Scapula, and lost. His wife and daughter were captured but he fled to the northeast of England. There, Cartimandua, queen of the Brigantes, handed him over to the Romans, who took him as a prisoner to Rome. The emperor Claudius pardoned him, and he probably spent the rest of his days in Italy with his family, long outliving Ostorius Scapula who had defeated him.

According to the historian, Tacitus, who was born some years after the battle, it took place where 'On one side rose steep hills. ... In front of the position flowed a river with an untested ford, and all the defences were bristling with armed men'. The description has allowed many claims as to the site of the battle, including the Herefordshire Beacon in the Malvern Hills (but this is a considerable way from any river and was not in Ordovician territory), and both Caersws and somewhere near Newtown in Montgomeryshire (the latter favoured by the historian, Peter Salway).

Shropshire has several contenders, including Cefn-y-Castell (castle ridge) on the Breidden Hills, which also provided a cave as temporary refuge for Caratacus, and Coxall Knoll at Bucknell, some 30 miles south. Caratacus is supposed to have marched to the latter from a camp either at the nearby Gaer (castle) Ditches at Bedstone or on Wapley Hill in Herefordshire. Further claims, unsurprisingly in view of the name, are made for two hills called Caer Caradoc. One of these, in the Stretton Hills, has a small cave said to be Caratacus's head-quarters, and also a field called Battlefield. Local names are also adduced in favour of the other Caer Caradoc (see chapter 2), though there is little chance they existed some 2,000 years ago.

However, a plausible argument suggests that the Romans marched from a camp at Leintwardine along the south bank of the Teme, forded the river and turned north, just short of Stow, then climbed Stow Hill to the plateau where the action took place. This would have placed the last stand at Caer Caradoc, close to the present hamlet of Chapel Lawn. When Humphrey Lhuyd, the Welsh antiquary and map-maker, visited the area in the 1560s 'the inhabitants informed him that the place was called Caer Caradoc ... and that formerly great battles had been fought there against a certain king called Caractacus, who at last was conquered and taken by his enemies'. As Charles Kightly has pointed out, 'Since Tacitus' unique account of Caratacus, lost in the Middle Ages, was not published in Britain until 1534 and not translated into English until the 1570s, it seems likely that the story [related by Lhuyd] preserved a genuine folk-memory'. Lhuyd himself concluded that 'this must be the identical spot where Ostorius contended with Caractacus'.

A reconstruction of Viroconium *(Wroxeter)*

Of this we shall never be completely sure, but by contrast a powerful and unequivocal presence in the landscape is maintained by the Roman town of *Viroconium*, Housman's Uricon. Building there began only 40 years after Caratacus's defeat. The town, with its 5,000 inhabitants, became the fourth largest in Roman Britain, after London, Cirencester and *Verulamium* (St. Albans). Only half its 180 acres have been excavated: to complete the task would take 100 archaeologists 100 years. The Romans abandoned *Viroconium* at the end of the 4th century. Evidence includes two coin hoards of that time and the skeleton of a man who had apparently hidden in the hypocaust of the public baths. Besieging forces caught sparrows from the town, stuck wildfire to their feet, and released them. The birds flew back to their nests in the thatched roofs and set them ablaze. The same story is told of Cirencester. However an artist's impression of *Viroconium* as it was shows all the Roman buildings with tiled roofs.

There is a notion that King Arthur took over what was left of the town. Certainly, Philips and Keatman in *King Arthur, The True Story* (1993) associate Arthur with *Viroconium*, though Higham in a more recent book, *King Arthur* (2002), sees him as 'essentially a folkloric figure whose name derives from the Latin Artorius, perhaps suggested by an early Roman leader in Gaul'. There are other possible Arthurian sites in Shropshire. Yr Hên Ddinas (old castle), the hill fort at Old Oswestry, had the alternative name of Caer Ogyrfan; and the giant, Ogyrfan, one of the gods of the underworld, was Guinevere's father and thus Arthur's father-in-law. Another giant who lived in the Red Castle at Hawkstone supposedly went to fight against Arthur when the latter held court at the nearby Bury Walls. The antiquarian, William Camden, wrote in his book, *Britannia*

(1586), that local people still talked of the association between King Arthur and Bury Walls. The mediaeval Welsh tale, *Breuddwyd Rhonabwy* (Rhonabwy's dream), describes how Arthur musters 'a great host' on an island in the Severn just below Rhyd-y-Groes, two miles from Welshpool, and plays a chess-like game with now-forgotten rules, called *gwyddbwyll*. The name (cross ford) came from the mediaeval cross which guided pilgrims across the river. Henry Tudor camped there on his way to Shrewsbury and the crown of England.

Gerald of Wales (?1145-1223) wrote of 'Pengwern in Powys, now known as Shrewsbury' and added that 'The place where Shrewsbury Castle now stands used to be called Pengwern, which means head of the alder grove'. Yet the normal Welsh name for Shrewsbury is Amwythig, and the place has no archaeological record before the late Saxon period. The Wrekin hill fort, Din Gwrygon, has also been identified with Pengwern, but Wroxeter seems a more likely bet. It was in the territory of the Cornovii, the tribe to which Cynddylan, 7th-century king of Powys, belonged. It was sacked in the 650s by Mercian Angles who killed Cynddylan, the last British prince to rule east of Severn:

> Stand out, maids, and look on the land of Cynddylan;
> The court of Pengwern is ablaze, alas for the young who mourn their brothers.

As time passed Shropshire people came to believe that giants had lived in the long-abandoned ruins of *Viroconium*. This did not prevent their pillaging the site for its stone, some of which can be seen built into the churches at Wroxeter and Atcham. Thoughts of antiquity lingered in the occasional name such as Bloody Romans' Field at Lydham, near Bishop's Castle. Roman objects, including swords, were indeed found there. Archaeologists concluded that they had been ritually cast into water as propitiary offerings. A well near Plaish is known as Roman Bath, for reasons which remain unclear. Some Roman structures were ascribed to the devil. Part of the road from Wroxeter to Rushbury which survives between Cardington and Acton Burnell was thought to have been laid in a single night and is called the Devil's Causeway. The same name was given to the Roman by-road connecting Nordy Bank with the Watling Street near Acton Burnell.

Bridge over the Devil's Causeway

Saxons

At Selattyn, near Oswestry, a 19th-century hilltop tower commemorates Gwên, a British warrior killed in battle with the Saxons. The story is told in *Cân Llywarch Hen* (the song of Llywarch the old), a series of poems written in the 9th and 10th centuries, not in fact by Llywarch but about him. The old man's burning desire for glory leads in turn to the deaths of all 24 of his fighting sons including Gwên, who was the last.

Saxons are said to have defeated invading Danes in 894 at Rhyd-y-Groes (see above). They were beaten at the place themselves over a hundred years later by Gruffud ap Llywelyn. For helping Vortigern the Saxon, Hengist, was offered as much land as an oxhide would cover. He cut the hide into thin strips and by this means was able to enclose enough land for Tong Castle to be built.

In due course the Saxons had to resist Norman invaders. A powerful thane, Edric Guilda—nicknamed the Wild, latinized as Sylvaticus—was lord of the manor of Lydbury North as well as owner of land in Radnorshire, Herefordshire (especially round Wigmore) and all over Shropshire (his main holdings were at the Long Mynd, the Stiperstones and in the Clun Forest, where Caratacus had made his last stand a thousand years earlier).

One farm near Clun, Llanedric, is said still to bear his name. After William the Conqueror's coronation Edric submitted to him and was confirmed in his lands. In 1067, however, with Bleddyn of Gwynedd and his brother, Rhiwallon of Powys, both former allies of King Harold, Edric 'devastated Herefordshire as far as the bridge over the River Lugg [at Leominster] and carried away much plunder'. Two years later, wrote a chronicler, 'The Welsh and the men of Cheshire besieged the king's castle at Shrewsbury, aided by the townsmen under Eric the Wild, that powerful and warlike man, and other fierce English'. The castle held out but much of the town was burned down.

Edric seems to have been reconciled with William in 1070, and is recorded as having been in his retinue during an expedition to Scotland, two years later. He apparently rebelled again in 1075: according to one account he was captured at Wigmore and delivered in chains to the king, who consigned him to perpetual imprisonment. His property had all passed into Norman hands, especially those of Ralph Mortimer, by when the Domesday Book was compiled in 1086. An appealing story suggests that Edric escaped from confinement and took refuge in the mountain fastnesses of Wales, where he died a free man.

A century after his own time, Edric featured in Walter Map's book, *De Nugis Curialium* (courtiers' trifles), written between 1180 and 1193. Map describes him as 'Eric Wild, that is the Forester, so called for his nimbleness of body and his merry words and deeds: a man of great prowess, lord of Lydbury North'. One day, he relates, Eric is on the way home in the middle of the night after hunting when he sees on the edge of the forest a mysterious mansion in which fine ladies are dancing: 'they were most beautiful to look at, provocatively clad only in elegant linen shifts, and were taller and nobler than human women'.

Edric is captivated by one outstandingly beautiful woman. He and his page burst in and, after a struggle in which the women defend themselves literally with tooth and nail, they drag her out. Back at Lydbury, for three days and nights Edric 'did with her as he wished, but all this while he could get no word from her, though she surrendered passively to his love-making'. Then, on the fourth day she suddenly speaks:

> Hail, my sweetest one, and hale shall you be, healthy in body and pros-
> perous in your doings, just as long as you do not taunt me either about
> my sisters from whom you have seized me, or with the place and sacred
> grove whence I came. ... On the day you do so you will lose all happi-
> ness.

News of the story reaches William, who summons Eric and his bride to hear it from their lips. They live happily for many years until one night as Eric returns from hunting she is slow in responding when he calls for her. In anger he shouts: 'Was it your sisters that kept you so long?' She hears the word, 'sisters', then disappears. Edric searches day and night for her, in vain. He dies of grief.

A later tradition returned to the theme of Edric's imprisonment—below the Stiperstones—as a punishment not for resisting William the Conqueror but for submitting to him. Lead miners professed to hear Edric and his companions knocking below ground, and thus pointing to the best lodes. When danger threatened the nation Edric, his wife and their retinue rode out over the Shropshire Hills. Charlotte Burne printed this account from a young Rorrington woman:

> It was in 1853 or 1854, just before the Crimean War broke out. She was
> with her father, a miner, at Minsterley, and she heard the blast of a horn.
> He father bade her cover her face, all but her eyes, and on no account
> speak, lest she should go mad. Then they all came by; Wild Edric himself
> on a white horse at the end of the band, and the Lady Godda his wife,
> riding at full speed over the hills. Edric had short dark curly hair and very
> bright black eyes. He wore a green cap and white feather, a short green
> coat and cloak, a horn and short sword hanging from his golden belt. ...
> The lady had wavy golden hair falling loosely to her waist, and round her
> forehead a band of white linen, with a golden ornament in it. The rest of
> her dress was green, and she had a short dagger at her waist.

The description smacks suspiciously of a Robin Hood saga but the informant assured Burne that her father had seen the Wild Hunt once before, 'and then Napoleon Bonaparte came'. Others have claimed further appearances, though the vision presaged death for those who saw it. Edward Armstrong has argued that tales of the Seven Whistlers may be echoes of the Wild Hunt: six of these birds—possibly either curlews or whimbrels—fly calling through the sky for a seventh of their number. When they find it the world will come to an end.

Welsh

At Montford Bridge, five miles north-west of Shrewsbury, a traditional place for Anglo-Welsh meetings, Dafydd ap Gruffud was in 1283 handed over as a prisoner to the English. Dafydd, prince of Wales since the death of his brother Llywelyn a few months earlier, had been fighting against the king he had once served, Edward I. Edward summoned Parliament which met at Acton Burnell, if local tradition is to be believed, in the great barn, and agreed that Dafydd should be executed for treason. In October 1283 he was hanged at the High Cross in Shrewsbury after being dragged through the streets tied to a horse's tail. Then his heart and entrails were removed and burned, his body decapitated and quartered. The head went to London for display at the Tower; body parts were exhibited in different towns in the kingdom. When the executioner threw the heart on a fire, people said that it leapt out and blinded him in one eye.

Just over a century later a further Welsh revolt against English rule began. Its leader, Owain Glyndŵr, had Shropshire blood: his grandfather married Elizabeth, one of the daughters of Sir John L'Estrange of Knockin. The Breidden Hills are said to have been a favourite resort of Owain's; Sycharth, his main residence, was only a handful of miles west of Oswestry, near Llansilin. In happier times the poet, Iolo Goch, celebrated the splendour of the company and the excellence of the Shrewsbury ale served there.

The war for Welsh independence began in September 1400 when Glyndŵr's forces attacked several towns in north-east Wales, together with Welshpool and Oswestry, which they burned (though the latter's castle held out). When the earl of Arundel granted a new charter to Oswestry in 1401 only English burgesses were given rights, which included being tried only by Englishmen; and only Englishmen could perform the duty of guarding the four gates of the town for three days and nights after each of the two annual fairs.

Although Hugh Burnell, a Shropshire landowner, inflicted a defeat on the Welsh somewhere on the banks of the River Vyrnwy, raids and incursions continued, reaching as far as the suburbs of Shrewsbury. Indeed, Buildwas Abbey some 12 miles east of Shrewsbury was sacked and looted. By 1406 'In Clun Deanery', wrote Geoffrey Hodges, 'few churches west of the Long Mynd were intact'. They were not demolished, merely stripped of anything moveable or useful, and then fired. The same treatment would have been meted out to secular property.

Glyndŵr's last raid into Shropshire was in 1409. Three 'men of fame' on his side were captured and sentenced to the same grim ordeal as Dafydd ap Gruffud in Shrewsbury, Chester and London respectively. The victim at Shrewsbury was Philip Scudamore of Troy, near Monmouth, formerly master-sergeant of Monmouth Castle, who had defected to Glyndŵr.

The Welsh struggle ended in defeat. Glyndŵr's last recorded action was in 1412, after which, no doubt still dreaming of a Welsh church, parliament and university, he contrived to disappear. The Welsh remembered him, and so too did Shropshire people, partly in the context of the battle of Shrewsbury, fought on 21 July 1403. It is highly likely that the English rebellion against Henry IV suited Glyndŵr's strategy, and there are suggestions that John Kynaston of Ellesmere acted as a link between him and the insurgents, Sir Henry Percy (known as Hotspur) and his uncle, Thomas Percy, earl of Worcester.

Although Shakespeare puts Glyndŵr at the battle he was in fact on campaign in South Wales at the time, but the story spread that he had watched the fighting from an oak tree at Shelton, a mile or so upriver from Shrewsbury, long enough to see that the rebels were losing, and then retired with his men. The edition of Camden's *Britannia* by Richard Gough (not the man of the same name from Myddle) put it like this:

About a mile and a half from Shrewsbury, where the Pool road diverges from that which leads to Oswestry, there stands an ancient decayed Oak. There is a tradition that Owen Glendwr ascended this tree to reconnoitre; and finding that the king was in great force, and that the Earl of Northumberland had not joined his son Hotspur, he fell back for Oswestry, and, immediately after the battle of Shrewsbury, retreated precipitately to Wales.

The Shelton Oak in 1810

However, a detailed description of the tree in a document of 1543 on 'the Grette Oake at Shelton' makes no mention of the story, which could have been a belated piece of black propaganda against Glyndŵr, especially as the site is over three miles from the battlefield.

In 1810 a D. Parkes of Shrewsbury sent to the *Gentleman's Magazine* an engraving he had done of the tree, together with the information that it was over 40 feet in height and also in girth at the base. He added:

> Within the hollow of the tree, at the bottom, there is sufficient room for at least half a dozen to take a snug dinner; and he, whose signature follows, would have no objection to make one of the party, and drink to the memory of Owen Glyndwr.

By the end of the 19th century the tree was known as Glendower's Oak. It stood until the 1950s, when the dead trunk was removed in the interests of road widening. A sapling now marks the site.

Across the river from Shelton, half a mile upstream, is Berwick House (built 1731) where in a forerunner of the present dwelling Hotspur spent the night before the battle. When he reached the field on the day he asked for his favourite sword. After realising that he had left it behind he enquired where. On the answer, 'Berwick', he remarked: 'I perceive my plough is drawing to its last furrow, for a wizard told me that I should perish at Berwick, which I vainly interpreted of that town in the north'. A further tradition adds that at Berwick House Hotspur traced the outline of his hand on a wooden panel and that a wise woman who saw the result prophesied: 'Whoso by chance shall lose this hand / Will lose both name and house and land'. What she foretold came true when Richard Belton, whose family had owned the land for at least a century had to sell everything, after losing the panel.

Hotspur fell in the battle, shot in the head. His body was removed to the parish church at Whitchurch on the orders of Lord Furnival, but Henry IV insisted that it be taken to Shrewsbury, placed between two millstones in the market place, then quartered and hung on the gates. Hotspur's ally, the Scots earl of Douglas—Black Douglas—attempted to flee after the battle on horseback but his mount fell on Haughmond Hill at a place thereafter called Douglas's Leap. The earl was captured, though later released.

Another tale tells that the queen was watching the battle by a group of fir trees on the top of Haughmond Hill and that when the king prevailed she shouted 'Amen, the battle's won', thus giving the hill its name (in local pronunciation) of Aymon Hill (see also chapter 2). The narrative continued, erroneously, that she rejoiced too soon because the king lost, and she had to flee. To put off pursuers the queen arranged for the blacksmith at Uffington to reverse her horse's shoes, then shot the man dead with a pistol as she rode off, for fear he should betray her. Henry IV's queen, Joan of Navarre, became very unpopular, and the story may have been intended to help discredit her.

Three years after the battle Henry IV ordered that a church be founded where fighting had been fiercest. The building still stands, alone apart from a vicarage, just outside the hamlet of Battlefield.

Richard Gough of Myddle wrote of a time when fear of Welsh raiding parties caused every town to construct a fenced and ditched enclosure where cattle could be driven and guarded overnight; and when

> there was a light-horse-man maintained in every towne with a good horse, sworde, and speare, who was always ready, upon the least notice, to ride strait to the Platt Bridge, there to meet his companions; and if they found any Welshman on this side the Platt Bridge, and the river of Perry, if they should apprehend him hee was sure to bee put to death.

Platt Bridge still exists on the B 4397 road between Baschurch and Ruyton-XI-Towns. Gough adds, incidentally, that the Welsh reciprocated by hanging any Englishmen found on their side of the bridge.

Lord Audley's Cross, Market Drayton

Civil Strife

Some 50 years after the battle of Shrewsbury there was a further inter-necine struggle at Blore Heath, near Market Drayton but just over the Staffordshire border. One of the Kynastons of Ellesmere killed Lord Audley in this battle between Yorkists and Lancastrians. Audley, supporting the latter and Henry VI, set out that day—23 September 1459—from the Red Castle in Hawkstone Park. Like another queen at Shrewsbury, Queen Margaret watched the fighting from a vantage point. She spent the night before at Belton, north of Drayton, and then took up position on the top of Mucklestone Church tower. 'At Mucklestone', wrote Hare in 1898, 'still exist, with the same name [Skelhorne], descendants of the blacksmith who shod the queen's horse backward for her flight'. (She fled to the bishop of Lichfield's castle at Eccleshall).

The Kynaston on the winning Yorkist side was the grandfather of Wild Humphrey (for whom, see chapter 1). Charlotte Burne believed that 'the dim remembrances of an earlier outlaw, who also rode with horseshoes reversed and fell upon his enemies under Nesscliff Hill, may perhaps have led to the importation into the legend of Wild Humphrey of places with which the Kynastons had nothing to do—such as the Breidden Hills and Loton Park, the present "great house" of Alberbury [seven miles west of Shrewsbury], which was the Fitz Warines' earliest Shropshire home'.

The family chiefly owes its fame (or notoriety) to Fulk fitz Warin, the third of the name, who when his father died in 1197 or 8 took over a long-standing claim to the barony and castle of Whittington. (As a very young man, incidentally, during fighting at Ludlow Castle he saved the life of the unlucky Joce de Dinan—see above). King John, remembering a childhood quarrel with fitz Warin, and in any case bribed by his opponent, ruled against. In 1200 fitz Warin waylaid and killed his rival, according to tradition, in the space opposite what is now the Three Pigeons Inn, just below Kynaston's Cave at Nesscliffe. For so doing he was outlawed. Hare puts things the other way round:

> He lived as a freebooter, robbing the king's merchants in the Breidden Hills. At the foot of Nescliff Hill he lay in wait for his supplanter at Whittington, Meuric FitzRoger de Powis, and slew him, after which he fled to take refuge with Llewellyn of Wales [presumably Llywelyn ap Iorwerth, known as Llywelyn the Great]. But King John came with such a force against Llewellyn, that Fulke fled beyond the seas, till, suddenly returning, he caught the king whilst hunting in the New Forest, carried him on board ship, and forced him to restore his lands. So he returned to Whittington in peace, and lived there till he died, and was buried in the New Abbey at Alberbury, which he had founded on the banks of the Severn.

Whittington Castle

Other sources add that fitz Warin was pardoned by John in November 1203, and restored to Whittington the following year. In 1215 he joined the baronial rebellion in support of Magna Carta, but was reconciled with John two years later, though he did not recover Whittington again until 1223. He then rebuilt the castle and founded Alberbury Priory. He died in 1256 or 7, having been blind for the last seven years of his life.

His time as an outlaw, particularly the period from 1200 until 1203, inspired an Anglo-Norman verse romance of the late 13th century. This is now lost but a prose narrative in the same language, copied by a scribe in Hereford between 1325 and 1340, has survived. This, written probably by Francisque Michel, a *trouvère* in the service of the fitz Warins, displays, wrote Thomas Wright, 'an extraordinarily minute knowledge of the borders of Wales, and more especially of Ludlow and its immediate neighbourhood'. In it, fitz Warin, disguised as a charcoal burner, lures King John into an ambush by offering to show him a fine stag in the forest. The captured king swears to restore the sequestered estates and is allowed to go. Fitz Warin seizes the king's merchants and forces them to dine with him at their expense. John de Rampaigne, fitz Warin's nimble-witted *jongleur*, enters the service of the usurper, Meuric, in order to spy on him, and succeeds in rescuing a prisoner. And so on, with reckless daring, hairbreadth escapes, and even sea fights from Orkney to Barbary, in a series of episodes which have led to comparisons with the deeds of Robin Hood. Unfortunately, Charlotte Burne concludes that 'the name of Fulk Fitz Warine ... has utterly vanished from popular traditions' in Shropshire.

Even so, later outlaws in the county seem to pale into insignificance by comparison. Lawley's Cross between Much Wenlock and Buildwas is said to be a corruption of Lawless Cross, so called because highway robbers either gathered or operated there. The Swan Inn at Munslow is thought to have harboured Dick Turpin. Wilfred Byford-Jones writes:

> The story has been handed down in bar gossip from a Mrs. Francis, daughter of a licensee of long ago, who collected the legend in the village and set it down in a manuscript, now lost. Turpin was said to have arrived in Corvedale in a brewer's dray early one morning. He was interested in some fine cattle in the meadows. To bolster up this yarn we are given the 'facts' that Turpin was the member of a gang of cattle stealers as well as being a highwayman. After the gang was broken up he was said to have visited Salop with Tom King [another notorious highwayman].

Turpin was hanged at York in 1739. Highwaymen were still causing trouble 80 years later in Shropshire: in 1820 the Hawk and Buckle, one of the 12 inns at Prees, was closed by magistrates for accommodating such criminals.

Civil War

The internecine warfare of the 17th century features in the collective memory less in the form of military strategy and political debate than of individual mishaps and adventures. Oliver Cromwell occurs in a few anecdotes only: he has a church pulled down at Colemere and the bells thrown into the lake; he feeds his horses with grain kept in the long chest still displayed in the church at Oswestry; he and his bodyguard rest in the church at Alveley, or alternatively they stay at the adjacent Three Horse Shoes Inn (which claims to be the oldest in the county). Cromwell's opponent, Charles I, leaves equally little in Shropshire tradition. Shrewsbury burgesses are said to have declined in 1642 his offer to make their town a city (as they had refused Henry VIII a century earlier—see chapter 2). Charles is reputed to have stayed in 1645 in the old hall (demolished in 1961) at Chetwynd, near Newport, on his way to the battle of Naseby. At some point he hid in a priest-hole at Greete Court, near Ludlow, and rewarded the owner with a ring and his portrait. In 1649 when he was beheaded in London he divided his cloak between his two pages, William Walcot took his half home to Bitterley Court, where his family preserved it for many generations.

Alveley Church

Such traditions are very minor, compared with the wealth of knowledge of Charles II in the tree at Boscobel, which is reflected in scores of Royal Oak public houses and their signs. After his overwhelming defeat by Cromwell's forces at Worcester on 3 September 1651 Charles rode northwards 40 miles to Whiteladies, a house then standing next to the ruins of the priory of the same name, close to Boscobel in the Forest of Brewood. He spent the next day hiding in a wood, Spring Coppice, then had a meal at Hobbal Grange, the home of Richard Penderel, before setting off on foot with the latter at dusk for Madeley. The plan at this stage was to go to Swansea and thence to France. At the bridge over the River Worfe by Evelith Mill the miller came out and the pair felt constrained to run away. At Madeley they were told that bridges over

Boscobel House with the wood in which the future Charles II hid

the Severn were secured, and the ferries strongly guarded by Parliamentary soldiers, so Charles after hiding till dark in a barn at Upper House decided to turn back to Boscobel. On the return journey he and Penderel waded through the Worfe so as to avoid alerting the miller. Back at Boscobel Charles—for whose capture by this time a reward of £1,000 had been advertised—and a Major Richard Careless hid in a leafy oak, where they were to spend 15 hours.

'While we were in this tree we see soldiers going up and down, in the thicket of the wood, searching for persons escaped, we seeing them now and then peeping out of the wood': so said Charles himself in the account which Samuel Pepys took down from him many years later. When the hue and cry died down Charles moved into the house at Boscobel, where his hosts were William and Joan Penderel, but then decided to transfer to Moseley Hall, five miles away in Staffordshire. Richard Penderel and his brothers, including John, escorted Charles to Moseley. After many vicissitudes he reached the south coast and then France, travelling part of the time in the guise of servant to Joan Lane, daughter of Colonel Lane of Bentley Hall, near Moseley.

After nine years in exile Charles II returned as king in 1660. The Penderels were received at Whitehall and awarded pensions which continue to be paid to their descendants today, and now amount to about £50 a year. Joan Penderel was buried at White Ladies Priory in 1689 with the epitaph:

Here lyeth
The Bodie of a Friende
The King did call
Dame Joane, But Now Shee is
Deceast and Gone.

Spring Coppice still exists, as do Hubbal Grange and Evelith Mill. Boscobel House may be, in Nikolaus Pevsner's judgement, 'architecturally of little interest either externally or internally', yet it attracts large numbers of visitors, drawn by the high adventure of Charles's escape. The Royal Oak is still marked on the OS Explorer maps just south of Boscobel House.

As soon as its story became known at the Restoration people not only flocked to see the tree but removed pieces as souvenirs. Although the land-owner had a protective wall built in 1680, by 1713 William Stukeley described the oak as 'almost cut away by travellers'. The present tree, a descendant, was damaged by gales in February 2001, so Prince Charles—the future Charles III—planted a sapling grown from one of its acorns so as to provide a replace-ment. The footpath which Charles II would have taken from Hubbal Grange has been designated as Monarch's Way.

Many other places in Shropshire have their own Civil War stories, on both sides of the conflict. High Ercall rejoiced in the claim that it was the place in the country to hold out longest in the royalist cause. In 1645 Sir William Vaughan so vigorously conducted the defence of the old castle at Shrawardine during a five-day siege by Parliamentary soldiers that he was dubbed 'the lion of Shrawardine'. Another zealous royalist, Major Thomas Smallman, discov-

Wilderhope Manor

The monument to Sir Roger de Pulestone, erected at Newport in the 13th century, was deprived of its crosspiece by Parliamentary soldiers during the Civil War

ered that Wilderhope had been visited and robbed by some of Cromwell's troops. He rushed off to organise an ambush on the road to Ludlow, shot and killed two or three troopers, and recovered his goods. More soldiers chased him back to Wilderhope, where he hid in a secret room before sliding down a shute, mounting his horse and galloping away. Another pursuit followed. Either on this occasion, or another time when he was carrying despatches, Smallman managed to escape only by jumping his horse down a precipitous slope. The mount was killed but he fell into a crab tree and managed to scramble to safety. The place, on Wenlock Edge behind Lutwyche, inevitably became known as Major's Leap.

The town of Wem, occupied for Parliament in September 1643, was attacked the following month by Lord Capel with some 3,000 men. A force of only 300 musketeers, supported by the townspeople, beat off the royalists. A mocking rhyme celebrated the event:

> The women of Wem and a few musketeers
> Beat Lord Capel and all his cavaliers.

One of the defenders at Wem was Robert Clive of the Styche (great-great-grandfather of Clive of India), who became MP for Bridgnorth in 1646. He is said to have posted women in red cloaks round the town to deter the enemy, who took them for soldiers. From then on, royalists fervently prayed:

> From Wem and the Wich [Nantwich, captured for Parliament by Fairfax],
> And from Clive of the Styche, Good Lord deliver us.

The Wem garrison's reputation was no doubt enhanced when it took Oswestry in 1644, joined in attacks on Apley, Moreton Corbet, Powis

Hopton Castle

and Shrawardine Castles as well as Hawkstone and High Ercall Houses, and helped capture Shrewsbury for the parliamentary cause.

The saying 'Hopton quarter', meaning no quarter (mercy) at all, derives from the siege of Hopton Castle in February 1644. The castle's small Parliamentary garrison, commanded by Colonel Samuel More of Linley, resisted for a month and inflicted many casualties on the royalist attackers. When More finally surrendered he and his second-in-command were imprisoned in Ludlow Castle but the rest of the men were slaughtered in a particularly brutal application of the unwritten rule against over-zealous resistance. Two maid-servants were stripped, beaten and forced to watch the massacre, though they were later allowed to go. One remained traumatised for the rest of her life. The church register at Hopton carries this entry:

> Occisi fuere 29 in Castro Hoptoniensi inter quos Henricus Gregorye, senex, et comeranneus meus. [29 were killed in Hopton Castle including Henry Gregorye, an old man, and of my age].

Among the victims were John Arthurs, a servant of Richard Gough's father at Myddle, and another man from the same village, Reece Vaughan. 'It was said from that day', writes Veronica Thackeray, who lives within sight of the castle, 'the king's cause never prospered and that whenever a Royalist begged for quarter from a Parliamentarian he met with the icy reply, "None but Hopton quarter"'. Of ghosts in the castle, once reputed to be the most haunted along the border, she adds: 'I have never even seen a whisker'. However, Mrs. Ira Gandy, who lived for some years in Clungunford, only a couple of miles away, during the 1930s, met a shepherd at Hopton who said ''When I was a lad the old folk would tell of how the ghosts of the poor soldiers murdered there often wandered round at nightfall'. He added: 'Not that I believe it myself. Still, best to go in daylight'. Those who have seen the gaunt keep as night is falling may share his view.

Just behind the castle is a pond into which the bodies of some of the dead were thrown. It still bears the name of Bloody Pool.

CHAPTER 5

Worshippers

The prominence of churches, both physically and spiritually, placed them at the centre of parish life and death. No wonder, then, that their saints and sites loomed so large in local consciousness. Churchyards where 'the rude fore-fathers of the hamlet sleep' provide a wealth of social and human history in the shape of epitaphs supplied, to quote Gray's *Elegy* again, 'by th'unlettered muse', moralising, touching and sometimes humorous.

Bells marked the passage of time, summoned parishioners to prayer 'and to the grave', as inscriptions often reminded. They also celebrated joyous occasions, personal and public. The ringers had—as they still do—their own ways as a tightly-knit fraternity. For music within the church another group of villagers took on the role of singers and instrumentalists, until the latter at least were displaced by what became the ubiquitous organ. West Gallery music, as it was termed, has been enjoying a revival, and is represented in Shropshire by the John Moore Quire.

Inside churches (and sometimes out) the wealth of effigies and features in wood, glass and stone all had their place in a pious context. They sometimes also generated stories of their own, serving as either a starting point or a focus for local lore.

In addition to their regular routine, churches had their own customs such as penance and perambulation, wakes and feasts. Parsons—some individuals for decades at a stretch—went about their duties in exemplary fashion, though the occasional incumbent stood out from the rest as wayward or eccentric, for better or worse.

One Foundation?
With rare exceptions churches claim the patronage of a saint or saints. The most favoured owe their foundation to the personal intervention of a saint. St. Ethelfleda, renowned for bathing out of doors at nightime in the nude 'for ascetical reasons', is said in the 10th century to have founded both a monastery

Stoke St. Milborough Church in 1791

at Chirbury (of which a few stones survive in the present churchyard) and a church at Shrewsbury. The latter's site was later occupied by a new building of which the sponsors preferred St. Alkmund (or Alcmund), son of the Northumbrian king, Alchred. Alkmund died in battle against Mercians led by King Eardwulf in about 800, and was buried at Lilleshall. Miracles reportedly took place at his tomb, but his remains were later moved to Derby. The parish church at Whitchurch is also dedicated to him.

The village of Stoke St. Milborough owes its name and the church its dedication to St. Milburgh (or Milburga) whose story is told in chapter 3. The claim that the martyrdom of St. Wistan in 850 took place at Shropshire's Wistanstow is disputed by experts, who ascribe it to Wistow in Leicestershire. The bones of the Welsh 7th-century martyr, St. Winifred, were at one stage moved into Shrewsbury Abbey, though the church was not dedicated to her. The usual miracles were reported there, and wells associated with her are still visited at Holywell and Woolston (see chapter 3). St. Oswald's connection with Oswestry is described in chapters 3 and 4.

When wealthy people, in pursuance of a vow or simply a desire to demonstrate piety or power, set about establishing a church, they could nominate a favoured saint as patron. There is a tradition that Queen Edith, wife of Edward the Confessor, founded a church at Kinlet, though the earliest parts of the present building are Norman. At Quatford, overlooking the River Severn at Bridgnorth, the church owes its existence to the vow made by Adelisa (or Adelais). The grand lady was sailing from Normandy to join her husband, Roger de Montgomery, when a great storm blew up in the Channel. A priest in her party had a vision of 'a certain matron' (Mary Magdalene) who told him: 'If thy lady would wish to save herself and her attendants from the present dreadful danger at sea, let her make a vow to God and faithfully promise to build a church in honour of the blessed Mary Magdalene on the spot where she may first happen to meet her husband, the earl, in England; and especially where there groweth a hollow oak and the wild swine have shelter'. The priest told Adelisa, she took the vow, the storm abated. When she met her husband he was by a hollow

Quatford Church

oak on a hunting expedition. He paid for the church to be built at the spot, and it was consecrated in 1086. In 1100 the then owner, Robert de Belesme, abandoned the site and moved to Bridgnorth, but parts of the original building survive in the present church. The oak tree is shown in 20th century stained glass in a window in the south wall.

Others were less punctilious in fulfilling their vows. Three squires, Walcot of Walcot, Plowden of Plowden and Oakley of Oakley, set off from Lydbury North to fight in a crusade on behalf of their overlord, William de Vere, bishop of Hereford. They took part in the battle of Acre (1191), and according to one account were captured. Each swore that if he returned safely home he would pay to add a chapel to Lydbury Church. Eventually they all came home, but only one, Plowden, kept his promise. Local tradition said that while the Plowdens

Lydbury North Church

87

flourished the Walcots and the Oakleys declined. The Walcots did fall into financial difficulties, and in 1764 sold their estate to Clive of India, though they had in fact built a chapel at Lydbury in thanksgiving for the return of Charles II in 1660. The Oakleys held out till Victorian days.

One Plowden of Elizabethan times, a lawyer, made himself famous during the trial of a client charged with attending mass, when to do so was illegal. It emerged that the mass had been said by a layman masquerading as a priest, probably to entrap those who attended. Plowden observed: 'No priest, no mass. The case is altered'. His client was acquitted.

Lydbury North was presented to the bishop of Hereford in about 780 by a man known as Egwin Shakehead, a sufferer from palsy, who achieved a miraculous cure by visiting the shrine of St. Ethelbert in Hereford Cathedral. The story of the donation seems to have transferred to another palsy victim, Aelnoth, the son of Wild Edric (see chapter 4), who was also believed to have given Lydbury in thanksgiving for being cured at Hereford.

It is easy to understand why well known saints such as Mary, Peter and Michael were chosen as patronal figures, such was their prestige. Other preferences are mysterious. St. Eatha, a Northumbrian bishop who died of dysentery in 686, has only one dedication in the whole of England, at Atcham. St. Calixtus (or Callistus), who was born a slave but became a pope, died during the course of a riot in Rome in 222, yet over 900 years later, in 1138, he was chosen as patron of the newly-founded church at Astley Abbotts.

Deciding on the site for a new church caused hesitation, heart-searching and even dissension. Near Shifnal the parish churches of Albrighton and Donington (the latter village now more or less a suburb of the former) stand very close to each other. A local tale has it that two rich sisters wished to have a church built, but quarrelled over where, and opted to have one apiece. In fact the foundation of St. Cuthbert's at Donington dates from about 1085, that of St. Mary Magdalene at Albrighton from the following century. An alternative explanation for the nearness of the two churches has been advanced by Wilfred Byford-Jones: Donington's church (I paraphrase) was endangered by outlaws from the nearby Brewood Forest, who crossed from Staffordshire to Shropshire to take refuge when things grew too hot for them. When a church was mooted for Albrighton a site near to St. Cuthbert's won acceptance so that the two establishments could provide mutual support. The strategy seems to have failed. Simon, the Donington parson, was murdered in 1256, and his home burned down. Travellers were robbed, and horses hamstrung.

In some cases Christians merely adopted a site already venerated. The church at Llanyblodwel is said to stand where Druids once conducted their rites. Many venerable yews long pre-date the churches by which they stand, and they may indicate places of pre-christian worship. Round plots also point to pagan sites, and this applies to 40% of Shropshire churchyards, including

Melverley Church—at its 'satanic' site

those at Alberbury, Bucknell, Church Pulverbatch, Diddlebury, Easthope, Kenley, Kinlet (originally), Leebotwood and Stanton Lacy. Tradition says that Acton Round is so called because the church there was round. At Shrewsbury after the collapse of St. Chad's in 1788 a round building allegedly replaced it because the trustees mistook for a plan of the church a circle drawn on the map by the architect to indicate the site.

Changes of location were at times attributed to intervention by the devil. Building at Baschurch is said to have begun to the north of the village on a hill called the Berth. The conspicuous position so offended the devil that every night he threw the materials into the Berth Pool below. The masons lost heart and adopted the site where All Saints' Church now stands. At Melverley people suspected a practical joke when building materials several times disappeared from the place chosen for the church, on high ground above the Vyrnwy, only to be discovered down on the river bank. Then satanic involvement was feared, so the alternative site was accepted. The church is still there, five centuries on.

The first church at Worfield is reputed to have been endowed either by the Saxon, Leofric (husband of Godiva), or by the Norman, Roger de Montgomery. The preferred location was on top of a steep ridge, in full view of the whole parish, but the devil thought better, and repeatedly carried masonry down to the foot of the hill. The builders perforce took to the new site but retaliated by erecting a soaring spire—an unusual feature for Shropshire—visible from most approaches to the village. Any satanic influence must have been readily negated: Worfield boasted that only four vicars were needed to cover the two centuries from 1564 to 1763. Stoke-upon-Tern, too, has its tale of a church begun on high ground but moved down when 'the devil would not have it', and drew the stones away. The present building is Victorian.

Ancient yew trees, possibly more than in any other English county, are a feature of many Shropshire churchyards including those at Acton Scott, Ashford Carbonel, Bucknell, Church Preen, Claverley, Clun, Easthope, Hope Bagot, Loughton, Ludford, Norbury, Selattyn, Uppington and Whittington. They supplied boughs to be carried on Palm Sunday or to be placed on coffins

Worfield Church

Yew tree at Loughton churchyard

at funerals. They symbol-
ised death by their darkness
but immortality by their
longevity. They protected
the church physically from
wind and weather and
spiritually from witches
and warlocks. Beneath a
yew was a favoured place
for a burial. Conversely,
at Market Drayton in the
late 19th century people
refused to allow their dead
to be buried anywhere
near the many fairy rings
which they identified in
the churchyard. The north
side, reached through the
'excommunication door'
(now often blocked, as at

Yew tree at Church Preen

Alveley, Ashford Carbonel and Church Stretton) was avoided whenever
possible as the devil's territory. This had the advantage that the empty ground
could be used for other purposes such as sport. At Bishop's Castle the remains
of a line still visible on the north side of the tower show where until the early

Easthope Church and yew tree

The blocked up north door at Stanton Lacy Church

19th century the game of fives was played. The same pastime is recorded at Stoke St. Milborough until 1820, and no doubt there are similar examples elsewhere.

High windows on the north side of the church at Acton Burnell, according to Dean Cranage, 'may have displayed a lamp to scare away evil spirits from the church-yard'. A low-side window in the south wall of the chancel at Kinlet was also believed to serve the purpose of allowing a light to shine out to repel the spirits thought to frolic after dark in the churchyard. It is likely, though, to have fulfilled the useful function of allowing the acrid smoke of candles and incense to escape from the church during services.

Resting in Peace

The rich and famous formerly had the privilege of being buried within churches, their tombs

Monument to Sir Robert Broke and his two wives at Claverley

*Monument to Francis Gatacre and
his wife in Claverley Church*

surmounted by elaborate effigies
of the occupants in the pomp they
had enjoyed in life. For example,
the richly-dressed Sir Robert Broke
(died 1588) is depicted with his two
(successive) wives at Claverley. In
the same church Francis Gatacre
(died 1599) and his wife, Elizabeth,
appear in a lavish funereal plaque.
Such monuments have great dignity
and sometimes pathos: the swaddled child shown on a painted tomb
at Moreton Corbet with Richard
Corbet (died 1566) and his wife was
their only son, who died in infancy.
Verses on the magnificent tomb of
Sir Thomas Stanley (died 1576) are
claimed to be by Shakespeare but
more likely came from a local poet,
Richard Barnefield:

The swaddled child on the painted Corbet tomb at Moreton Corbet Church

> Not Monumental Stone preserves our fame,
> Nor Sky-aspiring Pyramids our name.
> The Memory of him for whom this stands
> Shall outlive Marble and Defacers' hands:
> When all to Time's consumption shall be given,
> Stanley, for whom this stands, shall stand in heaven.
>
> Ask who lyes heare, but do not weep;
> He is not dead, he dooth but sleep.
> This stony register is for his bones,
> His fame is more perpetuall than theise stones;
> And his own goodness not himself being gon,
> Shall lyve when earthlie monument is none.

Either way, it is a handsome tribute. Stanley's contemporary, Edmond Cornewayll (or Cornwall) of Burford, once sheriff of Shropshire (died 1585, aged 50), preferred a bleaker style:

> For as you are so once was I,
> And as I am so you shall be,
> Although that ye be fair and young,
> Wise, wealthy, hardy, stout and strong.

The dead regularly addressed messages of this kind to the living, through the medium of inscriptions on gravestones, tombs or memorial plaques. The Latin epitaph at Stanton Lacy to Richard Heynes (died 1649, aged 24) regrets his untimely end, invites us to 'bewail this wrongful deed' which has caused it, and reminds us that all mortals are 'but dust and shadow'. Tradition says that Heynes was killed by Parliamentary soldiers during the Civil War, but this may merely be an attempt to explain the obscure circumstances of his death.

Moralising turns to melancholy in the epitaph at Clun to Charles Dilke of Mainstone (died 1825, aged 45):

> Joyous his birth, wealth o'er his cradle shone,
> Generous he proved, far was his bounty known,
> Men, horses, hounds were feasted at his hall;
> There strangers found a welcome, bed and stall;
> Quick distant idlers answered to his horn,
> And all was gladness in the sportsman's morn.
>
> But evening came and cold blew the gale,
> Means overdrawn had now begun to fail;
> His wine was finished and he ceased to brew,
> And fickle friends now hid them from his view,
> Unknown, neglected, pined the man of worth,
> Death his best friend, his resting place the earth.

Sadness from deep disappointment in love predominates in the inscription at Shifnal to Mary Adley (died 1803, aged 29), addressed specifically to women:

> Reader, attend, look at my name,
> And if thy sex it be the same,
> Look at my age, and then beware
> Of what hath been my early snare:
> Too hastily I fixed my mind
> Upon a youth who proved unkind;
> No sooner were we wed than he
> Took what I had, and then left me.

A more acerbic tone is adopted at Worthen, where Thomas Davies (died 1797) observes:

> This world's a city full of crooked streets,
> Death's the market place where all mankind must meet.
> If life was a merchandise that men could buy,
> The rich would always live, but the poor must die.

A similar verse is found throughout the country. The first couplet comes from *The Two Noble Kinsmen*, by Fletcher and Shakespeare, written in about 1613 and published some 20 years later. A particularly bitter epitaph composed for the tomb at Ludlow of a clearly unpopular Chief Justice of Cheshire and President of the Council of the Marches (died 1637) was not in the end engraved:

> Here lies Sir John Bridgeman, all clad in his clay;
> God said to the devil, 'Surrah, take him away'.

Genuine grief, on the other hand, is expressed for the passing of those who die in untimely fashion, by accident or illness. Robert Cadman was a steeplejack who supplemented his earnings by balancing on ropes stretched across heights. While he worked on the weathercock of St. Mary's Church, Shrewsbury, in 1739, he rigged a rope from the spire to Gay Meadow on the banks of the Severn, some 800 feet away. He entertained crowds by walking up, then sliding speedily down, but on 2 February the rope parted and he fell to his death. A memorial tablet is still in the church.

> Let this small Monument record the name
> Of CADMAN, and to future times proclaim
> How by'n attempt to fly from this high spire
> Across the Sabrine stream he did acquire
> His fatal end. 'Twas not for want of skill
> Or courage to perform the task he fell;
> No, no, a faulty Cord being drawn too tight
> Hurried his Soul on high to take her flight
> Which bid the Body here beneath good Night
> Feb? 2ᵈ 1739 aged 28.

Cadman's epitaph

95

A natural phenomenon killed Samuel Perkins and his wife and son at Wentnor, six miles north-east of Bishop's Castle, in 1772:

> On Sunday morn 'Bout nine o'Clock as we lay in our Bed,
> By Hurricane of Wind and Snow all three were killed dead,
> The House and we were Blown away as many well did know,
> And for that day could not be found all for the depth of snow;
> Fourteen poor souls were under it, but with us were killed seven,
> I hope the Lord hath Pardoned us and Received our souls in Heaven.

The need for pardon is explained, according to Magdalene Weale, because the Perkins family

> had gone one Saturday night to Asterton, a good mile away, for a 'caking'. This is a sort of gaming party in which the stakes are cakes baked and sold to the guests at a profit by the hostess who also provides a barrel of home-brewed ale. The Perkins family and other guests, no doubt, played long and merrily and drunk deep of the housewife's good home-brew, and then slept the night at the house. The next day being Sunday they, fourteen souls all told, lay long abed and sleeping off no doubt the effect of the night's carouse. At 9 am a terrific hurricane of wind and snow arose and the house and its occupants was blown away and buried deep in snow.

Caking went on for another hundred years or so after the Perkins' deaths. Gleanings from the fields after harvest provided corn for the flour for the cakes, and the gatherings would be held until Christmas. 'A right good cakin'' could make a hostess the useful sum of 8 or 10 shillings.

Edwin Tudur, killed in a railway crash near Telford in 1864 when he was 26, is commemorated in the churchyard at Stokesay:

> A fearful accident in youth and strength
> Cut short his life How well that a career
> Approvable of God lies not in length
> Of days but in his holy faith and fear
> Walk so and whether slow or sadder end
> Come late or no, Christ will be thy friend.

A Mrs. Lancett also died on the railway line, in 1882, struck by an engine near Ludlow when she was picking up nuts which had fallen from an earlier train. She is remembered at Ashford Carbonel:

> A sudden shock - I in a moment fell;
> I had not time to bid my friends farewell.

Beware! Death happens into all;
This day I fell - tomorrow you may fall.

Benjamin Giles (died 1795, aged 37), who fell from his horse at Hope Bagot, is described as having been 'snatched suddenly away by the King of Terrors'.

The trades and occupations of the dead are from time to time mentioned in epitaphs. One wonders whether Edward Knott (died 1759, aged 80) of Hope Bowdler was still working at the time of his accident:

In the quarry where this stone was got
Edward mischanced to fall it was his lot
Time for preparation it was small
God will have mercy on us all
That was all that could be said
Then in one minute he was weel and dead

In Benthall churchyard the cast-iron tomb of a trowman, Eustace Beard (died 1721) carries the prayer: 'From rocks and sand the Lord deliver us'. Edward Gittin (died 1842) received at Westbury the verse traditional for blacksmiths:

My Sledge and Hammer lie reclined,
My Bellows, too, have lost their wind.
My Fire's extinct, my Forge decayed,
And in the dust my Vice is laid.
My coal is spent, my Iron gone,
My Nails are drove, my Work is done.

John Abingdon (died 1817), 'who for 40 years drove the Ludlow coach to London, a trusty servant, a careful driver, and an honest man', was rewarded with an appropriate epitaph:

His labour done, no more to *town*
    His *onward* course he bends;
His team's *unshut* [unharnessed], his whip's laid up,
    And here his journey ends.
Death *locked his wheels* and gave him rest,
    And never more to move,
Till Christ shall call him with the blest,
    To heavenly realms above.

William Nott of Bitterley, shoemaker, parish clerk, churchwarden and rate collector, died in a blizzard in 1830 at the age of 73. The local schoolmaster, Herbert Green, wrote these verses for him:

He was NOTT born of womankind
And so it may be said
Although within this grave he lies
We know he is NOTT dead

No one possessed a better SOLE
When death gave him a call
He to the LAST was firm and strong
And calm gave up his AWL

To church he regularly went
Upon the Sabbath day
It was his duty to do so
As clerk and NOTT to pray

Foolish or bad he never was
And yet it strangely appears
He lived a very quiet life
In Bedlam [see page 38] for forty years

Then underneath this verdant sod
We'll let him now remain
For sure and confident we are
WILL NOTT will rise again.

Rather more irreverent were the lines to Thomas Davies of Langley House (died 1760) on a gravestone now badly weathered near the south door of the chancel at Stanton Lacy:

Good natur'd, bold and free,
He always was in company.
He loved his Bottle and his Friend
Which brought on soon his latter end.

Still more direct was the verdict on Francis Hick (died 1802) at Church Stretton:

Here lies the barber Hick,
Who cut and shaved and was so quick,
And now has gone to his long whum,
He killed himself with drinking rum.

Equally laconic was the inscription in the same churchyard (now gone, but formerly, according to Hare, near the sundial) to Ann Cook (died 1814):

> On a Thursday she was born,
> On a Thursday made a bride,
> On a Thursday her leg was broke,
> And on a Thursday died

Just as economical are the lines to William Jones (died 1836, aged 30) at Stokesay:

> When I was young and in my prime
> The Lord did please to end my time
> My race is run my work is done
> The Lord did call and I am gone.

The tomb of William Churchman (died 1602) at Munslow shows a man in a shroud, together with a skull and an hourglass, and bears these words:

> IN.THE.HOWER.OF.HIS.POWER.ONE.DEAD.
> BY.CHRIST.DOE.RISE.
> AND.WEE.WHOSE.BOANES.ROT.UNDER.STONES.
> OUR.DUST.HEEL.NOT.DESPISE.

One of the shortest — and most pessimistic — inscriptions must be the four words on the Leighton monument at Cardington: *Nemo ante obitum beatus* (no one is happy before death). Yet many memorials celebrate long life. At Ellesmere William Parks (died 1746) earned high praise:

> Interr'd here lies one hundred years and four,
> No one knew Scripture less and virtue more;
> Peace his ambition, contentment was his wealth,
> Honesty his pride, his passion's health,
> The father's duty and the husband's guide,
> By nature good, the age's wonder dyed.

Five years later Rowland Doukin died, aged 95, at Astley, four miles from Shrewsbury. His epitaph comments not on the man but on his experience:

> Many years I've seen, and
> Many things I've known,
> Five Kings, two Queens,
> And a Usurper on the throne;
> But now lie sleeping in the dust,
> As you, dear reader, shortly must.

A touching story at Stokesay concerns William Thomas, a gardener at the castle, who died in 1879, aged 94. He was much admired by a young lad who, when he returned to the village after a long absence, found his old friend uncommemorated, and so arranged this memorial:

> Autumn came and Thomas had
> Nuts and apples for the Lad.
> He to Manhood Having grown,
> Determined to erect this stone,
> The Soul of Thomas having flown.

The oldest of all Shropshire's old, at 152, was Thomas Parr (1483-1635), whose memorial brass in the church at Wollaston reads:

The old, old, very old man, Thomas Parr, was born at the Glyn, in the parish of Winnington, within the chapelry of Wolaston, in the parish of Alberbury, in the county of Salop, in the year of our Lord 1483; he lived in the reigns of ten kings and queens of England, viz. Edward IV and V, Henry VII and VIII, Edward VI, Mary, Elizabeth, James I, and Charles I, died the 13th, and was buried in Westminster Abbey the 15th November 1635, aged 152 years and nine months.

Thomas Parr

Parr married his second wife, a Welsh widow, when he was 121, and three years later had to do public penance in Alberbury Church for seducing Catherine Milton.

He was celebrated in verse by John Taylor, the 'Water Poet':

> Good wholesome labour was his exercise,
> Down with the lamb, and with the lark would rise;
> In mire and toiling sweat he spent the day,

Old Parr's Cottage in 1814. Rodney's Pillar (see chapter 1)
can be seen on the hilltop in the background

And to his team he whistled time away:
The cock his night-clock, and till day was done,
His watch and chief sun-dial was the sun.
He was of old Pythagoras' opinion,
That green cheese was most welcome with an onion;
Coarse meslin [mixed flour] bread, and for his daily swig,
Milk, butter-milk, and water, whey and whig [whey fermented and
flavoured with herbs]:
Sometimes metheglin, and by fortune happy,
He sometimes sipped a cup of ale most nappy [strong],
Cyder or perry, when he did repair
T'Whitsun ale, wake, wedding, or a fair;
Or when in Christmas-time he was a guest
At his good landlord's house amongst the rest:
Else he had little leisure-time to waste,
Or at the ale-house huff-cap [heady] ale to taste;
His physic was good butter, which the soil
Of Salop yields, more sweet than candy oil [syrup];
And garlick he esteemed above the rate
Of Venice treacle, or best mithridate [universal antidote].
He entertained no gout, no ache he felt,
The air was good and temperate where he dwelt;
While mavisses [thrushes] and sweet-tongued nightingales
Did chant him roundelays and madrigals.
Thus living within bounds of nature's laws,
Of his long-lasting life may be some cause.

After Parr's death, some expressed doubts as to whether he had really attained the age of 152, but there do seem to have been genes of longevity in the family: a grandson of Parr's called Robert, born at Kinver in Staffordshire in 1633, died in 1757, 124 years later. One enterprising man, a journeyman printer, made £100,000 from the 'life-pills' to which he gave Thomas Parr's name. The bottle bore the old man's likeness after the painting by Rubens.

One grave at Tong is bedecked with flowers but untenanted: it belongs to the fictional Little Nell whom Charles Dickens, ignoring desperate pleas from readers of the serialised *Old Curiosity Shop* (1840-1), killed off in the village.

Bells and Bands

Bells had their own inscriptions, almost as though when they rang the message of the words would be conveyed. *Sancte Petre* and *Sancta Maria Ora pro Nobis* ('O Saint Peter' and 'Saint Mary pray for us') inscribed at Astley Abbotts on bells cast in 1455 reflect standard pre-Reformation sentiments, but a different theology is implied on a third bell, of 1651, and therefore during the Commonwealth: *Cantate Domino Cantatum Novum* ('Sing to the Lord a New Song').

At Wroxeter a bell of Queen Elizabeth's time carries the words:

> God save the Church Our Queene & Realme
> send us Peace in Christ. Amen.

At St. Peter's, Chelmarsh, a bell dated 1700 announces: 'I call the Quick and the Dead / Prepare to Church and Bed'. The sixth bell of 1768 at St Peter and

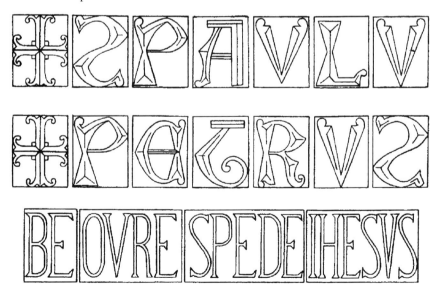

Inscription on bells at Ashford Carbonel

St Paul, Wem—in common with many elsewhere—is inscribed 'I to the church the living call, and to the grave do summon all'. Four of the 18th-century bells at St. Alkmund's, Whitchurch, are respectively engraved: 'I first begin to lead our ring', 'God preserve our gracious King', 'Prosperity to this Parish' and 'God preserve this Church and Benefactors'. The second bell at Stokesay, cast in 1822, proclaims:

> Here let us pause and now with one accord
> Salute the Church Triumphant in the Lord.

Ordinary people had their own rhymes to mimic the sound of a church's bells, or perhaps simply to create a memorable jingle. V.S. Lean amalgamated many such rhymes here:

> A nut and a kernel, say the bells of Acton Burnell.
> A pudding in the pot, say the bells of Acton Scott.
>
> Pitch 'em and patch 'em, say the bells of old Atcham.
> Hold up your shield, say the bells of Battlefield.
>
> Wristle, wrastle, say the bells of Bishop's Castle.
> Up Severn and down Morfe, say the bells of Bridgnorth.
>
> Roast beef and mutton, say the bells of Church Stretton.
> Hop, skip and run, say the bells of Clun.
>
> Axes and brummocks [billhooks], say the bells of Clungunus.
> Under and over, say the bells of Condover.
>
> A stick and a stone, say the bells of Edgton.
> You're too fond of beer, say the bells of Ellesmere.
>
> Why don't you ring louder? say the bells of Hope Bowdler.
> Because we are eaten, say the big bells of Eaton.
>
> Buttermilk and whey, say the bells of Hopesay.
> An old lump of wood, say the bells of Leebotwood.
> (Or: Lay a bottle in the wood, say the bells of Leebotwood).
>
> Roas' goose an' gonder, say the bells of Longnor.
> How dare you do so? say the bells of Ludlow.
>
> We must all die, say the bells of Norbury.
> Three crows on a tree, say the bells of Oswestry.

Roast beef and merry, say the bells of Shrewsbury.
Itchy and scabby, say the bells of the Abbey.

Up the ridge and down the butt, say the bells of Smethycote [Smethcott].
Roast beef and mutton, say the bells of old Upton.

Jack and Jim the tailor, hang the rogue the ringer.
Ivy, holly and mistletoe, say the bells of Wistanstow.

There is no indication as to whether the Upton mentioned is Upton Cressett (St. Michael's) or Upton Magna (St. Lucy's). There is a further sequence for Shrewsbury's churches:

Three naked lads (or golden spades), say the bells of St. Chad's.
Three silver (or golden) pikels [pitchforks] say the bells of St. Michael's.
Three golden canaries (or buttercups and daises or a new-born baby) say
                the bells of St. Mary's.
A boiling pot and stewing pan, say the bells of Julian.
You're a rogue for sartin, say the bells of St. Martin.

In his book, *The House in the Cornfield* (1957), Cledwyn Hughes, writing about an unspecified Welsh village close to the Shropshire border, describes a Mr. Sykes who claimed that 'in all the years he had been ringing he had never known a bellringer, either in the parish or for twenty miles around, who had died of cancer'. He added: 'They all live old and long because God looks after them that rings bells'. Even so, a ringer at Newport was killed in 1701 by the second bell. Like other objects and indeed animals which caused the death of a person, this was then forfeited under the law of 'deodand' (repealed only in 1846) to the lord of the manor, in this case, the earl of Bradford, who promptly re-donated it to St. Nicolas's Church. (Two millstones which became deodand in 1292 after killing Valentine the Miller at Hope Bagot can be seen at the base of the church tower. In 1796 a horse which kicked and killed Samuel Cook at Middleton Scriven was forfeited to the lord of the manor as deodand).

Ringers' indiscipline—*pace* Mr. Sykes—could be a problem. Several churches felt it necessary to display placards with detailed rules for behaviour: for example, at Bridgnorth St. Mary's, Cardington, Culmington and Tong (dating, in the last case from 1694):

If that to Ring you doe come here,
You must ring well with hand and care.
        keep stroak of time and goe not out;
        or else you forfeit out of doubt.
Our law is so concluded here;
For every fault a jugg of beer,

if that you Ring with Spurr or Hat;
a jugg of beer must pay for that.
If that you take a rope in hand;
These forfeits you must not withstand.
or if that you a Bell ov'r-throw;
It must cost Sixpence ere you goe.
If in this place you sweare or curse;
Sixpence to pay, pull out your purse.
come pay the Clerk it is his fee;
for one (that swears) shall not goe free.
These laws are old, and are not new;
therefore the Clerk must have his due.

A century later, when a similar verse was cut in stone at Church Stretton, the fine for swearing had increased to 12 pence. The names of the ringers of the day were added: Jo^n· Phillips, Jo^n· Roynolds, Jo^n· Poston, Jo^n· Evason, Jo^n· Nicholls, Edwd· Home, Rich^d· Phillips, Thos· Gough, Thos· Cole, Fran^{cs}· Loyd, Wm. Poston, Wm. Home and Wm. Gough.

As well as for routine services ringers rang on special occasions, and were paid for doing so. Churchwardens' accounts record the details. For example, at Cheswardine, four miles from Market Drayton:

1556	for a drink to the ryngers on corpus cristi deye [Thursday after Trinity Sunday] iiiid.
	to the ryngers on all Halo nyght [All Hallows, 1 November] iid.
1560	to the ringars on holy thursday [Ascension Day] iid. viiid.
1574	at the day of the Ryngynge for our queen [Elizabeth] iis.
1603/4	payde to the Ryngers for ye Kynge [James I] 4s.

Or Church Pulverbatch:

1683 to ye Ringers ye 5th November ls. 6d.

Many towns and villages had a curfew bell, though the legal requirement to do so ended as early as 1100. Among them, until the late 19th century at least, were Baschurch, Condover, Edgmond, Newport, Much Wenlock, Shifnal, Shrewsbury St. Mary's and Tong. Such a bell at 8 pm from Michaelmas (29 September) until the Annunciation (Lady Day, 25 March) rang at Cleobury Mortimer. There is a story that in the 1830s a lady out with a fox hunt that went through Acton Reynald, Twemlows, Lee Bridge, Iscoyd Park and Hawkstone became separated from other riders as dusk fell, and found herself in treacherous marshy ground by the River Roden between Wem and Loppington. She wandered all night until she heard the 6 am bell at Wem and was able to find her way to safety. In gratitude she donated a sum of money to the church to enable such a bell to be rung in perpetuity. In fact, together with a 6 pm curfew bell, it came to an end in 1912.

At Llanyblodwel a single bell in the spire called people to service but on Sunday mornings it was rung afterwards, too, to warn those left at home to put the dinner on. In much of England this was known as the pudding bell but at Llanyblodwel they used the Welsh term, *y gloch botes*, the broth bell, since the first course of the meal consisted of a basin of broth (*potes*). Formerly the clerk rang this bell, and was paid at harvest time by *yr ysgub y gloch*, the bell sheaf.

Churches had their own variations in ringing. On Sunday at Moreton Corbet they chimed the bells for 15 minutes, then two bells for five minutes, followed by the tenor and then the treble for a further five minutes in turn. At Cleobury Mortimer the passing bell was rung not on the day of a death but on that of a funeral, beginning at 8 am. For a man there were nine strokes on the second, third and fourth bells in turn, followed by the tolling of the tenor bell for half an hour—a whole hour, 'if desired'. The same procedure applied for a woman, though with eight strokes instead of nine. By 'old custom' at Morville, according to Hare, the 'joy-bells' were rung at a funeral.

The ringers sent a message far and wide. Music in the church, especially after the Parliamentary act of 1644 which banned organs from churches, was provided by a group of singers and musicians assembled, often, in a

West gallery at Wroxeter Church

gallery at the west end. One Shropshire blacksmith is said to have made himself an iron 'cello so that he could join the church band. Church records at Wem show purchases of a bassoon (1780) and a 'large fiddle' (1814). A pitch pipe (1807) would have been intended for the singers, who were paid until 1840. The serpent—a wind instrument so called from its convoluted shape—played in Shrewsbury St. Chad's before the tower collapsed in 1788 has been preserved in the town museum. The clarinet and bassoon

Church gallery musicians,
as drawn by Gordon Ashman

purchased in 1828 were played for 50 years at Mainstone. Before the church at Hope Bowdler was re-built in 1862 members of the Croxton family played violin, oboe and 'cello in the west gallery there. By coincidence, in the same year at Llanyblodwel an organ replaced west gallery performers. In the middle of the century these were William Jones, the sexton ('clarionette'), John Jones, Junior, of Glanyrafon (violoncello), Richard Pugh ('clarionet') and Thomas Hughes of Tŷnycoed (accordion). Two instruments, a 'cello and a bassoon,

West gallery at Tugford Church

were still kept in a chest in the church in the early 20th century. The latter's purchase, in 1797, appears in the churchwardens' accounts: it cost £5 13s. 1d, made up of £2 14s. 6d. in donations and £2 18s. 7d. from parish funds.

Mary Cholmondeley wrote that her father, who retired as rector of Hodnet in 1892, 'remembered the trombone and fiddle still in use in the gallery of country churches'. (She added that he also recalled at Hodnet 'how the church clock was set by "old Peg", presumably the churchwarden, who used to stroll down to the mail coach occasionally and "take the time" from the driver').

The rector at Tugford remarked on the flute, clarinet and melodeon which had been played there as late as 1899. At Stokesay bass viol, flute and clarinet were replaced in about 1855 by a harmonium. The present organ is now back in the gallery. The string band at Clun, of whose instruments only the double bass has survived, gave way to a barrel organ. A similar change occurred at Stanton Long, where a combined finger and barrel organ was installed in 1854. A barrel capable of playing 12 tunes is still concealed somewhere within the conventionally-played organ at Llanfair Waterdine. An organ with two barrels, each with 10 tunes, was last used at Cardeston in about 1879. The west gallery at Ashford Carbonel, built in 1752 to seat 25, was removed in the 1880s, and the old-fashioned choir gave way to a harmonium. In 1959 followed a new organ in a new loft.

As well as the names of instrumentalists at Llanyblodwel those of some of the singers have been recorded from the mid-19th century: M.A. Roberts, School House; Maria Williams, Wengwta; Mary Price; Edward Jones, Glyn; John Davies, Penrhiw; Matthew Roberts, conductor. In 1905 John Davies, who

The Horse Shoe Inn, Llanyblodwel

by then had emigrated to Minnesota, wrote to the local historian, Isaac Watkin to say that 'the singing was remarkably fine'. He went on to relate an occurrence shortly after he joined the choir:

> Mrs. Thomas Hughes of Tynycoed, a much respected parishioner and an esteemed member of the choir died suddenly, and at the *ail gladdedigaeth* (as the memorial service was then called) on the Sunday morning following the funeral, the minor tunes of the requiem selected had barely been sounded when every chorister broke down except Mr. Davies [the writer], who was unacquainted with the deceased, and he launched into the soprano and sang the hymn through alone.

The psalm singers' annual supper at the Horse Shoe Inn was financed from parish funds: the fairly generous sum of £3 3s. 3d. is listed in 1822, for example. Other expenditure included:

1766	Drink for Xmas Carols 5s. 0d.
1768	Drink for Xmas Carrols 5s. 0d.
1770	Treating the Psalm Singers 5s. 6d.
1790	Xmas Carols 5s. 0d.
1795	Ale for the strange singers 5s. 0d.
1806	Candles for the Plygen [*plygain*: see chapter 12] 5s. 6d.
1813	Reeds for the Psalm singers 6s. 0d.
1815	Paid for singing a Christmas Carol 1s. 0d.
1818	Mr. Davies for teaching the Psalm singers £1 Is. 0d.
	Psalm singers Salary £3 3s. 0d.

West galleries remain in many churches, including those at Bolas Magna, Cardeston, Eyton, Frodesley, Leighton, Melverley, Minsterley, Moreton Say, Stokesay, Tugford, Wem, Wroxeter, and no doubt elsewhere. The raw and powerful sound of the old singers has gone, though enthusiasts in the late 20th and early 21st centuries have brought about a revival. With Gordon Ashman as director, a group in Shropshire has taken its name and inspiration from John Moore, a Wellington nurseryman and seedsman born in 1819. He was still living at New Street, Wellington, in 1841 but then disappeared from the record, probably because for some reason he left the area for good. Four manuscript music books of his were turned up by Ashman in the Vaughan Williams Memorial Library at Cecil Sharp House in London, and some of the secular tunes were published by him under the title of *The Ironbridge Hornpipe* (see chapter 10). One of Moore's books, though, contained 55 psalm and hymn tunes, mainly scored in four parts. It provided a useful insight into what the villagers of Llanyblodwel and so many other places would have been singing and playing.

The hare in the porch at Llanyblodwel Church

Effigies and Objects

Churches at Cound, Easthope, Stanton Long and Wistanstow still have a ring or knocker on the door—also called by the curious name of hagoday. A person who grasped this could claim sanctuary in the church, at least for a time. The right was abolished in 1623 and the rings became merely objects of curiosity.

On arriving at a church one quickly becomes aware of visual signals, not only in the ensemble but the detail. Over the south porch at Clungunford there is a statuette of the church's patron, St. Cuthbert, with two emblematic swans. Unfortunately, these should have been the two otters which licked the saint's frozen feet and dried them with their fur. Again in the south porch, this time at Llanyblodwel, a stone shows a hare being chased by a greyhound (and the former also appears on the chancel screen). The allusion is to St. Melangell (or Marcella), a 7th-century princess who took refuge in the Montgomeryshire hills near Pennant to escape the advances of a predatory nobleman. One day the man came across her when he was out hunting. His quarry, a hare, dashed under Melangell's skirts and his dogs, sensing her saintliness, drew back. The prince, deeply impressed, renounced his own pursuit of Melangell and granted her land on which to found an abbey.

Detail of Owd Scriven
at Berrington Church

110

Other objects have less edifying stories. In the church at Berrington, three miles from Shrewsbury, is what Nikolaus Pevsner briskly dismisses as 'oak effigy of a knight, crosslegged, late C13 (S aisle)'. The parish clerk gave a far more colourful account to Dean Cranage:

> The people of the neighbourhood called him 'Ould Scriven', of Brompton, and the story was that in former times Scriven was going from Brompton to visit his lady-love at Eaton Mascot, and, when he came to a stile at the bottom of the 'Banky Piece' near Eaton Mascot he encountered a great lion, 'the terror of the neighbourhood', that 'Ould Scriven' had brought his great sword and had a combat with the lion, and 'a terrible tussle it must have been'. However, 'Ould Scriven' slew the lion and cut him in twain, and you may observe a lion, so cut in twain, lying under the 'image'. But the lion with his forepaw gave 'Ould Scriven' a terrible scratch on the face, and tore away all his right cheek, and you will also see this on the effigy.

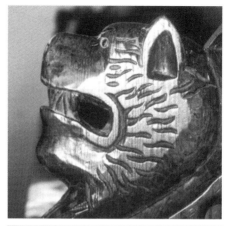

Strangely enough, when Maisie Herring questioned a local man about Scriven he replied:

> I never 'eered of 'im. But there was a woman murdered 'er 'usband an' set up a monyment to 'im. In time the monyment growed a thread o' red round its neck. 'Er 'ad it tuk down and another put up. Same place, made o' different stone brought from a distance. But it weren't any gainer. They couldna stop the red line coming. Thee can'st see un today in Berrington.

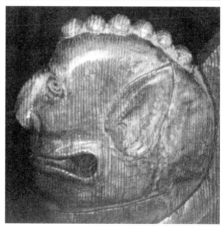

Carvings by Brewster on the bench ends at Middleton-in-Chirbury

Carvings on the sanctuary rail at Llanfair Waterdine Church

The Ludlow 'tapster' misericord

Seating arrangements in churches at times led to dispute. To avoid this pews reserved for the people of different farms were clearly labelled at Bettws-y-Crwyn and Llanfair Waterdine (see chapter 2). In the latter place the chancel rail bears the odd inscription: *SYR MADE AMURAC PICHGAR COL UNW AGOSOD ODDEC PUND CYRUFUDD* (Sir Matthew and Meyrick Pichgar of Clun set it up for ten pounds together). At Middleton-in-Chirbury, over a period of 13 years ending in 1890, the bench ends were carved by Rev. Waldegrave Brewster with caricatural likenesses of members of his congregation, including an old lady in a mob cap, an elder with a long beard and a bulbous-nosed man. The work was done by candlelight on winter evenings in the unheated church.

Another form of wood carving is to be seen in misericords, wooden projections fitted to the underside of seats. (These gave support as a singer or cleric stood during lengthy services, even when the seat was raised). One set can be seen in the choir at Tong. Fifteenth-century examples at Ludlow show the white rose with falcon and fetterlock which were the emblems of Richard, duke of York, manorial lord and owner of the castle. Very few—a bishop with mitre and an angel with shawm, for example—have ecclesiastical subjects. Some show vignettes of daily life (an alewife, a drunken tapster, a porter or pedlar preparing for the road) and entertainment (a scene from a play, wrestling). An owl symbolises not wisdom but ignorance. A harpy and a mermaid both stand for female guile. Several representations of foliate heads are echoed in the carved ceiling above the choir.

Examples of the green man or foliate head in churches have inspired extensive debate, with suggested explanations ranging from pagan fertility symbol to christian token of mortality. The siting of one green man—above the north door at Linley, near Bridgnorth—may be significant. Yet the stone with three upside down cat heads, each with foliage issuing from the mouth, was within the church at Much Wenlock Priory. (It is now in the Victoria and Albert Museum in London). Apart from these mediaeval examples—there is another at Tong, a misericord—when St. Mary's Church at Burford was restored in the late 19th century the architect, Sir Aston Webb, added a whole series of green man figures on the embattled north and south external walls.

A mermaid on the pulpit at Much Wenlock

113

Misgivings about the green man were insignificant, compared with reactions to the sheila-na-gig, a carving of a woman displaying her genitals. The term, meaning 'immodest woman', was not used by ordinary people, who probably said 'whore' or 'trollop'. Suggested explanations again range widely, and include Celtic earth mother, warning against lechery, and mediaeval obscenity. There is one

A green man on the outside of Burford Church

at Church Stretton, over the south door of the church, which Timmins guardedly calls 'an archaic little image'. Other sightings in Shropshire seem to be confined to Corvedale, with an 18-inch figure at Holdgate (on the external south wall of the chancel), two more at Tugford (inside, one on either side of the Norman entrance arch), and another at Abdon.

Rather more fragile items are preserved in some Shropshire churches: maiden's garlands. These are chaplets of white paper flowers with a pair of

Stone carvings by Brewster, that may be green men, at Middleton-in-Chirbury

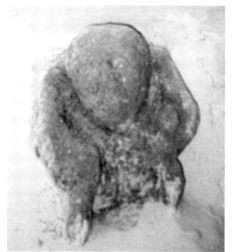

Sheila-na-gigs at Tugford (left) and Holdgate (right)

white gloves, also paper though sometimes of leather, which were carried at virgins' funerals and afterwards hung in the church as mementos to the departed. The practice is mentioned by a number of writers, including Shakespeare, with reference to Ophelia; and in the 18th century John Gay wrote:

To her sweet memory flow'ry garlands strung,
On her now empty seat aloft were hung.

Acton Burnell, Hanwood and Little Ness all have records of the custom. At Shrawardine, wrote Hare, 'are, or were a number of the funeral garlands, which the natives used to say were placed there by giants. With one were a pair of white gloves, "in memory of a much-loved young female of this village, who about half a century ago lost her life in crossing the river Severn"'. By coincidence Hannah Phillips lost her life in the Severn in 1707, on the eve of her wedding, and her garland still hangs in the church at Astley Abbotts. Several more can be seen in the church at Minsterley, dating from between 1726 and 1794.

*Maiden's garland
at Astley Abbotts*

Wall paintings at Claverley Church

Such reminders of mortality, part of the basic message of religion, recur in wall paintings at Cound and Claverley showing the last judgement. In the latter case there is also a quite different series of frescoes illustrating in striking fashion the combat between seven christian virtues and seven pagan vices. Apparently this followed descriptions given by the Roman, Prudentius, in his poem, *Psychomachia*.

Customs and Parsons

An offender against the church's code of conduct could be required to do public penance. John Munslow was in trouble at Rushbury in 1621 'for using unlawfull sportes in the churchyard ... on the saboath daye ... running and playnge at stooleball leapinge & iumppinge'. When reproved by the parson, and threatened with having to do penance, he 'said it was but the wearinge a sheete & for that he did not care'. On reflection, though, he confessed and accepted the error of his ways. Those doing penance did have to stand draped in a white sheet, which is exactly what happened in 1665, when

> Dorathy Penworth of the Parish of Stockton [five miles from Bridgnorth]
> ... did doe penance in the Church in the time of Divine Worship, making
> her confession, and habited in forme and manor as injoyned.

In 1742 a woman from Little Hereford, then a joint parish with Ashford Carbonel, for committing 'the foul Sin of Fornication', was ordered to do penance, specified as standing in the church porch from second bell till the first sermon was read, 'bare Headed, bare Legged and bare Footed, having a White Sheet over her Wearing Apparell and her hair hanging on her shoulders, holding a White Rod of an Ell [a yard and a quarter] long in her hand after the manner of a Penitent Sinner', and then to confess her sin publicly in church. She must have felt utterly humiliated. Old Parr's penance was mentioned earlier.

Writing in 1894, Catherine Gaskell commented:

In the last century and even up to the twenties of this I have been told by Mrs. Swyney that girls who got 'overseen' - in other words, who had lost their good name - had to pay penance in church. 'I mind me', my old friend once told me, 'of a certain Betty Beaman. She and I used to meet at the pump when us did the washing for Farmer Smout. One day as I was holding the pail and she was a-pumping in 'er burst into tears, for 'er was a-thinking, poor crittur, of 'er young days. Er said, "Sally, I bain't what I was, and never shall be, afore I paid penance. That's many a year agone, but standin' up in that there white sheet 'a took something out of me that'll never cum back. The spirit left me, and ever sin', though I can eat my wittles regler, somehow I 'ave a-lived like in the dust. Sure, I 'opes when I goes; as some un will 'elp the good Lord to misremember all about me".'

At Norbury a rough stone step by the sanctuary is said to have been used as a penitence seat. The same role may have been played at Claverley by the curious niche in a tower buttress in the nave.

The yearly round in some churches had unusual features. At Ellesmere, Rushbury and Wellington, according to Rev. G.S. Tyack, children 'clipped' the church—that is, joined hands to form a circle all round it—'with a good deal of tumult and shouting'. In the last place a boys' band gathered in the town centre before making its way, 'each lad blowing lustily on his tin trumpet' (? kazoo) to the church. By the 1860s the custom had died out but Edgmond defied the trend, revived 'clipping', and keeps it going still, accompanied by the singing of the hymn, 'We love the place, oh God'. 'Until 1939', Michael Raven has pointed out, 'this was followed by the Edgmond Wakes, a time of fun and frolics'.

Palm Sunday, a week before Easter, was known as Flowering Sunday in parts of Shropshire (as in Wales), and family graves were bedecked. Albrighton, near Shifnal, is one of the places where the custom was recorded. In contrast, Midsummer Day (24 June) was chosen for the placing of roses on the Vernon tomb at Tong, until the mid-19th century. Tyack remarks:

? Penitence seat at Claverley

117

It is said that this is the relic of an ancient land tenure, by which Henry de Hugefort held certain lands in Norton and Shaw by the service of bringing a chaplet of Roses to Roger de la Zouch, lord of the manor, on St. John Baptist's Day; and if he were absent from Tong, the flowers were to be offered at the shrine of Our Lady in the church. The shrine having long since disappeared, the custom arose of placing the wreath on the nearest tomb, which chanced to be that of the said Vernon.

Another 'relic' of earlier times was the Easter 'love feast'. At Berrington this was provided by the rector, and held in the church. Far from being the 'orgy' suggested by Michael Raven, this was probably a version of the church's dedication festival. Even so, the event was suppressed, perhaps because the vicar resented the expense, because the parishioners feasted too well, or because the church was no longer considered a seemly venue. However, on behalf of the congregation the church patron and local magnate, Sir Richard Lea (or Lee), petitioned the bishop of Coventry and Lichfield for the feast's restoration. The bishop, on a visit to Newport in 1639, accepted the request and confirmed that the Berrington parson should provide the love feast, though on Easter Monday, 'in any place convenyent for the same (the church only excepted), in as good and ample a manner as at any tyme heretofore it hath beene usually celebrated'. Not until 1713 did the custom come to an end.

A similar pattern was followed at Clungunford. In 1637 when the parson stopped the Easter feast the parishioners protested to Laud, the archbishop of Canterbury, at the loss of the traditional bread, cheese and beer enjoyed especially by the poor and old on Easter Day. Laud replied:

> I shall not go about to break this custom, so it be done in the parsonage house, in a neighbourly and decent way, but I cannot approve of the continuance of it in the church; and if I hear it to be done so again, I will not fail to call the offenders into the High Commissioners' Court.

It is unclear what subsequently happened at Clungunford. No doubt a study of local documents would provide enlightenment.

From the 7th century, Rogationtide and Ascension Day were marked by beating parish bounds and blessing crops. Ascension Day is 40 days after Easter, and it is preceded by the four days (Sunday to Wednesday) of Rogationtide. The perambulation of parish boundaries was known as 'bannering' (from the banners carried) to some in Shropshire. In Ludlow they preferred 'processioning', which they once did (until the early 19th century) on Ascension Eve. Boys from the various schools with a clergyman set off from the church, then went to a mound by Corve Bridge where a cross stood, and paused there for a reading of the epistle for the previous Sunday. Then they went eastward round the town to the Weeping Cross, where the gospel was read, and then followed the river bank back to Ludford Bridge, where a decorated birch bough was fixed. A battle for the possession of this bough followed between the boys of the different schools, who were already armed with the birch boughs they had been carrying. Then everyone marched to the Guildhall for a feast of plum buns.

The procedure at Much Wenlock seems to have been similar, but secular, though it may have originated as bannering. A former town clerk described a procession, 'in the Easter week, Holy Thursday, or in Whitsun week' consisting of 'a man who wore a hair-cloth gown and was called the bailiff, a recorder, justices, town clerk, sheriff, treasurer, crier, and other municipal officers. They were a large retinue of men and boys mounted on horseback, begirt with wooden swords ... They, when I knew them, did not go to the boundary but used to call at all the gentlemen's houses in the franchise, where they were regaled with meat, drink, and money; and before the conclusion they assembled at the pillory at the Guildhall, where the town clerk read some sort of rigmarole which they called their charter, and I remember one part was, 'We go from Beckbury and Badger to Stoke on the Clee [Stoke St. Milborough], / To Monk Hopton, Round Acton, and so return we'".

This ceremony died out at Much Wenlock by about the 1760s but when a new church, St. Mary's, Cleeton, was completed over a century later, in 1878, the vicar, schoolmaster and 60 schoolchildren set out the following year to walk the boundaries of the new parish, pausing to eat gingerbread, nuts and biscuits at one place, buns and cakes at another. The route passed over Titterstone Clee, through gorse bushes and briar hedges. Those who completed the arduous course received a substantial tea.

A somewhat pitiless version of the same thing remained well into the 20th century in the memory of an old man at Claverley interviewed by Wilfred Byford-Jones; he explained:

> Every year ... folks used to have processions which were the terror of us boys. They used to march us to the village boundaries or to the footpaths and then take off the trousers of us boys and give us a good tanning, sometimes drawing blood.

The idea, of course, was to ensure that the boy learned boundaries and rights of way so that he could pass on the knowledge, but Byford-Jones noticed: 'The old man winced as he told me the story. He seemed almost afraid to sit down lest the pain, so vividly remembered, should return'.

During these perambulations, as Cledwyn Hughes pointed out, particularly in the west of Shropshire, 'there was a local custom that a man could trespass on the squire's land on this particular day, and should suffer no penalty'. The bible readings at various points *en route* gave rise to a series of Gospel Oaks and, in one case, on Clee Hill near Bitterley, to a Gospel Stone. At High Ercall, though, the Gospel Oak took its name not from boundbeatings but because Methodists, forbidden by the local landowner from holding services indoors, even in their own homes, did so under the hospitable branches of the tree.

When a parson began his incumbency in a parish he would toll a bell. The number of rings forecast the years of his stay, ''E's on'y knouped the bell seven times, so 'e'll on'y be 'ere seven year', a parishioner was heard to say on one occasion. Inevitably, there were black sheep among clergymen. Stanton Lacy had two in the 17th century. Ralph Clayton had to be ejected from the living in 1637 for

> haunting alehouses, and once continuing in several alehouses in Ludlow from Thursday to Wednesday, neglecting to come to his church, being within two miles, or any other church on the Sunday; for tempting the chastity of divers women; for causing the bells to be rung at the bringing of beer into his house, making those who brought it drunk, and giving the ringers 2s.

Finally, for good measure, Clayton after beating his sexton with a staff in the church was imprisoned in Ludlow Castle.

Even worse was Robert Foulkes, who arrived in 1660 and served in exemplary fashion for 18 years but then had an affair with a young woman lodging in his house, and killed the resulting child. He was hanged in London in January 1668/9, though not before writing a confession later published under the title of *An Alarme for Sinners*.

One reason why parish boundaries had to be delineated so carefully was the assessment of liability for the payment of tithes to the

An Alarme

F O R

SINNERS:

Containing

The Confeffion, Prayers, Letters, and laft Words of

Robert Foulkes,

Late Minifter of *Stanton-Lacy* in the County of *Salop*; who was Tryed, Convicted, and Sentenced, at the Seffions in the *Old Bayly, London, January* 16:ʰ 167⅞, and Executed the 31ᵗ following.

With an Account of his L I F E.

Publifhed from the Original, Written with his own hand, during his Reprieve, and fent by him at his Death to Doctor Lloyd, Dean of Bangor.

Let him that thinketh he ftandeth, take heed lift he fall. 1 Cor. 10.12.

Licenfed, *Jan.* 29. 1678.

L O N D O N,

Printed for *Langley Curtis*, on *Ludgate-Hill*, 1679.

rector or vicar. Tithes, Easter dues and routine fees, all meticulously listed, payable to the incumbent, were not always popular, to say the least. An unnamed vicar, 'famous all over the county for his peculiarities and general shrewdness', according to E. Moore Darling, had difficulty with a farmer who would not pay his tithe:

> Again and again the vicar tried, and again and again the farmer grinned and said, 'Sue me', which was the last thing the vicar wanted to do. The amount wasn't much, but the old man was much too fond of his own way to take defiance lying down. What he did was to wait, having apparently given up all hope, and then send his groom to buy some hay and oats from the recalcitrant farmer, the latter being told that if he'd call at the vicarage on market day the vicar would pay him. He did so, and was shown into the vicar's study. 'Ah, Mr. Brown', he said, 'just make out the receipt. I've got your money in an envelope here', opening his secretaire and taking from it an envelope in which money chinked. The farmer handed over the receipt and received the envelope which he opened. It contained a receipt for his tithe and the sum of 4s. 6d. in odd money, the balance of his bill. So much for that.

At Myddle, Richard Gough relates a tithe story very much to the credit of the parson, Rev. Kinaston:

> This Mr. Kinaston kept good hospitality and was very charitable. An instance of the latter, I will briefly mention. There was a poor weaver, named Parks, who lived in Newton on the Hill, he had eleven children, all baptized by Mr. Kinaston; at the baptizing the tenth or eleventh, Mr. Kinaston said (merrily), 'Now one child is due to the Parson', to which Parks agreed, and Mr. Kinaston choase a girle, that was about the middle age among the rest, and brought her up in his own house, and she became his servant; and when she had served several years, he gave her in marriage with thirty, some say sixty pounds' portion to one Cartwright, who lived beyond Ellesmeare, and had an Estate to balance such a portion.

Other stories of good parsons include this, relating to two villages near Ludlow, told by P. Thoresby Jones:

> The vicar of Hopton Cangeford, with eighty inhabitants, was also rector of Cold Weston, a parish of thirty-two people. The way between them is two miles by a footpath under a 1000-foot whaleback; the four miles of a roundabout road are steep even for Shropshire. One Easter Sunday the old clergyman arrived at Cold Weston, and in his shirtsleeves pulled the oldest bell in the county, while a visitor knocked up people from the scattered cottages to get a congregation of seven, nearly a quarter of the

parish population. The damp had got into the harmonium, so the visitor whistled the hymn-tunes, selected by the congregation themselves.

Mary Cholmondeley (1859-1925) is remembered for the novel, *Red Pottage* (1899), a satire on the rural clergy. Of her father, rector of Hodnet, she wrote that 'The parish with him at its head had a sort of homely but tough freemasonry'. Rev. Cholmondeley did not feel it beneath his dignity to settle a trivial dispute:

> I have known Father intervene with success in matters of extreme delicacy, as when one of Mrs. Brown's caps spread on her side of the hedge to dry had 'got blowed' on to Mrs. Jones's side, and had been appropriated by her; the situation, already grave, having been further complicated by Mrs. Brown actually calling her neighbour 'Woman Jones' across the hedge. Possibly no self-respecting person, much less Mrs. Jones, could restore a cap after that. Anyhow, Father probed the difficulty, obtained the cap, and took it back himself to Mrs. Brown.

Mary Cholmondeley, after long experience of the country clergy, came to the conclusion that 'there is no class so charitable, so quixotically charitable'. Of 'a certain Shropshire archdeacon', she wrote:

> As a curate it had been his duty to visit the cast-off mistress of one of the large landowners of Shropshire, who allowed her three hundred [pounds] a year. At the man's death his son refused to continue the allowance or any part of it. She was left entirely destitute. The young curate, who had private means himself, paid her the same allowance till her death many years later. This action hampered him during all the years in which he was educating his children, but he did it without flinching, and without speaking of it.

No clergyman, perhaps, could outdo the devotion of Rev. G.O. Brown, vicar at Gobowen during the 1920s, who resolved to be buried facing west, rather than the customary east, so that on the day of resurrection he would rise to face his congregation.

CHAPTER 6

Witchery

The weird phenomena most publicised in the late 20th and early 21st centuries may have been crop circles and flying saucers. The former, after causing initial wonderment, have been exposed as fraudulent, that is to say, man-made. The latter, according to the carefully considered view of David Clarke and Andy Roberts in their book, *Out of the Shadows* (2002), were the product of mass hysteria occasioned by the Cold War.

Old-fashioned ghosts continue to attract their share of attention: the haunting of a public house or a stately home warrants immediate coverage in the press or on the television. Dorothy Nicolle of Wem claimed in her book, *Shropshire Walks with Ghosts and Legends* (2003), that at least 500 sites in the county were known to be haunted. Instead of the word, 'known', many would prefer 'believed'. Some would share the sentiments expressed by Daniel Karlin when in 2002 he reviewed a different book on the subject: 'The beauty of ghosts is that they don't exist. As a product of the imagination they are among the most lively and long-lasting human phenomena, the immaterial material of some of our greatest stories'.

Fairies, imps and goblins have long moved into the realm of children's stories, yet they were once feared by adults. The devil himself, a formidable figure in the past, now commands little attention, save through the willing suspension of disbelief in the reader or hearer which is essential for the appre-ciation of any fictional narrative.

It is some 200 years since the last conviction in Britain for witchcraft, yet during much of that time fear of its practitioners lingered. The latter-day witches of Wicca have devised a new mumbo-jumbo to replace the old, but its credibility is limited to a narrow circle of initiates. The old tales of witches retain the power to engage the listener, thanks to the human emotions involved in them.

Edric and Exorcism

Edric the Wild was a historical person who lived in the 11th century. After his death he was believed to roam the hills with a phantom retinue when danger threatened the country. One woman and her father saw them just before the Crimean War (see chapter 1). A later witness claimed to have seen the ghostly party in 1939 at the outbreak of the Second World War. Variations on the story suggest that Edric is confined to a cave in the Stiperstones until the day when an English king sitting on an English throne restores his rightful lands to his descendants. Alternatively, Edric is seen sitting on the Stretton Hills in the form of a fiery-eyed black dog.

Such beasts were considered to be of extremely ill omen. 'A headless black dog', reported Augustus Hare, 'haunts the road where a man was murdered between Baschurch and Yeaton'. A century on, the animal seems more likely to be a puma. Veronica Thackeray saw one in Hopton Titterhill Woods—Titrell in the local pronunciation—and another in nearby Twitchen Lane. In 1999 the RSPCA announced that a further specimen, some six feet long from nose to tail, had been spotted on a security videotape at Blockleys brick factory in Telford. Then in August 2003 police closed for a time the main road at Bayston Hill and sent in a search helicopter after reports that a large black cat had been seen.

The bull of Bagbury was another troublesome creature whose tale is still told. Bagbury Bridge, some $3\frac{1}{2}$ miles north of Bishop's Castle, spans a stream (or 'prill') which marks the boundary between two counties (Shropshire and Montgomery) and two countries (England and Wales). There, an abusive and overbearing farmer, cruel to his workers and cursed by a witch, came back after death in the guise of a fiery-eyed bull which bellowed so loud that shingles and shutters flew off buildings. The blind parson at Hyssington and 11 of his colleagues assembled to exorcise the apparition. They failed at first, but drove the beast into the church, and there, with bell, book and candle, succeeded, but not before his enormous bulk had cracked the building from top to bottom. The chastened spirit pleaded to be laid under Bagbury Bridge, knowing that every pregnant mare which crossed would lose her foal, and every woman her child. Clearly, this could not be allowed, and he was shut in a snuff box and consigned to an old boot buried beneath the church doorstep, or (depending on which story is followed) to the bottom of the Red Sea for 1,000 years. A further belief persisted until at least the 1930s that the unquiet spirit was buried beneath a flat stone in the marsh 'at Pennerley, where the road branches right for Shelve'. So wrote Magdalene Weale.

Another story of exorcism concerns Kinlet, where hall and church stand high on the hill, some distance from the village. The Blounts lived in the hall, and their splendid monuments can be seen in the church. The family emblem was the sun until one Blount, sleeping at an inn at Mamble, rushed out in his slippers to fight Welsh raiders, and then ordered a commemorative slipper

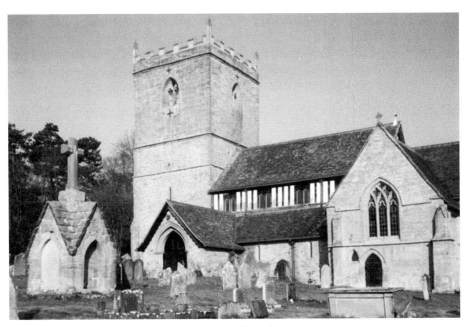

Kinlet Church

*Detail of Sir George Blount's tomb in
Kinlet Church*

to be added. A later member of the family, Sir George Blount, vehemently disapproved of his daughter's choice of a social inferior as husband. After his death in 1584, his vengeful spirit came back and charged over the dinner table on a warhorse, or in a coach and four, when his daughter had guests. The perturbations ceased only when the old hall was pulled down in the 1720s, and another built. According to John Wood, 'there is an intriguing story that the old cellars still contain buried store of wine and ale which may not be unearthed for fear of raising the ghost'.

Another version says that Blount haunted both hall and park on horseback, and also a pool (now dried up, though the site is still called Blount's Pool) from

*Further detail of the same tomb in
Kinlet Church*

which women who went to wash clothes saw him emerge. They believed that he was on his way to visit the cellar beneath the hall to check the pipes of wine and hogsheads of ale. The clergy, alerted, carried out the ritual of exorcism and confined Blount's spirit to a bottle, which was then put on his tomb in the north transept of the church. The bottle, seven or eight inches long, with a green stopper, has now gone but Sir George's restless wandering has long ceased. Kinlet Hall houses a happy and peaceful school. Whether its cellars still hold stocks of wine and beer is another question.

Haunted Halls

Like Kinlet Hall, many a mansion had its ghost story. One almost has the feeling that no self-respecting country house of any standing would be without its terrifying tale. Some, such as Cann Hall, where Charles I and Prince Rupert once stayed, at Bridgnorth, simply had the vague reputation of being haunted. Others provide elaborate detail.

F.H. Groome's book, *In Gipsy Tents* (1880), contains this story:

> It was at Chetwynd End, near Newport, just by the parson's house; and there was a young lady, Miss Pigott, out hunting; and the horse run up a great big sandy bank, and threw her off his back, and killed her. And they said she used to come night and day, and squeak awful. It got so terrible, that people couldn't go along the road for fear of her, but then they laid her, threw her into Chetwynd Pool. And somehow the bottle they'd put her in got broken (somebody skating, I think it was); and she come as bad again after that, and got jumping on the men's horses. It seems she would run after everything, carriages and all; so long and by last they got twelve priestes [*sic*], and they were all round a table with the bottle on it till it seemed no mannerable good, and they were very near giving it up.

But the oldest of them told them to stick to it, and their candles went out all but his; and he prayed till the sweat dropped off his hair. All the rest, you know, were so afeared; and if his candle went out, the devil would have fetched them, and she would have scratted them all to pieces. Ay, bor, and as fast as they lighted the candles, they were blown out, all but this one; and the priest as belonged to that, he prayed and prayed; and at last they saw her come in between the candles, drawing to the mouth of the bottle; and they kept on praying hard as ever they could. Long and by last they got her in. And then she begged of them not to be thrown into the Red Seas; but the priest he wouldn't hear of it. And so they threw her in, and the place has been in quietness ever since. Why! you can see the palings in the road, put in the wall right again the pool where they laid her first.

Almost 20 years later, Hare offered this version:

The old rectory .., pulled down in 1864, was connected with the ghost story of 'Madam Pigott'. She was a neglected and ill-used wife, who used to issue at midnight from a trap-door in the roof and wander through the park to Edgmond, rolling over a great boulder-stone by the roadway on her way. In the high-banked lane called Cheney Hill was a curious old tree-root which became known as 'Madam Pigott's arm-chair'. Here she would sit at midnight, 'combing her baby's hair', and if a horseman passed, would spring up behind him - impossible to displace - until they came to running water, when she would go no further. It has often been thought necessary to summon the clergy 'to lay Madam Pigott': yet it is believed that if you cover your head as Madam Pigott passes, she will do you no harm.

It has been suggested that there is no evidence of Pigots at Chetwynd, but a Thomas Pigot died there in 1665 and a Walter Pigot in 1669. In 1967, though, Byford-Jones advanced the view that the events leading to the hauntings dated from the 1770s. The unfortunate woman's husband, the squire, badly wanted an heir. He was delighted when she became pregnant, but shortly before the birth became due the doctor warned that because of complications he could save either mother or child but not both. Without hesitation, the squire declared: 'Lop the root to save the branch'. As she died, his wife cursed him. The child survived only for a short time.

Since then [Byford-Jones continues], at widely spaced intervals, the ghost of the ill-fated mother is said to emerge ... and to wander about the fields near the Windy Oaks [also called Madame Pigot's Hill], sometimes to haunt the hilly road at night, especially when the weather is bad. Richard Talbot ... saw the terrifying apparition ... right in front of the handlebars of his motor cycle as he rode one dirty night through the Wintry Oaks.

Returning to the subject in another book of his, *Midland Murders, Hauntings and Odd Characters*, Byford-Jones identified the place as Windy Oaks, and said that an exorcism conducted there by 12 clergymen led by Mr. Foy, curate at Edgmond, had appeared effective until a brake (carriage) full of young people again encountered Madam Pigott: 'The horses reared and the driver was nearly scared out of his wits', Byford-Jones decided to visit the scene himself one night with two companions. All three men were thoroughly alarmed when they saw 'a column of vibrating light' and repeatedly heard 'a repulsive noise, something like a snarl'.

Rather less frightening, apparently, was the White Lady of Oteley Hall, near Ellesmere. At successive re-buildings—in the 1770s, the 1830s and the 1960s—a chimney from the mediaeval house has been retained as a refuge for her, the ghost of a nun ejected when a Saxon convent on the site was sacked.

When the 17th-century Badger Hall, six miles from Bridgnorth, was demolished in the 1930s a Mr. Cecil Jasper recalled his experiences there with the Lady in Grey. In his own house nearby, late one Christmas Eve, he heard a rustling noise, turned, and saw a dark-eyed, golden-haired woman, dressed in grey. He greeted her and moved towards her but she disappeared. A few days later he woke in the night to find her standing smiling by his bedroom window. When he stretched out an arm towards her she again vanished. He then saw her at a Christmas party in the Hall, with the same enigmatic smile. Then her lips moved and she seemed to be trying to tell him something. Another Christmas Eve, some years later when the hall had been demolished, Jasper saw the grey lady again by moonlight in the park.

At the beginning of the Second World War when bulldozers set about clearing the last remains of the Hall an ancient jewel box came to light, containing an engagement ring. From that time the Grey Lady appeared no more. Jasper concluded that she had been disappointed in love and had

Oteley Hall, Ellesmere

Shipton Hall

returned to the place of previous happiness. Alternatively, she might have failed to rest in peace until the lost ring were found.

Styche Hall at Moreton Say, three miles from Market Drayton, belonged for many generations to the Clive family. It not only had the reputation of being haunted but brought a good deal of ill-luck to the Clives. Robert Clive (of India) died by his own hand in 1774. One Lord Clive died in the First World War, another in the Second. Two women members of the family met their deaths in car accidents, the later of the two in 1964. In the late 1940s phantom lights and unexplained footfalls gave concern in the hall. A decade earlier during a seance a William Tallis manifested himself and claimed that he had been shut up in the grounds of Styche to prevent his pursuing his courtship of one Arabella.

Shipton Hall, six miles from Much Wenlock, is supposed to have both a secret passage and a ghost, though details are sketchy. The place was built in 1587 by a Lutwyche. One of the family, Sir Edward, a judge who died in 1686, apparently continued to perambulate Lutwyche Hall near Easthope for the best part of 250 years. The same hall had 'a pleasant ghost - that of an old nurse dressed in grey': so wrote Lilian Hayward in 1938, adding that 'the daughter of a former occupier' of Millichope Hall at Munslow 'had often seen the "old squire" walking up the drive carrying his head under his arm'.

At the Lower Hall, Beckbury, the clattering hooves and the whinnying cries of a phantom horse 'have been heard many times', according to Michael Raven. The animal has been identified as 'one of Squire Stubbs's horses, possibly ridden by the ghost of the squire himself' (see also chapter 9).

Misfortune and Murder

A sense of injustice in life often seems to persist in death, if certain stories are to be believed. At Whiteladies, near Tong, the tradition lasted for 400 years that the oldest of the nuns, dragged away shrieking when the abbey was suppressed in the 1530s, vowed she would haunt the place till the White Ladies returned. She kept her word, and ceased to appear only when the order built a new nunnery nearby at Brewood, in the early 20th century. Another long-lived local anecdote claimed that a team of horses refused to plough what had been the nuns' cemetery at Whiteladies.

Horses are also involved in a story about the bells of Wenlock Abbey. A wizard stole the bells and hid them in a hill. People avoided the place but one day the landowner decided to plough. 'The horses sweated and swot, but they wudna move. So of course the folk knew that there must be summat there, so the parson came and dug and found the bells, and now they be hangin' in Wenlock church'. The phantom bells of a lost monastery can be heard in Monks Field at Hope Bagot.

A rather different ecclesiastical spirit is that of a Reverend Pritchard who in the 18th century spent the very large sum for the time of £5,000 on Pradoe Park near Eardiston, six miles from Oswestry. Ruined by the expense, he never lived there, but turned up after death. 'An apparition dressed in a black frockcoat', writes Michael Raven, '... was seen many times by the very sane and sensible mother of the present owner-occupier, Colonel Kenyon'. Easthope Church is haunted by a vicar, Will Garmston, who for unknown reasons killed the patron of the living, John Esthope, in 1333. The two monks buried side by side in the churchyard who killed each other in a drunken fight also re-appeared as ghosts, but later only the phantom sounds of their mortal struggle could be heard. Either way, some avoided the place at night, until the 1960s at least. The monks came from a grange (now a farmhouse) of Wenlock Abbey. A further unlikely tale suggests that some of the abbey's treasure is buried with them, but thanks to a curse on their graves, anyone attempting to disturb them would be struck dead.

Gravestones of warring (and haunting) monks at Easthope

Condover Hall

According to a primitive belief, blood spilled during the course of a murder remained indelible. Such a stain at Condover Hall, which is now a school, purported to date from the time of Henry VIII. Burne had the story in 1881 from a Condover person. I summarise: While he is in bed Lord Knevett is stabbed by his son. He rushes through the chapel, calling for help, but falls dead, leaving the indelible pool of blood. The butler, John Viam, is accused of the crime by the son. He is tried at Shrewsbury, found guilty, and hanged. From

The Lion Inn, Shrewsbury

the gallows he vows that no son at Condover will ever succeed his father in peace. A lawyer called Owen, himself the son of an ostler at the Lion in Shrewsbury, happens on the transcript of the trial and, suspecting perjury on the part of the young Lord Knevett, persuades Queen Elizabeth to order a new trial. The queen decides to attend in person, under the pretext of seeing a play performed by the boys of

Shrewsbury School (see chapter 11). She has only reached Coventry when she receives Owen's message: 'The play is played out'. She turns back. Knevett is hanged. Owen is granted the Condover estate but Viam's curse holds good, and he dies before receiving his rents.

It is interesting to set some facts against the story. Henry VII granted Condover in 1544/5 to Sir Henry Kinjett (or Knyvett) but the latter soon sold it. Several owners later, it was bought in 1586 by the son of a wool merchant at Shrewsbury, Thomas Owen of Lincoln's Inn. Owen's son, Richard, had the old hall demolished in 1598, and the existing building erected. Elizabeth did set out for Shrewsbury in 1575, but at Lichfield heard of an outbreak of plague there, and diverted to Worcester. Part of Condover which belonged to Shrewsbury Abbey was bought at the Dissolution by George and John Isam, and soon re-sold. There is no chapel.

Nevertheless, the bloodstain story continued to be told, sometimes with the variation that the imprint of a bloody hand appeared on a staircase. When this was wiped away it immediately came back, until early in the 20th century when the piece of stone balustrade with it was chipped away.

Plaish (pronounced 'Plash') Hall has its own indelible blood. In the neighbouring village of Cardington the effigy of Sir William Leighton (died 1607) can be seen in the church. Leighton, squire of Plaish, Chief Justice of North Wales and member of the Council of the Marches, is playing cards in the hall with two clerical friends. The locked doors fly open once, twice, and then a third time, when the devil appears. The two parsons flee, leaving Leighton to his fate. He is never seen again but bloodstains in the shape of a human form remain for ever on the floor. Alternatively, on the door, 'where they came through every coat of paint'.

A further story of Judge Leighton was noted by Byford-Jones:

> One day the judge was at Salop Assizes, and 'e asked someun if there were anyone who could build ornamental chimneys, as 'e was rebuilding Plaish. The clerk told 'im that by a stroke of luck the prisoner 'e'd just sentenced to be hung was one of the best chimney builders in the county. What did the judge do? Why, he sent for the chap and 'ad 'im taken to Plaish, where, with coppers sittin' below, 'e built the chimneys, the like o' which ai [aren't] to be seen hereabouts nor nowhere else. After that the chap was sent back to Salop and strung up. He thought he were gettin' off, and 'e were so upset about it all that his ghost worrets them who lives there.

Lilian Hayward, who was 'frequently' shown the recurring bloodstains on the door at Plaish by the then owner, claimed that the chimney builder had to die because Leighton did not want him to do similar work anywhere else. She added:

His ghost is sometimes heard moaning on the roofs. A bedroom is haunted by a man who walks through it carrying a knife dripping blood. A rather psychic young man told me that he had seen this manifestation. The ghosts of Plaish were so troublesome that some ten years ago [1920s] the owner got the rector of the parish to come and exorcise them - or so I was told.

Petsey

Petsey, a black and white house at Stoke-upon-Tern, dating from 1634, has its own ghost, another victim whose bitter resentment, that of an itinerant pedlar-woman, persists beyond the grave. She was always allowed to sleep in the house when she passed that way. After being murdered on the road she continued to return from time to time to her room at Petsey.

The Civil War, hardly surprisingly in view of the extreme emotions it engendered, was perceived to produce eerie phenomena. Stanton Lacy Church is said to be haunted by a young man killed there by Cromwellian troops. but the story may simply be an attempt to explain the inscription cut into the chancel arch to Richard Heynes of Downton 'which urges readers: *flete nefas* (weep for the crime). (For more on the epitaph, see chapter 5). Jean Hughes comments that 'a presence of evil' has been felt in the church, and that a Ludlow man taking photographs in the chancel suddenly felt terrified; and until he made the sign of the cross his hair stood on end. A Cromwellian soldier is said to appear at Heath House, a mile from Hopton Castle. Two murders have taken place at the house, and the garrison was slaughtered at the castle (see chapter 4): any of these events could be responsible for the ghost.

The widely-held (but unfortunately erroneous) notion that murder could not ultimately be concealed goes back at least to the 14th century. 'Modre wol out', says one of Chaucer's characters in *The Prioress's Tale*. The belief, deriving from a powerful sense of natural justice, lies behind a story told by Richard Gough:

There was one Thomas Elks, of Knockin, who had an elder brother, who married and had one son, and soone after died and his wife also, and left the child very yong. The grandmother was gardian to the child. This grandmother was mother unto Thomas Elks, and was soe indulgent of him, that shee loved him best of any of her children; and by supplying him with money to feed his extravagances, shee undid him. But when shee was gon poore, and could not supply him, hee considered that this child stood in his way between him and the estate, and therefore contrived to remove him: and to that end he hired a poore boy, of Knockin, to entice the child into the corne feilds to gather flowers. The corne was then att highest. Thomas Elks met the two children in the feilds; sent the poore boy home, and took the child in his armes into the lower end of the feild where hee had provided a pale of water, and putting the child's head into the pale of water hee stifled him to death, and left him in the corne. Att evening, the child was missing, and much enquiry made for him. The poore boy tould how his uncle had hired him to entice the child into the corn feilds, and there tooke him away in his arms. The people suspected that the child was murdered, and searched the corne feild. They found the child, wheather buryed or not or wheather hee intended to bury him that night, I know not. Elks fled, and tooke the roade directly for London. (I thinke hee was a jurnyman shoemaker). The neighbours had intelligence which way hee went, and sent two men to pursue him, who followed him almost to London; and as they were passing on the roade neare Mimmes, in Hertfordshire, they saw two ravens sitt upon a cocke of hay, pulling the hay with theire beaks, and making a hideouse and unusuall noyse. Upon this, the two men alighted from theire horses and went over to see what the matter was, and there they found Tom Elks fast asleep in the cocke of hay, and apprehended him, who beeing tormented with the horror of a guilty conscience, confessed that these two ravens had followed him continually from the time that hee did the fact. Hee was brought backe to Shrewsbury, and there tryed, condemned, and hanged on a Gibbet, on Knockin Heath.

Even inanimate objects could contrive to point to a crime. At Longville-in-the-Dale near Wenlock Edge a man killed his father and dragged the body through a hedge to conceal it. He carefully filled with thorns the hole ('glat' in the vernacular) he had made. Next morning the hole had re-appeared. It continued to do so for generations, or so local people believed until the 1940s at least. They called the hole Clattering Glat.

Pubs and Places

Public houses often have ghosts, the promotion of which is by no means bad for trade. The Dun Cow in Shrewsbury's Abbey Foregate, which takes its name from the beast of Mitchell's Fold (see chapter 1), stands on the site of a hostel in which 11th-century masons lived while they were building the abbey. They do not haunt it but a Dutch officer does. During the Civil War he murdered one of Prince Rupert's stewards who was staying there, and was hanged himself in the stables for his pains. His ghost, in Dutch cavalry uniform, appeared until the 1970s. The Nag's Head in Wyle Cop has the ghost of a coachman who hanged himself in the 17th century. Footsteps, crashing noises and heavy breathing are its methods of haunting. The Acton Arms at Moreton Say claims the ghost of Richard Marshall, 28th abbot of Shrewsbury Abbey, who once lodged there. It is unclear why his spirit cannot rest.

The writer, Veronica Thackeray, heard this from the landlord of the Bull Inn at Ludlow:

> It was a Sunday evening about seven o'clock. He and his wife had had a small altercation earlier and he was alone in the bar when he felt a hand placed firmly on his shoulder. Thinking it was a loving, peace-making gesture from his wife he turned at once, but there was no one there. The same feeling of a hand being firmly placed on the shoulder happened again three months later, and once again when he turned there was no one to be seen. ... He believes that the hand belonged to the ghost of an old woman who, according to the residents around the Bull Ring, manifests herself to any newcomers in the area.

The Mytton and Mermaid Inn is at Atcham. The mermaid of the name seems to be unexplained, though the hotel's proximity to the River Severn may provide a clue. The Mytton connection is that the body of Mad Jack Mytton (see chapter 9) was kept in the building (then a coaching inn) the night before his funeral in the chapel at Halston Hall, near Oswestry. Mytton's ghost is said to appear at the hotel each year on 30 September, his birthday.

The Swan at Dawley had a ghost—or poltergeist—known as Humphrey, who moved pictures about. His footsteps were sometimes heard and his figure seen, clad in long coat and leather breeches. The suggestion is that he had been robbed and murdered in the inn. A spectacular incidence of poltergeist activity at Wem

Sign of The Mytton and Mermaid at Atcham

reached national newspapers in 1883, and remained a talkingpoint in the town for half a century afterwards. At a farmhouse between Burlton and Loppington, called The Wood, burning coals leapt from the fire, and crockery on the table jumped up and then fell back. The contents of a locked cupboard flew round a room, and a servant girl who tried to close the door temporarily lost the power of movement and speech.

Some time before the Second World War the isolated house of the school-master at Knowbury was the scene of poltergeist or ghostly activity in the form of a long-faced girl of 11, dressed in grey. Wilfred Byford-Jones, who wrote for the *Express and Star* newspaper under the pen-name of Quaestor, wanted to see for himself. The schoolmaster, a Mr. Barber, his wife and children, related disturbing experiences, and the local rector declared 'I am convinced ... that this ghost is a visitant spirit ... I believe in its existence'. Late at night Byford-Jones heard unexplained tapping and banging in the house, then saw a securely-fastened window fly open. Outside, after midnight, he heard a low sob and then a deep-throated laugh. After that he saw sparks soundlessly flying off the masonry on a corner of the building. Back inside he felt a tight grip on his ankle, and began to see lights jumping before his eyes. By this time he had become so uneasy that his host drove him back to Ludlow, where he arrived at 2.30 am and spent the rest of the night sleeping in a hotel's sitting room. Records of subsequent developments at Knowbury seem to be lacking.

To return, briefly, to public houses, when the Four Alls re-opened after refurbishment in March 2001 at Market Drayton, a carpenter reported that when he was working in a cellar he felt a sudden drop in temperature and saw the figure of a woman who muttered something incomprehensible. Local people connected the experience with the story of two sisters, inseparable until one, Alice, was married, and after that were never again together. So deep did the rift become that when one died the other did not even receive an invitation to the funeral.

Ghostly manifestations are by no means confined to buildings. Ippikin's Rock on Wenlock Edge, near Presthope, is a case in point. The eponymous Ippikin with his band of travellers preyed on travellers and hid their booty in a cave where they perished as a result of a landslide. Anyone with sufficient nerve who stands on the rock and shouts: 'Ippikin, Ippikin, / Keep away with your long chin', will (paradoxically) see the robber's ghost but run the risk of being pushed off the top to his death. Byford-Jones heard this version of the story:

> Old Ippikin was a bandit, a real bold, bad lad. ... 'E used to live in a cave there and 'e robbed everybody with money round 'ere in the old days, and in that cave, which was his stronghold, 'e kept a sight of the cash. One day there was a thunderstorm and old Ippikin and his robbers were

in the cave when the lightnin' struck it and smashed it in. They were all buried wi' the money, an' they died together as robbers should. An' if any man goes down there and cries out 'Old Ippikin! old Ippikin!' the ghost of the robber will come and he'll slash out with a chain.

At Hope Bowdler by a disused mine called Copper Hole stood the toll house known as Hazler Gate. A dairy maid called Sarah Duckett—perhaps the 19-year-old listed in the 1861 census as working at Upper Farm, Chelmick— moved away, but from time to time visited relatives at Soudley. On the way she paused at the toll house and talked to the people who lived there. On the last occasion after arriving by train from London she called at the toll house but failed to reach her relatives' home, and was never seen again. Some time later people began to say that she was haunting the Copper Hole, which they started to call the Ghost Hole. Money raised by public subscription paid for the mine shaft 'as deep as a church steeple' to be explored, but no body came to light. Articles appeared in the press under the heading of 'The Shropshire Mystery'. Some said Sarah had gone to Australia; Charlotte Burne suggested that she had died in Worcester Infirmary.

A poem quoted in George R. Windsor's *Handbook of Church Stretton* (1885) takes a different view:

> Why does this poor ghost haunt the roads in the night?
> Does she know of some treasure she wants brought to light?
> Suppose she was murdered. Oh! horrible thought,
> And to stern justice wants her foul murderer brought.
> A wandering maiden, Miss Duckett by name,
> Who by movement erratic was well known to fame,
> Was seen, years before, on the Hazler highway
> And had never been heard of, or seen since that day;
> She had been just before of her father bereaved,
> He had left her some money, and it was believed,
> She had then on her person the cash she received.

During the 1930s the ghost story was still potent enough to deter people from walking past the Ghost Hole at night—rather inconveniently, since this was the only road from Church Stretton to Hope Bowdler. The fear induced a cyclist to turn back on Hazler Hill one night when he heard footsteps coming down and saw a white figure. Only at the bottom, in the lamplight, did he realise that the ghost was in fact a man wearing cricket whites. A shoemaker walking home from Church Stretton with his son turned out to be more valiant. When a ghostly, white-clad figure approached he set about it with a heavy stick. Next day a would-be practical joker sported a black eye and a cut forehead.

Even in the 20th century murders could result in talk of haunting. In 1912 a miller called Wiggins, as he returned from Wolverhampton market to his home at Eardington, near Bridgnorth, was confronted by a robber. When he resisted the thief shot him in the chest, and ran off. Wiggins chased him for 100 yards, then collapsed. People who had heard the shot carried him into a house, where he died. The murder spot soon acquired the reputation of being haunted. A red cross was believed to appear on an ash tree by the side of the road each year on the anniversary of the miller's death: 26 November. The murderer remained undetected. Wiggins's Tree was felled after the Second World War because of road widening, and the ghost story faded away.

Other tales continued to circulate. In November 2002 BBC Television's Midlands Today programme interviewed people from Hughley, near Much Wenlock, who said that horses jibbed at crossing a ford in the brook, and one girl claimed that as she reached the footbridge her torch regularly dimmed. Apparently a stage coach had crashed at this point—obviously, many years before—as it carried a bride and her father to a wedding. The woman and a horse were killed.

Carry On Haunting

Tŷn-y-Rhos Hall at Weston Rhyn, near Oswestry, has been described as 'the most haunted house this side of the Welsh border'. Among its ghosts is that of a wealthy industrialist's son who died on a day-bed in the dining room during the First World War. Members of staff at Hopton Court, Hopton Wafers, saw during the same war a member of the Woodward family walking towards them. They called out excitedly, 'Captain Leslie's home, he's coming up the drive'. On looking again they found that the sight had vanished. Later the news came that the captain had been killed at that time in France.

One wet night when his cycle tyre sustained a puncture, a Mr Henry Evans asked a couple at Titterstone Cottage, near Bitterley, to put him up for the night. The date is unrecorded but it is known that Evans's father was an admiral who attained that rank in 1928. Upstairs at the cottage Evans noticed an old woman dressed in black, who ignored him. When he went down he asked about her, and the woman of the house immediately fainted. Later Evans discovered that 'on many occasions she had seen the ghost but that the husband had always scoffed at her and told her that she suffered with nerves'.

Titterstone Cottage

A Lincoln bomber in the Royal Air Force Museum at Cosford has apparently generated a series of stories summarised by Raven:

> Strange and unexplained phenomena have occurred .... whistling noises; discrepancies in temperature within and without the aircraft; a phantom airman wearing a white polo-necked sweater and bomber jacket; and mysterious faces appearing on photographs. It has been suggested that the apparition is that of a Major Miller who knew the aeroplane well and who died in an air accident near Codsall.

In fact the plane, built in September 1945, did not take part in the Second World War, as some have claimed. Indeed, it never flew in anger, so to speak. It was retired in 1963, and moved to Cosford five years later. After restoration the aircraft went on display, and can still be seen. The stories attracted attention from various paranormal investigators, notably Dr. Stephen Ray and Dr. David Young of Wolverhampton University, whose report in 1992 on the Cosford haunting concluded that any phenomena could be explained by physical factors such as cooling and luminescence. Disappointing for some.

Until the 1990s at least at Wem a fire of some 300 years earlier continued to have strange repercussions. The disastrous conflagration of March 1677 in the town is said to have been caused by a little girl called Jane Churm, whose candle ignited the thatched roof of a house on the corner of Leek Street and High Street. According to one story she was in the attic gathering dry kindling; another suggested that she was trying to read under the bedclothes. Either way the fire spread rapidly and widely, though only one person, a shoemaker, died. Throughout her long life Jane Churm was wracked with guilt.

In 1995 after another fire at Wem had engulfed the town hall a photographer took pictures of the still-smouldering building. When he developed the film he was staggered to see the faint image of a girl in a cap and petticoat peering through a doorway. The thought that this could have been the wraith of Jane

Is this ghost of Jane Churm caught by a photographer in 1995?

Churm was reinforced by the series of bizarre events which followed. As the heavy square of plaster which commemorated the earlier fire was being removed from the town hall for renovation it fell and broke a workman's left foot. The factory to which the object went caught fire, and burned down. Once the work was completed elsewhere, the engine of the van taking it back to Shropshire also caught fire, and the vehicle had to be written off. Finally, when the plaster plaque reached Wem it fell on the same unfortunate builder as he set about installing it, and broke his right foot.

The plaster plaque commemorating the fire in Wem of 1677

Ghosts which remain unexplained are the phantom girl seen at dances and by a bridge at Longnor in the 1970s; another female apparition which announces a bereavement in the family, of the owner of Combermere Abbey, near Whitchurch; bargemen's wraiths at Stern's Cottage, Chelmarsh, near Bridgnorth; and insubstantial figures of miners seen by the old shaft and engine house on Chelmarsh common. Finally, modern technology meets ancient mythology (not to say credulity) in the accounts of car drivers' sightings of angels on the A 4117 road one and a half miles from Hope Bagot Church, in 2003.

Hope Bagot Church

Fairies and Imps

The agents responsible for clearing the Clattering Glat (see above) were thought by some to be fairies. These beneficent creatures lingered in some Shropshire imaginations until the early years of the 20th century. Lilian Hayward wrote that the servant of a friend of hers at about that time 'was the last person I know of to claim to see fairies dancing in a ring, wearing little red jackets'.

> She said that anybody could see the fairies—or the little people as she called them—if they'd a mind to. All they had to do was to walk round a field where cattle were grazing and finish the circuit *exactly at midnight*. That seems to be the catch in the recipe. When I was a young girl there were plenty of farm lads who swore that the fairies had got at their horses and plaited their manes during the night. ... the horses were 'never no good after'.

Fragments of pipes dug up at Broseley were called 'fairishes' pipes', which is surprising because churchwarden clay pipes were manufactured in the village and would have been familiar to everyone. Edmund Vale identified as clay pipes, probably dropped by peat cutters, the fairy variety found on Fenn's Moss, near Prees.

Fairies were thought to dance in a field at Coalbrookdale; anyone who tried to interfere would be drawn into the enchanted circle and kept there. In 1862 Thomas Wright observed:

> There are remote districts in our county where the ignorant part of the population still put their faith in witchcraft; and the fairies are still believed to hold their assemblies at the Beacon ring on the Long Mountain, and to keep possession of the deserted mines of the Romans in the hill of Llanymynech, from which latter place the benighted miner sometimes imagines that he sees them coming forth to perform their gambols on the grassy slopes of the mountain.

Some 20 years later T.H. Groome noted this story from a gipsy:

> The curiousest thing that ever happened to me was at Ditton Priors just by the Clee hills yonder. It must have been about twelve o'clock at night and we were camping in a bit of a wood with a little brook running down below. It was Lemmy here, she heard some very curious tunes right atween the tents but nigher the boys' than ourn. Just like the sound of a lot of fiddles, it was, a long way off, but wonderful clear and sweetsome, and Lemmy kicked me - leastwise so she said next morning. And the boys, they hadn't heard nought neither, but the bailiff of the fine doctor said, 'Oh, I've often heard that myself; that's the fairies.

Well over a century on, we find such a narrative charming and we relish the language ('clear and sweet-some') used, but we can attach no credence to it. Wood's brewery at Wistantow can refer to fairies in an advertisement on the Internet (see illustration), but strictly with tongue in cheek. The same applies to tales of hob-goblins, bogies and imps.

Owd Lad, Nick or Scrat

Such were the names given by Shropshire people to the devil, who is still literally on the map at Devil's Armchair by the Rock o' Woolbury near Clun, the Devil's Chair on the Stiperstones, the Devil's Mouth to the east of the Long Mynd, the Devil's Dingle near Buildwas, and the Devil's Causeway in several places (see chapter 2), including near Acton Burnell. A newspaper report of December 1938 told how a geologist called George Vardy was studying the rock formation on the Stiperstones known as the Devil's

This Wood's beer is brewed 'to mark the myth of the Bury Ditches fairy who is said to have hidden a pot of gold on the ancient south Shropshire hillfort ... Anyone discovering a fine gold thread on the site will be led to the long-lost treasure'

Chair when the daylight began to fade prematurely. As he began to make his way downhill he felt a dramatic change in temperature:

> It had suddenly become very cold - bitterly cold - in a weird, unnatural way. Immediately after this, he saw what looked to be several shadowy figures not very far from where he was standing. They appeared to be swaying in the mist, and he got the feeling there were many others he could not see. ... Then he realised that the people he could see seemed to be quite oblivious of his presence. A chill wind had sprung up from nowhere and he suddenly caught sight of a faint light illuminating a hilltop. As he did so, he saw that some of the figures were completely naked. They were of both sexes, and appeared to be performing a weird ritual dance. How long this went on he couldn't remember. All he could later recall was that he had been too afraid to move until the figures had vanished as suddenly and completely as they had appeared. When that moment arrived, Vardy couldn't move quickly enough.

Dragons and imp carved at Wenlock Priory

He later made enquiries, and found that others reported similar experiences. Local people told him that on the longest night of the year the ghosts of witches and warlocks assembled by the Devil's Chair to re-enact their rituals.

If such fear could be aroused in a professional man in 1938 it is easy to understand people's terror in earlier times such as the mid-19th century in Shropshire, when a particular stile acquired the reputation of being 'a favourite resort of the adversary', which no one could pass without turning an item of clothing inside out. 'So strongly is this superstition implanted', wrote R.C. Warde, 'that I have heard of women deliberately turning their gowns before crossing the stile'.

Even on holy ground the devil's power caused apprehension. The weeping pear tree by the front porch of Bucknell Church was known as the devil's tree. Not far away, between the River Clun and its tributary, the Kemp, at Clunbury, Chapel Farm, formerly a chapel, became a farm when the congregation fled, convinced by unexplained nocturnal noises that the devil was haunting it. Hare quotes a manuscript account of when the devil did (allegedly) appear:

> This yeare 1533 uppon twelffe day in Shrowsbury, the dyvyll apearyd in saint Alkmonds, churche there, when the preest was at highe masse, with great tempeste and darknesse, so that as he passyd through the churche, he mountyd up the Steaple in the sayde churche, teringe the wyers of the clocke, and put the prynt of hys clawes upon the 4th bell, and tooke one of the pynnacles awaye with hym, and for the tyme stayed all the bells in the churches within the sayde towne that they could neither toll nor rynge.

Women from Prees and Whitchurch told Edmund Vale in 1915 that a rector at Ightfield had secret dealings with the devil. He sacked a garden boy for being cheeky, and later met him in Prees and asked him what he was doing. 'Trying to find a new place'. 'You'll never get one', said the parson. The boy fell ill, and told the doctor that after the rector had driven off a strange shadow appeared in the road, and would not leave him. Three days later the boy died, having shivered ceaselessly since the meeting. Still in Ightfield, a squire, Mainwaring, gambled with the devil and won. The loser had under the terms of the wager to plant an avenue of trees leading up to the church. When Mainwaring died he had his tomb placed half in and half out of the church, so as to cheat the devil. Even so he re-appeared after death, driving a spectral coach to his old home, where indelible bloodstains remained.

The equivocal burial indicates a pact with the devil, or rather the attempt to avoid the consequences of losing one's soul after making such an agreement. Ida Gandy noted before the Second World War from a Mr. Powell and his sister of Graig Wood, Llanfair Waterdine, a long narrative about a lad called David who was born at Skyborry and worked on a farm close by. When Llanfair Wake came round the farmer insisted that David 'mun stay and scare the crows' but 'an unknown personage, who, you must understand, was the devil himself' offered to shut the offending birds in a barn. Off went David to the wake, to be confronted by the irate farmer, who was later more than surprised to find that the birds were indeed confined, as he had been told.

The devil came again when David was sowing wheat, and asked in his simple way whether he would choose the tops or the bottoms of the crop. Of course, he chose tops. Faced with the same option another time in a potato field David bested the dimwitted devil by picking bottoms. He won a third victory when the devil failed in a challenge to carry water in a sieve from Skyborry to Llanfair.

These encounters made David deeply afraid of adverse consequences, and when he died he left instructions that his heart was to be thrown on a dunghill where a raven and a dove would fight for it. If the raven won his soul would go to 'Uncle Joseph' (another euphemism for the devil); if the dove prevailed his soul would go to 'a better place'. His body was not to be taken though a door or a window, not carried along any road or path, and buried neither in the church or the churchyard.

David's relatives, afraid of falling foul of his curse, carefully complied with his orders. After removing slates they lifted his body through a gap in the roof, then carried it along the dykes (stone field walls) and buried it with the head in the church and the feet in the churchyard. A raven and a dove were carved on his tombstone, though which won the contest for his soul remains a mystery. When the church was restored (in 1854) the grave had to be opened, and David's skull proved to be missing. Later, a man's skull and a great key were found in a cellar at Skyborry, though no one could open the door which led from the cellar to an underground passage believed to run to Craig-y-don Rocks above Knucklas on the Radnorshire side of the River Teme.

The Pritchards insisted that David had really existed, and claimed that their uncle had possessed a book with details of the barn where the crows were penned and of the potato field where the devil had appeared. F.H. Groome adds the detail, contributed by Silvanus Lovell, waggoner's boy at Chapel Bottom, that the boy 'growed up to be an old, old man, and was a regular sort of conjuror [see chapter 7]. Why, the farmers have told us that scores and scores of times when we went up to the farms a-fiddling'. Brenda Davies and Jocelyn Williams, long-term residents at Llanfair, state in their pamphlet on the village that the boy's name was David Syr Evan, and that, having sold half his soul to the devil he was buried half in and half out of the churchyard. Fragments of a tombstone, thought to be his, showed birds in flight, perhaps those of the story. David's ghost sometimes appears, it is said, sitting on the gatepost of Nether Skyborry.

Witches

Well into the 20th century witches were feared because of their perceived ability to bewitch, or 'o'erlook', as the Shropshire term had it. Early records mention Thomas Owen's curses which kept the vicar of Mainstone awake at nights in 1616/7. At about the same time the rector at Greete, five miles from Ludlow, excluded Joan Davies from Easter communion on the grounds that she had put a curse on her neighbour, Beatrix Hall. In the 18th century Mary Bebb was charged at Shrewsbury with 'profanely uttering sixty-seven curses'.

Those concerned were not necessarily considered to be witches. A man called Jasper, thrown out of the Bear Inn at Hodnet some time in the 16th century for being unable to pay his bill, perished in the winter snow. Before dying, he cursed the landlord, who then died himself, of heart failure. A puritan, Paul Holmyard, given shelter at Moreton Corbet in the time of James I, was later told to leave. After being arrested he delivered this anathema to Sir Vincent Corbet:

A woodcut showing a witch-hanging in the seventeenth century

Rejoice not in thy riches for neither thou nor thy children nor thy children's children shall inhabit these halls. They shall be given up in desolation and thy house shall be full of doleful creatures.

'These last words', writes C.J.R. Errington in his pamphlet on Moreton Corbet, 'are believed to be a reference to glum and rainsoaked tourists wandering around the castle in search of a hot cup of tea or a toilet, neither of which is normally in evidence'.

Catherine Gaskell's narrative, written in 1894, clearly shows ordinary people's deep fear of witchcraft and its practitioners, and is worth quoting at some length:

> In the middle of this century there lived at Westwood, near Wenlock, a woman who was known in the neighbourhood as a famous witch. Nanny Morgan, for such was her name, was a black or evil witch. She was described to me as 'the wickedest woman as ever I saw'. 'When Nanny met me', that old woman said, 'she could make me break out in a cold sweat all over, for 'er had two grey eyes as could strike through you like knives, and seemed to burn you inside like devil's fire. We was terrible afeard of Nanny, and none durst say her nay, because she knowed everything about a body, more than a body could know hersel''.
>
> Nanny was employed by her neighbours to 'ill-wish' those against whom they owed a grudge, to prepare love philtres, to bring recalcitrant lovers to the feet of love-stricken maidens, and to curse those who 'could not work out their own hate' unaided. 'There's no use going against the psalm', I have been told by an old friend, 'for when 'tis read out of a prayer-book it finishes a Christian, body and soul; but when 'twas read by sich a curser as Nanny Morgan there's no angel in heaven could flit by safe'.
>
> In the early part of this century Nanny as a young woman was tried for stealing a coat at Bourton; but, owing to her being at that time a 'queen of hellish beauty', she was acquitted. She subsequently married a man who used to work on the roads. He fell ill some years after, and the neighbourhood believed was starved to death by her. There was an inquest, but not enough was proved against Nanny to convict her. One of the officials who went up to inspect the corpse declared it was a loathsome sight. 'Three dogs and four cats, rested on the poor body, and the face fair swarmed black wid fleas'.
>
> Eventually, however, the devil got his own, and Nanny came to a tragic end. She was murdered in her sixty-ninth year, in September 1857, by her lodger Wright, a young man from Baschurch, for who, it is said, she had conceived an unholy passion, and who killed her, it is alleged, to escape from her spiritual thraldom. During the trial the judge said to him, 'Prisoner, what have you got to say in your defence?' Wright replied, ''Tis no use my speaking, for 'tis all on one side, like the Bridgnorth

election; you be all agin me'. Wright was sentenced to death, but recommended to mercy by the jury, and eventually transported for life.

Dr. Brookes [for whom, see chapter 9] has told me that he was one of the party who went with the chief constable to Nanny's house when they heard that she was murdered. They found the wretched sorceress lying with her head on the first steps of her staircase, her long hair hanging about her shoulders in mats, clotted with blood. One of her dogs, her sole mourner, was howling piteously by her side. Nanny kept innumerable cats and many dogs. 'The house foul reeked of cats', I was told, and one 'a grey sheeny Tom, was known by the evil name of Hell-Blaw'. She kept also toads in a box, and 'called unto her azgals (lizards) from the garden'. After her death wheelbarrows full of letters were found in the cottage, which had been written consulting her on various matters, and some of them were said to have been penned by most 'respectable people'. These notes, with her books, some of which were MSS., were written in the 'Devil's tongue', and 'in various speeches'. They were all burnt, by order of the mayor, in the yard of the Talbot Inn, before all the townsfolk of Wenlock.

I once expressed my keen regret to an old man who had been present on this occasion at the destruction of the witch's library. For this display of what he considered evil curiosity I was rebuked. 'Mam', he said severely, 'no clean-livered woman could have perused them books'. Such was the horror Nanny inspired that I have been told the men who found her put her into her coffin 'in any how', for it was explained to me, 'we was terribly afeard of the curse that might come to us if we was but touched by the witch's blood'.

Some ten years later, in 1905, Gaskell wrote that her gardener believed that his brother had been 'overlooked' by Becky Smout,

> an old gangrel [vagabond] body, weazen, dark as walnut juice, and the look of a vixen in her eyes. Some folks say she came to Shropshire on a broomstick some seventy years agone from Sliverton [Silvington] on the Clee-side. 'Tis a land of witches that Clee Hill, and allus must have been a stronghold of the devil.

The gardener believed that an ash whip was a useful implement for keeping witches at bay.

Such fear and beliefs by no means ended with the 19th century. W. Haye wrote in 1954 that he grew up near the Wrekin (possibly this was at Little Wenlock) 'in an atmosphere half religious, half-immersed in witchcraft that seemed to have a bearing on most happenings in the local daily life':

> There stood the cottage of Molly de Leyte who was credited - amongst other accomplishments of a like nature - with the ability to change

herself into a cat, and many a story in support of it was told to me. Did I believe them? After almost half a century I shall still not commit myself. Why did she keep a huge toad in a large earthen vessel known as a spigot stein, used by most country folk in those days ... for the storage of home-made wine? Why did she feed it, according to eye-witness accounts, on sacramental bread and converse with it on occasions in strange and unknown words? I know that no villager would willingly pass her on the road, nor would they intentionally be guilty of any act likely to offend her, but rather try and keep on the right side of her if at all possible.

People had recourse to a variety of mechanisms to defend themselves against witchcraft. Jean Hughes lists making a cross in the flour when baking or in malt when brewing, putting silver or a slip of mountain ash in a churn or pail of milk, and wearing a left stocking inside out. In 1882 a man found in the kitchen of his house near Madeley a paper sealed with red wax and bearing the words 'I charge all witches and ghosts to depart from this house, in the great names of Jehovah, Alpha and Omega'. It is possible that another protective charm lies behind the children's formula:

> Dead horse, dead horse.
> Where, where?
> Prolley Moor, Prolley Moor.
> We'll come, we'll come.
> There's nought but bones.

This was recited on seeing a carrion crow. Prolley Moor, five miles from Craven Arms, had the reputation of being a meeting place for witches.

Hair clippings and nail parings were carefully burned to prevent their use in witches' spells. Lest they might be similarly used the fonts at Clunbury and Neenton had staples, the marks of which can still be seen, to secure the lid. Glass 'witch balls' — made, among other places, at Wrockwardine — were hung by windows and door to keep witches out. Another expedient was certain patterns made on doorsteps or hearthstones with juice squeezed from elder or dock leaves. 'The Shropshire patterns', wrote Lilian Hayward, 'are for the most part very simple - a border of crosses between two lines; a series of vandykes [zigzags] with or without a circle in the wide part of each vandyke; two large crosses, divided by a vertical line; a figure resembling the Union Jack with the cross of St. George intersecting the cross of St. Andrew'. It would be interesting whether any such pattern has ever been sketched or photographed in Shropshire.

CHAPTER 7

LIFE

The two incontrovertible stages in existence are birth and death, though their accompanying rituals and beliefs change. Within these perimeters other important waymarks included that of marriage. This, too, is changing: in 2001 only some 250,000 couples married in England and Wales, the same number as a century earlier, when the population was much smaller. As a result 40% of children were born outside wedlock (76% where mothers under the age of 26 were concerned). However, some have suggested that the statistics of marriages are skewed since between 55 and 60,000 choose each year to be married abroad. In addition, lavish and highly publicised celebrity nuptials may have helped the number of weddings to rise in 2002 for the first time in a decade. Even so, in one survey, the question, 'Do you think that marriage is essential to ensure a lasting relationship?', received a negative response in 52% of cases. There is nothing new, though, in a couple's deciding to cohabit without benefit of clergy: the old Shropshire expression for it, borrowing a term from the world of work, was 'to butty'.

During life, health is a major preoccupation which in the past sometimes led people to seek the advice of cunning folk or charmers. A feeling of confidence in a practitioner remains an important factor in therapy, especially in complementary medicine. Some of the herbal remedies of yesteryear have also regained favour. Fears of the unknown, of the future, of possible catastrophe—and also of how to avoid trouble—continue to feature strongly in people's preoccupations. In 2003 a survey by Dr. Richard Wiseman, a psychologist at Hertfordshire University, showed that only one person in ten claimed to be not at all superstitious. Lucky people were less inclined to be superstitious; unlucky people, more so: they were often worried about life, and unable to tolerate ambiguity or uncertainty. The most frequent superstitions—some requiring positive, some avoiding, action—were touching wood, crossing fingers, not walking under ladders, not breaking mirrors, carrying a charm, having one's path crossed by a black cat, not putting shoes on a table, saluting a single magpie. Shropshire has its own priorities in this field.

Birth

Lilian Hayward described in 1938 the 'common belief' that if an expectant mother were frightened by an animal her baby would resemble it in some way such as hairiness or shape. The withered arm of one child was attributed to the mother's refusing when she was pregnant to buy from a one-armed pedlar who called, and then cursed her.

According to Augustus Hare, on the Clee Hills people believed that if a hare crossed the path of a pregnant woman the baby would be 'hare-shotten' (have a hare-lip) unless she immediately stooped and tore her shift. Further rules of conduct were: 'You must never rock an empty cradle, unless you wish another child to occupy it'; and 'it is very unlucky to put a baby in a cradle before it has been baptised - the fairies may take it'.

Fear of fairies featured strongly in the story of a very old Shropshire woman related in the periodical, *Woman*, in May 1953. She thought it risky to speak at all of an expected baby, lest the fairies be alerted and injure or steal it. She therefore referred to her daughter's expected children as 'pot lids', since such humdrum objects would be unlikely to attract the fairies' attention. In the Clun Valley in the 1950s it was considered unlucky to take a pram into a house before the birth of the child due to occupy it.

The notion that a new-born child must go up before it went down, requiring a neighbour or grandparents to stand on a chair, baby in arms, survived until the late 20th century. The increasing number of babies born in hospital may well have put paid to it.

Alf Strange was born at home in 1925 at Welsh Frankton. The local midwife, Nurse Jones, attended: she only charged what people could afford, and accepted payment in kind, including (from one gipsy family) a roasted hedgehog. Alf's mother, after having three sons, tried walking backwards up stairs during her pregnancy in the hope that this would ensure that a daughter came. In vain. She tried the same again three years later but the outcome was a fifth baby boy.

Mrs. Strange, a strict Congregationalist, was properly married. An illegitimate child in Shropshire was called a 'by-blow' or 'come-by-chance'. The term, 'barley child' (after the time between the sowing and the harvesting of barley), designated one born in wedlock, but within six months of its parents' marriage.

'According to a fancy prevalent in Staffordshire and in west Shropshire, if one of the God-parents [at a christening] looks into the font, the infant will grow up to resemble him'. So wrote Rev. G.S. Tyack in 1899, adding: 'In Shropshire it is also considered to be unlucky to mention a child's name until it is announced at the font; the father selects it, as a rule, and keeps it as a secret until the last moment'. A deep fear of human vulnerability at times of transition underlies such anxieties.

Courtship and Marriage

Young women employed various ways of discovering the identity of a future husband. One formula, dated 1861, runs as follows:

> Procure the blade-bone of a lamb and prick it with a penknife at midnight, repeating ...
>> 'Tis not this bone I mean to prick,
>> But my love's heart I mean to prick;
>> If he comes not, and speaks to me tonight,
>> I'll prick and prick till it be light.

A decade or so later, girls tried something else:

>> This is the blessed Friday night;
>> I draw my stocking into my right,
>> To dream of the living, not of the dead,
>> To dream of the young man I am to wed.

At the same time young men might be carrying a bachelor's button plant, wrapped in damp moss, in a pocket. If this continued to grow he would be assured of success at some future date with the woman he had in mind. The problem is that the name, Bachelor's Buttons, is given to well over a dozen different plants. Perhaps of all these the periwinkle, with its alleged ability 'to cause love', was intended.

In July 1891 Widow Mary Preece of Rorrington described to Rev. Waldegrave Brewster how when she was a servant at Parson Williams's in Chirbury the three daughters of the house went 'permanenting' at Hallowe'en:

> The oldest prepared a piece of ground intending to sow hempseed and, as the clock struck twelve, sing:
>> The hempseed I take, the hempseed I shake;
>> He who shall love me come after me and rake.
> In the meantime the two other sisters, having forced the maid [Mary] to get their father's watch while he was asleep, went down the path alongside the vicarage garden to a sage bush. Leaving the maid with a lantern a little way up, they intended each to pick a leaf from the sage bush at every stroke of twelve, expecting or hoping to see the intended picking on the other side of the sage bush. But just before the hour their own large black tom cat ... plunged through the sage bush, whereupon the two ran screaming and scampering, which frightened also the other sister. The clock struck twelve, and they lost all their chance for that year.
> Another way of permanenting would have been to drop a pea out of the window at every stroke of the clock, when 'he' would have appeared. The risk of being caught taking the watch seems to have fixed this in the

Preece mind. The watch was wanted to warn of the coming striking of the clock.

Ira Gandy tells the sad story of Frances Hatton, who became the step-daughter of the noted politician and jurist, Sir Edward Coke (1552-1634), when he married her mother in 1598. Coke decided that the girl, aged 15, should marry Sir John Villiers, brother of the 1st duke of Buckingham. When she refused, Coke beat her, tied to a bedpost, every day, until she consented to the match. It proved disastrous. Villiers went mad. His family disputed his baby's parentage. Frances was imprisoned, and, when she refused to perform the penance of walking barefoot in a white sheet from St. Paul's to the Savoy, excommunicated. Eventually, she escaped in disguise from her implacable relatives, and was taken by her lover, Sir Robert Howard, to the Hall of the Forest, his retreat (now a farmhouse) in a narrow valley above the village of Newcastle. She stayed there for some five years, alone much of the time except for servants.

In attempting to ensure that marriages were less unhappy than this, people tried to avert ill omen. Wednesday and Saturday weddings were considered unlucky, the former bringing poverty, the latter threatened by untimely death. Rain at a wedding meant an uncomfortable relationship for the couple; sunshine augured comfort and prosperity. Until recently—perhaps still—it was thought unlucky for the groom to see the bride's dress before the wedding, or the bride herself on the day of the ceremony. In 1957 near Clun when church services were held only in alternate weeks the sexton-cum-verger insisted on reading the banns outside the building on the Sundays when the clergyman did not attend, so as not to interrupt the sequence, which would have been unlucky. A similar case is recorded from Hopesay where the sexton in 1948 read the banns 'to the four winds', turning to the cardinal points of the compass as he did so. Another bad omen would be if the ring were dropped during the ceremony: at Ellesmere they believed that whichever of the bridal couple did so would be the first to die.

An unusual custom described at Stoke-upon-Tern in 1829, and continuing in the county for at least another decade, involved decorating the church gate with white cloths to which were fastened silver spoons, tankards and watches lent by neighbouring farmers for the occasion. More widespread in Shropshire was the belief that wedding carriages should not turn after reaching the church. Instead they went back by a different route, but if this were impossible they had to go on beyond the church before turning. At Madeley, wedding and funeral processions arrived by different routes, and at St. Luke's, Hodnet, separate gates to the churchyard were used by weddings, christenings and funerals.

Stephen Price, waggoner, and Ethel Cornes, housemaid, were married at Worfield in 1919 (see illustration opposite). 'The wedding photograph', wrote their son, Derek (born 1927), 'shows the moustached bridegroom looking proudly handsome with bowler hat, black drainpipe trousers and polished boots, whilst the bride has a long elegant dress and wide-brimmed hat like her bridesmaid sister Leah'. He adds the family story of when his father, mother and aunt went to see the vicar to arrange the wedding. Asked which of the sisters he was marrying, Stephen Price replied: 'I'd have them both if I could afford them'.

A rather heartening tale of fidelity is variously placed at Caus Castle, Moreton Corbet and Wattleborough, but always involves Thomas, a member of the Corbet family who went on pilgrimage to the Holy Land, leaving the care of the family estates to his younger brother, Robert. Some four or five years on, Robert, despairing of Thomas's return, decided to marry the woman intended for him. On the day of the wedding a pilgrim arrived at the gate and was invited to join the festivities. Only after the ceremony did he reveal himself to be Thomas. Robert offered the estate back — if not the bride — but Thomas asked only for a small piece of land on which he could live out his life as a hermit.

Such asceticism is far removed from the thoughts of most people at weddings. At Clee Hill the family and guests, after the newly-weds' departure, would retire to a public house, taking two or three chamber pots which were filled with beer and handed round for all the company to have a drink.

The wedding of Stephen Price and Ethel Cornes

Discord

In the male-dominated societies of the past sanctions in dysfunctional marriages were much more common for women than for men. However, a husband is the target in the ritual of 'burning the mawkin' in which Charles Peskin took part as a boy in the early 1870s:

> We would make an effigy of straw and old clothes, and then form a procession, and with tin whistles, clappers and tin cans for music we would carry the 'mawkin' to the door of a wife-beater and fire it.

Charlotte Burne gives details from the 1880s of several cases of 'riding the stang', a public expression of disapproval directed against either husband or wife when he or she proved unduly quarrelsome or blatantly unfaithful. 'Formerly, we may suppose', she writes, 'the offender must have been made to mount the "stang" or pole in person; now a "mawkin" (or effigy) takes his place, or else a youth is carried by his companions in a chair fixed upon a ladder, shouting at intervals a doggerel verse abusing the offender'. The mawkin went round, accompanied by 'tin-pot music' as far as the offender's house, where it was ceremonially burned. 'Tin-panning', when youths turned out to serenade a couple deemed quilty of some offence, was remembered in Wem until the mid-1970s. Earlier, effigies of a man and woman 'having illicit acquaintance' would have been carried through the town to a similar accompaniment.

Ducking stool for a scold

The ducking stool—or gumb stool, in Shrewsbury—could be used for either sex by women seem to have been its more frequent victims. At Much Wenlock the cucking stool (as they termed it) served quite simply 'for ducking women of evil life'. A Mrs. Swyney also described the use there of another device applied to women: 'often have I seen poor Judy Cookson walked round the town in the shrew's bridle. 'Er was said to be the best abuser in the borough, and 'er would go and curse anybody for three-ha'pence - that was the fee'. As with other punishments, this was inflicted on a Monday—market day—so as to receive maximum exposure. Judy, though, remained incorrigible:

> Judy used to abuse Sir Watkin's agent something terrible, 'im as they called 'King Collins', for 'e did what 'e listed and none durst say 'im nay. She was a fearsome pelrollick, it is true, was Judy, but I never knowed as the bridle did 'er any good. It makes me swimmey-headed only to think of those Mondays, with the relatives all cursing and crying, the lads laughing and jeering, and the lawyer men looking on to see as their law was carried out.

At least one other woman at Much Wenlock was subjected to the same treatment; Mrs. Swyney remarked that 'the poor creature's face streamed with blood, and two teeth fell out in removing the bridle'. An example of the device has been preserved in the museum at Ludlow. Another, formerly in the work-house at Oswestry, has disappeared: it was 'last used when a pauper inmate named Mary Jones, otherwise "Red Moll", being ordered to keep silence, threw a basin of broth over the head of the master in the dining-hall'.

Burne records the belief among 'less educated folk' in Oswestry that if a husband failed to maintain his wife she could return his ring and look for a better match. Repudiation often went the other way. Mrs. Swyney recalled this occurrence at Much Wenlock from the 1830s:

> A man by the name of Yates sold his wife, Mattie, to a man called Richards. Yates brought in his missus in a cart, with a halter round her neck, from Brockton, and sold her for 2s. 6d. When Yates got to the market-place 'e turned shy, and tried to get out of the business, but Mattie mad' un stick to it. 'Er flipped her apern in 'er gude man's face, and said, 'Let be, yer rogue. I wull be sold; I wants a change'.

'Contrary to what might have been expected', Gaskell commented, 'Mattie's second marriage turned out very happily, and she and Richards lived for many years amicably in the Bull Ring'.

The ritual of wife selling—a form of divorce perceived to be legal (though not in fact so) among consenting parties—has been recorded only a handful of times in Shropshire, almost all in the Much Wenlock area. The account by Charles Peskin must date from about 1875:

When I began work sixty-six years ago, there was an old man named John Aston living in the Strawbarn, who had been married four times. He was generally known as Drummer Aston, and his last wife, who, he declared, was the best of the four, he 'bought' at Wenlock fair for 1s. 6d. and brought her to Coalbrookdale with a halter-rope round her neck; this was supposed to clinch the bargain.

From somewhat farther afield is the rather flowery report which appeared in a local newspaper in 1810:

A circumstance of a melodramatic nature occurred at Bridgnorth on Saturday se'nnight. A forgeman in the neighbourhood having resolved to dispose of his better half by public sale, thought he could not choose a more eligble spot for that purpose than the market at Bridgnorth: accordingly on the above, he, with a considerable number of his Cyclopian bretheren conducted the forlorn fair-one to the destined spot. It being 'high change' at they entered Bridgnorth, the good women in the market perceiving the assemblage approaching towards them, insistently concluded that it was the intention of the black brethren, who composed it, to make a general attack and deprive them of the commodities they had for sale; flight was instantly the order of the day, and in the confusion of the retreat, the pavement was strewed with a mixed multitude of ducks, fowls, pounds of butter, halfpence etc., which being perceived by the salesmen, they thought they could not do better than take the dispersed commodities into their keeping. This being done, the business of the sale commenced, and half-a-guinea being bid for the lady, her tender husband knocked her down, with much satisfaction and immediately after the convocation was dissolved in a very peaceable manner.

Ballad writers took up the theme of wife selling. One song, sold in the streets in the 18th century as well as being performed in theatres, circulated orally for many years afterwards. This version of 'John Hobbs' was sung in 1907 to Janet Blunt by a Miss M. Glover of Kingsthorpe, Northamptonshire, who learnt it as a child in about 1870 from her old Shropshire nurse.

He took her to market, did Hobbs, John Hobbs,
He took her to market, John Hobbs.
She made such a ruction he threatened destruction:
'I'll sell her by auction', says Hobbs, John Hobbs,
So he put her to auction, did Hobbs.

'Who'll buy a wife?' says Hobbs, John Hobbs,
'A very good wife', says Hobbs;
But somehow they tell us, these wife-dealing fellows
Were most of them sellers like Hobbs, John Hobbs,
Were most of them sellers, like Hobbs.

'Bring me a rope', says Hobbs, John Hobbs,
'Bring me a rope', says Hobbs.
'I'll not stand to wrangle, Myself I will strangle',
So he hung dingle-dangle, did Hobbs, John Hobbs,
He hung dingle-dangle, did Hobbs.

Down his wife cut him, did Hobbs, Jane Hobbs,
Down his wife cut him, did Hobbs,
With a few hubble-bubbles they settled their troubles,
Like most married couples, did Hobbs, John Hobbs,
Like most married couples, did Hobbs.

JOHN HOBBS, JOHN HOBBS.

Fears and Hopes

In 1855 John Noakes wrote from Worcester to the *Gentleman's Magazine* in London to say that 'in parts of this county and Shropshire, the following occurrences are considered unlucky':

> To meet a squinting woman, unless you talk to her, which breaks the charm.
> To go on a journey on a Friday.
> To help another person to salt at table.
> To be one of a party of 13 at Christmas.
> To have crickets in the house.
> To have a female come into your house on New Year's morning
> To have a cut onion lying about in the house breeds distempers.
> To cross knives accidentally at meal times.
> To walk under a ladder.
> For the first young lamb you see in a season, or a colt, to have its tail towards you.
> To kill a lady-cow.
> To see the first of the new moon through a window, or glass of any sort, is also unlucky. But if you see it in the open air, turn the money in your pocket, and express a wish for luck in the ensuring month, you are supposed to ensure it.
> To have apples and blossoms on a tree at the same time is a sign of a forthcoming death in the family.
> To have a long succession of black cards (spades or clubs) dealt to a person whilst at play is prophetic of death to himself or some member of the family.
> When a corpse is limp it is a sign that another death will happen in the house.
> As to cutting your nails on a Sunday, the following couplet is very expressive: Better a child was never born / Than cut his hoofs on a Sunday morn.
> The itching of the nose is a sign of bad news; if the ear itches, you may expect news from the living; if the face burns, some one is talking about you; and when you shudder, a person is walking over the spot where your grave will be.
> To leave a tea-pot lid open is a sign that a stranger is coming; and when a cock crows in your doorway, or a bit of black stuff hangs on the bar of the grate, it is a sign of a similar event.
> A bit of coal popped from the fire must resemble either a purse or a coffin, and consequently good luck or death.
> Tea-drinking is made to foreshadow a large number of the casualties of life, including the receipt of presents, the visits of strangers, obtaining sweethearts, and the like, merely from the appearance of the tea and the grounds. A bright speck in a candle is a sure indication that a letter is coming to the individual to whom it points.

If the sun shines warmly on Christmas day there will be many fires in the ensuing year.

'A great year for nuts, a great year for children', is a common saying.

To present a person with a knife is supposed to have the effect of cutting a friendship.

A donkey braying is an infallible sign of rain.

To cut your hair during the increase of the moon is said to ensure its favourable growth.

The horse-shoe is still to be seen over doors in many places, and fastened to bedsteads, to keep witches away.

A pillow filled with hops, and laid under the patient's bed, is an undoubted cure for rheumatism.

In the rural districts great faith is put in rings made of shillings and sixpences given at sacrament, and many clergymen have told us of repeated applications having been made to them for sacrament shillings for the purpose of keeping away the evil spirit, or as a remedy for fits. Omens or tokens of death adhere to the popular belief to a more general extent than any other relic of superstition, perhaps one-third of the population attaching more or less credit to them. It would be impossible to enumerate all these idle fancies, but among them are prominently the howling of a dog, a winding-cheet in the candle, and the issuing of light from a candle after it is blown out.

Several of these recur in a list supplied by Colin Bird, who was born in 1928 at Stow, near Knighton. Unlucky actions include to walk under a ladder, open an umbrella indoors, kill a spider, see a new moon through a window, wear green at a wedding, put new shoes on a table, spill salt, cross knives, stir with a knife (which causes strife), cut finger nails on a Friday or a Sunday, pass someone on the stairs, change an item of clothing put on inside out, leave a house by a door other than the one used on entering, and see a cross-eyed woman. The last item is illustrated by a story heard 'many years ago: "I were going to look for a job and on the way I met a ooman with one eye and a ball of chalk. I knowed I wouldna get the job and I didna, her put the black stick on me"'.

Mr. Bird's lucky list is confined to seeing a 'chimley' sweep or a black cat, apart from the practice of a darkhaired man's opening (by arrangement) the door of a house and walking through on New Year's morning. His version of the well-known magpie rhyme, like others, has a mixed message:

> One for anger, two for mirth,
> Three for a wedding, four for a birth;
> Five for rich, six for poor,
> Seven for a witch, I can tell you no more.

In the 1950s children at Llanfair Waterdine, not far from Stow, said:

> One for sorrow, two for joy,
> Three for a present, four for a letter,
> Five for something better.

Mary Webb took the title for one of her novels from the penultimate line of this variation:

> I saw seven magpies in a tree,
> One for you and six for me.
> One for sorrow, two for joy,
> Three for a girl, four for a boy,
> Five for silver, six for gold,
> Seven for a secret
> That's never been told.

Charles Swainson, who published a book on the folklore of birds in 1885, wrote that a north Shropshire friend of his, when he saw a magpie, took off his hat, spat towards the bird, and said, 'Devil, devil, I defy you'. The magpie's bad reputation is explained by the suggestion that it alone refused to go into the ark with Noah, preferring to perch on the roof and chatter at the other animals.

Various superstitions are (or were) connected with working practices. In 1940 a farmer ignored local wisdom at Llanbrook that young trees should not be cut down when the sap was rising. He found, or so people said, that his lambs died in the spring, and that his mother endured a year's illness. Rev. Brewster found at Middleton-in-Chirbury that his parishioners would not work on a Good Friday, nor would they throw out ashes or suds since this would be to fling them 'in the Saviour's face'. An exception to the taboo was baking. Mary Preece told the classic story of a woman preparing to bake bread, one Good Friday. A beggar comes to the door asking for bread. The woman says that the dough is not yet in the oven, but she takes a small piece and puts it to bake specially for him. When she looks a little later she finds that it has risen and grown into a big cake. 'Oh', she says, 'this is too large for thee'. The beggar—Christ in disguise—turns away and says, 'A hoohoo [owl] shalt thou henceforth be, and all the birds of the wood shall follow thee'. The woman's owlish face is sometimes seen on gnarled old trees to this day.

Remedies

Good Friday bread, believed to last up to seven years, could be grated and swallowed to cure stomach upsets and other ills. The bizarre application of 'bletch' (grease) from church bells to cure 'the chick-pox' is mentioned in *Precious Bane*. John Rorrington of Rorrington Green described to Rev. Brewster in 1891 how to deal with rupture: split a growing she-ash sapling and pass the patient nine times through it, then bind the tree together with strips of bark from a male ash, then as the two halves re-unite the rupture will disappear.

The same kind of sympathetic magic applied in the procedure mentioned by Hare which required that a child suffering from whooping cough should be taken to Ludlow Castle to 'waken the echo'. The appeal, 'Echo, please take away my cough', would prove effective. For the same widespread complaint, 'one rather heroic cure', wrote Lilian Hayward, 'was to put hair from the cross on a donkey's back into milk and make the patient swallow it'. Alf Strange's version prescribed that a cutting of the sufferer's hair should be put in an envelope and buried beneath a yew tree in a churchyard. Late in the 20th century in the Acton Burnell area a hairy caterpillar was put in a bag tied round a child's neck. When the caterpillar died the cough would have gone. More simply, sufferers were taken to breathe copious draughts of air near a gasworks. At Clee Hill the time-honoured expedient remembered by Alf Jenkins consisted of applying goosefat to the chest, and covering it with brown paper.

Vegetable resources at Clee Hill included a piece of onion inserted in the ear to cure an ache, and whipping the legs with nettles to combat rheumatism. Many herbal remedies remained in use in the 1930s, according to Lilian Hayward:

> Tea made of agrimony and wood betony for the blood, 'floppy dock' tea for the heart - floppy docks are foxgloves, and I know of a case where a girl made floppy dock tea for her grandmother. She made it too strong, and the grandmother died. Poultices made of the root of comfrey for sprains and boils; house leek (called house rue in Shropshire) for sore eyes; herb rue for flea bites; eyebright tea for sore eyes. Though as regards eyes, most districts had their healing well or spring [see chapter 3] to which people resorted to bathe their eyes.

In the late 20th century a poultice of house leeks—plants also thought to be lucky when growing on the roofs of cowsheds and pigsties—was considered good for earache. One woman at Ketley poured hot water over comfrey and marshmallow leaves and then bathed a sprained limb with the liquid. Blackcurrant tea treated a cold, broom tea, rheumatism. Nasturtium leaves (also eaten in salads) could be used to make an infusion drunk 'to enrich the blood'.

Charmers and Cunning Folk

Charms intended to bring good luck or good health could take verbal form, either spoken or written, or be various objects, worn, carried or displayed. Charmers were people thought to be specially gifted in administering or applying such charms in order to treat a range of natural ailments in humans and animals. Only rarely did they combine this activity with other kinds of magic, though sometimes a charmer doubled as a herbalist.

Charmers are sometimes confused with cunning folk (see below), though the two were separate. Mary Webb's Wizard Beguildy mistakenly combines the two roles when he rhetorically asks:

> Dunna I snare souls like conies, and keep 'em from troubling the lives of men? Canna I bless, and they are blessed, curse, and they are cursed? Canna I cure warts and the chincough and barrenness and the rheumatics, and tell the future and find water, though it be in the depths of the earth? Dunna the fowls I bless beat all the other fowls in the cock-fighting? Ah, and if I chose, I could make a waxen man for every man in the parish, and consume them away, wax, men, and all.

Warts, mentioned by Beguildy, are famously susceptible to suggestion. Possible treatments listed by Hayward include stealing a piece of beef, rubbing it on the wart and burying it; rubbing with and burying a bean pod; taking a piece of wood and burying it at a crossroad; burying for three days a golden celandine picked at midnight, then squeezing its juice on the wart. These all involve self-help but Hayward also mentions cases where assistance came from a third party such as the farmer in her parish who 'had the power' and could will warts away without even seeing them or the sufferer. Two old ladies near her house could effect a cure, 'one by rubbing the wart with a silver thimble, and the other by tying a bit of string round the sufferer's fourth finger'. A child near Pontesbury went to a charmer who 'spoke over her', but the treatment failed because, contrary to the strict instructions of the charmer, she talked about it. A young girl with bleeding warts on both hands consulted an old gardener from just over the Staffordshire border who told her carefully to count the warts. As she did so he put a knot for each in a piece of wool. Refusing both thanks and payment, he went off with the wool. Within a few weeks the warts disappeared, never to return.

The power of suggestion is clear, but what of charming in the case of animals? Hayward reports the case described to her in 1937 but dating from 50 years earlier of a heifer which bled at the nose. Hughes, a charmer at Church Stretton to whom the owner applied for help, said, 'Well, I'll see what I can do. You go back whum and take a little can or summat and put it under 'er nose, and maybe you'll find the bleedin's given ower'. So it happened. Another farmer, near Clun, had an animal with a troublesome kneejoint. A different charmer wrote a verse from the bible on a piece of paper and put it in the boosey (manger) for the beast to eat with its hay. The problem cleared up.

When Hayward's own house had a plague of rats in 1922 — 'we even had them walking up and down the stairs' — a man professing to be a rat charmer offered to get rid of them (unusually, because charmers did not normally ask for cash) for a fee of £1, payable in advance.

> I showed him the places where we had seen many rats. He asked for some flour; this he put about in little heaps, sprinkled with some powder that he had with him. He muttered some sort of incantation over them, but refused to repeat this clearly. Next day I expected to find a score of dead rats. Not one was to be found; but the rats had all disappeared, and they never returned while I lived in that house.

Ira Gandy was told of Isabella Pearce, an old lady dressed in a grey cloak, who collected herbs to make into medicines and salves. People travelled long distances to consult her. One of her remedies was the briar-boss (otherwise called briar ball or Robin's pincushion, once collected from wild roses and sold by apothecaries). 'If you han the tuthache', said Isabella, 'and you light on a briar-boss accidental, and you wear un in your buzzom it'll cure un'. Gandy also met a woman from Llanbrook Farm who 'made a drink of wormwood sometimes, when a body needed a tonic, or a nice tea from the mugwort in the hedges'.

At much the same time, Magdalene Weale met 'the local wizard' by the outlet of the Boat Level, an underground waterway from Pennerley Mine, two miles distant. A man, having announced in the local pub that his wife, Gert, was 'as gwold as a guinea', received advice to consult the wizard, who told him to wind some strings nine times round the patient's leg and to read some of his charms over her. A few days later the woman's daughter enthusiastically confirmed the cure, adding that in addition to 'yellowert' (jaundice) the wizard could deal with other problems.

> She herself had worn in a little bag on her chest a folded-up paper which he had given her, and her toothache had disappeared by magic. You must on no account, however, she warned me, read what is written on the paper, neither must you offer him money or say 'thank you' at the time. Armed with these instructions I called upon the witch-doctor and told him I had heard of his clever cures. He looked at me suspiciously out of the corner of his eye. ... I repeated my compliment rather nervously. Then a light came into his eye and, one esoteric to another, he confided: 'It's like this. They thinkenen as the charms does 'em good, anna does'.

As it happens, a number of written charms have survived. John Davies (1786-1876), a farmer in Llanyblodwel parish, served as churchwarden on several occasions. His activities in the Tanat Valley as a charmer do not seem to have conflicted with his religious duties. When he died, aged 90, he was found to be wearing a charm intended for his own preservation. This has not survived, nor has the manuscript book he possessed, though two items were copied. These run:

> Charm for Beest Bewitched Abrasac
> Lord of Demons & Eric Spirits
> propitious powers preserve this cow
> of John Davies of the township of
> Blodwell in the County of Shropshire
> from all ill accidents that may happen
> to John Davies is cow. In the name of
> the Father & the Son & of the Holey
> Gost amen.

> Plead my cause O Lord with them that
> strive with me fight against them that
> fight against me Take hold of Shield
> and buckler and stand up for mine help
> Draw out also the Spear and stop
> the way against them that perse

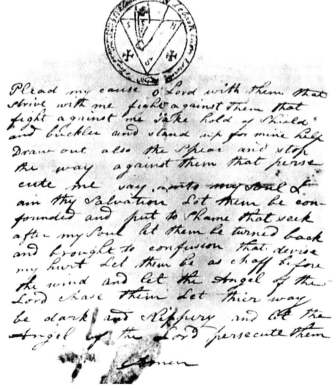

The second charm quoted above beginning: 'Plead my cause O Lord'

cute me say my Soul &
am thy salvation Let them be con-
founded and put to shame that seek
after my Soul let them be turned back
and brought to confusion that devise
my hurt Let them be as chaff before
the wind and let the Angel of the
Lord chase them Let their way
be dark and slippery and let the
Angel of the Lord persecute them
Amen

The second of these texts is a fairly faithful version of the first six verses of Psalm 35. Other charms also came from the bible or apocrypha, or at least used biblical language. Seven more have survived in the early 19th century manuscript book which belonged to a blacksmith-farrier at Clun. Here are some.

A C[harm] to stop blud. – Our Saviour Jesus Crist was borne in Bethalem was Baptised of Jon in the river of Jordan. God commanded the water to stop & it stoped So in his name do I command the blood to Stop that run from this orrafas [orifice] vain or vaines as the water Stoped in the River of Jordan wen our Saviour Jesus Crist was baptized in the name of the Father. Stop blud in the name of the sun Stop blood in the name of the Holeygost not a drop of blud proceduth Amen Amen Amen – to be sed 3 times but if the case be bad 9 times and the Lords praier before & after holding your rit hand on the place and marck the place thus + with your midel finger.

[For ague and fever]
When our Saviour Jesus Christ Saw the Croos Where on he was to be Crusified his bodey shaked the Juse said unto him shure you have got the Ague Jesus ancered and said Woso ever beleveth in me and wereth these wordes shall never have the ague nor fever Amen Amen Amen + to be wore in the Bosom of Shurt.

[For scalds and burns]
Mary mild has burnt hur child by the sparkling of the fire out fire in frost in the name of the father son and Holey gost Amen Amen Amen – to be said 9 times and the Lordes praier before & after.

[For strains and sprains]
Our Sauiour Jesus Crist roate on a marbel Stone Senow to Senow Joint to Joint Bone to Bone he Roat thes wordes everey our In the Name of the Father Sone and Holey Gost Amen Swet Jesus Amen Swet Jesus Amen. Going round the afflicted place each time with your hand and the Lordes praier each time and marck it thus + 3 times or if verrey bad 9 times.

To Draw a thorn. – Then came Jesus forth whering the crown of thorns and the purpel robe and pilat said write then behold the man Amen Amen Amen – to be said 9 times and the Lordes praier before and hafter hold your midil finger on the place or go round it each time and marck it thus +.

Cunning folk, otherwise known as conjurors, wise men and women, and, confusingly, as wizards or white witches, were diviners and magicians as well as being concerned with healing. Of their number Owen Davies has calculated that about two-thirds were men and one-third women. One of the earliest recorded in Shropshire was perhaps John Talbot of Sheriffhales, about whom people complained to the authorities in 1623 for being a wizard and a finder of lost objects.

Richard Gough tells the story of Reece Wenlock, who lived in the Mere House at Haremere. When his cow was stolen he went to consult a wise woman at Montgomery. To test her powers he put a stone in his pocket to see whether she remarked on it. 'Thou hast a stone in thy pocket', she unerringly commented, 'but it is not so big as that stone where-with thou didst knock out such a neighbour's harrow tines'. Gough omits to say whether she helped the man find the cow.

Thomas—'Wisdom Tom'—and Martha Carter, of Chelmick Valley, Church Stretton. In 1851 Martha was 53 and Thomas, whose nickname may have indicated cunning man status, 60

Richard Morris (1710-93), trained as a youth in Derbyshire by a fortune-telling aunt, set up in Oswestry, where he became known as Dick Spot the Conjurer. To fortune-telling he added magic and healing. He became prosperous, helped the poor, and at his death left several properties in Shrewsbury's Frankwell, including the White Horse Inn, to the newly-founded Manchester and Salford Lying-in Hospital. In the *Life and Mysterious*

Transactions of Richard Morris (1799) his anonymous biographer set out to establish 'whether good or evil' had come from his doings. On the whole, the writer inclined to the former, with reservations about his 'charms and spells and such Magic delusions', yet recognising that 'he had performed some notable cures, such as old inveterate agues, removed by burying three bits of paper sealed up, in a secret part of a field, and other disorders, by burning scraps and looking into the contents'. He concluded unequivocally 'that a country conjuror is more useful of the place he resides in, than the fat vicar, who only sleeps and stirs about his tithes'.

Thomas Light of Walton, near High Ercall, could reputedly influence the outcome of cock fights, advise on love affairs, cure sick animals and recover stolen property. In addition he dabbled in astrology. At his death—brought about, apparently, by a rival, Jack o' the Weald Moors—he was found to have possessed a prime work: on geomancy and astromancy, John Heydon's *Theomagia; or, The Temple of Wisdome* (1664). A contemporary of Light's was the unnamed wizard from Whitchurch called into Twemlow's Farm (which still exists) at Prees Higher Heath when hay ricks were fired. The wizard led the farmer into a small back room where a kind of vision appeared of two youths in the act of arson. The farmer recognised them. They were arrested and convicted. Then they confessed, but this did not save them from the gallows. In view of the details given, it should surely be possible to find a precise record, but the story could be a distorted reflection of another event: for example an arson attack on a farm near Whitchurch which occurred in December 1830 during the disturbances known nationally as the Labourers' Revolt.

Burne mentions several conjurors by name. John Malpass of Kinlet in the 1840s had a written copy of a verse from the bible which could protect anyone who carried it from witchcraft. John Thomas of Bishop's Castle told her of Todley Tom:

> Oh, iss, I knowed Todley Tum well. He was a labourer, and lived o' the side o' Todley 'Ill - that was how he got his name. He had three daaters - the chaps used to go courtin' to the daaters. He was this sort of a man - if anybody had any grudge, if I had anything of a grudge at you, Mr. B., sir, and was to go to him (and give him something, you know), he could bring trouble on you by *working a spell*, and that was what they called it. I knowed a man as had a cock for a cock-fait [fight]. (There was a jell [deal] o' cock faitin' about those parts when I was a lad). Well, this man, he wanted to know very bad which cock 'ud win, so he went to old Todley Tum an' give him something, and he was to make the cock appear. Not the *real* cock, you know, but like the *likeness* of it. He *kest* [cast] *the planets*, I suppose, to show it. Oh, iss, he showed it to him, and that was the cock as won.
>
> Job Rogers, I remember him well, 'e anna bin jed [dead] so many 'ears. He lived at Mr. Berwick's at the More Farm, and he went to Todley

Tum to know if he should be drawed for the militia or nod. Todley Tum was a good while afore he towd him, and so Job Rogers got in a bit of a pet, and axed him, whi didna he tell him? So Todley towd him nod to put himself in a pet, for he should be at home in no time. (Todley Hill, where Tum lived, is three mile from More Farm). So when Todley Tum had towd him about whether he should be drawed for the militia or not, he axed him how he would like to go wum, whether he'd go high, low, or level. He choosed to go high, for he was afeard o' being dregged through the brairs [briars], and then Todley Tum gave the word, and off he went, up in the air, iver so haigh [high], and dropped him down in the More farmyard. Job Rogers told his butties in the farm yard that he could remember coming over the poplar trees at the bottom of the cow pastur'. The poplar trees bin there now. He was livin' when I left that part, old Tum was, but that's fifty years back, and I dunna know how he died.

Burne also wrote of a conjuror then still living at Yardington, near Whitchurch, whom she identified as W.T.

He is a tinker by trade, and his magical powers were formerly in great request. About 1874, an old woman of Bletchley, near Moreton Say, lost some potatoes, and also a pair of sheets which she had hung out in her garden to dry, and she went all the way to Whitchurch, to consult this man about it. It was a nine miles' walk, but 'there *was* none nearer', so she trudged off bravely. The tinker assured her that the potatoes 'was eat', but that she would get the sheets back, and in about a fortnight she found them hanging on the hedge off which they had been stolen. One would think that W.T. must have had private reasons for the information he gave. He was not so happy in another case, when he was consulted as to the whereabouts of a young man who was 'missing'. He replied that he was 'quite comfortable and with his friends'. Shortly afterwards the poor fellow was found under the ice in the canal. Probably this shook public confidence in the conjurer, for I am informed that few people seem to know of his pretensions now-a-days.

Despite Burne's comment, belief in some kind of magic persisted for the next hundred years and more. Many thousands still buy *Old Moore's Almanac*. Its originator, Francis Moore, doctor and astrologer, came from Bridgnorth, where he was born in 1656. His *Kalendarium Ecclesiasticum* (church calendar), published to promote both pills and predictions, changed its title in 1700 to *Vox Stellarum* (voice of the stars) before settling to a very long run as the familiar almanac.

Quacks and Doctors

Tim Williams wrote in 1994 of being in a country inn when talk turned to the National Health Service: 'it was rather disconcerting to be told by an old boy that he didn't bother with doctors; he went to "an owd witch as lives on

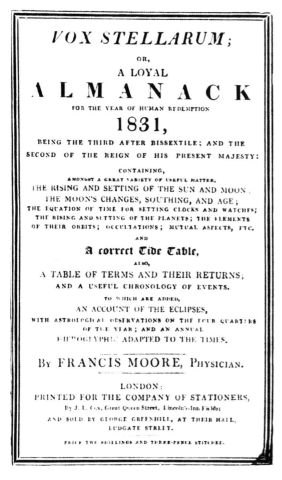

VOX STELLARUM;

OR,

A LOYAL

A L M A N A C K

FOR THE YEAR OF HUMAN REDEMPTION

1831,

BEING THE THIRD AFTER BISSEXTILE; AND THE
SECOND OF THE REIGN OF HIS PRESENT MAJESTY:

CONTAINING,

AMONGST A GREAT VARIETY OF USEFUL MATTER,

THE RISING AND SETTING OF THE SUN AND MOON;
THE MOON'S CHANGES, SOUTHING, AND AGE;
THE EQUATION OF TIME FOR SETTING CLOCKS AND WATCHES;
THE RISING AND SETTING OF THE PLANETS; THE ELEMENTS
OF THEIR ORBITS; OCCULTATIONS; MUTUAL ASPECTS, ETC.

AND

A correct Tide Table,

ALSO,

A TABLE OF TERMS AND THEIR RETURNS;
AND A USEFUL CHRONOLOGY OF EVENTS.

TO WHICH ARE ADDED,

AN ACCOUNT OF THE ECLIPSES,

WITH ASTROLOGICAL OBSERVATIONS ON THE FOUR QUARTERS
OF THE YEAR; AND AN ANNUAL
HIEROGLYPHIC ADAPTED TO THE TIMES.

By FRANCIS MOORE, Physician.

LONDON:

PRINTED FOR THE COMPANY OF STATIONERS,

By J. L. Cox, Great Queen Street, Lincoln's-Inn Fields;

AND SOLD BY GEORGE GREENHILL, AT THEIR HALL,
LUDGATE STREET.

PRICE TWO SHILLINGS AND THREE-PENCE STITCHED.

the Mynd"'. To the statement that at least the health service would be carrying on indefinitely, the man retorted that he had no problem with his practitioner because "er's taught 'er daughter the trade'.

Richard Gough mentions 'that famouse Dr. Goddard, who when I was a youth was much conversant and had great practice in this country. Hee gave that soveraine potion called Goddard's drops. Hee was used to say that hee was confident that many English people were buryed alive; for if they had been kept in theire warme bedds for forty-eight houres many of them would have recovered'. Especially, perhaps, if they had taken his 'soveraine' potion.

The desperation occasioned by problems for which appropriate treatment was unavailable or unknown is illustrated by Gough's account of Margaret Davies, who died in 1701. For over 20 years she suffered 'paine and lamenesse in her limbs, and made use of severall remedyes for cureing thereof, butt all proved ineffectuall'.

> At last, shee was in an Apothecary's shop buying ointments and ingredients for fomentations [poultices] my uncle, Mr. Richard Baddely, an able chirurgeon, saw her and asked her how shee gott her lamenesse: shee sayd by takeing could in child-birth. Then says hee spare this charges and labour, for all the Doctors and Surgeons in England cannot sure it.

When during his short reign (1685-8) James II visited Shrewsbury, Margaret Davies 'was admitted by the King's Doctors to goe to His Majesty for the Touch, which did her noe good' — which is not surprising, since the royal touch was supposed to cure scrofula. (James held a further session of touching in the almory at Much Wenlock. Its results are unrecorded),

Too late for Davies to try came the preparation made from Pitchford bitumen, sold during the 18th century as Betton's British Oil. Later still followed Hopewells Salve (known in the Clee Hill vernacular as 'Okwel Soov), an ointment applied to bruises, cuts and wounds, and also chapped hands.

Other expedients were rather more fanciful. Hayward heard from the wife of a Church Stretton doctor that when he called to see a patient and asked what had been done the man's wife replied, 'Oh, there be naught that I unna done. I've even crossed 'is stockins under 'is bed'. Yet a local remedy—this time, herbal—led a skilled doctor to an epoch-making discovery. William Withering (1741-99), born at Wellington, was the son of an apothecary. He studied medicine in Edinburgh and Paris before starting work as a doctor at

Stafford Infirmary. When in 1775 he moved to Birmingham Infirmary he drove back to Stafford once a week for a time to see patients there. During the 30-mile journey the horses had to be changed, and on one occasion Withering was asked to look at an old woman with dropsy. Despite his unfavourable prognosis he later heard that she had recovered, thanks to a herb tea made from a family recipe jealously guarded by an old woman in Shropshire. This, it was asserted, sometimes succeeded where the ministrations of regular practitioners failed. When Withering managed to buy a sample of the mixture used he found that it contained over 20 different herbs, 'but it was not very difficult to one conversant in these subjects to perceive that the active herb could be none other than the Foxglove'. Withering tried the dried and powdered foxglove leaves on poor patients at Birmingham Infirmary and realised that they had 'power over the motion of the heart to a degree not yet observed in any other medicine'. So he wrote in *An Account of the Foxglove* (1785). The substance, digitalis, is still used to treat heart ailments. Withering had a distinguished career not only as a physician but also botanist, mineralogist and campaigner. He was a member of the enlightened Lunar Society of Birmingham. As he lay dying, a friend of his commented: 'the flower of physicians is Withering'.

The foxglove

Death

Of a farm called Marton in the parish of Myddle, Gough wrote: 'It is observed that if the chiefe person of the family that inhabits ... doe fall sick, if his sicknesse be to death, there comes a paire of pidgeons to the house about a fortnight or a weeke before the person's death, and then goe away. This I have knowne them doe three severall times'. Such beliefs in tokens of impending death were common until within living memory, and may not entirely have disappeared with the advent of the 21st century. In the 1990s a bat's (unlikely) clinging to the outside of a window pane was thought a sure sign of death. A century earlier Brewster recorded at Middleton-in-Chirbury various death omens: partridges flying against a window (soon); hearing the Seven Whistlers (within seven days); seeing a corpse candle or will o' the wisp: this would move from house to house until it settled on the one in which a death was to occur. 'The Gwilliams say, that on the night that Jimmy Whittall of the Marsh died in 1875 there were three double knocks at his door about the time Mrs. Gwilliam was with Jimmy Whittall'. In 1891 the knowledgeable Mary Preece told Brewster that the previous year at Hallowe'en John Francis and another man from Longfords Farm walked 12 times round Chirbury Church at midnight, then went into the porch. There they saw a man with a pick and spade pass by. They went back to the house and told what they had seen. Francis's companion scoffed, but was buried before the next Hallowe'en.

A belief widespread in Shropshire held that the church clock's striking during the announcement of the text for a Sunday morning sermon—and alternatively at Baschurch during the singing of the final hymn—portended a death. (A variation forecast a funeral within a week if the clock struck during the first psalm).

Hayward lists a large number of random occurrences, including owls hooting and dogs barking, as death tokens. She also gives death-bringing activities which can and should be avoided, such as burning elder. It was also unlucky to bring elder into a house or even use it as a stick with which to drive cattle. Worse still, if elder were put on the fire in a house the devil would come down the 'chimbley'. (The elder's evil reputation may derive from the notion that Christ's cross was made from elder wood).

The presence of pheasant or pigeon feathers in pillows or a mattress prevented those ready to die from doing so. One woman, finding her husband's passing to be unduly prolonged, remembered the pigeon feathers in the bed, and laid him on the floor. 'He went off as nice and easy as you please'. Bees had to be told of a death in the family: Gideon in *Precious Bane* gives them news of his father's death. In 1961 bees in the 14 hives of Sam Rogers at Myddle were told of his death to prevent their flying away, but they turned up in a huge swarm at his memorial service and settled all over the flowers on his grave. Perhaps his family had omitted to raise each hive an inch or two at the

*Graves at Bettws-y-Crwyn, curiously
decorated with white stones*

time his coffin was lifted to make its last journey.

Before the coffin left a sin-eater would step forward, eat the bread and drink the wine placed at its foot, and announce: 'I give easement and rest now to thee, dear man [or, presumably, woman], that ye walk not over the fields nor down the by-ways. And for thy peace I pawn my own soul'. Such is the formula given by Mary Webb in *Precious Bane*. However, the sole evidence for sin eating in Shropshire comes from the antiquarian, John Bagford, who wrote in 1714:

> Within the memory of our Fathers, in Shropshire, in those villages adjoyning to Wales, when a person dyed, there was notice given to an old Sire (for so they called him) who presently repaired to the place where the deceased lay, and stood before the door of the house, when some of the family came out and furnished him with a Cricket [stool], on which he sat down facing the door. Then they gave him a Groat [4d. coin], which he put in his pocket; a Crust of Bread, which he eat; and a full bowle of Ale, which he drank off at a draught. After this, he got up from the Cricket and pronounced with a composed gesture, *the ease and rest of the Soul departed, for which he would pawn his own Soul*. This I had from the ingenious John Aubrey, Esq. [1626-97].

Efforts to prevent the dead from walking 'the fields and byways' are a different matter. Gough had a long narrative about a Richard Clarke who 'in a mellan collicke fytt of greife' walked to Wem to buy poison, 'which hee eat up as hee came homeward', and then died. As a suicide he was buried on Myddle Hill 'att that crosseway where the road-way from Ellesmeare to Shrewsbury, called the Lower-way, goes over crosse the way that goes from Myddle toward the Red Bull, butt was removed next night: and some say hee was interred in a rye-filed of his owne'. Some two centuries on, Claverley's last suicide was buried at night with a stake through his body at a crossroads near Chyknell Park.

According to Cledwyn Hughes, coffins were left open, a row of candles stuck road the edges with clay, during the night before a funeral, for a wake. On the day of the funeral the coffin lid was not sealed until the mourners had filed past to pay their last respects to the deceased.

Even the poor, at least in charitably disposed parishes, were given a proper send-off. At Llanyblodwel entries such as these can be seen in the church-wardens' accounts:

1756	Wid. Harris's levy and in her illness	£1	4s.	5d.
	Her coffin and grave		6	
	Carring [*sic*] the Bier		1	
	Shroud for Ditto		3	
	Drink allow'd at her burial		3	
1758	Buring [*sic*] a child of Elizth Littlehale's (viz) -			
	A shroud		1	10
	Coffin for Ditto		3	
	Laying the child out		1	
	Making the Shroud			6
	Minister's and Clark's ffees [*sic*]		3	4
	Ale at the burial		2	

The expenses total respectively £1 17s. 5d. and 11s. 8d., not negligible sums for the time.

At Wem, as in a number of other places, friends and relatives unable to attend a funeral were sent cakes in black-edged paper, sealed with black wax. Such cakes in Shropshire were normally of sponge, but in Wem sweet biscuits or pieces of cut cake were sometimes substituted. Until the mid-20th century

Grave digger at Bishop's Castle, 1902. This was probably Jeremiah Ellis, later found dead one Christmas at Oakley Mynd, where he had been gathering holly

people there remembered sombre funerals, with black velvet trappings and black plumes.

Bearers walked in front of the hearse, and then carried the coffin into the church; others preferred to carry the coffin all the way. Alf Strange wrote that he had seen one 'carried and pulled for up to two miles, with a sledge being used in winter'. There was no option but to carry coffins from some remote farms at Clee Hill, with pauses when the bearers were refreshed with bottles of beer. In the same place digging graves could be difficult because after the depth of a spade's blade clay, rock or water could be encountered. Quarrymen supplemented their income by digging graves at 2s. 6d. a time.

At Clee Hill, as in many localities, people were anxious that a deceased person should be sent in due form to his or her 'long home'. Alf Jenkins writes:

> Anyone who has a Welsh ancestry is well aware of the 'feast' which follows a funeral and the tradition of laying the corpse in the parlour for all to view. This was the accepted tradition on Clee Hill. Many visitors were expected at the house of the bereaved and so there had to be a plentiful supply of food and drink. Each visitor after expressing his sympathy was given refreshments.

CHAPTER 8

Labour

Farming, massively transformed in the second half of the 20th century, remains of central importance in Shropshire. The seasonal round of animal husbandry and arable production perforce continues, but the old ways and attitudes are progressively less well remembered or even known at all. Institutions like the Acton Scott Historic Working Farm help to bring understanding; so do the songs, stories and memories of those who hired themselves out for a year at a time, drove herds of cattle for many miles, and laboured by hand in the harvest fields.

Shropshire's place in the industrial revolution is assured, but this, too, lies in the past. Even the physical evidence of its existence calls for an observant eye, except, that is, in museums such as those of the Ironbridge Gorge, which draw many thousands of visitors every year. Yet the traditions and tales of miners and pit girls, quarrymen and wenches, retain their savour in post industrial times.

Changing Places

For centuries, farm workers went to hiring fairs, sometimes known as 'mops', where they contracted to work for a year at a time. In the north-east of Shropshire servants of both sexes hired from Christmas to Christmas. They left one place on Boxing Day and enjoyed a brief holiday before starting at the next on 2 January. Burne found that this applied 'in the districts round Ellesmere, Wem, Wellington, and all the country to the north and east of them (including the market towns of Whitchurch, Drayton, and Newport'. Hiring took place on the appropriate market day, known as the Gauby Market, in Christmas week. Burne believed that this had died out in her day, but at least one woman remembered in 1992 how 73 years earlier her grandmother had taken her 'to see the Gauby Market in High Street, Wem, where farm servants were given a day off to receive their wages for the previous year, and to offer themselves for hire in the coming year'.

Earlier, in the mid-18th century, hiring at Wem took place on Holy Thursday (Ascension Day). The maids dressed all in white and gave the occasion the alternative name of Rig Fair. The young men and women seeking places were respectively called Johnnies and Mollies.

By contrast a changeover in May was the rule 'at Oswestry, Shrewsbury, Much Wenlock, Bridgnorth, and all the country to the south and west of them (including Church Stretton, Ludlow, Clun, etc.)'. Burne believed that the dividing line between the two systems corresponded both with a marked change in dialect and also the ancient boundary between Mercians (north-east) and Magonsaetans (south-west). 'Then the farm men', wrote Cledwyn Hughes of the May changeover, 'can be seen going from an "old place" to a new one, carrying all their worldly possessions in a tin trunk balanced on the handlebars of a bicycle'. The hiring fairs here continued much longer. Of Much Wenlock in 1894 Gaskell noted: 'Servants are hired in the market-place, as of yore, and linen embroidered smocks are still worn by countrymen'. At Church Stretton hirings endured until the 1930s, on or about 14 May. Young women would approach a farmer or his wife with the ritual question: 'Do you want a sarvant wench to milk and shift the muck?' Alan Dakers quotes some interesting details from the account books of the Croxtons, who were blacksmiths in the village of Hope Bowdler and perhaps also had some land:

> 1855   May 14 1 hired Thomas Yap for £8 8s. 0d.
> 1856   I hired Charles Smout 14th May to serve me for one year is
>   time to be up 14th May 1857 To give or take a Month notice
>   or a Months wages [in lieu] £7 7s. 0d.

Perhaps the lower rate was because of the get-out clause. Charles Smout must have found the place to his liking because in 1857 he 'stopped a Gain' (stayed on), as he did, at increased wages, the following year. At the year's end in May 1857 he received only 9s., but this was because of a series of advances against his wages totalling £9. £2 7s. 6d. went to the shoemaker, and 26. 6d. for a 'broadhook'. (Did he have to provide his own tools, or was this to pay to replace one he had lost?) £1 10s. was spent on a watch. Recreation accounted for £2 10s., made up of 5s. at Shrewsbury Show, £1 3s. at Church Stretton's Michaelmas Fair, and £1 2s. at Christmas. Smout would have been a single man, with bed and board—'all found', as it was termed—provided by his employer.

The quality of food and lodging, as well as the level of wages, determined whether a worker would 'stop again' or move on. The ballad, 'Country Hirings', of which a manuscript copy was preserved at Clun, makes an uncompromising appeal:

Brook Farm in Much Wenlock, a preserved glimpse of bygone Shropshire

> Servant men, stand up for your wages,
> When to the hirings you do go,
> For you must work all sorts of weather,
> Both cold and wet and snow.

Complaints at poor diet are mitigated by joy at the approach of hiring day, and there is a sly coda:

> The description of your living, I am sure it is the worst,
> For the pottage it is thin and the bread is very coarse,
> While the masters they do live as you shall understand
> On butter and good cheese and the fat from the land.
>
> A roasted goose for dinner likewise a leg of lamb,
> With soups and potatoes and everything that's grand,
> While servants in the kitchen they do both sport and play,
> Speaking about the fun they'll get on the hiring day.
>
> But I could tell you of a better plan, without any fears or doubts,
> If you would only kiss the mistress when the master he is out:
> You may kiss her, you may squeeze her, you may roll her roundabout,
> And then she would find you better grub without any fear or doubt.

The anecdote related by his grandfather to Derek Price (born near Bridgnorth in 1927) may be apocryphal but it carried a wealth of feeling:

> A farmer and his wife had a young boy living in. One day at lunch time the farmer said, 'Would anyone like a second helping of pudding?' The boy said, 'Yes, please, sir'. 'What did you say?' roared the farmer. 'No, thank you', said the frightened lad. 'That's a good lad. Speak up', replied the farmer, and proceeded to finish the pudding himself.

As here, on some farms, workers living-in sat at the same table as their employer and his family. In others, they ate separately, like the shepherd remembered by a farmer's daughter at Condover, who 'would sit in the kitchen with Lucy, the maid, and we loved to go and listen to his tales which were often very frightening - he had a firm belief in ghosts'.

Arthur Lane (1884-1975), who spent many years as a hired man, recalled how workers sat at table in hierarchical order of shepherd, waggoner, cowman. At one farm,

> used a lump of beef to come from Bishop's Castle, some time in the week. The end of the week, used to boil it in a great furnace in the corner of the back kitchen. Boil it, that was on a Sunday morn; Sunday dinner time, we had a lump off that, that was a good ration. We had some good food there, but we always had our pudding before our meat, dinner time. We've been as many as four, five, to nine men there, living; in. ...Six o'clock was our time at night. Whether it was dark at five at night, we'd got to stay out till six, work in the dark as well as we could. Well, then we'd have supper. Go in and have our supper after we'd ungeared the horses and give them something - oh, it'd be getting on for half-past six again. Used to have a loaf of bread at the farmhouse, home-made bread, great big loaf, much as you could do to get your arm round, and get the knife to take a piece off. Another basin of broth, broth 13 times a week from that lump of beef, and it

Arthur Lane

The farm where Arthur Lane grew up

was good. We used to put the bread in, bread our own basins, go and ladle our own broth out of the pot. Bread, puts the second lot of bread in, the spoon'd stick up straight in the basin, and we'd eat that; that was all right.

Lane, born at Vernolds Common between Craven Arms and Ludlow, began work at perhaps the age of 13 as a groom earning £5 a year. He resented the lack of freedom, and one Sunday walked home, a mile away, to take his washing to his mother. On the way back his employer spotted him and threatened to give him a good hiding for absence without leave. 'But when May came he wanted me to stop again. "No, I've had enough on it", I said. My mind was made up. I was going to leave there'. He therefore went to the hirings:

The young chaps goes to the May Fairs. Chaps goes, then the farmer comes. 'You want a job, young man? You want a job?' 'Yes'. 'What to do?' 'Oh, go with the horses'. 'Oh, I want somebody to go with horses. What wages do you want?' Like that, that's all we can do at the May Fairs. The waggoners - some used to have a bit of whipcord in here [lapel], and some had a little bone horse-shoe on the side of their hat, like. That was for a waggoner. They go for them.

They gave you a shilling. Once you'd made the bargain, they gave you a shilling and you'd gotta go then. Some did give the shilling back but some had refused it. 'Twas the same as joining the army. ... Well, you could give a month's notice it it was not satisfactory, you could give a month's notice, or he could give you a month's notice. 'Twas either way.

I made the bargain for the twelve months. He'd pay me £9. I'd gone £5, £7, £9, I had. Then he wanted me to stay again. If a job suited you and the farmer says, 'You staying along with me again?' 'I don't mind'. 'Well, what wages you want?' You tell him that, we make another bargain for the next year, from May to May. [Or] the farmer says, 'I daresay you want to go to Ludlow Fair today, do you?' - he said to the men in the morning, giving them their orders. One says, 'No, I'd rather go to Craven Arms Fair, I should see the old folks there, perhaps'.

With the shilling advance—otherwise known as an 'earnest' or 'yarnist'—together with the wages at the previous year's end, workers, especially single men and women with no family responsibilities, fell on the joys of the fair. Apart from the public houses there would be stalls selling fruit and sweets, shooting galleries, boxing booths, roundabouts and swings (see also chapter 9). Many had affectionate memories of the hirings on the first Friday in May at Bishop's Castle, which went on almost until the beginning of the Second World War—though some there changed jobs on Lady Day (25 March), which they called Flea Fair. (Should this be Flee Fair?). Farm workers dressed in their Sunday best—riding breeches, leather leggings, boots, jacket and cap—waited in the market place or just below the town hall. Alf Shakespeare (1904-92) as a boy noticed how potential employers would feel a man's muscles before deciding whether to offer him work.

Livestock market held in the Burway Road in Church Stretton, c.1900

Many Shropshire people went over the Welsh border to hirings at Knighton in Radnorshire which continued until 1947. Mrs. Deakins of Cwm Farm, Llanfair Waterdine, found maidservants there. Colin Bird (born 1928) very clearly recalls the May Fairs at Knighton, 'something that everyone looked forward to':

The farmer would ask a man or lad if he wanted a job. If they agreed they were paid the princely sum of 2s., known as 'earnest money'. It had been known for a young lad to agree to go and work at a certain farm and then meet someone who would say, 'I wouldna go there if I was thee, boy, he be a hard ald devil to work for and dunna keep a very good table'. The

'Saturday morning after the May Fair', Bishop's Castle, c.1890

lad would have to find the farmer and cancel his agreement. Not a very pleasant task, I imagine.

Sheep-shearing

'May is the month usually', wrote Cledwyn Hughes, 'when shearing is due on a farm ... to make the sheep cool and comfortable for the summer, and to have the fleece as a tidy preserved unit for selling'. He looked back wistfully at 'the old days':

> Gone are the old social shearing times, when gangs of men came to a farm in the daytime and talked or sang in the evenings; gone are the patient ways of shearing. ... Modern power and geared clippers do not allow conversation ... there is an ungodly clatter and rattle, and no voice can be heard above the all-pervading mechanical hum. The only sound, when hand-shears were used, was a 'snip-snip'; shearers talked to their friends standing about, to the other shearers, and to the servant-girls of the farm, whose job it was to wrap the fleece into a neat bundle.

John Dyer, who wrote in his poem, *The Fleece* (1757) of 'those notes which once the Muse / Heard at a shearing, near the woody sides / Of blue-topped Wreakin', may have been referring to songs sung at feasts to celebrate the end of shearing. These continued in Shropshire until the 1870s. One farmer, a Mr. Thomas Powell, told Charlotte Burne: 'The man who sheared the biggest fleece

Shearing near Cleobury Mortimer, early 1900s

was always the chief contributor of songs and riddles at the supper. The master and family always joined in, with a neighbouring farmer or two; all were on a level that night'. The songs he remembered from such occasions included 'The Painful Plough', 'John Barleycorn', 'God Speed the Plough', 'The Carrion Crow' and 'The New-mown Hay'. The last of these is said to have been inspired by the story of Henry Cecil, who at Great Bolas, near Newport, met, courted, and in 1790 married Sally or Sarah Hoggins, the daughter of a miller and small farmer. On the death of his uncle in 1794, Cecil became the 10th Lord Burghley and inherited the palatial Burghley House at Stamford in Lincolnshire. He took his wife, who remained in ignorance of his standing, past the mansion, and when she expressed admiration for it, said, 'Then, dear Sarah, it is yours'. She did not enjoy it for long, since she died soon after the birth of her fourth child in 1797.

Bolas Villa—later renamed Burleigh (sic)

The charming tale omits a few uncomfortable elements. When Henry Cecil married Sarah Hoggins he described himself as John Jones, bachelor yeoman. Yet he had a wife, Emma (née Vernon), heiress to Hanbury Hall in

Worcestershire, who after 13 years' marriage had decamped with the local curate, Rev. William Sneyd. Cecil's bigamy seems to have been overlooked. In June 1791 an Act of Parliament authorised his divorce from Emma, and four months later he went through a second marriage ceremony with Sarah, this time at St Mildred's Church, Bread Street, London. They then returned to Great Bolas and lived in their 'villa' (in fact a substantial house) until the move to Burghley.

Haytime and Harvest

During the childhood of Alf Strange (born 1925) at Welsh Frankton, to make the most of good weather during haymaking people would work up to 16 hours a day. Small farmers helped each other, 'satisfied enough to get their food and drink in the field, and have the favour returned when the time came'. On the bigger farms gangs of itinerant scythemen, having agreed on a price with the owner, would work in echelon across a field. (I have seen this done myself, not in Shropshire but—in the late 1990s—in northern Spain). The last man, who set the pace, would, if he found it too slow, tap with his scythe-blade on the heel of the man in front of him, who would pass the message up the line in a similar manner. At Weston Lullingfields near Baschurch, Cobbler's Meadow takes its name from the artisan would wagered that he could scythe it in a day. Those who stood to lose laced his beer with Epsom salts. Undaunted, the cobbler won his bet, but completed the task minus his trousers.

One haymaking gang which operated round Broseley went by the name of the Long Company. The advent of the horse-drawn mowing machine brought

Break in haymaking, 1920s

Harvest gang, Ness Strange, c.1887

an end to this way of working, but not before Alf Strange's story of men from his village, who formed themselves into a team of six to cut hay in the evenings. At one farm there was no one in but they had cut a field there for several years, and did so again. After three hours' hard work they went to the farmhouse, some distance away, and, seeing a light on, knocked at the door and politely asked to be paid. The farmer had bad news: 'I sold all that hay as a standing crop two months since and as far as I know the new owner planned to use his mowin' machine on it'. The men not only had no pay, but missed the customary drink of beer or cider.

Harvest—'the greatest event of the year', according to A.B. Tinsley—was also very much a matter of team work. Bands of itinerant labourers arrived from Wales, Ireland or the Black Country, and bargained by the acre to cut the corn. As late as the opening years of the 20th century, some still used a sickle, though scythes soon became the norm, and lasted until the reaper-binder replaced them. Band-tiers, often women, followed the reapers, gathering an armful of corn and tying a few stems round it to make a sheaf. The sheaves were then piled upright in groups or stooks. Tinsley called sheaves 'shoffs' and stooks, 'mows'. Wheat needed eight shoffs, four facing four; oats, six: two against two, with one at either end; barley, seven: three by three, with one resting lengthwise on the top.

The mows had to dry in the wind and sun long enough 'to hear three lots of church bells', according to one prescription, which seems rather generous.

Cidermaking at Bucknell, c.1900

Then the sheaves were carefully loaded on carts, carried to the farm and built into stacks. In due course these were taken apart and the corn was threshed, to separate grain from straw. All this, now, is accomplished in a few hours by one or two men and a combine harvester.

Food and drink for the workers were delivered to the fields. Gangs staying overnight also had to be fed. In the 1890s Mrs. Swyney of Much Wenlock looked back to her youth:

> I went to work at the Downes farm. Harvest time was very different to what it is now. In them days there was brewing and baking. Why, we used to bake eight bushels [of flour] in a day when us 'ad the thirty Welshmen for the mowing, as slept in the barn, and the maister used to kill a sheep every day, and there was nought but the bones left at candle time.

At the end of reaping came the custom of 'cutting the gonder's [gander's] neck off'. Several ears of corn left standing for the purpose were knotted together. The reapers retired to an agreed distance, ten paces or so, and took turns, leading man first, to throw their sickles at it. Whoever succeeded in severing the neck was declared 'the best mon', and carried it to the farmer's wife, who would give a mug of drink in exchange and keep it for good luck until the next harvest.

Two young women who talked to Charles Kightly at Bishop's Castle in the early 1980s said that whoever cut the gonder's neck made a corn dolly from it. This was then kept in the farm for luck for a year. By then the custom was long gone, but one woman still made corn dollies from corn carefully left standing for her in the middle of the field by the combine harvester driver.

A second ritual, 'crying the mare', was performed by the reapers at the first farm in a district to finish the harvest. The men gathered in the stackyard, or on high ground in one of the fields, and after a lusty 'Hip, hip, hip, hooray', bawled this dialogue. The names mentioned are those of different farmers:

> I have her! I have her! I have her!
> What hast thee? what hast thee? what hast thee?
> A mare! a mare! a mare!
> Whose is her? whose is her? whose is her?
> Will Beacoll's! Will Beacoll's! Will Beacoll's!
> Where shall we send her? where shall we send her? where shall we send her?
> To John Lathom's, John Lathom's, John Lathom's.

Other farms completing their harvests would follow suit, but in the case of the last one to do so, the final line of the dialogue would be changed to: 'Keep her all the winter, all the winter, all the winter'. Burne mentions such ceremonies up to the 1870s but Hare suggests that they continued 'in some parts of the county' until the last years of the century.

Still to come after the crying of the mare was the harvest home celebration, with the triumphant shouting of such verses as: 'We have ploughed and we have sowed, / We have reaped and we have mowed, / And we have brought home every load'. Traditional toasts were proposed:

> Here's health to the maister, who drives the harvest-cart!
> And health to the missis, she always takes her part!
> Here's health to the ploughman, he ploughs and sows the corn!
> And health to the huntsman, who merrily blows his horn!

In October 1784 *The Nottingham Journal* published this account of an event in Shropshire:

> On Wednesday last a Harvest-home was celebrated at Hawkstone, the seat of Sir Richard Bill, Bart, which seemed to revive the idea of ancient English hospitality. Early in the afternoon Sir Richard's domestics and workmen were called to attend divine service in the chapel, for the purpose of offering up public thanksgiving to Divine Providence for a season distinguished by an uncommon profusion of the fruits of the earth, when part of the 65th psalm was sung ['Thou crownest the year with this goodness; and thy paths drop fatness'], as being particularly adapted to the subject. After the service no less than two hundred workmen, reapers, &c. repaired to a regale, given them by Sir Richard and managed under the direction of his servants, consisting of five sheep, two of which were roasted whole, several pieces of beef pies, plumb puddings &c, when all was conducted with so much regularity,

as happily to blend temperance and hospitality together, a union which it was so much to be wished, was always observed upon such occasions. Though the number of guests was so great, yet they behaved with the utmost decorum, and returned early to their respective families, without the least appearance of clamour, riot, or excess. The whole was concluded with three cheers of gratitude, and then the company went off highly delighted with the entertainment, and full of thankfulness to the amiable and hospitable founder of the feast.

Harvest suppers of rather a different stamp continued into the 20th century. Arthur Lane recalled:

'Twas after the harvest had finished. Then there'd be some Saturday night, there'd be preparation made - big do for all the men as was in the harvest, and they'd take their wives if they liked, but the wives had to help with the harvest supper. They could take a friend, but that was after the supper: they could come and have some of the beer. There was singing then, same as us here now, only had a good supper and having some beer. This was how they did the singing: 'Beer, beer, glorious beer, / Fill us right up to here'. There'd be a barrel of beer for that night [paid for by the farmer] on a Saturday night, and they'd be there till two, three o'clock in the Sunday morning, singing.

However, just before the Second World War, Lilian Hayward noted:

Few harvest customs survive. Here and there a large arable farmer may give his workmen a supper. If a stranger sees the last load carried the workmen will say that 'he did ought to stand 'em a goose'. This is not now meant to be taken seriously. But it is a relic of the days when a stranger in the harvest field was covered with corn, or ducked, and must ransom himself by gifts of food and drink. One fairly frequently sees little affairs made of wheat hanging up from the beams of farm houses ... 'for luck'.

Wimberries and Weather

Another harvest came from wild fruits. In *The Golden Arrow* Mary Webb described 'the great wimberry market' at 'Silverton' (Shrewsbury): 'The berries were brought in hampers that needed two men to lift them, and the purple juice dripped from them as in a wine-vat'.

People for centuries must have gathered the berries to supplement their diet and also their budget. On the Long Mynd Walter White saw 'Troops of women, boys, and girls, who have come from Stretton, ... dispersed about the summit picking the plentiful fruit, which they say fetches a good price this year [1860], because of the scarcity of other kinds'. Rev. E. Donald Carr, famous for being

Wimberry pickers, c.1900

lost in the snow for 22 hours in January 1865, noted that up to 500 pounds' weight of fruit used to be collected in a season on the Long Mynd:

> To the poor people for miles around the whinberry picking is the great event of the year. The whole family betake themselves to the hill with the early morning carrying with them the provisions for the day; and not infrequently a kettle to prepare tea forms part of their heavy load. I know no more picturesque sight than that presented by the summit of the Long Mynd towards four o'clock on an August afternoon when the numerous fires are lit among the heather and as many kettles steaming away on top of them, while noisy chattering groups of women and children are clustered around, glad to rest after a hard day's work.

Perhaps Rev. Carr might have avoided his ordeal if he had paid more attention to weather lore, of which there was a good deal in Shropshire. Snow, frost or hail were forecast when a cat turned its back to the fire. On the other hand, if it washed its face, rain threatened. Other portents of rain included donkeys braying, bulls bellowing or taking the lead when a herd of cattle walked to pasture. Swallows flying close to the ground, crows cawing loudly, the heigh-ho (woodpecker) calling, and rooks flying high were further signs, not forgetting: 'When the cock goes crowing to bed / He's sure to rise with a watery head'. To see the hills clearly outlined against the sky also meant rain; and there were local indicators such as, from Market Drayton: 'When the cock has his neb in Hodnet Hole, look out for rain'—the reference being to the church weathercock's pointing south-west, towards Hodnet. Alternatively: 'As soon as Hodnet sends the wind / A rainy day will Hodnet find'.

The famous rhyme about St. Swithin's Day (15 July) had a variant noted at Middleton-in-Chirbury by Rev. Brewster:

> If St. Swithin weeps, the proverb says,
> The weather will be foul for forty days.

This had the encouraging sequel:

> All the tears that St. Swithin can cry,
> St. Bartholomew's mantle wipes them dry.

St, Bartholomew's Day is on 15 August.

In the early summer people looked, as they still do, to the oak and ash:

> When the ash is out before the oak,
> Then we may expect a choke [drought];
> When the oak is out before the ash,
> Then we may expect a splash.

At about the same time the cuckoo can bring good news:

> If the cuckoo sings when the hedge is green,
> Keep thy horse and sell thy corn.

The meaning, far from clear now, is that corn will be plentiful, so it need not be conserved.

The Tinsley family—farmers in Shropshire, though A.B. Tinsley's autobiographical book does not say precisely where—treated their well as a sort of barometer:

> Whenever the question of weather arose, as it so often does on a farm, someone was sure to ask, 'What does the well say?' In fact it 'said' quite a lot if one interpreted its behaviour correctly, because it 'blew up' for stormy weather, and 'drew down' for fine weather. When the well was 'doing nothing', the weather would generally be classed as fair or changeable.

Drovers

Cattle on the hoof were once driven by tough men, 'droviers' in Shropshire parlance, from Wales to various markets (and later railheads) in England. Several routes led to or through Shropshire. One, from Newtown in

189

Clun sheep on sale at Craven Arms, 1940s

Montgomeryshire, went by Forden, Welsh House and Westbury to Shrewsbury, then on to Wellington, Fazeley and Northampton. Another, from Llanidloes, crossed Kerry Ridgeway to Kerry Pole (now a fox-shaped weathervane mounted on a telegraph pole). From this point, one route continued on the ridgeway, past the Cantlin Stone (see chapter 1) to Pant Glas (where it joined the coach road between Aberystwyth and Shrewsbury), and over Offa's Dyke down to Bishop's Castle. Then the herds went on across Oakley Mynd to Edgton, and from there either by Plowden over the Long Mynd to Leebotwood (and from there to Shrewsbury or instead on to Wednesbury, Kenilworth, Buckingham and London); or past Wart Hill and Long Lane to Craven Arms.

At Kerry Pole an alternative itinerary went to the Anchor Inn, a favourite resort of the drovers, where a resident blacksmith could if necessary renew the temporary shoes with which the cattle were equipped for their journey. From the Anchor one route led to Poundgate Farm, Llanfair Waterdine and Knighton. The Red Lion at Llanfair welcomed drovers, who could pen their sheep or cattle in the space over the road. Or, again from the Anchor, the flocks or herds followed a dramatic way past Bettws-y-Crwyn, Spring Hill, Twitchen, Clungunford and Onibury to Ludlow (and then on, if need be, to Bewdley and Birmingham).

Individual drovers had their own variations. The name of Welshman's Meadow at Clun may indicate an overnight stopping place; the common by the Seven Stars Inn at Cold Hatton, six miles from Hodnet, was certainly another. Bromlow Callow, a distinctive wooded hill six miles from Pontesbury, is thought to have been used by drovers for orientation, and Michael Raven has written that Woore, seven miles from Market Drayton, has 'a long-standing tradition that there should always be an ash tree in the village, especially on the shooting butts high ground, where it could have acted as a drovers' landmark'.

Miners and Quarrymen

Shropshire's metalliferous mines, some of them worked in prehistoric and Roman days, were mainly in an area south of Minsterley, though some distance away at Llanymynech, copper, lead and zinc ores were extracted. By the mid-20th century the last mine—at Snailbeach, once the foremost producer of lead in Europe—was closed. Now all that can be seen of a lost industry are occasional reminders here and there in the shape of spoil heaps, overgrown workings and crumbling engine houses.

Coal mining—even more widespread, with fields at Coalbrookdale, the Clee Hills, Shrewsbury, the Wyre Forest and (in part, near Oswestry), the Denbighshire coalfield—went the same way. It lingered rather later, with the last deep mine—Granville Colliery, at Donnington Wood, near Oakengates—closing in 1979. The pits at Clee Hill shut down over 50 years earlier, but the quarries—where between 1,500 and 2,000 men worked in the heyday of the 1860s—continue on a small scale.

Yet what of the men, women and children who worked? What of their culture, customs, traditions, and even vocabulary? Of the metal miners little seems to have been recorded. Lead miners preserved the story of Wild Edric whom they believed had been confined with his retinue below the ground as a punishment for submitting to William the Conqueror. 'The miners call them the "Old Men"', wrote Burne, 'and sometimes hear them knocking, and wherever they knock, the best lodes are to be found'. It was a miner's daughter who with her father claimed to have seen Edric and his men near Minsterley (see chapter 1), William White recorded a rather more pedestrian scene at the Bog Mine, where he saw a cider cart:

> The cart was a wagon containing half a dozen barrels of cider, one of which was tapped and placed peeping out at the tail, convenient for draught. The women to whom it belonged had drawn up under the shadow of a shed, so, availing myself of the same screen, I sat down, took a pint of cider, and making an exploration of my pockets, discovered a forgotten crust, wherewith I dined. On the opposite side of the road, a number of miners lounged in the sunshine, enjoying the idleness of pay-day, and calling now and then for 'Another point, missus!' ... The woman told me that she brewed forty hogsheads of cider every year, and came up out of Herefordshire to find customers along the road. 'Twas hardish work travelling in the hills; but the miners always lightened the load.

Cider was important, too, at Clee Hill, where boys were employed to carry earthenware jars of it to the quarrymen. The cider cost 4d. a pint, and the jars were protected by a wickerwork jacket called a 'whisket'.

Miners feared the cry of the mysterious birds which they called the Seven Whistlers, and some would refuse to go down the pit after hearing it. The cuckoo, on the other hand, was a good omen. In 1898 a contributor to the periodical, *Byegones*, wrote:

> In accordance with this custom, colliers and other workmen, especially the colliers of Shropshire, stopped work on hearing the cuckoo, obtained a holiday from their employers, and drank beer and ale in welcome to the cuckoo. The custom ... called 'cuckoo foot-ale' ... was discontinued about the year 1870. Usually, the drinking took place in the open air, but colliers of Oakengates, St. George's, and Donnington invariably celebrate the custom within doors.

Drawing by M. Newton of miners photographed at Waxhill Barracks Mine (Donnington Wood), shortly before it closed c.1900. It shows the costume worn by the women who worked on the surface screening coal and working on the spoil heaps

Visitors to pits were also expected to contribute to a foot-ale; that is, to give a tip which went into a kitty to be spent on ale for the miners. When John Randall of Madeley went underground in 1859 he commented: 'A group of pit girls and boys pass a sly joke at your expense, and a hope is expressed that you will pay your foot-ale'. Miners were notorious for their reluctance to work on Mondays. Pig Monday was the name given at Clee Hill, Saint Monday at Ludlow, where the public houses traditionally had extended opening hours on Mondays.

At Moat House Colliery, Annscroft, near Longden, boys loaded coal on to 'dans' (sledges) and hauled it with a harness round their waists and a rope through their legs to where it could be transferred to 'tubs'. Each boy was paid jointly by five miners whose coal he removed in this way. Boys also worked in the Clee Hill pits. They were known as 'donkeys' or 'carvers', the latter word deriving from 'carve', a wooden box with skids beneath which was dragged on a chain fastened to a harness much like those illustrated in the Royal Commission reports of the 1840s. In 1916 a boy received 15s. for a six-day working week. His career progression might be from carver to waggoner, who pushed laden tubs to the main tunnel, where a pony hooked on to pull them to the bottom of the shaft. Going up the scale, a waggoner could become a filler, who packed stone beneath worked out areas to hold up the roof, then a pickman or holder, who cut a grooves into the solid coal, one yard deep and five yards wide. The latter earned 4s. a day. Only after this stage could a man graduate to being a miner or collier: he removed the coal above the holer's stint, and received 4s. 6d. a day for his work.

Women, too, worked, though within living memory on the surface—the pit bank—rather than underground. In many places this provided the only alternative to domestic service for women. In 1992 one woman remembered how when she was a child at Dawley pit girls went past her home at 6 am on their way to work:

> They always wore clogs and we could hear them pattering down because they always came in groups. As they came they were nearly always singing; they were so happy although it was such laborious work, picking out the rubbish from the parts that were of value either as iron-stone or small pieces of coal from the pit bank.

At Clee Hill women carried coal on their backs down steep slopes. Richard Jones of Ashford saw at Titterstone Wake in 1846 'fine and handsome wenches .., and well dressed too', but remarked that 'you wouldna know 'em the next day with a bag of coal strapped on their backs'. A big boulder called 'the resting stone' stood near Watsall Pits, where women could rest their loads without taking them off their backs, before continuing to the road where the coal could be transferred to carts to go to Hereford or elsewhere.

Accidents were an inescapable concomitant of mining. A fatalistic attitude is revealed in the story of the death of a man at Moat Hall during the First World War. When a workmate arrived at the man's house to bring the news to his wife she said: 'You needn't tell me, Ern, he's dead. After he went through the gate this morning he came back and kissed me again. He put his arms round me and said, "Ta, ta, chuck", and he never done that before'. Apart from the steady attrition of individual deaths and injuries there were major accidents when many lives were lost. Such occasions were sometimes publicised in printed ballads which offered commiseration but also attempted to raise funds for the victims' dependants. The author of 'In Memoriam', S.T. Morgan of Ketley, declared that 'part of the proceeds from the sale' would be donated to 'any fund for the relief of the bereaved ones'. Seven 'men and youths' had died at Kemberton Pit, Madeley, in December 1910:

> Snaps the wire rope, grinding, crashing,
> To the sump the cage has sped,
> Carrying with it those poor fellows,
> To be numbered with the dead.
> Providentially that those others
> Missed their comrades' hapless: fate,
> So it seems on some occasions
> It is well to be some late.

An earlier accident in a shaft, this time at Springwell Pit, Little Dawley, in 1872, inspired W.R. Morgan of Dawley to write:

> 'Twas on the sixth day of December,
> At Springwell Pit, sad to relate,
> In Dawley Field, in brave old Shropshire,
> Eight healthy men met their sad fate.
> Their work being done, for home preparing,
> And to the bottom they had come,
> Little thinking their days were numbered,
> And that they'd never see their home.

Three years later toxic gases caused loss of life at Lodge Pit, Donnington Wood:

> Pray listen to these feeling verses,
> Which we now relate to you,
> At Donnington and miles around it
> There is much grief and misery too
> For eleven poor hard working colliers
> Went to labour under ground
> But by fire in the coal mine,
> A dreadful death they have all found.

The mine thereafter became known as 'the slaughter pit'.

The sentimental style of such pieces is replaced by a harder attitude in 'Lines on the Shropshire Strike', by 'Nil Desperandum'. The strike of some 400 men, one of the longest recorded in Shropshire, lasted 22 weeks in 1886. Arbitration finally resolved the dispute:

> All this is the greatest struggle
> Mill or forgeman ever knew;
> Let it teach us all the lesson,
> Unity has brought us through.

Miners during the strike of 1912 at the Nabb Pit, St. George's

To obtain free fuel during strikes miners opened their own 'jackey' pits where coal seams were near the surface. At St. George's, three miles from Wellington, in 1912, with the aid of an upturned bicycle, a riddle and an old bath, strikers extracted coal from seven yards down. Others were photographed at an outcrop at Foxholes, Benthall.

Like mining, quarrying could be a dangerous occupation. In the Limekiln Inn at Porth-y-Waun a poem is displayed on the subject of the explosion at Cooper's Quarry which in May 1872 killed six men and boys whose ages ranged from 13 to 63. Quarrying was also arduous. Alf Jenkins interviewed several men who had begun work early in the 20th century. Tom Jones started in 1908 as a tool carrier, aged 13, earning 1s. a day. George Turner's hours were from 6 am to 5.30 pm, with 30 minutes for breakfast and 60 for lunch. Saturdays were from 6 am to 4 pm—2 pm after 1918 when the 8-hour day came in. Many of his workmates walked long distances from places such as Coreley, Knowbury, Hope Bagot, Bitterley, Cleobury Mortimer, and even Leominster. Fog on the hill was often dense, and pieces of broken crockery were dropped on the paths and trodden into place to help show the way. Lambert Matthews started as a horseman in 1911, aged 13, and for his first fortnight's work received half a sovereign (10s. 6d.). He eventually graduated to quarryman at 5s. a day, but was perhaps fortunate, since when boys attained the age of 18 and became eligible for men's pay they were often dismissed.

Workmen at a quarry at Titterstone, 1930s

Men wore a 'Clee Hill collar and tie': a knotted handkerchief, known as a muffler. Dennis Crowther has celebrated in a poem the garb of hobnailed boots, ridged corduroy trousers, woollen gansey, shiny waistcoat, red kerchief and flat cap perched at a rakish angle. The uniform of the limestone quarrymen

Clee Hill quarrymen

Traditional dress for Clee Hill quarrymen:
mufflers and trousers tied below the knee

at Porth-y-Waun and Pant was similar, with cord trousers tied below the knee with strings known as yorks, union shirt and muffler, thick boots waterproofed with dubbin or goose grease. In wet weather a hessian sack was draped round the shoulders and held in place by a big safety pin in front. Explosives from the quarry found their way to wedding celebrations, where they were known as bangers or cannons.

The quarryman's typical lunch, tied in a coloured handkerchief, was a loaf with the centre pulled out and replaced by a piece of butter and cheese, supplemented at times by a big onion. To drink, cider. Holidays were few, only four days a year: Good Friday, Easter Monday, August Monday, Christmas Day. Breaks in work because of weather conditions were eagerly filled with card playing, joke telling, singing and drinking. Jenkins in his fine study of Clee Hill relates the story of Enoch Tennant, who when trotting back to work after clearly consuming a skinful, was warned by the foreman: 'You'll have to be very careful with that drink, Enoch, otherwise you'll kill yourself under the

The last sett makers on Clee Hill, 1958

Clee Hill village in 1903

face'. Enoch, skinful or no, tartly replied: 'Well, I work for bloody nothing, I may as well die for the same'.

One of the specialised tasks at Clee Hill was that of making setts for kerbs and roads. Despite the extreme hardness of the stone a good man would produce a ton of setts per day. Such work ended in 1958, but quarrying continues on a modest scale. The village of Dhustone (pronounced 'jewstone' or 'joostwun') continues to bear the name of the hard rock of the hill.

Iron Men

In her poem, 'Colebrook Dale' (1785), Anna Seward lamented the advent of industry:

> Scene of superfluous grace, and wasted bloom,
> O, violated COLEBROOK! in an hour,
> To beauty unpropitious and to song,
> The Genius of thy shades, by Plutus brib'd,
> Amid thy grassy lanes, thy wildwood glens,
> Thy knolls and bubbling wells, thy rocks, and streams,
> Slumbers! - while tribes fuliginous invade
> The soft, romantic, consecrated scenes;
> Haunt of the wood-nymph, who with airy step,
> In times long vanish'd, through thy pathless groves
> Rang'd ... Now we view
> Their fresh, their fragrant, and their silent reign
> Usurpt by Cyclops; - hear, in mingled tones,
> Shout their throng'd barge, their pond'rous engines clang
> Through thy coy dales; while red the countless fires,
> With umber'd flames, bicker on all thy hills,

Dark'ning the Summer's sun with colums large
Of thick, sulphureous smoke, which spreads, like palls,
That screen the daed, upon the sylvan robe
Of thy aspiring rocks; pollute thy gales,
And stain thy glassy waters. - See, in troops,
The dusk artificers, with brazen throats,
Swarm on thy cliffs, and clamour in thy glens,
Steepy and wild, ill suited to such guests ...

In turn, the 'tribes fuliginous' and 'dusk artificers' were looking to advance what they considered to be profit and progress. John—'Iron Mad'—Wilkinson (1728-1808) kept the cast-iron coffin in a conservatory made for him and proudly showed it to guests after dinner. His house, The Lawns, still stands at Broseley, and indeed is open to the public as a museum. In 1787 Wilkinson designed, built and launched on the Severn at Willey Wharf *The Trial*, an iron boat which drew only nine inches of water. His firm produced steam engines, iron cylinders, pipes and cannons. His enterprise was celebrated by an admirer in ballad form:

You workmen of Bilston and Bradley draw near,
Sit down, take your pipes, and my song you shall hear.
I sing not of war or the state of the nation,
Such subjects as these produce nought but vexation.

But before I proceed any more with my tale,
You shall all drink my health in a bumper of ale.
Fill it up, and without any further parade,
John Wilkinson, boys, that supporter of trade.

South-west prospect of Coalbrookdale, by François Vivares, 1758

May all his endeavours be crowned with success,
And his works, ever growing, prosperity bless.
May his comforts increase with the length of his days,
And his fame shine as bright as his famous blaze.

That the wood of old England would fail, did appear,
And though iron was scarce because charcoal was dear,
By puddling and stamping he cured that evil,
So the Swedes and the Russians; may go to the divil.

Our thundering cannon too frequently burst,
A mischief so great he prevented the first,
And now it is well known they never miscarry,
But drive all our foes with a blast to old Harry.

Then let each jolly fellow take hold of his glass,
And drink to the health of his friend and his lass.
May we always have plenty of good beer and pence,
And Wilkinson's fame blaze a thousand years hence.

When Wilkinson died in 1808 he was buried in the grounds of the house to which he had by then moved, Castle Head, near Lindale in his native Cumberland. Ironically, the iron coffin proved to be too small. His body had to be temporarily buried while the 20-ton cast-iron monument he had designed was constructed. After the second burial the ground turned out to be unable to bear the weight of the monument, so Wilkinson had to be buried a third time, where the underlying stone would support the structure. Oddly enough, there

Ironbridge by George Robertson, 1788

was a fourth interment: when new owners of Castle Head in 1928 wanted neither body nor monument the former was moved to Lindale Chapel and the latter, ignominiously, to the roadside.

Less has probably been written of iron workers than of iron masters. Charles Peskin in *Memories of Old Coalbrookdale* described the treatment meted out to slackers:

> It was not unusual in the early [18]seventies for dilatory and presumably idle workmen - fellows who persistently lost morning 'quarters' - to be fetched forcibly from home, put in a wheelbarrow, and in the middle of a procession accompanied with tin cans, gongs, whistles, rattles, and anything noisy, conveyed triumphantly to the foundry and upset there. This was called 'ringing them in'.

One more than adequate worker was the ancestor of J. Ball, grocer and sugar-boiler in the village where Ellis Peters spent her childhood. William Ball, otherwise known as the Shropshire Giant or John Bull, worked as a puddler in the ironworks. In his later years he weighed 36 stone, but was as famous for his great strength as for his girth.

Maisie Herring knew men at Horsehay, three miles from Wellington, from whom she learned, 'much of the lore and ways of the ironworker'. One of them, whom she calls George, started work in a foundry in the last decade of the 19th century. 'One of his jobs was to fetch water from a well for the moulders to drink, with a handful of oatmeal scattered in it. He and the other boys shovelled up dung for the men to mix in "loam cores"'.

The iron bridge today

Of the old days he has many stories: how he used to fetch coal for his mother at $4^1/2$d. per bag from the pit head; how women would line up outside the works with men's dinners, some hearty enough to fill a great washing-up bowl. He will tell of his amusements, choir outings, cricket matches, trips in horse-brakes (infinitely better in his opinion than cars for seeing the country). He laments that there are not the 'characters' at work that there used to be, and cites the story of one, a simple-minded foundryman who would obediently roll in the dirt like a horse when bidden, who could turn the handle of a ten-ton jib crane by himself, and who could when asked, recite the collect for any day of the year, and sing the psalms in a good round bass. 'I went to see him in his box', said George. 'And we sang the hymn he asked for over him. It was "Now the Labourer's Task is O'er". He'd always asked for that'.

CHAPTER 9

Leisure

Those who had little leisure, and often less money, eagerly grasped every opportunity for diversion or recreation. People in parts of Shropshire delighted in the bloody and barbaric sports of bull baiting and cock fighting, as their ancestors had in bear baiting. Several towns and villages still have a space bearing the name of Bull Ring. The last bull baiting in Shropshire took place at Oakengates in 1833. The practice was outlawed nationally two years later. Cock fighting became illegal from 1849, though it continued clandestinely, and perhaps still does.

The establishment of the 'Olympian games' at Much Wenlock in 1850 by Dr. William Penny Brookes may have been intended to fill the void left by the suppression of bull baiting and cock fighting. Within 20 years they had become a leading track and field meeting; the baron de Coubertin visited in 1890 before launching his own, better-known revival of the Olympic Games. Much Wenlock's are still held in great affection, as this account, published in 1992, shows. It comes from an anonymous Women's Institute member:

Monument in the church at Much Wenlock to William Penny Brookes

203

The games are held every August Monday on what are called the Linden Fields or the Games Ground. Every kind of sport was competed for. ... There was always a big carnival procession, led by a boy on a pony dressed as a herald. Then came the Wenlock brass band, and of course the Town Crier, lots of decorated drays drawn by horses ... and lastly people on foot all dressed up hoping to win a prize. During the afternoon there was maypole dancing ... What I am writing about is when I was a child about 70 years ago, but the Olympic games are still held today.

Brookes's house at Much Wenlock

Indeed they are, and when Queen Elizabeth visited the town in 2003 she was treated to a demonstration of some of the athletic events.

The passionate debate aroused by the suppression of blood sports in the 19th century was paralleled in the last years of the 20th and the first of the 21st when fox hunting came under scrutiny. At least the fox has a chance to escape, and the humans involved risk limb and sometimes life in their pursuit. Proponents spoke of age-old tradition, and in Shropshire of past luminaries such as Jack Mytton (see below). Mytton was scarcely a good role model, but his haunts are now commemorated by a long-distance path opened in 1993 for the peaceful pastimes of walking and horse riding.

Perhaps the greatest opportunity for collective recreation in the past was provided by wakes (originally religious occasions) and fairs. Of the latter, David Kerr Cameron lyrically writes: 'They exploded ... across the firmament of the year like starbursts on bonfire-night, punctuating the rural calendar and changing destinies - beacons that marked the passing of the seasons and quietly regulated the country's economy'. Among the plethora of events now available, from music festivals to car boot sales, 'the Show' at Shrewsbury—the oldest such horticultural occasion in the world—is a descendant of the fairs of old.

Bears and Bulls

The last bear baiting in Shropshire was apparently in 1825, at Loppington, as part of the festivities in celebration of the vicar's daughter's wedding. (The ring to which bulls were fastened stayed in place, and any stranger who turned it over was deemed to issue a challenge to fight the best man in the village). The sport is recorded at Shrewsbury as early as 1483/4 and at Ludlow 60 years later. The town records list payments to the bearwards of various noblemen and monarchs. For example, at Shrewsbury in 1516/17:

> *dato ursinario domini Regis pro agitacione bestiarum suarum ultra denarios tunc ibidem collectos vjs. viijd.* (given to the bearward of the lord King for the action of his beasts over and above the money then collected in the same place 6s. 8d.)

On some of these occasions a dancing bear is mentioned, but baiting is specifically recorded at Shrewsbury in October 1606 and at Ludlow in 1543/4 ('Item Spent upon your bretherin atte berbayting ijs. xd.'). In September 1606 two men from Bridgnorth called Bird and Millard baited a bear at Munslow 'without the licence of any of the parrishe'. As a result, charges were tabled in the ecclesiastical court against Thomas Arundel, for being present and collecting money, Thomas Shepard of Balcot, his wife, and their son, Isaac, for being present, and Humphrey Law, 'for being present at a bearbaiting ... upon

Bull baiting c.1800, from Country Life, *14 Nov. 1941*

The Bull Ring, Claverley

the saboath daie and putting his dogg then and there to the said Beare'. In 1622/3 during another bear baiting on the Castle Green at Ludlow a purse with 5s. 8d. in it was stolen from Hugh Stevens of Disserth in Radnorshire by Elizabeth Powell of the Lye in Worcestershire and Anne Price of Llanafan Fawr in Breconshire. The details show the distances which some people travelled in order to attend such events.

As with bears, bulls fastened to a stake or ring were baited by dogs trained for the purpose. This was not only seen as a sport but a necessity, since an act of Parliament laid down that bulls should not be killed unbaited. At Shrewsbury Thomas and Edward Clarke in 1585/6 and Thomas Jones in 1591/2, all of them butchers, were fined for slaughtering unbaited bulls.

Three centuries later, in 1878, James Grice of Myddle described a bull bait he had seen as a boy at Loppington, which would have been in the space by the Dicken Arms Inn: 'It was a young bull, and had very little notion of tossing the dogs, which tore his ears and his skin off his face in shreds, and his mournful cries were awful'. Colliers and bargemen, the most dedicated supporters, flocked to the wakes at Oakengates or Madeley to see bulls baited. The latter's wakes were held in October, with baitings at three venues on each of three days. At Oakengates, one of Burne's informants said,

> It was a sight to see the colliers ranged on either side to may a lane [make a lane] for the bull to pass along [to where he was to be fastened], each man holding a dog eager for the fray by the collar, to let him have a glimpse of Taurus. It was a question which looked the most ferocious, the bull, the dogs or the men.

Bull Baiting,

COCK FIGHTING,

AND

DOG FIGHTING,

AT AN END

BY ACT OF PARLIAMENT.

In an Act of Parliament, passed on the 9th of September, 1835, is the following Clause:

" **Whereas,** Cruelties are greatly promoted and encouraged by Persons keeping Houses, Rooms, Pits, Grounds, or other Places, for the FIGHTING OR BAITING OF DOGS, BULLS, BEARS, or *other Animals*—and for FIGHTING COCKS—and by Persons *aiding or assisting therein;* and the same are great Nuisances and Annoyances to the Neighbourhood in which they are situate, and tend to demoralize those who frequent such places. Be it, therefore, enacted—that, from and after the passing of this Act, if any Person shall *keep or use any House, Room, Pit, Ground, or other Place,* for the purpose of *running, baiting, or fighting any Bull, Bear, Badger, Dog, or other Animal,* whether of domestic or wild nature or kind—or for *Cock Fighting*—or in which *any Bull, Bear, Badger, Dog, or other such Animal, shall be baited, run, or fought;*—every such Person shall be liable to a Penalty not exceeding FIVE POUNDS, nor less than TEN SHILLINGS, for every Day in which he shall so keep and use such House, Room, Pit, Ground, or Place, for any of the purposes aforesaid. —Provided always, that the Person who shall *act as the Manager* of any such House, Room, Pit, Ground, or other Place—or who shall *receive any Money* for the admission of any Person thereto—or who shall *assist in any such baiting, or fighting, or Bull-running,* shall be deemed and taken to be the Keeper of the same for the purposes of this Act, and be liable to all such Penalties as are by this Act imposed upon the Person who shall actually keep any such House, Room, Pit, Ground, or other Place, for the purposes aforesaid."

We, the undersigned Constables of Wolverhampton, beg to draw the attention of the Public to the above Act of Parliament.

WILLIAM SAVAGE, } Constables.
HENRY CRUTCHLEY, }

Wolverhampton, October 12, 1835.

Printed by WILLIAM PARKE, Wolverhampton.

Only one dog was loosed at the bull at a time, thus giving rise to the Shropshire expression, 'one dog, one bull', meaning fair play. Many did not see the sport as fair play. Local feeling ended it at Ellesmere in 1812 or 13, and even at Oakengates in 1833, two years before it became illegal nationally. Broseley, Ketley and Rodington were other places once keen on bullbaiting, the last by the Bull's Head Inn. Other villages and towns— Claverley, Much Wenlock, Ludlow—still have Bull Ring name plaques. Mary Webb devoted a chapter of *Precious Bane* to a baiting at 'Lullingford' (Ludlow).

The Bull Ring, Ludlow, with the Old Tolsey
(see p.220)

'Feaste of Mischiefe'

This is what the puritan writer, Philip Stubbes, called cock fights in 1583. Dr. Taylor's manuscript history of Shrewsbury described one five years later in rather more favourable terms:

> This yeare in aprill and in the ester weeke was a great cockfeight and other pastymes kept in shreusbury at Richard hortoons house beine geylar [gaoler] of the towne upon whose backsid a house and the pitt was made for the people to stannd and see ... unto the which cam lordes knightes and gentilmen at the which was grete soms of money woon and lost, the matche was made betweene the Cockes of Cheshire and lanckashir against the cockes of shropshire and wales thider came lundeneres with their cockes whiche held with shropshiremen but in the ennd the chesiremen and lancashir had the victory and wennt away with the gaynes of greate soms of Money.

Parliament came round to Stubbes's view in 1645 and banned cock fighting, but 15 years later Charles II brought it back. In 1835 the sport again became illegal, together with 'the fighting or baiting of dogs, bulls, bears, or other animals'. The act must have been ineffective in some way because further

Tradesman's token of 1666, issued by Robert Huddell of Newport which may show a fighting cock

legislation followed in 1849. However, cock fighting apparently continued in Shrewsbury during race meetings until 1857. A century later at Bridgnorth, according to Brian Waters, 'A certain element ... still takes part in the beastly and illegal practice of cock-fighting'. His informant said: 'They clears out a bedroom of everything that's in it', so as to hold a clandestine contest. In 1985, according to Michael Raven, the kennelman of the Wheatland Hunt, whose dogs were kept at Eardington, a mile from Bridgnorth, was convicted of organising cock fights.

A cockpit from behind the Crown Inn at Bridgnorth, partly reconstructed and partly replicated, can be seen in the Avoncroft Museum of Buildings near Bromsgrove, Worcestershire (where a fine old inn, the String of Horses from Shrewsbury, has also been re-erected). The original structure, with tiered seats

Cock-fight by Thomas Bewick (1753-1828), who commented: 'A wayside Public House; and worse still – a cock fight. The Rain-bow emblem of peace is not regarded by these 50 cruel, ignorant Clowns'

round a circular dais on which the birds fought, covered by a roof, dated from the 1770s. Another cockpit once stood at the Red House Farm, Lydbury North.

More simply, fights could be held in a natural or artificial hollow, or even on level ground. The cockpit at Much Wenlock was simply a field so named. At Farlow, near Oreton, Green Meadow was another venue, near the church and Maypole Inn (now Hillhead Farm).

Gamecocks were carefully bred and fed. John Randall wrote in 1862 of 'Old Joe':

Cockpit building at Red House Farm, Lydbury North

He knew the great breeders, assisted at 'burning the feathers' and casting spells at mains [matches] of cocks, when that gentlemanly sport was at a premium. He picked up the feathers when a lad at a main in Worcester, when Lord Spiker and Prebend Shirkum fought out a disputed battle of their favourites. He knew all the great cockers, feeders, and fighters of the time; and could cast spells, and raise the devil with any of them.

The mains consisted of an agreed number of fights by pairs of cocks. There would be prize money on the result of each fight, and on the side winning most fights in total. For example, at Lee Bridge on Easter Monday and Tuesday in 1779 when the birds of the gentlemen of Cheshire and Shropshire met the prizes were two guineas a battle and 20 guineas for the main. Side bets would also have been placed. The encounter went badly for Shropshire. A celebrated trainer whose name Burne disguises as Thomas Martin had the humiliation of being obliged to pick up his bird, so acknowledging defeat, and returning to the Pack Horse (later called the Horse and Jockey) at Wem. A ballad recording his discomfiture later featured at his funeral, at Horton, near Wem.

A Welsh main—'one of the great contests of the Border countryside', wrote Cledwyn Hughes—matched eight pairs of birds, then four, two, one, in a sort of knock-out competition. In a battle-royal a number of cocks were put together and allowed to fight on until only one remained. They were equipped with metal spurs which, allied to the birds' instincts, meant that all fights were fatal. Brian Waters:

> A Broseley tradesman some years ago made a bet that a gamecock would sooner fight than feed. A pair of cocks were starved for days and then put into a room with plenty of grain and a sheet between them. They started to feed hungrily, then the sheet was raised, and the two birds fought to the death.

Fox Hunting

Cock fighting, once favoured by the county's gentry, increasingly became the sport of colliers and bargemen, which may be why Parliament outlawed it, while fox hunting retained both legality and respectability. Traditions of daring and eccentricity were part of the heritage which it claimed as its own.

The fox itself purports to relate the events of a hunt in 'A True Salopian Hunting Song' of the late 18th or early 19th century:

> One morning last winter as it came to pass,
> A noble fox hunting on Moreton Wood was
> By Squire Hill of Prees, and Squire Roberts of Wem,
> Besides a large company of gentlemen.
>
> There's tailors and weavers, there's labourers enow,
> With these gentlemen there's a jovial fine crew,
> They are all comen here for to see me die
> But I am an old fox, and am got very sly.
>
> They turned me out about ten of the day,
> And to the Old Fields I hasted away,
> And finding that road would do me no good,
> I turned to the right and came to Igen's.
>
> And from Igen's Wood I tried my skill,
> I gave them a ring and came by Moreton Mill,
> They gave me a view holloa, I liked it the worst,
> I took up the valley and ran round the Hurst.
>
> Then off to Kempley I led them a chase,
> And to the Tremlows which is a rough place,
> And over Prees Heath for to make them amends
> I am going to Esquide [Iscoyd] for to see my old friends.
>
> And when I came there, they used me ill,
> They forced me off then for Harmer Hill
> And when I came back I vow and declare
> The hair of my back it began for to stare.

O'er hedges and ditches I led them a flight
Till I thought it high time to bid them 'Goodnight'.
So we'll drink his good health – so cheerful drink
To this noble fox hunting that never will sink.

Chorus
Tally-ho, tally-ho, hi tally-ho,
Hark forward, hark forward, huzzah tally-ho!

There are affectionate stories of fox hunting men such as the clergyman at Greete who was dressed in his pink ready for a meet when the bishop unexpectedly called. He dashed upstairs, jumped into bed, and sent down word that he was indisposed. When the bishop offered to go up and see him the parson sent down the further message, true but ambiguous, that he was suffering from scarlet fever.

Another clergyman regularly said morning prayer with a surplice over his hunting rig, his horse tethered outside the church, and the clerk keeping watch from the top of the tower. If the hounds drawing a nearby covert swung away from the church, mattins would continue; but if the clerk reported that the pack was moving that way, the parson whipped off his surplice, mounted his horse and joined in the hunt, leaving the congregation to fend for itself.

The same man, also a keen angler, turned down a parishioner's request for him to baptise her baby on a Monday, on the grounds that he was going fishing on Tuesday, and if he were to perform the ceremony on the Monday he would have nowhere to keep his live bait (which, of course, was in the font). The woman sympathised with his predicament, and agreed to Wednesday.

Squire Stubbes (born 1671) of Lower Hall, Beckbury, seven miles from Bridgnorth, followed the South Shropshire hounds six days a week in the season. He rode 20 miles a day at a steady trot which acquired the affectionate designation of 'Stubbes's pace'. His image is far removed that that of John—'Mad Jack'—Mytton (1796-1634) of Halston Hall, near Whittington. Mytton, who came from an ancient and distinguished Shropshire family, was expelled as a boy from both Westminster and Harrow Schools, and joined the 7th Hussars at the age of 19. Two years later he became heir to extensive estates which brought in £10,000 a year. During the course of 15 years he spent some £500,000 on gambling, drinking, hunting, and breeding and racing horses. In between times he was briefly MP for Shrewsbury and high sheriff of the county.

He was powerfully-built, utterly reckless, and completely fearless. He had two wives and innumerable amours. He could be 'kind and beneficent to a degree very rarely witnessed', wrote his friend, the sporting writer, Nimrod (C.J. Apperley). As a result, he was extremely popular in Shropshire. He died in London's King's Bench Prison, where he was confined for debt. Some 3,000 people turned out for his funeral; mourning peals rang from the churches of Oswestry, Shrewsbury, Ellesmere, Whittington and Halston.

After his death stories of his rash exploits continued to circulate for over a hundred years. He drank from four to six bottles of port a day, starting the first as he shaved in the morning. He tipped friends out of gigs, took over the reins of the Holyhead mail coach, jumped the Ellesmere canal on horseback, played practical jokes with a bear and a monkey, rode across the Severn though he could not swim, jumped the palings at Attingham Park, set fire to his nightshirt to cure himself of hiccoughs, outfought colliers and outdrank bargemen (at the Barge Inn—now Barge Cottage—at Mountfields, Shrewsbury). He was a habitué of many other pubs, including the Lion at Shrewsbury. The Mermaid and Mytton Hotel at Atcham (see chapter 6) still bears his name, as does Mytton's Dingle. The story behind the latter (at the back of the Stiperstones Inn) is not to his credit: he drove his second wife down it in a tandem, a two-wheeled vehicle drawn by two horses harnessed one before the other, at such a pace that an upset broke her leg temporarily and her nerve permanently. Very much the squire, Mytton once knocked down a dealer who addressed him as 'Johnny'.

The gentry rode to hounds fed and exercised by a kennelman, and, during a hunt, partly controlled by a whipper-in. Very unusually, one whipper-in, Tom Moody, became famous in his own right. He worked for Squire Forester at Willey Hall, near Bridgnorth, and was celebrated in several poems and ballads.

'What! never upset in a gig?' One of Jack Mytton's exploits, drawn and etched by H. Alken

Tally Ho

THE HOUNDS.

The hunters are up, and the ruddy fac'd morn,
Most cheerful salute with the musical horn,
The blue misty mountains seem'd join'd with the
    skies,
And the dogs yelp aloud as away Reynard flies,
Tally ho, tally ho, see the game is in view,
The sportsmen all cry as they nimbly pursue.

The high-mettled steed sweeps away at the sound,
And the hills seem to move, as they fly o'er the
    ground,
Each prospect is charming, all nature is gay,
And promises sport and success thro' the day,
Tally ho, tally ho, see the game is in view,
The sportsmen all cry as they nimbly pursue.

The goddess of pleasure, sweet rosy cheek'd health,
Gives joy more abundant than titles or wealth;
An appetite gives, to their viand a zest,
Above all the sauces by cooks ever drest.
Tally ho, tally ho, see the game is in view,
The sportsmen all cry as they nimbly pursue.

Huzza! then my boys to the chase let's away,
Nor in indolence lose the delights of the day;
From fashion and folly we borrow no grace,
But joy paints the cheek as we follow the chase.
Tally ho, tally ho, see the game is in view,
The sportsmen all cry as they nimbly pursue.

J. Kendrew, Printer, York.

TOM MOODY.

You all knew Tom Moody, the whipper-in well,
The bell just done tolling was honest Tom's knell,
A more able sportsman ne'er follow'd a hound,
Thro' a country well known to him fifty miles round.
No hound ever open'd with Tom near the wood,
But he'd challenge the tone and could tell if 'twas good,
And all with attention, would eagerly mark,
When he cheer'd up the pack,—" Hark !
    To Rockwood, hark ! hark !
    High ! wind him ! and cross him !
    Now Ratler, boy, hark !"

Six crafty earth stoppers, in hunter's green drest,
Supported poor Tom, to an earth made for rest,
His horse, which he stil'd his "Old Soul" next appear'd,
On whose forehead the brush of his last fox was rear'd ;
Whip, cap, boots, and spurs, in a trophy were bound,
And here and there follow'd an old straggling hound.
Ah ! no more at his voice yonder vales will they trace!
Nor the Wrekin resound his first burst in the chace !
    With high over ! Now press him !
    Tally-ho !—tally-ho !

Thus Tom spoke his friends, ere he gave us his breath,
" Since I see you're resolved to be in at the death,
One favour bestow—'tis the last I shall crave,
Give a rattling view-hollow, thrice over my grave ;
And unless at that warning I lift up my head,
My boys ! you may fairly conclude I am dead !"
Honest Tom was obey'd and the shout rent the sky,
For ev'ry voice join'd in the Tally-ho ! cry,
    Tally-ho ! Hark ! forwards,
    Tally-ho !—Tally-ho !"

His ghost has been reported in the area, accompanied by a favourite hound, though he is buried at Barrow, two miles from Much Wenlock.

Moody inspired a song, 'Bachelor's Hall', by the celebrated Charles Dibdin (1745-1814). Dibdin was a friend of George Forester's, and visited him at Willey in about 1787 when, incidentally, he complained about air pollution caused by industrial activity in the Ironbridge Gorge. A street ballad, 'Tom Moody', was in print for at least two decades after Moody's death in 1796.

The social divisions in hunting continued until well within living memory. An apt illustration is provided by Alf Strange (born 1925), whose father Joseph was the village blacksmith at Welsh Frankton, near Ellesmere:

> Only the gentry could afford the hunt. They would gather in the red coats and tall, black, shiny hats astride their magnificent, shiny hunters, ready prepared and saddled by personal grooms before the riders arrived in their chauffeur-driven cars. The ladies too looked like something from out of a colourful hunting picture as they sat side saddle with their long black dresses and black-veiled hats sipping sherry served by a butler holding a silver tray of drinks.

Joseph ambled up to Hardwick Hall as if to join the hunt, though wearing his working overall and apron, and riding 'old Peg', a working cob pony. 'The major' immediately called for a drink for him, and politely enquired whether he would be hunting. Joseph excused himself on grounds of pressure of work:

> His face beamed with delight. He had gone to meet on an old cob pony in all his working gear, been presented with a free drink, sat amidst the gentry, and now was on his way back to the smithy to collect the half crown won in his bet with the farmers who waited there for him now.

Alf Strange was very much a down-to-earth hunt follower, but something of the reckless extravagance of Jack Mytton lingered into the 20th century. Charles de Courcy-Parry, brought up in Cumberland, served with the Seaforth Highlanders in France during the First World War, during which time he was wounded, buried alive and shell-shocked. In 1926 he moved to North Herefordshire, and two years later became master of the United Hunt, whose kennels were at Bishop's Castle. One afternoon at the end of a long chase he reached the Anchor Inn, some eight miles west of Clun. He called for drinks, but the landlord declined: 'out of hours'. The thirsty huntsman invited him to name his price for the inn, bought it on the spot by cheque (for £700), and poured himself and his companion, expensive pints of beer, at £350 each. Various riotous parties followed. De Courcy-Parry wrote to Veronica Thackeray: 'Some stories are not true, nine virgins did not dance naked in the Anchor yard at midnight on New Year's Eve, only seven of them did'. He sold the inn during the Second World War when he returned to the army, but bought it back again at the end. As well as riding with the Ludlow and South Shropshire Hunts he followed the Clun Beagles in search of hare and otter.

Wakes

The annual parish feast or wake was an important occasion. Originally a vigil of prayer on the eve of a religious festival, it became a celebration of a church's patronal saint. At Llanyblodwel, where they called it a *gwyl mabsant*, it took place on the first Sunday after Old St Michael's Day (10 October). In the parish of Church Stretton for good measure there there were four wakes: Little Stretton, on Old St. Lawrence's Day (21 August); Caradoc, on Trinity Sunday (Sunday after Whitsun); All Stretton, on the Sunday after Trinity; and Minton, on the Sunday after St. Thecla's Day (15 October).

The church at Norton-in-Hales is dedicated to St. Chad, whose day is 2 March. Burne quotes a song taken down from the recitation of an old man which reflects how the wake went in the 1830s:

Last March, it being a holiday time,
When I was young and just in my prime,
To Norton Wake it was my intent,
I dressed myself up and away I went.

There was Roger the ploughman,
Sally and Ally and Nan;
We each took a lass, we tripped it along,
And when we got there, there was a great throng.

There was some crying Banburys and some crying cakes;
My lads and my lasses, let's keep up the wakes.
Some crying Banburys as big as the egg of a pout [pullet],
And gingerbread junks [lumps] as big as my foot.

We eat and we ate, we ate and we eat,
Till we could not eat more, they were so good and sweet;
So Bob treated Ally and Ralph treated Sally,
And I bought a fig cake for my Mally.

Then the next was a bull that they brought to the stake,
And this was all done some fun for to make.
He gave them a toss and a terrible throw,
Threw the dogs in the air, and the folks tumbled o'er,
Such pulling and hauling and shouting and bawling,
As I never saw in my life before.

The Banbury cakes and gingerbread mentioned were universally popular. Fig cakes were a speciality at Norton, together with Billy Hayward's mint cakes. Frumenty, made from new wheat grains was favoured at Market Drayton, where the wake followed the feast of the Assumption (15 August). Wake-goers in Shrewsbury's Abbey Foregate district preferred cherries (Sunday before 3 July) and eel pie (Sunday before or after 15 August, on which the authorities disagree). As well as at Norton, bull-baiting (see above) flourished at Oakengates Wakes in early October, then at Madeley's, five weeks before Broseley's, on St. Leonard's Day (6 November).

Even tiny places, as long as they could provide a patch of land for the purpose, had a wake. The Beach (now known as the Beeches) was a hamlet with four houses, yet until 1837 Beach Dingle Wake attracted some 300 or 400 people for dancing, drinking, playing pitch and toss, and prize fighting. Wakes at wells and on the hills also attracted large numbers. Halliwell Wakes, originally connected with a holy well, took place at Rorrington Green on Ascension Day. There was a maypole and, in the evening, dancing to a fiddle. Richard Gough disparagingly refers to John Hall, 'a weaver, and a common fidler, who went abroad to wakes and merriments, butt tooke care to spend what hee had gott beefore hee came home'.

During Wrekin Wakes, on the first Sunday in May and the three successive Sundays, according to a Wellington man, looking back in 1873 to the early years of the century, 'The top of the hill was covered with a multitude of pleasure-seekers, with ale-booths, gingerbread-standings, gaming-tables, swingboats, merry-go-rounds, three-sticks-a-penny, and all the etceteras of an old English fair'. The main feature of the wake was a fierce annual battle between colliers and countrymen for possession of the hilltop.

Titterstone Wake began on the last Sunday in August and lasted a week. To mark its opening young men and women dressed in their best marched together down Tea Kettle Alley. The tea soon gave way to beer and, if some commentators are to be believed, bacchanalia. Wakes were widely judged to promote immorality, drunkenness and disorder. In 1608 Catherine Jones fell foul of the rector at Whethill, eight miles from Bridgnorth, because on the Sunday after Michaelmas (29 September) 'at Evening Praier there to be catechised she cam not but went to a wake at Aston [Botterell]'. Evidently she was a bad lot: the following month, 'being reproved by some of the parishioners for dancing on the Saboath daie and not comming to be catechesed, said, I care not for parson Acton toord in his teathe [turd in his teeth]; I will dance on the Saboath-daie in despite of him even at his nose'. Three young men, David Lewis, Thomas Bridges and Griffith ap John, were in trouble in 1637 for going 'to the wake & pastime in New Castle', and thus absented themselves from evening prayer.

Those were times when puritan doctrines held the ascendancy. In the Victorian era the suppression of wakes came to be seen as desirable, along with the activities they featured. Wrekin Hill Wake was ended by the arbitrary action, sometime in the 19th century, of the Cludde family which had bought the manorial rights to part of the land. The Crab Wakes held at Michaelmas at Chetwynd, near Newport, were so called because it was customary for boys to pelt each other with the fruit. In about 1862 a policeman intervened to stop the rector of Newport from being 'crabbed', and the practice came to an end.

Georgina Jackson quotes this brief conversation in her *Shropshire Word-Book*: "'They'd 'n a pretty rout [party] at Powtherbitch [Pulverbatch] Wakes". "'Adna? Whad wun a doin?" "W'y, fightin' like mad"'. Despite opposition, wakes lingered, especially in remote places such as Bettws-y-Crwyn, where in 1899 Timmins reported that the 'time-honoured' custom 'still holds its own'. In another small community, Llanfair Waterdine, the wakes finally lapsed, though a revival began in 1952. In the 1930s Ira Gandy described the wakes at Kempton, near Clun, in the past tense: 'in the first week in July, when the Foresters and Oddfellows marched round the village with banners flying, and a Robin Hood on horseback behind them, he [Earl Powis] produced a grand supply of cakes and cider'.

According to Maisie Herring, writing in 1949, only 'a shadow' survived of Oakengates Wakes, though older people retained affectionate memories:

> There were rows o' gingerbread stalls an' they sold sweets called Tommy Dodd and Little Joe. Dunna ask why. They were red and white, some shaped like cakes and others like a walking stick. Yo' could walk on the heads o' the people at that fair and I never saw the stall-holders put the money in their pockets; they used buckets for it.

Fairs

By royal charter, fairs were set up as large-scale annual markets, to which merrymakings attached themselves. The earliest in Shropshire seems to be that in Clun, though King John's charter of 1204/5 could merely have confirmed an existing fair. The following year John granted a weekly market and an annual fair to Wem.

Church Stretton's charter came in 1214, when John conceded both a weekly Wednesday market and an annual fair on the Feast of the Assumption. In 1342 under Edward III the market changed to Thursdays and the fair to the eve, day and morrow of the Exaltation of the Holy Cross (14 September). The latter charter also provided for the hiring of servants (see chapter 8). Shrewsbury's first charter dates from 1273/4, during the reign of Edward II. William Cobbett arrived in the town on a fair day in 1830 and wrote:

> Shrewsbury is one of the most interesting spots that man ever beheld.
> ... The town lies in the midst of a fine agricultural country, of which it

is the great and almost only mart. Hither come all the farmers to sell their produce, and hence they take, in exchange, their groceries, their clothing, and all the materials for their implements and the domestic conveniences.

The opening of a fair called for due civic ceremony. At Market Drayton in 1878, for example:

> The annual custom of walking the fair was celebrated ... on Thursday, the 19th of September. The officers of the Court Leet, the javelinmen, constables and others paraded the bounds, and the crier made the usual proclamation about tolls and privileges, and warned all prospective breakers of the law to leave the fair.

A similar ritual, once broadcast on the radio, continued until the 1940s. In 1912 J.E. Auden wrote that at Drayton

> the old manorial customs are still kept up, a court leet being held every October, and the fairs declared open by the steward of the manor. Dressed in his scarlet robes of office, and attended by constables, searchers, sealers, and scavengers, he calls upon the official ale-taster to read the proclamation that all may come and go free from arrest except for outlawry, treason, and murder, but that all thieves, rogues, vagabonds, cut-purses, idle and disorderly persons must immediately depart. A court of piepoudre is held to settle any disputes which may arise during the fair.

Sheep Sale at Craven Arms in 1935

The court of pie-powder takes its name from the French, *pieds poudrés* (dusty feet), an expression designating the fairgoers. Ludlow, too, had such a court, held in the Tolsey, so called since fair tolls were collected there, a building which still stands in the Bull Ring. Ludlow's fair continues, as in Housman's day, to attract 'the lads in their hundreds'. Newport's was held on 28 May in the High Street until the late 1930s, when increasing traffic caused its banishment to a field off Wellington Road. As the same period Phyllis Crawford noted at Bishop's Castle: 'This fair [on St. Hubert's Day, 3 November] is now practically extinct, but in the same county, the traveller calling in spring or autumn, will find at Church Stretton, the rounding-up fairs for the shaggy little ponies that roam this lovely stretch of moor].

Still in the 1930s, Magdalene Weale came across a sheep fair at the Horse Shoe Inn, Ratlinghope. Autumn sheep sales at Craven Arms—perhaps the last vestiges of mediaeval practice—included as many as 16,000 ewes, mainly of the Clun Forest and Kerry Hill breeds, sold in pens of 20 or 40 at a time. Farmers living within four or five miles would drive their ewes in, so 'it seemed that all roads leading to Craven Arms were a mass of heaving sheep, followed by collie dogs and men with sticks'.

A century earlier the full list of Shropshire fairs (including some places later transferred to other counties) was:

Albrighton	May 23, July 18, November 9
Bishop's Castle	Friday before Feb. 13, Friday before Good Friday, first Friday after May Day, July 5, September 9, November 13
Bridgnorth	Thurs. before Shrovetide, May 1, June 30, August 2, Oct. 29
Broseley	Easter Monday
Cleobury Mortimer	April 21, Oct. 27
Clun	Whit-Monday, Nov. 22
Ellesmere	Third Tuesday in April, Whit-Tuesday, Aug. 25, Nov. 14
Hales Owen	Easter Monday
Hodnet	May 15, October 20
Llanymynech	May 29, Sept. 29
Ludlow	Monday before Feb. 13, Tuesday before Easter Sunday, Wednesday after Whit-Sunday, Aug. 21, Sept. 28, and Dec. 6
Market Drayton	Wednesday before Palm Sunday, Sept. 19, Oct. 24
Newport	Sat. before Palm-Sunday, May 21, July 27, Sept. 24, Dec.10
Oswestry	March 15, May 12, Wednesday before Midsummer Day, Aug. 15, Wednesday before Michaelmas Day, Dec. 11
Powder Batch	September 27
Ruyton	July 5
St. Kenelm's	July 29
Shifnal	August 5, Nov. 22
Shrewsbury	Second Wednesday in every month
Stretton Church	May 14, Sept. 25

Wattlesbury	August 5
Wellington	March 29, June 22, Nov. 17
Wem	May 6, Holy Thursday, June 29, Nov. 22
Westbury	August 5
Whitchurch	Whit-Monday, October 28

Of all these, it was perhaps the May Fairs, coming as they did at the beginning of summer, which provided the greatest thrill. 'Bishop's Castle, Ludlow, Craven Arms, Knighton and Clun each had its fair in succession', wrote Ira Gandy. 'People from all the villages for miles around flocked to ride on the roundabouts, have their fortunes told, see the Fat Lady, buy gingerbread and clever toys that the gipsies made'. Time and time again people lovingly recalled such occasions.

At Bishop's Castle children went on the swings and roundabouts, women caught up with a year's gossip, and men disappeared into the Boar's Head, the Six Bells and the Three Tuns. 'Everyone went home happy and, in some cases, it was the horse who knew the way home'. At Craven Arms where 'the May Fair was one of the social highlights of the year', the excitement began when great steam engines arrived laden with roundabouts, helterskelter, chair-o-planes, swingboats, cakewalk, ghost train, Noah's Ark, not to speak of side-shows, circus tents, boxing booths, wall of death, freak shows, rifle ranges, hoop-la stalls and coconut shies. The 'great day', when the sun always seemed to shine, was 24 May.

By contrast, at Clee Hill, in the recollection of Alf Jenkins, the weather, 'always cold and windy with occasional heavy snowfalls, was not expected to improve until the May Fair had left'. Children nevertheless keenly looked forward to the occasion, with its brandysnaps, hot dogs and toffee apples. Music played a big part. In a singing contest to win a pig, 'the idea ... was for

Fair at Newport

221

each competitor in turn to hold a piglet in his arms and sing a song, without the pig squealing'. In the local band the 'leader ruled his players in an unorthodox manner. While playing at the flower show, one member who had partaken of a few drinks put his instrument down in the middle of a tune. The conductor marched up to him and struck him so forcefully that he was knocked out. No one seemed unduly distressed, and when the victim recovered he sat up, picked up his instrument and continued to play as though nothing had happened'.

The Show

During its two days every August, Shrewsbury Flower Show, held in Quarry Park, attracts some 100,000 visitors, and apart from being 'the major event in the county calendar' is the oldest horticultural show in the world. It has a venerable ancestor.

The feast of Corpus Christi (the body of Christ) on the Thursday following Trinity Sunday (the first Sunday after Easter) was enjoined by Pope Urban IV in the 13th century, though it did not become widespread in observance until John XXII issued a bull on the subject in 1317. In Shrewsbury the first recorded reference occurs in a minute book of about 1389/90, *Ordinacio procescionis*

The Procession at the Show in 1863

*Drawings of the procession at the Show in 1831,
made by Samuel Hulbert, aged 11*

Artificum Ville Salopie (order of procession of the craftsmen of the town of Shrewsbury), which lists millers, bakers, fishermen, cooks, butchers, boatmen, shoemakers, goldsmiths, cellarers, carpenters, fletchers, coopers and bowyers, weavers, barbers, apothecaries. After assembling by the castle a solemn procession, led by priests, monks, the parish clergy, town bailiffs and corporation, and followed by the craft guilds, walked two miles to the Weeping Cross, and then back to St. Chad's for high mass. (According to local tradition, the Weeping Cross at Sutton was the site of a gallows, or alternatively a place where coffins were rested on their way to burial in Shrewsbury. However, it seems likely that a penitential cross stood there). After the service at St. Chad's the members of each craft repaired to its 'hall' or pavilion in the Gullet (a former quarry) for several days of feasting and merrymaking.

The religious element in the proceedings had to be abandoned after the Reformation, and the event moved to a Monday. Even so, puritans continued to disapprove. In 1588, according to Dr. Taylor's history:

> This yeare in the moonths of maye, and Iune was soom contraversie in the towne of salop about the setting upp of maye poales and bonyfiers mackinge, and erection of tresse [trees] before the shermans haule and other places the whiche one mr tomkys publicke prechar beinge preseunt at then perswadinge reformacion was then thretenid and push'd at by certen lewde persoons but in the ennde it was reformid by the bayliffes.

Tomkys, a reforming zealot, minister of St. Mary's as well as public preacher of Shrewsbury, bitterly opposed not only what he saw as superstition, but jollification in general. The young shearmen in particular clung to their traditions. (The name comes from the heavy shears used for trimming the nap on cloth). In 1590, 500 people gathered protectively round the tree at shearmen's hall, but the following year the town bailiffs intervened to forbid that it should be set up. A party of shearmen defiantly planted a symbolic sapling during the night. Four of them, Richard Fernes, John Bickerstaff, Thomas Evans and Wilfred

Heath, were indicted and imprisoned. Very enterprisingly, they obtained a writ of *habeas corpus* and were released. However, they made their peace providing that 'all lawfull custome of our company may be saved and reserved'.

In 1594 two shearmen were hanged for a murder which seems to have been motivated by the victim's having sawn up the revered tree. The following year the guilds began to go to Kingsland, a less prominent site. Shortly afterwards, the corporation, which owned the land, allocated to each company a plot on which a semi-permanent 'arbour' was erected, inside a fenced and ditched enclosure. The shearmen persisted with their tree: early 17th-century records show payments for gunpowder for fireworks 'at the bringing in of the tree'. Later, the tree was allowed to remain in place and grow permanently.

Two centuries on, the show continued, despite reports of its imminent demise. Show Monday remained a general holiday. In 1831 eight guilds attended, together with mayor and corporation, two MPs and the Earl of Powis. 'The poor were fed with plenty, and the rich not sent empty away'. In 1844 according to the *Salopian Journal*, after the show the people adjourned to the inns 'where they tripped merrily to the light fantastic till long after Sol had enlived the earth with his rays'. Two years later:

> Kingsland on Monday was the tented field of glorious pastime in all its enticing forms, from fun show to shindies of every sort - shooting, 'slap-bangs', wines, cakes, comfits, beef and ham sandwiches, coffee, brown stout, beer and backey [tobacco].

Burlesque figures were always a feature of the procession. Crispin and Crispianus preceded the shoemakers, Vulcan led the smiths, and Rubens, the house painters. Henry I owed a place to his having granted Shrewsbury its first charter. 'The reasons why the tailors and skinners were led by Cupid and the Stag, the builders by Henry VIII, the cabinet makers and hatters by the Black Prince, the hair dressers and bakers by Queen Elizabeth, and the flax dressers by Katherine of Aragon are no longer apparent', wrote P.E. Price.

The arrival of the railway at Shrewsbury had a great impact on the shows— an excellent example of a new technology helping an old tradition. In 1849 for

Shrewsbury School at Kingsland, built on part of the old site of the Show

The tailor's arbour at the Show, 1863

the first show after the line opened, 'The cheap trains from the Chester line, from Oswestry, &c, and those from Stafford, Wellington and Oaken Gates stations poured forth visitors in their thousands'. Each year, the numbers brought by train increased: 15,000 in 1850, 2,900 in a single train; 32,000 in 1853, in 42 special trains besides 56 regular services.

Despite, or because of, this huge popularity, opposition to the shows increased. Since stallholders and others had to prepare for the show on the day before, a Sunday, there were complaints of Sabbath-breaking, as well as 'beastly intoxication, ... and tremendous oaths and cursing'. Middle class opinion turned against 'this ridiculous pageant ... and the usual array

1867.

SHREWSBURY SHOW

PATRONIZED BY THE
NOBILITY GENTRY,
AND THE PUBLIC OF THIS AND THE ADJOINING COUNTIES.
PRESIDENT. MR. J. R. PICKERING.

Oh, come to the Shrewsbury Show!
For June in her sunshine robe is there
All glowing and bright on the Kingsland hill,
And the wild flowers spangle the grass so fair,
Where blessings of gladness to the Severn repair.
At it flows at will—
And thus they go
Through the upward sward to the Shrewsbury Show.

Oh, come to the Shrewsbury Show!
Though the Quarry's sweet walks may invitingly say—
"Come wanderer, come, to my sylvan shade,
For the shrine of nature is seen this way,
In the foliage that circles the infant spray,
In my green arcade,
Her waviness go,
From my bower of blooms to the Shrewsbury Show."

Oh, come to the Shrewsbury Show!
Should the Severn beguile with its wandering song,
And zephyrs wend there with their cooling wings—
The voice of the stream is of sadness! for long
Has it echoed through ages! and runs among
Like an old harp's strings!
But away let's go—
With a step of delight—to the Shrewsbury Show.

Oh, come to the Shrewsbury Show!
Where laughter is seen with her pearly eyes,
And maidens are threading the dance so gay,
As light as the air from the smiling skies,
And love is breathing her languishing sighs,
Then away we'll go—
On this holiday,
To the old and long famed Shrewsbury Show.

ON MONDAY, JUNE 24th, THE

ANCIENT SHOW PROCESSION

Which, so far back as 1448, appeared to be a "Tyon out of mynde Festival" will be carried out with the Customs and Honours of former days; forming in the Market Square at 12 o'clock, and proceed up Pride Hill, Castle Street, under the Railway Bridge opposite the Old Thrashers, up Chester Street, St. Mary's Street, Dogpole, Wyle Cop, over the English Bridge, Abbey Foregate, back to High Street, round the old Market Hall to Mardol Head, through Shoplatch to Bellstone, Claremont Street, Mardol, over the Welsh Bridge to Frankwell and KINGSLAND, in the following order; the Characters either representing the "Monarchs who granted their Charters or some principal Personages of their Trades" being gaily dressed with "Crownlets and Gauds of rare device.

MARSHAL and TRUMPETERS on Horseback.
Splendid New Banners—THE SHREWSBURY ARMS and THE STANDARD OF ENGLAND.

CRISPIN AND CRISPIANUS.
BAND OF MUSIC   Representing Shoemakers.   Flags, Banners, &c.

BANNER.—"The Patrons of Shrewsbury Show!
With the Armorial Bearings of The noble Lord Lieutenant; The High Sheriff, George Tomline, Esq. M.P.; W. J. Clement, Esq. M.P., and the Members for the Northern and Southern Divisions of the County.

KING HENRY THE FIRST.
Who granted the first Charter to the Borough of Shrewsbury.

CUPID, in Splendid Car, drawn by Grey Horses
Accompanied with the Seasons—"Spring, Summer, Autumn & Winter"
Representing Tailors, Drapers, Skinners, &c.

A KNIGHT OF THE CLEAVER.
Representing Butchers and Tanners   Beautiful Flags and Banners

KING HENRY THE EIGHTH.
Representing Bricklayers, Carpenters, Joiners, &c   BAND OF MUSIC.   Flags, Banners, Streamers &c.

KING EDWARD THE SIXTH.
The Youthful Founder of Shrewsbury School.

A Beaver Hunter. | Vulcan, in Chain Armour.
Representing Hatters, Cabinet Makers, &c.   Representing Smiths, Wire Workers, Ironmongers, &c.

Queen ELIZABETH, | Queen CATHERINE,
Representing Hairdressers, Bakers, &c.   Representing Flax Dressers, Thread Manufacturers, &c

RUBENS, the Eminent Artist,
Representing Corn Brethren of Painters, Printers, Tinmen, &c. BAND OF MUSIC. Flags and Banners, an dernation of their Craft

Sir John Falstaff. | Jenny Jones & Edward Morgan,
Robin Hood and Little John,
And a variety of other Characters &c., which will be introduced with Bands of Music.
Splendid New Flags, Banners Streamers, &c. supplied by Mr. T. Darlington & Mr. R. Andrews.

On Tuesday, June 25th, commencing at 2 p.m.

A VARIETY OF OLYMPIC GAMES

Consisting of a HANDICAP FOOT RACE! Distance 120 yards. First Prize £3., Second £1. Entries 1s.6d.
Open to the County of Salop Also ONE MILE HANDICAP! on same conditions, all to run in one heat.
Entries to be made on or before 8 p.m. on June 22nd., at Mr. Bowen's Spirit Vaults, High Street, Shrewsbury.

Honorary Secretary, Mr. DAVID LEWIS,   Assistant Secretary, Mr. THOS. LLOYD.

of drunken kings and factory queens promenading the streets ... [in] a straggling procession'. Debate became particularly keen in the 1860s, and 'a variety of Olympic Games' was introduced, presumably on the lines of Much Wenlock's, as an added attraction.

Nevertheless, in 1878 the local magistrates recommended to the Home Secretary that the show should be abolished, since it was a pleasure rather than trading fair, which

Shoemakers' arbour at the Show, 1863

attracted the lower orders and caused much drunkenness. He complied, and the corporation promptly sold 27 acres of the Kingsland site to Shrewsbury School, which moved out from the town centre in 1882. On Show Monday in 1878 the Black Prince and Rubens, accompanied by a small band of die-hards, marched through the town and up to Kingsland. For the next ten years 'a pale shadow of the former festivities could be observed on some waste ground outside the closed Abbey Foregate railway station', wrote Price.

Meanwhile, the new show had started (in 1875) in the Quarry. It would be kinder to remember the old in the glory of its heyday, rather than the ignominy of its decline. Michael Peele summarises descriptions from the *Shrewsbury Chronicle*

of the mustering of the trades, with their standards, streamers, music, and a crowd of lads huzzahing in the rear; of the procession in all its glory, and its characters, Crispin and his pious brother, the apprentices' king with towering feathers, the iron man 'mounted on a Flanders mare, somewhere about 8 feet high, which capered and frollicked like an elephant with its castle, to the high glee of the young Vulcans who followed', the kingly Henry, who 'bowed and rolled from side to side till he captivated all hearts', Venus, 'nestled in finery unspeakable'. There are glimpses of Kingsland: the visit and entertainment of the mayor and his his retinue; the booths and merry-go-rounds and games of roly-poly and prick-the-garter. 'Here was a stout, jolly wench with Market Drayton buns, all spiced so nicely, and studded with a solitary raisin - there the unwilling halfpenny was lugged forth from the pocket to buy the crimping, yellow-faced, buttery Ellesmere cake - here was a load of Everton toffee, all twisted into blessed mouthfuls - and there a delicious basketful of Oswestry dumplings, claiming many a sigh from those whose exchequer could not muster twopence for their purchase'. Then come the closing scenes, the trades marshalled again, behind kings, queens and cupids, and one faint hint of the more bedraggled return - 'but Crispin and his partner were obliged to abandon their steeds and lead the van as humble pedestrians, a sudden giddiness having visited the saints'.

CHAPTER 10

Music and Song

During his perambulation of the Midlands, published in 1860 as *All Round the Wrekin*, Walter White dropped into the Shakespeare Inn at Newport. There, he wrote,

> It was Saturday night, and while eating my supper, I heard the singing of a large party of working people in the taproom, who were making a hole in their wages as a happy finish to the week. The liveliest singer sang something pathetic, and one stanza so very touching, that I made a note of it:
>
> Come all you ladies drest in white,
> Come all you sailors drest in black,
> From the cabbing [*sic*] boy to the mainmast high,
> Pray shed a tear for my sailor boy.

Some 70 years later during a trip down the Severn Wilfrid Byford-Jones saw women 'squatting on their haunches before large boulders washing clothes in the river'. Some were talking as they worked, others 'chanting Shropshire dialect songs in a lilting cadence that consorted with the music of the rippling waters'.

Such scenes are charateristic of times when people sang for their own pleasure, drawing on a body of traditional material, and sometimes adding to it by their own compositions. Such songs continued to circulate in some circles well into the 20th century, and indeed, in the person of the Corvedale farm worker, Fred Jordan (see below), into the 21st. In the meantime, enthusiasts in folk song clubs and at festivals such as Shrewsbury's (every August) had taken to performing songs which for the most part they had learned from books and recordings rather than in the old, oral tradition.

Of course, the oral transmission of songs has long been supplemented by written and printed material. A manuscript collection, now world-famous, was found by Thomas Percy at the house of a friend of his, Humphrey Pitt, at

Shifnal. Percy (1729–1811), the son of a Bridgnorth grocer, went to Newport School, then Oxford University, before becoming a parson in Northamptonshire. While visiting Pitt at Haughton Hall, probably in 1753, he noticed a battered volume 'lying dirty on the floor, under a bureau in ye parlour ... being used by the maids to light the fire'. In due course this provided a starting point for Percy's anthology, *The Reliques of Ancient English Poetry* (1765). Percy doctored some of the ballads in an effort to 'please the most delicate and correct Taste'; he also omitted bawdry as well as politics or protest. Even so, the three-volume work was not only immediately successful but came to be considered a land-mark in European literature.

Thomas Percy's house, Bridgnorth

Percy supplemented his manuscript source with other material, including ballads originally printed for sale in the streets. The ballad trade had its prac-titioners in Shropshire who reissued nationally-known items but also covered local events such as executions and disasters. The authors of such texts are often unknown. Shropshire has, however, produced identifiable writers, of whom John Audelay or Audley, the blind and deaf chaplain from Haughmond Abbey, in 1426 completed a book of poems dealing mainly with religious themes. He may also have written 'Wolcum Yole' (Welcome Yule: see p.320). Almost 600 years on, *The Land of Lost Content*, a collection of songs, settings and arrangements by Michael Raven, published in 1999, has many links with Shropshire; and Alan Bell's song, 'Letters from Wilfred' (2002), commemo-rates the Oswestry poet and soldier killed days before the end of the First World War.

As with songs, tunes circulated by ear, in manuscript, and in print. Instrumental players—'musicianers', as they were once called in Shropshire— have a long history in the county, from mediaeval minstrels to village players of the 19th and 20th centuries, from wandering gipsy fiddlers to the folk musi-cians of today.

Minstrels and Waits

The word, 'minstrel', first recorded in English in 1297, appeared in the Shrewsbury town records until the early 17th century. For much of the time it was interchangeable with *histrio*, meaning actor in classical Latin, but later a musical entertainer. Entries in the Bailiffs' Accounts for 1473/4 place three terms on a par:

> *Et in denarijs solutis tribus Mimis sive histrionibus Regine, xx s. Et ...*
> *pro vino dato dictis Minstrallis .... iiij s. ix d.* (And in the usual money to
> three mimes or entertainers of the queen ..., 20s. And ... for wine given
> to the said minstrels ..., 3s. 9d.)

Any doubt as to what the *histriones* did is dispelled by frequent references, such as this, to their music, or rather melody:

> *Et expenditum per Ballivos & Compares suos audientes melodiam*
> *histrioni domini Regis vij s.* (And spent for the bailiffs and their
> colleagues listening to the music of the entertainers of the lord king 7s.)
> (1536/7).

The Ludlow accounts, too, record payments to 'the Kynges mynstrelles' (1535/6), 'Mr pakyngton Mynstrell' (1543/4) and, in 1544/5:

> Item to the maior of Chesters Mynstrelles in rewarde viijd.
> Item gevn to mr packyngtons mynstrelles at Candlemas [2 February] xxd.
> Item gyven unto the Kynges mynstrelles vjs. viijd.
> Item spend upon the Kynges mynstrelles besyde theyre wyne xxd.
> Item gyven unto my Lordes mynstrelles that cam from lychfeld iiijd.

In the same year even a small village like Worfield made payments of 16d. to 'the syngers of dudley' and of 11d. 'to the mynstrell for old dette'.

Both *histrio* and minstrel could be used for the waits—musical watchmen who also played on civic occasions (see below). At Shrewsbury an entry of 1437/8 mentions the fees of '*clamatoris & duorum Ministrallorum vocatorum Waytes ville*' (the crier and two minstrels called town waits), and, four years later, those of '*clamatoris & trium histrionum vocatorum waits*' (the crier and three entertainers called waits). Finally, musicians (in various spellings) enter the records in the mid-16th century. For example, at Ludlow: 'Item gyven agaynst Crystemas to the officers of the Castell: to the musyssions, ijs.' (1567/8).

The performers, like the dramatic players of the next chapter, often came from royal or noble households, which presumably sent them on tours funded by others, so as to offset the expense of maintaining them. The king's *histri-*

Waits, as depicted in an early broadside

ones are mentioned over and over again, the king's mother's, once (in 1502/3 at Shrewsbury), the queen's, several times. The Marquess of Exeter, the earls of Powys and Shrewsbury, the dukes of Buckingham, Clarence, Gloucester and York, Lords Arundel, Derby, Ferrers, Stafford, Strange and Tankervile, are some of the nobles whose men are listed as appearing in Shropshire towns. Both the abbot and the town of Shrewsbury maintained musicians. In addition, municipal players from Bridgnorth, Bristol, Chester and Nottingham performed in Shrewsbury.

The occasions on which they played are not always specified, and one has the feeling that any pretext would have justified a performance. The opening of a court session at Shrewsbury in January 1437/8 warranted the expenditure of 6s. 8d. on Lord Stafford's minstrels, who happened to be in town. The Ludlow accounts for 1616/17 record ten shillings paid to one 'love the musissioner & his Coompany for all theyre musicke at the feaste & the law day & my lords coming the 26 of May'.

Certain religious festivals—the Easter and Whitsun weeks, and especially Corpus Christi (see chapter 9)—were marked by civic feasts and/or processions, invariably with music. St. George's Day (23 April) was favoured by the craft guilds for their feasts. In 1597, for example, the shearmen of Shrewsbury paid out 8s. for 12 gallons of ale, 12s. 3d. for 49 gallons of beer, 4s. for a gallon of sack, 14s. 6d. for bread, one shilling for another quart of sack (perhaps an oversight), five shillings for 'our mynstrell' and one shilling to his apprentices, and finally, 4s. 6d. for 'cuppes trenchers bowes and Rosshes [rushes]', a total of £2 10s. 3d.

St. John's Day (24 June), or rather its eve, features in entries such as this, also from Shrewsbury (1450/1):

> *Item uno Minstrallo Comitis Salopie eunti coram Ballivos & aliis probis hominibus in vigilia Nativitatis Sancti Iohannis Baptiste pro honestate ville, iijs. iiijd.* (Item to one minstrel of the earl of Shrewsbury going in the presence of the bailiff and other honourable men on the eve of the nativity of St. John the Baptist for the honour of the town, 3s. 4d.).

This seems to have been some kind of nocturnal perambulation.

Corpus Christi usually fell in June. For several years in the early 16th century the Mercers', Drapers' and Ironmongers' Company of Bridgnorth paid for a feast, together with a light, banners and torches for a procession and also the services of a minstrel. Corpus Christi records at Shrewsbury begin in *c.*1389/90, though music is listed only from 1468/9, with 'the waites of the towne'—though minstrels for the event were paid by the Drapers' Company from 1487 until 1511.

Waits originally blew on horns and other instruments to warn of dangers such as fire or to mark the passing of the hours through the night. The Black Book of Edward IV (reigned 1461-83) details their duties: to pipe four times a night from Michaelmas to Shrovetide, three times the rest of the year. In the Ludlow records they are mentioned a few times only. In 1446/7 provision is made for 'too gownes ... for the waites'. Exactly a century later there are payments to 'the waites of Salop' (Shrewsbury), and in 1600/1 to 'the waites of Hereford'. Ludlow certainly had waits of its own because in 1614/15 they were paid 3s. 4d. 'for plaijnge upon the tower [of the church?] at the cominge of my lord and lady Ewre into this towne'.

Bridgnorth, too, had waits, but they seem to have been recorded only in the accounts at Shrewsbury, where they were paid on one occasion in 1551/2. There are frequent references to Shrewsbury's own waits. Three of them were paid £2 between them for the year 1435–6 but a decade later they had to share that sum with the town crier, John Calverhall (1446–7). The three (or their successors) were back to £2 in 1509–10, and were paid the same amount in 1537–8, which seems to be the last time their salary is mentioned. They seem to have received further small sums from time to time, presumably for commitments beyond their normal duties. For example, the Shearmen's Company paid 'the waits of the towne' 4d. in 1468/9.

A minute of the town's accounts for 1537 states that 'the waytes shalbe hyred for this yere folowying & to have suche lyverye as hertofore hath byn used & a customed and they to entre a thinvencion of the holy crosse' (3 May). The buying of gowns—the Latin word, *toga*, is used—for three 'toun minstrels called waits' is recorded in 1450/1, at five shillings apiece. The garments lasted ten years and were then replaced at exactly the same cost. The identical transaction appeared again in 1477/8, and in 1486/7, an indication of the stability of prices at the time. The waits' garments and equipment then disappear from the record until 1549/50, when new tunics were supplied at a cost of 27s. 6d. In 1567/8 two waits, Francis Stenton and John Challenger, wrote on the subject to the bailiffs:

> Your obedient oratours [petitioners] ... now present that ... beinge comon travelers Every mornynge with theire instruments for that all artificers myght know the due owre for theire ffamylye to goe to theire nessaris buisiness & also for all travilers [workers] to Knowe like wise Intended consideracion whereof maye hit pleas yowr worships uponn your accustumable goodnes to shewe your lefull favor for to grant us beinge poore men some what towardes the byinge of us to leverey cottes & thus for godes Love.

Several years elapsed and then, somewhat puzzlingly, 'waittmens cottes' at 44s. 11d. and 'waytmens coattes' at 13s. 4d. appeared in quick succession (1573/4 and 1575/6). Soon afterwards it was decided that 'there shalbe geven to the wayte men newe coates of broad clothe of the color of oringe tawnye in Respecte of their paines takinge to playe every morning' (1580/1).

In 1607/8 the number of waits was increased to five. Sums of £3 15s. were spent on coats and £4 6s. 3d. on badges and chains. More coats were bought in 1611/12 at a cost of £3 15s. The Shrewsbury men are recorded as having performed at Coventry in 1616 (twice) and 1633. The waits may have continued for a further two centuries in Shrewsbury, until the Municipal Reform Act of 1835 brought them to an end, but documentation on this period awaits a researcher.

In the early accounts musicians are usually identified by the titles of their royal, noble or municipal masters. From time to time a personal name does appear, the earliest example of which seems to be with the payment of five pence in Shrewsbury in 1269/70 to 'Symoni filio Hugonis le harpare' (Simon the son of Hugo the harper). Often the player is identified but not his instrument: at Ludlow Edward Perkins (1533/4) and Walter Tailor (1551/2), the latter paid 'for hys playeng at crystenmas', and Arthur Braite (1602/3), another Christmas performer. The Shrewsbury records also name the earl of Shrewsbury's minstrels, John Goss (1452/3), John Jamins (1506/7) and Bennett and Wells (1520/21), Lord Monteagle's Randolph Hubbard (three times between 1520 and 1526), and the town's William Breese (1525/6).

Often a musician is identified by his first name and that of his instrument, like Simon Harper at Ludlow in 1447, and probably Walter Harper in 1476/7 and 1468/9, and Roger Harper in 1547/8, at Shrewsbury. Thanks

Two fiddlers, one playing, the other tuning, on a carved wood panel of c.1800, formerly kept at the Coach and Dogs tearooms, Oswestry, but removed in 2001 when the premises changed hands

to a complicated agreement on the silver collars which the town minstrels wore we know the names of several, one of whom, Richard Ferber, played the *cithera*, which is usually taken to mean the harp (1507-9). Rather a remarkable entry of 1520/1 concerns money and wine given to William More, '*histrionum domini Regis eo quod est cecus & principalls citherator Anglie*' (king's entertainer who is blind and the principal harper in England). It recalls that of 40 years earlier concerning seven pence given to another of the king's minstrels '*via elemosinaria causa eius paupertatis & etatis*' (by way of charity because of his poverty and age).

Other players of stringed instruments mentioned were John Williams, paid 12d. at Shrewsbury for perambu- lating and playing the lute on St. John's Eve, 1446, and John Luter (the surname is no doubt significant), paid 6s. 8d. for playing in 1522/3. A remarkable letter written in September 1304 to the abbot of Shrewsbury by Edward, prince of Wales (the future Edward II), concerns the crowd or *crwth*, a kind of three-stringed fiddle which has left its mark on the language in the surname, Crowther:

> *Pur ceo que Richard nostre Rymour desire moult daprendre la menestracie de Crouther e nous avoms entendu que vus avez un bon croutheour que nus vus prions chierment que vus voillez comander a vostre Croutheour quil apreigne al dit Richard sa menstralcie.* (Because Richard our Rhymer [Bard] much desires to learn the minstrelcy of Crowther and that we have heard that you have a good Crowther that we dearly beg that you order your Crowther to teach the said Richard his minstrelcy).

The abbot's reply has not survived, but he is hardly likely to have turned down the royal request.

Among wind players were Henry Trumpet, paid after Easter in 1401/2 at Blackmere, and the five unnamed men entertained in 1616/7:

> gave unto v of the Kings trumpiters who cam to Ludlow to See the towne & the castell as they weare passing in to the northe to meete King. There was Spent uppon them in wine bred & beare & other things 2s. 2d.

The Blackmere accounts include annual payments of £2 to Thomas Piper and his colleagues, Bircestre, Stephan and Woodburn. John Philipps received two shillings '*pro suo labore*' (for his work) on St. John's Eve and St. Peter's Eve (28 June) in 1653. The pipe and tabor were widely played. The duke of Gloucester's minstrel, called 'le Taberrer', was mentioned at Shrewsbury in 1476/7. The queen's taborer was in town in 1586/7; the accounts of the Lord President of the Council of the Marches acknowledge the payment of 2s. 6d. to 'the Taber and pype in the hall at Christmas' in 1614/15.

Musicians fell foul of borough or church authorities in a number of cases involving their instruments. William Corser 'played upon a tabber *tempore divinorum*' (during divine service) at Stanton Lacy in 1588. John Davies, taborer, some time in 1628/9, 'was taken by master Bayliffe rowley upon saterday nighte laste aboutes Twelve of the Clocke in Playinge upon the Taber & pipe in a Bardge at the Key in ffranckwell amongeste a Company of Bardgmen'. After being

Richard Tarlton, actor, comedian and pipe and tabor player. He was reputedly herding his father's pigs at Condover when his witty, 'happy unhappy answers' to the questions of the passing earl of Leicester led to his becoming one of Queen Elizabeth's players. He became tremendously popular but died in poverty in 1588

confined in Stonegate prison he 'was discharged promising to leave of playinge on the Taber & pipe hearafter'.

The pipe and tabor are not quiet instruments, and they are cited in several cases of sabbath-breaking. At Little Wenlock Maria Blakeway on an August Sunday in 1619 'with others did manteigne a minstrell to play with Taber and pipe in the howse of one Edward harding ale seller ... she with others there dancing'. In the same place in 1636 John Binner failed to attend church on Sunday 8 May and on Ascension Day (26 May), 'being upon the said dayes tabouring and playing'. Five years earlier at Habberley Richard Cowper on another May Sunday played his pipe and tabor during divine service, and was excommunicated for doing so.

Thomas Crump, *musicus*, of Holdgate, played in service time at Shipton in 1635. Richard Collins, 'being a minstrell', offended at Pontesbury by not only 'plaieng at divine service upon trinitie sunday last [6 June 1596] & divers other sundaies' but by 'shoting of his gunne in the sermon tyme upon Whitsun munday [31 May] to the disturbance of the Preacher & hearers of the word'.

Others, like Maria Blakeway, were not musicians themselves but were responsible for inviting them to play. At Ludlow in 1614/5 at the Bull Inn musicians played all night while others drank sack and gambled. Andrew Mason was in trouble at Bishop's Castle in 1606/7 for bringing in 'two strange minstrels', Francis More Edward ap John and John Madox; and at the same place in the same year Hugo Watters organised not only music but dancing. In 1614/5, again at the Bull in Ludlow, people drank sack and played the tables all night while 'musiciens' entertained. Catherine Harris, widow, gave offence by inviting players to Stanton Lacy in November 1619.

Musicians, of course, sometimes fell foul of the law not for playing but for other offences. In 1593/4 two evidently tough performers, Edward Hughes and John Williams, were accused of breach of the peace against two other men apiece, one of the four victims being a bargeman. In the same town in the early 1630s two bagpipers, John Evans and Humphrey Ridge, were separately charged with 'wandering'. David Jones and David Williams, his boy (probably apprentice), minstrels by profession, were also charged with wandering because they lacked the necessary pass signed by two magistrates. They were discharged in June 1632 and supplied with 'a passe to travell to Monmorth where they confesse they were borne'.

Still in Shrewsbury, a labourer called Thomas Dawes was accused of 'stealinge of a violett otherwise called a fiddle with ij stringes beinge the goodes of one francis Uppon', in 1592/3. It seems that he had borrowed the instrument, then refused to give it back. The outcome of the case is not recorded, but probably the bailiffs, before whom Dawes appeared, simply ordered him to return it. In 1606/7 John Nunnely, John Edwards and William Cocks 'did walke abroad

Little Billy Martin's brass band at Clee Hill

the streetes ... att undue tyme of the night ... abysinge a pore harper in taking his harpe from him & playenge upon the same alonge the streetes after nyne of the Clocke att night'. Clearly, music after nine was unacceptable.

Village Musicians

Unlike minstrels and waits, many instrumentalists were occasional rather than professional music-makers. The advent of cheap printed music in the 1840s helped the spread of brass bands. Many musicians, though, played by ear. Perhaps Saul Adams did. He lived at Colebatch and Cefn Einion in the late 19th century, and worked as a gamekeeper. His accordion and melodeon can be seen in the little museum at Clun.

Many a village musician, like Thomas Hardy and his father in Dorset, played on Sundays for services (see chapter 5) and on Saturday nights for dancing and merrymaking. John Moore of Wellington possessed one manuscript book with the tunes of psalms and hymns, others with country dance and song tunes. One of the latter, with 148 tunes, has been edited by Gordon Ashman under

Music for 'The Ironbridge Hornpipe'

*Photograph possibly of
Edward Philpott, taken by
Jakeman and Carver, Hereford*

the title of *The Ironbridge Hornpipe*. Its contents include items popular in the 1830s, such as 'Auld lang syne', 'The Blue Bells of Scotland' and 'Pop goes the weasel'. There are waltzes, quadrilles and hornpipes. Standard traditional tunes include 'The Girl I left behind me', 'Drops of Brandy' and 'The Irish Washerwoman'. Some, to judge by their titles, are of local origin: 'Worster Hornpipe', 'Wellington Hornpipe', 'Shrewsbury Waltz', and 'The Ironbridge Hornpipe' itself.

Moore's repertoire, unsurprisingly, has a good deal in common with the manuscript tune books belonging to Edward Philpott, who was born at Easthope, and buried there in 1901. One of the books (now deposited with the Ironbridge Gorge Museum Trust) is marked 'Copyed Oct. 23rd 1852 by Edw.d Philpott'. Others are in different hands. Of the 200 or so tunes in all, some were novelties ('Kossuth Polka', presumably dating from the late 1840s), others old favourites ('The Lass of Richmond Hill', 1789), and still others from the traditional repertoire ('The Black Joke', 'Moll in the Wad', 'Soldier's Joy'). As with Moore there are (presumably) local tunes: 'Rakes of Shrewsbury' and 'Shropshire Quick Step'.

Music for 'Rakes of Shrewsbury'

Music for 'Shropshire Quick Step'

Unlike Moore and Philpott, gipsy fiddlers such as John Lock and his brother—possibly Polin (Napoleon) Lock—played only by ear. Mrs. E.M. Leather, the Herefordshire folklorist, heard them at Pembridge Fair in May 1908 and was so impressed that she arranged for John Lock to play to Cecil Sharp in Leominster the following year. Among the tunes were 'Blue-eyed Stranger', 'Boyne Water', 'Greensleeves', 'Herefordshire Hornpipe', 'Hunting the Squirrel', 'Mad Moll', 'Three Jolly Sheepskins' (see chapter 11) and 'Speed the Plough'.

John Lock spent much of his time in the area round Clun. The story was long cherished of how he was playing one evening at the Kangaroo Inn at Aston-on-Clun. His glass of beer was liberally replenished, but as he paused to drink his fiddle bow was surreptitiously given a rub on one of the sides of fat bacon hanging from the ceiling hooks. As he became more fuddled so his bow progressively failed to produce a sound—to his consternation and the collective hilarity. T.W. Thompson, the secretary of the Gypsy Lore Society, sought him out in 1923:

> August is bilberry time, and bilberries are amazingly plentiful on the hills near Clun, especially on the 'far' hills, where none but Gypsies go to pick them. There, we were told, John Lock and his family were sure to be, for they had passed through the town, bound thither, some ten days earlier. ... A jolting ride to the little village of Newcastle, succeeded by a steady climb of four or five miles against a buffeting wind, brought us without a hitch of any sort to a recently abandoned Gypsy camp amidst acres of bilberry bushes; and if from this point our progress was slow, since it had to be made in the teeth of what at 1500 feet was almost a gale, we had no doubt as to the direction in which the pickers were moving, wheel-marks being clearly visible along a green road leading over to 'the' Sarn ...
>
> But just then came the smell of wood smoke on the wind, and almost simultaneously the voices of bilberry buyers mounting up from 'the' Sarn. The Gypsies were close at hand, their waggons completely hidden by an encircling belt of trees, within which, on approaching, we saw huge fires burning. Besides John Lock and his family, there were Prices, Smiths, and Stephens; a purple-stained, windbattered throng, clamorous, most of them, for the food which the buyers had brought them from below.
>
> Refreshed, and warmed by the blaze from two young fir-trees, we learned from 'fiddling' John that he was a son of Ezekiel Lock, ... and of Amy Taylor ...; and that John's parents, who were taken to 'the' Rock, near Bewdley, to be buried ..., had eight children in addition ... Old Ezekiel, it appeared, had passed most of his life in upland country, round about Clun, Bishop's Castle, and Knighton, in the mid-Welsh shires of Montgomery, Radnor, and Cardigan, and on the Clee Hills; travelling

always, right up to the time of his death some eight or nine years earlier, with pack-donkeys and tents ... John himself had only lately taken to a waggon; and he, we gathered, was the first of the family to do so.

Even if Ezekiel Lock dabbled in witchcraft, as some of his relations aver, his chief occupation was fiddling; and three or four of his sons are said to play well, John, by common consent, being the finest performer among them, until, quite recently, rheumatism stiffened his fingers. The country dance tunes he knows were, for the most part, favourites of his father's, but some he learned from his Uncle Noah and other Gypsies, and some—not a large number—from gorgios [non-gipsies] encountered here and there in the course of his travels. Which of his brothers accompanied him when first he met Mrs. Leather I do not know; nor much about any of them in fact, except that one got into trouble near Monkland shortly before I was there in 1922, for pulling into a very narrow lane along which hay was being led, and refusing to make way, and for aggravating his offence by sawing the shafts off the obstructed haycart and burning them. Evidently he has inherited an undue share of his maternal grandfather's propensities; unlike John, who never forgets that he is one of the 'Gentleman Locks'.

Mrs. Leather noted that after her meeting with John Lock he often visited her at Weobley, 'introducing himself by playing away under our windows', but she added in 1925 that 'his wife tells me he is now crippled with rheumatism and unable to play'. In 1912 Cecil Sharp visited a James Lock, aged 60, at 17 Springfield Terrace, Newport. The relationship of James with other members of the family is unclear, as is that of James's (unnamed) father, a left-handed player who nevertheless strung his fiddle normally. From him, James learned 'Morning Star'. James, like John, knew 'Blue-eyed Stranger', 'Greensleeves', 'Mad Moll and the Cheshire Hounds', and 'Three Jolly Sheepskins'. Unlike him, he played 'Bonnets so blue'. James played for dancing at Albrighton (see chapter 11), where Gordon Ashman told me that when the sons of one of

Music for 'Morning Star'

Charlie Lock, brother of Esmerelda (see below), a rare photograph of c.1910

the Locks chose to go on a bike ride instead of washing his horses the father took an axe and chopped up their bikes. (The same man had a real beauty of a daughter, of whom he said ''Er could draw a duck off water').

Members of the Lock family carried up and down the border counties the family's reputation for fiddle playing. Until the 1940s at Llanfair Waterdine they played for country dancing in the old barn—variously known as Black, Tithe or Morris Barn—which stood opposite the Red Lion. John Lock's cousin, Herbert, is buried in the churchyard beneath a headstone with a pious and elaborate inscription in Romany which the village children believed to be a curse on anyone who interfered with the grave. The stone was erected thanks to Hubert Smith, town clerk of Bridgnorth and Herbert's brother-in-law. (Herbert's sister, Esmerelda, married Smith in 1874, and, after divorcing him, Francis Hindes Groome, in 1876. For Groome's book, *In Gipsy Tents*, see the bibliography).

Magdalene Weale met other Locks in 1935 in a disused quarry at Snailbeach, near where they were picking wimberries. The oldest of the women told her: 'This is the Lock family, a famous family', and asked whether she had heard of Gipsy Lock, the fiddler:

> I had, and of his retinue of younger brothers of all ages and sizes, with
> their improvised fiddles made out of biscuit tins, and of the merry music
> they made in the days before jazz banished the fiddle from inn and
> village dance. And how, one Christmas eve during a very hard winter,

he had stayed playing too late at the inn, had been overtaken by a snow-storm on his way home, had lain down to rest and never waked again. I had heard it all, and more too. So this old woman was all that was left of the beautiful high-spirited girl, not of Romany blood, who had fallen in love with the handsome fiddler and run away and married him. He had had some trouble, too, to break her into gipsy life, but a broken nose and many a 'lammering' had not dimmed her regard for her stalwart lover, and even now she tells in broken accents of her husband's death in the service of his beloved fiddle, and regrets that none of the later genera-tions has inherited his gift.

There is some confusion here. John Lock's wife, Amy (his cousin), was not a non-gipsy. One of the Locks did perish in the snow with his fiddle by his side, in about 1928, on the Long Mynd or near Church Stoke, depending on the version followed. This was not John, but could have been the elusive Polin, his brother. As to the statement that 'none of the later generations' continued to play the fiddle, Simon Evans relates how in 1938 he tramped four miles to a hollow by the River Rea to deliver a letter addressed to 'Gypsy Lock. Thumper's Hole, Nr. Cleobury Mortimer':

> When I arrived at Gypsy Lock's camp in Thumper's Hole he and all his family seemed as happy as could be. There was a great fire, and the break-fast Mrs. Lock was cooking made me feel hungry. Old Man Lock was playing his fiddle, and some of the little brown children were singing and dancing. Not one of them seemed a bit interested in the letter I had.

Singers

What were the 'little brown children' singing? Charlotte Burne took down songs from gipsy children, Eliza Wharton and her brothers, who travelled in North Shropshire and Staffordshire in the 1880s. These include ballads such as 'The Cruel Mother' and 'The Gipsy Laddie', the carol 'Now Christmas Day is drawing near at hand', and three short love lyrics, including:

My mother sent me for same water [For some water for my tea]
My foot slipp'd and in I tum-bled, My true love came whis-tling by.

> My mother said as I shouldna have him,
> 'Cos that he would break my heart;
> I don't care what my mother tells me,
> I shall take my true love's part.

He will buy me silks and satins,
He will buy me a guinea-gold ring,
He will buy me a silver cradle,
For to lap my baby in.

It so happens that the composer, Ralph Vaughan Williams,—who, incidentally, took down a tune from a Mr. Lock in 1910—noted songs at Weobley in Herefordshire in 1909 and 1912 from a Mrs. Esther Smith, née Whatton, who may have been one of the children listed earlier as Wharton by Burne. Certainly, her repertoire included not only 'My mother sent me' (tune given above) but 'Christmas now' and 'The Cruel Mother'. In turn, one of Esther Smith's 15 children, May (born *c*.1900 at Chepstow), shared some of her repertoire, including 'Under the Leaves' (see chapter 12). She was recorded in 1959 and 1966 as May Bradley, by Fred Hamer.

Vaughan Williams wrote memorable settings of Housman's poems in *On Wenlock Edge* (1909) but he did not visit Shropshire in pursuit of traditional songs. His friend and fellow composer, George Butterworth, did, in 1908. (He was later killed during the First World War). Butterworth noted 'As I roamed out', 'The Trees they do grow high' and 'Willie the waterboy' from a Mrs. Whiting at Broseley, and 'Green Mossy Banks of the Lea' from Mr. Lockly, the 80-year-old sexton at High Ercall. Cecil Sharp followed, with visits in October and December 1911, July 1912, and August and September 1913. He seems to have been mainly interested in finding carols (see chapter 12), and he noted only a handful of other items, including 'Dabbling in the Dew' from Mrs. Fanny Duff (aged 54) at Newport Union (Workhouse), 'A Good Jug of Ale' from Mrs. Halfpenny (64) at Lilleshall, and 'Van Diemen's Land' from Samson Price (58) at Little Stretton.

Sharp could have visited other singers like Arthur Lewis, who would have been in his middle 30s at the time, and Arthur Lane, some ten years younger. Lewis (for whom, see chapter 12) was recorded by Peter Kennedy in 1952, together with Bert Edwards of Little Stretton and others, including the 80-year-old Mrs Cook of Cardington. In 1968 by a happy accident John Seymour met Arthur Lane of Stanton Long (for whom, see also chapter 8), and described the occasion in his book, *The Countryside Explained*:

> I had been driving along this remote lane one flaming day in June, and had seen an old man scything grass on a very steep hillside. I stopped and climbed up to him. I had a strange sensation that he had been expecting me. 'I were just going to have a rest', he said. 'Come down and have a drop of wine'. Arthur Lane was his name, but they called him Lane the Drum because he lived in a house which had once been a pub called 'The Drum and Monkey'.

Lane, born in 1884, had been farmworker, small-holder, publican and council workman. As well as being a singer he played the mouth-organ and the melodeon. In 1974 he described to Charles Parker and Philip Donnellan how he had learned several of his songs at Ednop, near Mainstone, when he worked there as a farm labourer, living in. After supper the men would go into the barn, lie down in the straw, and entertain each other:

> One'd sing a song, then another'd sing a song, and then we used to have our eyes shut, singing, passing the time away. Well, it'd come on eleven o'clock, twelve o'clock, one o'clock; we used to go on singing, then perhaps we'd go to sleep - some would. When you wakened up it'd be two o'clock, perhaps. Then we'd get up to go to bed.

Lane also learned songs in pubs and at fairs and shows. He whistled and sang at the plough. Songs like 'All Jolly Fellows that follow the plough' and 'The Farmer's Boy' (see below) were relevant to his work, but he also sang of the wider world in 'Banks of Sweet Dundee', 'The Dark-eyed Sailor' and 'The Gallant Hussar'.

Arthur Lane

The sun went down behind yon hill, Across yon dreary moor. Weary and lame a poor boy came up to a farmer's door. "Can you tell me if any there be That will give me employ For to plough and sow, to reap and to mow, And to be a farmer's boy — To be a farmer's boy.

For my father's dead, and mother's left
With her five children small;
And what is worse for mother still,
I'm the oldest of them all.
Though little I be, I fear no work
If you will me employ,
For to plough and sow, *etc.*

'And if that you won't me employ
One favour I have to ask:
Will you shelter me till the break of day
From this cold winter's blast?
At break of day I'll trudge away
Elsewhere to seek employ,
For to plough and sow', *etc.*

The farmer said, 'Pray, take the lad,
No further let him seek'.
'Oh, yes, dear father', the daughter cried,
While the tear ran down her cheek;
'For those that will work it's hard to want
And wander for employ,
To plough and sow', *etc.*

In course of time he grew a man,
And the good old farmer died;
He left the lad the farm he had,
And his daughter for his bride.
So the boy that was now farmer is;
He sits and thinks with joy
Of the lucky, lucky day he came that way,
To be a farmer's boy, to be a farmer's boy.

One of those who heard Arthur Lane singing and playing his melodeon in pubs was a young farm worker called Fred Jordan, who was born in Ludlow in 1922. Jordan started work, aged 14, at a wage of three shillings a week, an arrangement confirmed at three successive annual hiring fairs, with a small rise each time. During the Second World War hiring changed to six-monthly contracts and wages rose to ten shillings a week. In 1952 Fred Jordan bought a one-up and one-down house at Aston Munslow, and from then on became a freelance farm worker.

Having learned songs not only from Arthur Lane but from his parents and also May Bradley ('May wasn't a bad singer. Different if she got drinking'), he reached the stage when he 'fancied himself as a bit of a singer so in the pub they'd say, "Give us a song, Fred", and I'd say, "What you want? Want

Fred Jordan

an owd un? 'Farmer's Boy' or 'Farmer's Daughter' [title which both he and Lane used for 'The Banks of Sweet Dundee'] or any o' them?". So, "Cost you a pint", I used to say'.

In 1952 Jordan was recorded for the BBC archives by Peter Kennedy, and so began a parallel career as a singer in folk clubs and at festivals. From these circles further songs entered his repertoire, though he assimilated them into his own style of singing and manner of delivery. He made LPs in 1966 and 1974, and a cassette in 1991. In 1998 he contributed to the prestigious series of CDs issued by Topic Records under the title of *The Voice of the People*. He died in July 2002, and the following year a memorial double CD appeared, entitled *A Shropshire Lad: English Folk Songs*.

I first heard him sing in 1966, and then many times subsequently. A song of his that I often asked for was the ancient and magical 'Six Pretty Maids' ('Outlandish Knight'), which he had learned from the Lock family. He often reflected afterwards on how rich a man would have been to boast 'thirty and three' horses in his stable.

'Come bring to me your father's gold,
And your mother's wealth', said he;
'And the two best horses that stands in the stalls,
Where there stands thirty and three'.

So she brought him out her father's gold,
And her mother's wealth brought she;
And the two best horses that stood in the stalls,
Where there stood thirty and three.

She mounted on a milk-white steed,
Him on a dapple-grey;
Many miles they rode till they reached the seaside,
Just as it was breaking the day.

'Come 'light, come 'light from off your steed,
Deliver him now unto me,
For six pretty maids I have drownded here,
The seventh one you shall be.

'Come strip me off your fine silken clothes
And all your jewels', said he;
'For better I sell them for what they are worth
Than they rot with you under the sea'.

'Oh stay, oh stay, you false-hearted man,
And turn your head', said she,
'For not fitting it is that a ruffian like you
A naked lady should see'.

So he turned his head while she undressed
To where the leaves grow green;
She caught him by the small of the waist
And she flung him into the sea.

He plungèd high, he plungèd low,
And at last the side reached he.
'Oh save my life, my pretty fair maid,
And my bride you shall be'.

'Lie there, lie there, you false-hearted man,
Lie there instead of me,
For if six pretty maids you have drownded here,
The seventh one have drownded thee'.

So she mounted on her milk-white steed,
And she led his dapple-grey;
And fast she rode till she reached her own house
Just as it was breaking the day.

Now the parrot that was in the window so high
Looked down as he saw her ride by:
'Oh where hast thou been, thou wilful child?
Some ruffian has led thee astray'.

'Don't prittle, don't prattle, my pretty Polly,
And tell no tales of me,
And thy cage shall be made of the glittering gold,
And the door of the best ivory'.

'Why shout you so loud, my pretty Polly,
So loud and so early, Polly?'
'Oh the cat has climbed up the window so high,
And I fear that he will have me'.

'Well done, well done, my pretty Polly,
You've changed your tale well for me;
So thy cage shall be made of the glittering gold,
And the door of the best ivory'.

Sources

Such singers drew upon the body of traditional material circulating orally. This was topped up by songs originating in the music halls. Arthur Lane, for example, sang 'Darkest House', 'Don't Go down the Mine, Daddy', 'Last summer time I went away to Dover by the sea' and 'We're best for one another'. Fred Jordan learned 'Break the News to Mother' (1897) from his mother, appropriately enough, and 'The Volunteer Organist' (1893) from his father. Other songs of local composition were taken into oral tradition and circulated for longer or shorter periods. Jordan's 'When the frost is on the pumpkin' appears to be of that kind, but the text is in fact by the American poet, James Whitcomb Riley (1849–1916):

When your ap-ples' been all gar-ner'd And your man-gold harvest's due When your ei-der ma-shings o-ver And your wo-men folk come through, It sets my heart a-ti-cking, Like the ti-cking of a clock, When the frost is on the pump-kin And the fodder in the shock.

Oh the canking of the gander as he leads his mighty flock,
The stepping and the stamping of the strutting turkey cock.

Oh the husky, rusky tussle of the husky, rusky corn,
I shall see the ploughshare shining on the headlands in the morn.

The earliest record of named singers in Shropshire may be that of 1581/2 concerning John Melin, a Shrewsbury shoemaker who 'did walke at undue time of night for to sing', together with Ellis Beddo, Humphrey Groome (both shoemakers) and Thomas Will (shearman). A decade later, Thomas Jones of Longdon-upon-Tern was apprehended as a rogue or vagabond for singing May songs (see chapter 12).

Altogether more serious were the verses circulated in Montford in August 1604 which alleged that Joan, wife of the vicar, Rev. Henry Cunde, was promiscuous. A copy preserved in the Public Record Office is signed 'Thy very good friend, Jack Straw', though the authors were probably John and Thomas Browne. The 'infamous libel' caused the unfortunate woman so much 'inward grief and sorrowe that she presentlye fell sicke and pyned, wasted and consumed away, and shortly afterwards dyed'. The text of a home-made song appeared in the documentation relating to a complaint made by William Meddins, the curate at Rowton, six miles from Wellington, that he was the victim of a libel, fixed on a post in the church, circulated in the form of written copies, and also read out and sung by another clergyman, Roger Low, Jane, his wife, and Richard Rocksby, yeoman:

Thereto it is and sure Ile laye my lief
That Richard the Myllnar [miller] hath Iaped [seduced] the parsons wief
The parson doeth not him blame
he knoweth it and wynkes at the same
She is a Iade he is a Cuckwold
A knave and a Bawde
The apparitor [officer of the ecclesiastical court] will beare blame
When Master Chauncellor doeth know that he wynkes at the same.

It seems that attacks made in the form of verses, placarded and sung, were fairly common at the time. An example in Welsh from Llansilin, just over the Denbighshire border, dates from 1612. Two years later, at Wellington, Jane, the wife of John Bennett, a tanner, was accused of being a whore in verses 'published dyvulged spoken sunge and repeated' by Thomas Forster, clothier, and others including a mercer, a feltmaker, spinsters and labourers. Again in 1614, at Sheinton, near Much Wenlock, two gentlemen, Richard Batley and John Shaw, were accused of contriving 'libellous songes and rymes' and fixing them 'upon postes and scattered in publique places', as well as 'singing the same and ... delivering copyes thereof to divers other persons'. The victim, Henry Wood, seems to have been targeted because of his catholic faith. An obscure, 30-line verse, which includes puns on Wood's name, ends:

> Sheinton for my grave thankes thou shalt have
> When woodecocke ends his lief
> Lend him a rome for hether he will come
> but lay him with Cooke his wief.

In 1615 William Pennell of 'Barnes Landes' appeared at the Ludlow arch-deanery court charged with 'making and singing a rhyme':

> Goodman Blake can knitt a knott
> hey dirrie sandie,
> and goodwief Blake can crusse [?cool] a pott
> that is as fine as can be
>
> William Blake is poor & bare
> &c
> he gaged [pawned] his sawe for a pott of ale
> &c
>
> Robert Blake can heele a hose
> &c
> the goodwief Camebridg will not parte from the droppings of her nose
> &c
>
> Ann Blake is as leane as a rake
> [&c]
> And Margerie Blake can cracke a cake
> &c

Proof seems to have been lacking, because Pennel's case was dismissed, but in 1619/20 a Ludlow man, William Sherwood, had to pay a fine of £3 6s. 8d. 'for singing of Rybaldry songs and using undecent speeches to Richard Bulkley Esquire in an alehouse'. Again in Ludlow, in 1636, Richard Jenkin failed to appear on a charge of 'singinge of Rimes against all the men and their wifes or the most parte of them in the parish'.

Such proceedings fell into disuse, but the habit of making songs continued. Richard Gough mentions Thomas Jukes of Myddle, who had 'three sons, and never a good one'. Of these, Vincent, the oldest

> went to be a seaman, and was taken prisoner by the Turks, of Tangiers, and another Englishman, his companion. These two, after some time, changed theire religion (if they had any before), and became Turks, and

soe gott more favour and liberty than other slaves. After some time, these two were sent roveing in a small vessell, and onely eight Turks in theire company; and these two, watching an opportunyty, when the Turks were all under deck, shut downe the hatches, and kept them there, and hoisted up saile for England, and put the Turks on shoare, and sold the vessell. Vincent Juckes bought a new sute of cloaths, and a good horse, and came done to Myddle, and was there att what time they were singing ballads abroad in Markett townes of this adventure. Hee went after to sea again, and was heard of noe more.

In the 19th century people still 'made a ballet' (ballad) on an event or person. Such parochial productions, like those of earlier times, often enjoyed only a brief vogue, and were not committed to writing or print. An exception was 'The Loppington Bear' which in about 1822 marked the occasion when a local shoemaker, Andrew Wycherley, took fright at an excavated treestump which he took for a bear on the loose. The collective authors were Joseph Harper and Richard Davies, shoemakers, Windsor, farmer, and Williams, blacksmith: 'We all on us maden a bit on it, and when we thoughten on anything we putten it down'. The song circulated orally for over half a century before the words and tune were taken down.

A farmer at Whixall incurred the resentment of villagers in the 1850s when he turned a fierce bull into his fields at nutting time to deter boys from venturing there. When the man was later killed by his own bull local people responded with a ballad of which Georgina Jackson quotes one verse:

The pound at Loppington

> 'E got 'is wealth by fraud an' stealth,
> As fast as 'e could scraup it;
> Theer com'd a bull, an' cracked 'is skull,
> An' 'iked [tossed] 'im in a sawpit.

Jackson gives a snatch of another 'old Shropshire song' which clearly derives from a printed ballad sheet of the late 18th or early 19th century:

> Cheer up your drooping spirits,
> And cease now complaining,
> Although you've suffer'd hard,
> Still fresh hopes there's remaining.
> You see the corn is falling,
> In every market town, sir,
> In spite of roguish badgers [dealers]
> The price it must come down, sir.
> Then thankful be to Providence,
> Who heard our wretched cry,
> And send us glorious crops of grain,
> Our wants for to supply.

Print

As early as 1577 a ballad registered with the Company of Stationers in London was entitled 'Figure of ij [2] monstrous children borne at Wemme in Shropshire'. Perhaps it was among those 'ballads and some good books' which a pedlar brought to Richard Baxter's father's door at Eaton Constantine. The mature Baxter might well have tolerated 'Salops supplicacion to almighty God', which dealt with the plague affecting Shrewsbury in 1632. However, neither 'Shrewsberry' (1658), beginning 'Come listen, young Gallants of Shrewsbury fair Town', nor 'The Shrop-shire Wakes or Hey for Christmas' (1672–95) with their celebration of pleasure would have gained his approbation.

'George Barnwell', registered in 1624 but only surviving in a copy of some 50 years later, turns up in Percy's *Reliques*, though not from the Shifnal manuscript. It relates how an apprentice, George Barnwell, takes up with a fast woman, Sarah Milwood. After running out of money he travels to Ludlow, where he kills and robs a rich uncle. Sarah is arrested in London, presumably as an accessory, and is taken to Ludlow, where she is 'jug'd, condemn'd, and hang'd, / For murder incontinent'. George escapes abroad but 'For murder in Polonia, / Was ... hang'd in chains'. For many years, Huck's Barn at Ludford was pointed out as being connected with the murder: George waited there until his uncle returned from Leominster Fair, and did the deed in an adjacent wood. The barn is still shown on OS maps, by a bridleway off Overton Road.

Huck's Barn near Ludlow, from the Gentleman's Magazine, *1810*

Rather more creditably than Barnwell, John Benbow (1653-1702) is commemorated in two ballads printed in his lifetime which remained in oral tradition for over 200 years afterwards. They do not mention his Shrewsbury connections, though inn signs remember him there, and he has a memorial in St. Mary's Church. According to one story, the Shrewsbury-born sailor once came back from sea after a long absence and his sister, Ellinor, failed to recognise him when he entered the coffee house she kept in St. Mary's churchyard. Admiral Benbow died a hero, and is buried at Kingston, Jamaica.

None of these ballads was produced in Shropshire, though there were some local sources. Roger Ward, a

Admiral Benbow Inn, Shrewsbury

254

Ruyton-born printer, had the contents of his Shrewsbury shop seized in 1585 for debt. The inventory of 546 items of stock and materials distrained showed that most of his publications were devotional manuals and grammar school textbooks. However, he also printed popular stories such as *Valentine and Orson* and jocular tales such as *The Jests of Scroggin*. A 'boxe for ballates' (whatever that was) is also listed, and one ballad is recorded by its title, 'fittes morries' (Fitzmorris)—it refers to an event of 1579 in Ireland. Ward is known to have printed two other ballads and it is possible that he produced more.

This is a fairly meagre output, and only in the 18th century did further local ballad printers emerge. Oddly

*Benbow monument
in St. Mary's Church, Shrewsbury*

enough, many of these produced 'new songs' and carols in Welsh. Thomas Durston issued some 30 such sheets or booklets between 1712 and 1762. Other Welsh language printers at Shrewsbury were Stafford Prys (1758-82), John Rhydderch (1715-68), John Rogers (1707-24) and William Williams (1765-68). William Edwards (1793-1810) and John Salter (1789-91) were in the same line of business at Oswestry. Collectively, they produced some 200 items which have survived. The earliest of these had the curious title of '*Ymddiddan Rhwng Gwr Ieuangc a'r Golommen Ynglwch Dewis Gwrair*' (1710) (Conversation between a young man and a dove concerning the choice of a woman). Many more sheets are known to have been produced in Shrewsbury, though they lack a printer's name. Some were commissioned by Welsh ballad writers, who presumably sold them on their own account, mainly no doubt in Wales, though it seems likely that there would have been a market in north-west Shropshire (see chapter 2).

The partnership of John Cotton and Joshua Eddowes published such material in English. Cotton (from 1740) and Eddowes (from 1749) were printers and

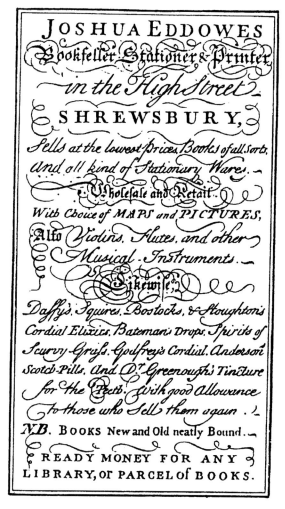

Joshua Eddowes advertisement,
in business 1749-75

booksellers in Shrewsbury who joined forces in 1761. One item the partners issued took the form of an 8-page booklet entitled 'An Elegy on the Much Lamented Death of Sir Watkin Williams, Bart. Who died by a Fall from his Horse in Hunting, near Wrexham, in Denbighshire, on Tuesday, the 26th of September, 1749'. Even this adds a Welsh translation of the title, with the indication that the tune prescribed is 'Nutmik and Sînsir' (Nutmeg and Ginger), a copy of which happens to have survived.

James Waidson, printing in Shrewsbury from 1776, was at Dog Lane in 1780, Barker Street in 1790, then back at Dog Lane until he went out of business in 1803. He may have been succeeded by the R. Waidson listed in directories in c.1815, and he in turn by Mary Waidson, 1821-2. Burne says 'I have had a great number of these [their ballad sheets] placed at my disposal', but mentions, in addition to 'election squibs', only 'Ben Block' and 'The Gallant Hero', and quotes two more. She gives the full text of 'An English lady in love with a Welsh Plough-boy', printed by M. Waidson, and points out that 'Young Welshmen were in the habit of taking service at Shropshire farms, coming to England to seek their fortune':

> All in the month of May, when flowers were a-springing,
> I went into the meadows, some pleasure for to find;
> I went into the meadows, I turned myself around,
> Where I saw a pretty Welsh lad a-ploughing up the ground.

And as he was a-ploughing his furrows deep and low,
Cleaving his sods in pieces, his barley for to sow;
It is the pretty Welsh lad that's all in my mind,
And many hours I wander this young man for to find.

An old man came a-courting me, a man of birth and fame,
Because I would not have him my parents would me blame,
It is the pretty Welsh lad that runs all in my mind,
A poor distressed lady, a Welsh lad to my mind.

I wish the pretty sky-lark would mount up in the air,
That my pretty plough-boy the tidings he might hear,
Perhaps he would prove true to me, and ease my aching heart,
It is for the pretty Welsh lad that I do feel the smart.

I'll wait until I see him to tell him my mind,
And if he don't relieve me I shall think him unkind,
And if he'll not grant me his love, then distracted I shall be;
Into some grove I'll wander, where no one shall me see.

Burne also reprints 'The Shropshire Militia Boys' from 'Waidson, Shrewsbury', which could have been R. Waidson. The Shropshire Militia went to Portugal in 1809, when the song was probably first written. After returning in 1814 it went off to St. Helena the following year to guard Napoleon, and this may have occasioned a revival. Burne points out that Lord Hill, who is mentioned, became a peer only in 1814. The whereabouts of any original copies of these ballads is unfortunately not known.

 William Baugh, established at Ellesmere in 1792 as a stationer, became from 1821-7 a printer, music seller, bookbinder and bookseller, and then from 1834-9 simply a printer. I have seen only one sheet printed by him, 'Death and the Lady', with a lugubrious woodcut of a skeleton, hourglass and fatal arrow in hand, hovering over a sleeping and doomed woman.

John France set up as a printer in Shrewsbury in 1827 and was in the Mardol from 1834-9. He issued a series of carols (for which, see chapter 12) and also

DEATH AND THE LADY.

DEATH,

FAIR Lady lay your costly robes aside,
No longer must you glory in your pride,
Take leave of all your carnal vain delight,
I'm come to summon you away this night.

LADY

What bold attempt is this, pray let me know.
From whence you come and whither must I go,
Shall I, who am a Lady, stoop or bow,
To such a pale-fac'd visage, who art thou?

DEATH,

Do you not know me? Well, I'll tell you then,
'Tis I that conquers all the sons of men,
No pitch of honour from my dart is free,
My name is death, have you not heard of me?

LADY.

Yes I have heard of thee time after time,
But being in the glory of my prime,
I did not think you would have call'd so soon,
Must my morning sun go down before 'tis noon,

DEATH.

Talk not of noon, you may as well be mute,
This is no time at all for to dispute,
Your riches, jewels, gold and garments,brave,
Your houses & land must all new masters have
Though thy vain heart to riches was inclin'd
Yet thou must die and leave them all behind.

LADY,

My heart is cold, it trembles at the news,
Here's bags of gold if thou wilt me excuse,
And seize on such, thus finish thou the strife,
On those as are most weary of their life,
Are there not bound in prison strong,
In bitter grief of soul have languish'd long,

All such would find the grave a place of rest,
From all their grief in which they are opprest,
Besides there's many with hoary beads.
And palsy joints by which their strength is fled.

DEATH,

Though they by age are full of grief and pain,
Yet their appointed time they must remain,
I come to none but when my warrant's seal'd,
And when it is, they must all submit and yield,
I take no bribe, believe me this is true,
Prepare yourself to go, I am come for you.

LADY.

Death, be not severe, let me obtain
A little longer time to live and reign,
Fain would I stay, if thou my life would spare,
I have a daughter beautiful and fair,
I wish to see her wed whom I adore,
Grant me but this, and I shall ask no more.

DEATH,

This is a slendour frivolous excuse,
I have you fast, and will not let you loose,
Leave her to Providence, for you must go,
Along with me whether you will or no.
I, Death, the King can make to leave his crown
And at my feet they lay their sceptres down,
If unto kings this favour I dont give,
But cut them off, can you expect to live?
Beyond the limits of your time and space,
No? I must send you to another place.

LADY,

You learned doctors now exert your skill,
And let not Death of me obtain his will,
Prepare your cordials, let me comfort find,
My gold shall fly like chaff before the wind,

DEATH.

Forbear to call, their skill will never do,
They are but mortals here as well as you,
I give the fatal wound, my dart is sure,
'Tis far beyond the doctors skill to cure,
How freely can you buy your riches fly,
To purchase life rather than yield to die,
But when you flourished in all your store,
You would not give one penny to the poor,
Tho' in God's name their suit 'o you did make,
You would not spare one penny for his sake,
My Lord beheld wherein you did amiss,
And calls you hence to give account for this.

LADY,

Oh! heavy news, must I no longer stay,
How shall I stand in the great Judgment Day?
Down from her eyes the crystal tears did flow,
She said, none knows what I do undergo,
Upon a bed of sorrow here I do lie,
My carnal life makes me afraid to die,
Lord Jesus Christ have mercy on my soul,
And tho' I do deserve thy righteous frown,
Yet, pardon, Lord, and send a blessing down,
Then with a dying sigh her heart did break,
And did the pleasures of this world forsake,
Thus may we see the high and mighty fall,
For cruel death shews no respect at all,
To any one of high or low degree,
Great men submit to death as well as me,
Tho' they are gay, their lives are but a span,
A lump of CLAY, so vile a creature's man, (care,
Then happy they whom CHRIST has made his
Die in the LORD, and then they blessed are.

PRINTED & SOLD BY W. BAUGH, ELLESMERE.

'The Last Farewell to England of Frost, Williams, and Jones', dealing with the penal transportation of Welsh Chartists in 1839.

Like their earlier counterparts, metropolitan printers took an occasional interest in Shropshire events. John Pitts of London's Seven Dials issued, some time after 1832, 'The Sorrowful Weeping and Lamentation Of Four Lovely Orphans, left by J. Newton, A Wealthy Farmer, who was Executed at Shrewsbury'. The sheet, with a hanging scene partly cribbed from William Hogarth's engraving of the death of the idle apprentice, has two parts,'The Orphans' Lamentation' and 'The Murder, Trial, Sentence, Execution, and [slightly illogically] Confession', written by a John Jackson. No doubt sensational events such as these—the murder of a pregnant wife discovered only at a second inquest, following by an execution which left four orphans—were needed to draw the attention of the wider world to Shrewsbury.

Various pit disasters commanded a local audience. Over a period of half a century members of one family called Morgan produced a series of ballads on the subject. 'Sudden Death of Three Poor Colliers' (1851) and 'The Stirchley Tragedy' (c.1861) were by Jeremiah Morgan. W.R. Morgan of 3 King Street, Dawley, wrote 'The Springwell Pit Accident' (1872), while S.T. Morgan of Ketley produced 'In Memoriam' (1910), on the seven lives lost when a wire rope snapped at Kemberton Pits, Madeley, and two items on a different topic, 'The Red Lake Murder' (1900) and 'The Stirchley Murder' (1909).

It is interesting to see the genre reaching the 20th century. Ivor J. Brown remembered 'at least one mine deputy, the late J. Lycett of Madeley, who in the

1950s, if so inspired, could produce in minutes a dozen verses on the smallest of incidents'. One wonders whether any of his work has been preserved.

Printed ballads were made for the needs of the moment. Many, perhaps most, were ephemeral. Some captured the collective memory and endured. We still sing of brave Benbow and of jolly ploughboys because of the songs' human and musical qualities, even if we had to learn the them at school or in a folk club rather than from workmates or relatives.

CHAPTER 11

Dance and Drama

In the early 17th century when puritanism pressed, dancing, if not a civil crime, could conflict with church law when it took place during church service time on Sunday, and since these were among the few hours available for leisure, offenders were not uncommon. Such cases provide valuable documentation which might otherwise have been lacking.

Men and women involved in general or social dancing are named, and the circumstances specified. A specific form of dancing, morris, also came in for censure. This was the preserve of men only, for the most part, and because of the higher degree of skill involved it could bring in rewards of money or of food and drink. Modern morris dancers often attempt to invest the activity with a certain mystique; they readily talk of pagan fertility rites. Yet the first recorded instance of morris was on St. Dunstan's Day (19 May) in London in 1448, when any fertility rites could have brought very serious consequences to those involved.

In one form or another the traditional morris lingered until the 1930s, which is remarkable enough, but then after a gap of several decades it enjoyed a renaissance. At the beginning of the 21st century six or seven revival sides were in existence in Shropshire, including men's, women's and mixed. Traditional social dancing of various kinds also managed to survive, thanks both to those keen to dance and musicians willing and able to play.

Village drama also proved to have perennial appeal. It, too, had to outlast persecution by religious zealots. Like morris, folk plays died out, only to be brought back to life—inevitably altered in purpose and in personnel—but still a living link with the past and an opportunity for present enjoyment.

'Drincking, dauncing and plaieng'

References in the church court proceedings are often to social—or anti-social, as they saw it—dancing, though the morris is sometimes specifically mentioned (see below). An inquest at Bridgnorth which can be dated roughly between 1305 and 1315 recorded the events of St. James the Apostle's Day (25 July) when some men of Sir Roger Mortimer's came to the town 'to a round dance for the sake of recreation'. A quarrel arose between the visitors and the Bridgnorth men, the outcome of which was the death of one of the latter.

In most instances, though, offences against religious practice were at issue, chiefly dancing on Sundays. They illustrate how widespread was the love of dancing, since they are recorded from Bitterley, Cleobury North, Farlow, Greete, Hopesay, Kinlet, Little Wenlock, Myndtown, Long Stanton (now Stanton Long), Neen Savage, Pontesbury, Stokesay, Stottesdon, Stow and Westbury. There must have been further cases which escaped notice or proceedings.

A typical expression of hostility towards dancing comes from Richard Baxter (1615-91), the puritan writer and preacher who spent the years between roughly 1625 and 1640 at Eaton Constantine (where the family house still stands):

> In the village where I lived the Reader read the Common-Prayer briefly, and the rest of the Day even till dark Night almost, except Eating time, was Spent in Dancing under a May-Pole and a great Tree, not far from my Father's Door: where all the Town did meet together: And though one of my Father's own Tenants was the Piper, he could not restrain him, nor break the Sport: So that we could not read the Scripture of own Family without the great disturbance of the Taber and Pipe and Noise in the Street.

Dancers recorded in the church proceedings are often of humble circumstances, such as Bridget Hare, servant (Greete, 1606), and 'Morrice Jones, Mr. Actons man' (Farlow, 1608), Thomas Dallow and Richard Harding, ale sellers (Cleobury North, 1619/20, and Kinlet, 1635, respectively), John Simons, servant to Richard Dike, Roger Duddell, servant to Maurice Fewterell, Anna Gefferes, maidservant to William Cox, and Anna Gittins, servant to Mr. Thomas (Long Stanton, 1635). As the list indicates, both sexes were involved. One could add Peter Edwards and Margaret, 'his wief' ('prophaning the saboath daie, viz. drincking, dauncing and plaieng' at Stokesay, 1606), Thomas Doughty and Margaret his wife, John Sharpe and Jane, his sister-in-law, Mr. Heynam's three daughters of Wheathill, with others (for similar behaviour at Farlow Wake, 1608); and Jane Chilton ('for keeping drinking & dauncinge in her house at tyme of eveninge prayer the xv[th] of Aprill beynge the saboath day' at Little Wenlock, 1621/2).

Clearly, dancers needed music, and musicians in several cases were also charged. 'Thomas yop minstrell' played at Greete, and Anthony Protherough, another minstrel from Brampton Bryan, at Stow (both 1606). Thomas Elcocks was the offending musician at Stottesdon (1618). In none of these cases is the instrument identified, but William Carpenter, piper, played for dancing at Stanton Long (1635). At Westbury, Richard Titherland played the pipe and tabor every Sunday in June 1637 'before the whole service was ended ... and by his meanes hath drawen divers to profane the saboath by daunceinge at unlaw-full times'. William Titherland, who must have been a relative, described only as a minstrel, faced a similar charge at the same place the following year.

Dancing was sometimes associated with other activities which gave offence. The churchwardens at Stow, Lewis Gough and John Griffiths (the latter from Lurkenhope), were themselves in trouble in 1622 for failing to report 'such persons as plaied ... at Keiles [?], at quoiting, and such as did dance, and tiple and drinck in alehowses ... in time of divine praier in the parish churche'. To make matters worse, 'there was tennys plaieng there the said yere *diebus dominicis* [on lord's days]'.

'Morice dauncers'

A very similar pattern exists for morris dancing, though in at least one instance support rather than opposition is shown: the bailiffs' and chamberlains' accounts at Ludlow for 1526/9 show a payment of seven shillings for 'gowne clothe to Morris piper ayenst cristenmas'. Some 60 years later a very different attitude lies behind the churchwardens' enquiry at St. Mary's, Shrewsbury, as to 'whether there have bene any Lordes of mysrule, or sommer lordes, or ladies or any Disguised persons, as morice dauncers, maskers, or mummers or such lyke within ye parishe ether in ye nativitide or in sommer, or any any other tyme, and what be their names' (1583/4).

At Stanton Lacy in 1611/12, William Wilkes allegedly 'counterfaited the divell in the morrice dance uppon the Saboath daie'. It may be that Isaac the drummer and Humphrey Brioley were also involved, the former for playing during divine service, the latter 'for plaeing then on his instrument, swearing, brawling, and quarreling and committing other disorders'. A few years earlier in the same village a minstrel called Malpas played 'and divers daunced after his music on Whitsondaie' (8 June 1617). Philip Abree, who hired minstrels on that occasion, in addition on St. John's Day (24 June) 'being ... [dis]guised and leading the way to a Morris dawnce, ... was the principall cause that all the Morice dawncers and divers other were absent the same daie from morninge praier'. Abree confessed the error of his ways, had to do penance (see chapter 5), and was dismissed with admonishment.

On Sunday 30 May 1619 at Shrewsbury a three-cornered fight erupted between members of the crowd, Francis France and other morris dancers, and Ralph Whoode, lord of misrule and the rest of his company. The list is full of graphic detail:

> William Cheshire, glover, wounded redd John ap Morgan, servant
> Richard Harries, corser [horse dealer], hit Richard de ffranckwell and hit
>   ffrancis ffrance with a staff
> George Cheshire, glover, broke Euan Jones's head
> David Plume, tailor, hit William Cock, tailor, on the head with a flagstaff
> Owen Williams, labourer, struck William Cock on the head with a staff
> David Raynoldes assaulted William Cock
> redd John ap Morgan made two affrays on William Cheshire Richard,
> Mr. Rock's man, made one affray on William Cheshire.

Only two of the eight morris dancers seem to have become embroiled in the fighting. The remaining six were Simon Holmes, David Stanley, Roger Adderton, William Oakley, Richard Machin and Richard Groves. Their trades are not given.

In the same year Thomas Chelmick of Abdon borrowed the cloth for the communion table from his local church and lent it to Nicolas Millichap of Clee St. Margaret for use 'as a flagg in a morrice dance' at Whitsuntide. As a result, a whole number of people had to make confession and do penance: Nicolas Millichap himself, together with Edward and William Millichap of Stoke St. Milborough, Thomas and John Chelmick of Abdon, Joseph Tedstell, William a Maund and John Barret of Clee St. Margaret, Nicolas Evans, alias Tudge, of Munslow, and Walker the servant of William Knott of the Heath. In addition, the same penalties were incurred by Adam Wilding, drummer, Nicolas Abdon, who was 'ffrier' (Friar Tuck), John Bottrell, for carrying a sword, Richard Endlick, the hobby horse, and Walter Millichap, the lord's fool.

On occasions, it appears, so as to economise on time lost to dancing, the morris men attended church services in full kit, much to the fury of people like Richard Baxter:

> And sometimes the Morrice-Dancers would come into the Church, in all their Linnen and Scarfs and Antick Dresses, with the Morrice-bells jingling at their leggs. And as soon as the Common Prayer was read, did haste out presently to their Play again.

At least his anger provided a vivid glimpse of the dancers in their costume.

In 1652 a petition sent to the magistrates at Much Wenlock declared:

> That all wee whoe names are subscribed Inhabitants of the Parishe of Astley Abbots doe certifye that upon Munday in Whitsunday week being the 7th of June last past there came a Morrice daunce forth of the Parish of Broseley with six sword bearers and a rude companye of followers throwe ye whole bodie of this our said Parish being uninvited by any one within the said Parish that wee doe know of. And coming to Nordley unto the house of Richard Pensham a lycenced ale seller

calling for what drinke they pleased left most parte thereof unpaid and nott onely insculted the people of the house butt also al the rest of the neighbors and people there present with som that were absent that have bine aproved frendes and servants to ye Parliament of England as likewise Mr. Crowther who desireing them to pay ye poore woman for their drinke they there upon presently called her bad names many tymes and in this way misbehaveing themselves in letting theire tongues run at large that yf there had bine a considerable partye to have mashed them yt is beleeved there would have bine a greate fray and blood shed yf nott murder comitted many of those rude persons haveing borne armes against ye Parliament as will be mad to apeare to your worships.

Morris On

With the Restoration, attitudes changed. The ballad, 'Shropshire Wakes', printed between 1672 and 1695, happily says:

> The Morrice-dancers will be ready,
> Meat and drink enough to lave ye:
> And in a Fools dress will be little Neddy,
> To entertain our Christmas Lady.

In 1688 and '89, far from opposing the 'bedlam morris', the Glovers' Company of Shrewsbury gave financial support. The meaning of bedlam here is unclear, but it may have implied dancing round sticks placed in the ground.

According to a statement quoted in guidebooks, a tombstone in Willey churchyard, near Much Wenlock, bears an inscription to a Margery Brider, who died in 1756 at the age of 113, and danced with the morris the year before. However, Gordon Ashman established that the woman was in fact buried at neighbouring Harrow, though no tombstone survived there. He also discovered that, as Margery Symonds, she had in 1701 given birth to a bastard son, Joseph, whom she blamed on a vagabond, Thomas Pritchard. Corroboration of her morris dancing is still lacking.

A touching story concerns the arrest in Queen Square, Westminster, in August 1817, of John Cadman, Rowland and William Fowler, Edward Herbert, and five other morris dancers. The magistrate, a Mr. Fielding, before whom they appeared, noticed a paper in one of their hats marked 'Colliers from Shropshire'. When he found that the nine men had only two shillings between them, all in halfpence, although he could have ordered their imprisonment as vagrants, he not only discharged them but instructed the clerk to give them half a crown apiece out of court funds. However he required them to leave London that day and to seek employment outside the town, and also to forfeit their morris gear.

The Times report of the occasion is doubly useful. It shows that the morris served as a fund-raising expedient for hungry men, and it provides details of the dancers' dress and activity:

these nine men were decked out in all the colours of the rainbow, by means of ribands of various colours, white, red, and yellow paper round the edges of their hats, to imitate silver and gold lace, and other absurd imitations of finery, made their appearance .., one of them bearing in his hand a tambarine, and the others with sticks in theirs, and began dancing in their usual grotesque way.

There is no information as to where these men came from, but in the 19th and 20th centuries morris dancers were reported for over a score of towns and villages in Shropshire, including Ashford Carbonel, Aston-on-Clun, Bishop's Castle, Bridgnorth, Bromdon, Broseley, Clee Hill, Coalbrookdale, Dawley, Grinshill, Harley, Hodnet, Homer, Ironbridge, Ketley, Lydbury North, Ludlow, Madeley, Madeley Wood, Much Wenlock, Newport, Onibury, Oswestry, Shifnal, Shrewsbury, Stretton Westwood and Whitchurch. Many more places would have received visits from morris sides. In almost every case at this stage (unlike the Whitsuntide of earlier times) the activity took place at Christmas or in the winter. The participants were working men, often unemployed because of the season. 'It is a common thing in hard winters for frozen-out bricklayers or quarrymen to get up a morris-dancing party, and dance in the streets of the neighbouring towns and villages to collect money'. So wrote Burne, adding that 'among the Severn-side watermen, the ironworkers, colliers, and potters

The Shrewsbury Arcadian Morris Dancers shown in the Square at Shrewsbury when they took part in a Cycle Carnival in 1906. They look decidedly downhearted in the rain, and bear no resemblance to morris dancers as we know them

of Madeley, Colebrook Dale, and Broseley, and also the Clee Hill quarrymen, morris-dancing is a living art'.

Several sources provide descriptions of dancers' costume and actions. At Ketley in about 1840 colliers dressed in grotesque, be-ribboned clothes, and clashed sticks. In Shrewsbury, one January in the 1870s, five bricklayers out of work because of frost carried trowels, and five others, short, thick staves. To the music of a fiddle they danced in two lines, trowels hitting sticks. A fool with ribbons on hat and coat also had a bell on the back of his belt. A few years later, the tune 'Nae luck about the house' played upon a concertina was heard.

At Broseley in 1885 a dozen or so men with blackened faces—a practice which may have come in after the Jim Crow craze for 'Ethiopian' minstrels was imported from America, starting in 1836—each carried a short stave. Two facing men alternately danced and tapped sticks. The dress was Ruritanian-style military, with plenty of coloured paper added. Performances continued at Christmastime until 1914. After this they were taken up by children and carried on until the 1950s.

A Much Wenlock side which also turned out at Christmas consisted of 12 (later, nine or seven) dancers with blackened hands and faces, some wearing top hats, some dressed as women. Tambourine, triangle and bones, together with a melodeon, provided the music. In the 1930s a troupe interviewed for the BBC said they still came out on Christmas Eve and danced from 6 until 12 pm, and then on Boxing Day—sometimes as far afield as Shrewsbury from midday until midnight, and after that might continue every day until the New Year.

The Much Wenlock morris dancers turned out in full costume in 1935
when they were interviewed for a radio broadcast

'The dying remnants', as she put it, of morris were observed in another village by Lavender Jones:

> In 1930, I spent Christmas with my husband's family in their home in the Clun valley. ... the lads of the village visited all the local inns at Christmas time. They called it 'going niggering', though the villagers called them 'the mummers'. There was practically no dance, 'just a bit of jigging about'. The music consisted of bones, a tambourine, a tin whistle and such like. They blacked their faces and dressed up in any old things they could beg or borrow.

Something similar was encountered by Maisie Herring some 20 years later, who wrote that at Much Wenlock 'Besides speech they have kept alive the traditional Morris dance':

> It began to waver and die out, as the curfew which the Norman church rang died out not so long ago. It was heard of two years ago in a farmhouse near Benthall, and then this year [1949] I came through Wenlock about dusk on a day near Christmas and there they were, half Nigger Minstrels, half make-do-and-mend, but still Morrisers with their known steps and their staves and the immemorial tune:

In fact, the 'immemorial tune' is 'Not for Joe', the music of which was written in 1867 by H.J. Whymark to words by Arthur Lloyd.

In the same year as Herring, Geoffrey Mendham made a much more detailed series of observations:

> I first met Shropshire Morris Men in August 1949 when ... the Westwood Morris Men performed out of season at Much Wenlock Abbey. There were five of them, all dressed carefully in carefully made 'fancy dress', mostly modelled on the circus clown's costume. ... Two carried short stout sticks and the third a small melodeon.
>
> We were told that the full team included another pair of stick men, but only those five were available that day. ... All five had blackened faces and hands and there was an 'aura' of alcohol about them. This they

attributed to the fact that they invariably washed in ale before applying the burnt cork 'because it comes off easier'. ...

The four dancers stood in a square of about 12 ft. inside, with the musician in the centre. ... The musician then played a 16-bar tune loud, fast and very inaccurately. The second strain was recognisable as that of the 'Three Jolly Sheepskins' ... During the first strain the three in motley moved rapidly round each other in a serpentine track ... The step was a rapid rolling walk, executed as if in a hurry to get somewhere.

Meanwhile the top-hatted tambourinist moved fairly slowly anti-clockwise round the set, and performed a variety of polka and rant steps in an almost sitting position. At the end of the first eight bars all were back in their places in the square but with the side joining the stick men shortened to bring them within reach of each other. ... All 'instruments' were played with extreme vigour - and almost ferocity.

In 1978 Dave Jones met Cyril Moseley (aged 63) of Much Wenlock, who provided him with a detailed description of what he called the 'Molly' dancers' costume, and also their ten-man performance, given on the evening of Boxing Day.

In the county at large very few traditional sides survived beyond the 1920s and '30s, and many died even earlier. However, just as Dave Jones was gathering the last recollections of one of the old sides, attempts at revival in Shropshire were already under way. Indeed, the Ironmen were founded in 1976, though instead of out of work quarrymen or the like their 18 members included teachers, systems analysts, a public health inspector, and an RAF officer, supported by a 12-piece band.

Cyril Moseley,
a 'molly dancer'
from Much Wenlock

The Much Wenlock
costume as worn by
Cyril Moseley

Morris dancing at the Show in 1972

The Shrewsbury Morris, which also first danced in 1976, grew out of the activities of the local folk club. Two separate teams or sides were established. The men's was called the Bull and Pump Morris, after the former name of the Castle Inn where they practised. The women's opted for the Shrewsbury Lasses, from the title of a dance tune. Both are still dancing, led respectively by Ray and Bev Langton. The men, in brown cord breeches, green socks, white shirts and green waistcoats, perform mainly dances from the border area, together with original inventions in the same idiom, including the Shrewsbury Bricklayers' Dance, based on a description made in the early 1800s. The pinafore-dressed women favour traditional and original dances with garlands, short sticks and handkerchives—and in one instance, garters. A third, mixed, team of clog dancers has also emerged.

Over the years people from a wide range of occupations, chiefly professional, have been involved. These include, with an age-range from ten to 60, students, teachers, nurses, doctors, college lecturers, clerical, retail and industrial workers, coalman, millwright, architect, optician, pharmacist, occupational therapist, conservationist, cook, chef. All members are encouraged to take up a musical instrument, and as a result a ceilidh band called Pump Action came into being, featuring combinations of melodeon, concertina, guitar, recorder, whistle, banjo and a wide range of percussion. The men and women of Shrewsbury Morris dance every year on the May Day bank holiday in Shrewsbury's Quarry Park, in the Square in the town, and also at local fêtes and shows. Their emphasis is not on historical re-enactment but on entertainment, with a variety of dances and a high standard of performance.

At the beginning of the 21st century in addition to the Shrewsbury Sides there were: the Ironmen, Merrydale Mixed Cotswold Morris, Severn Gilders, Shropshire Bedlams and South Shropshire Morris Men. Performing programmes were extensive, and publicity for many included websites.

Forfeits and Formality

Like the morris, social dancing attracted little attention once the religious tensions of the 17th century had subsided. Richard Gough mentions only in passing that Elizabeth Onslow of Myddle, a fugitive from justice, 'was found upon a hollyday, dancing on the topp of an hill amongst a company of young people'.

Itinerant musicians like the famous Lock family played for village dances such as those held until the late 1940s in the barn opposite the Red Lion at Llanfair Waterdine (see also chapter 10). The fiddler, James Lock, who must have been related to some of the musicians who played at Llanfair, told Cecil Sharp in 1912 how when he played 'Three Jolly Sheepskins' at Albrighton, 'youths would dance it any length of time with three hats on the ground. The first who touched a hat had to forfeit. Women danced as well as men'.

The barn (left) opposite the Red Lion in Llanfair Waterdine
once used for village dances

The music for 'Three Jolly Sheepskins'

Equally well-liked was the broom dance recalled by Alf Jenkins, who was born in the Dhu Stone Inn on Clee Hill in 1928:

> Frequently when my mother approached the bar to sweep up [as a signal for closing time], some one would grab it and perform a broom dance. ... The broom was held at one end and the dancer swung first one leg and then the other over in time to the music. Then he dropped the broom and danced along it, jumping from side to side.

Step dancing also had its adherents. Arthur Lane learned it at home in the kitchen from his father, though both father and son enjoyed dancing the waltz or quickstep on a village lawn or in a suitable room. Dennis Crowther describes just such an occasion in his poem, 'The Parson's Annual Ball'. Of her own father, rector of Hodnet until his retirement in 1892, Mary Cholmondeley wrote:

> He had a great belief in plenty of amusement for old and young, and gave many entertainments to his parishioners. He enjoyed the choir dances quite as much as the choir and their friends. We had a mixed choir, men, women, and boys, and many a time we have danced with about sixty parishioners in the drawing room of Hodnet Rectory, Father always leading off in the country dance with Mrs. Cross, our principal soprano. My brothers and brothers-in-law used to come in their pink hunt coats, and dance all night with the village maidens. What fun it was! And how very well every one danced! The village lads used to have quadrille parties in the fields beforehand, till they knew their figures much better than we did.

Such gatherings varied from the formality of Madeley, where the men wore white gloves and an MC presided, and of Highley, where ladies had programmes in which prospective partners booked dances by entering their initials, to the rough and tumble of Prees, where until the Second World War dances were held in suitable barns. Practical jokes played on people arriving included 'a parcel placed in the road tied to a length of string held by a suitable person behind the hedge. When someone stopped and dismounted for his or her bicycle, the string was pulled and the parcel disappeared'.

At Baschurch the station clerk with three other instrumentalists provided the music. 'He also made the piano dance, and kept "The Gay Gordons" and the "Highland Fling" going, with the floor of the hall moving up and down with all the couples prancing about'. Until the 1950s dances at Cressage took place in village halls and schoolrooms round about, with music supplied by local talent—'a pianist, a violinist, drummer, and maybe someone with an accordion'. Similar stories could certainly be told of many other villages.

Drama and Dumplings

Many of the venues for dancing also served for dramatic performances. William Hazlitt, later famed as an essayist, spent a good deal of his childhood in Wem, starting in 1787 when his father moved to the town as its Unitarian minister. Hazlitt junior never forgot how as 'a boy I lived within sight of a range of lofty hills, whose blue tops blending with the setting sun had often tempted my longing eyes and wandering feet'. Among his memories of Wem, whose grammar school he probably attended, was watching strolling actors performing. A few years later (in 1818) a boarder at the school wrote to his parents: 'The Players are here, and I went to see them on Monday last; ... the house was so full there was scarcely any stirring ... The Players are tolerably good if they had a larger theatre'. Other performances took place on the site of what is now the town hall, in a disused malt kiln, and in a canvas tent in the Talbot yard. Troupes such as Holloway's Theatre and Maggie Moreton's Company performed plays ranging from *Maria Marten* to *Hamlet*. Plays were given in the 1920s and '30s at Madeley in a converted chapel in Park Street and also in a hall called the Anstice, where travelling companies acted *The Murder in the Red Barn*, *The Man They Couldn't Hang* and *The Dumb Boy from Manchester*.

Local people put on annual pantomimes at Acton Burnell. In the Gothic Hall the Highley drama group performed *East Lynne* and *The Sign of the Cross*. In the decade before the Second World War, during a week-long annual drama at Llansilin 'contestants and spectators flocked from far and wide, and plays were performed in English and Welsh on alternate nights, with a reduced price for a ticket to cover the lot'.

Dawley ironworkers described to Maisie Herring the canvas theatre erected in Chapel Street:

The seats near the brazier in the middle were a shilling, gallery seats threepence. Plays shown included *East Lynne*, *The Silver King*, *The Little Drummer Boy*, *Old Folks at Home*. Effects were wonderful - tin trays for thunder and lightning a lighted candle thrown across the stage. After the play perhaps came a 'laughable farce', or a dumpling contest, when members of the audience ate hot dumplings to see who finished first.

The chapels, terming them concerts, put on biblical scenes. 'Easter plays', wrote Herring, 'are still a feature in the chapels round Horsehay'. Something similar emerges from the manuscript preserved at Shrewsbury School containing parts of three plays in Latin and English which would have been performed in churches early in the 15th century. The lines of only one character, the third shepherd, survive from *The Angels and the Shepherds*, and those of the third Mary from *The Three Marys at the Sepulchre*. The page illustrated opposite, from *The Two Disciples going to Emmaus*, features an extract from the part of Cleophas, beginning 'And gode wyne schal us wont non'. The words on the right are cues from Luke's speeches. Both actors join to sing the passage in Latin with music at the bottom, beginning '*Quid agamus vel dicamus*' (What we may do or say).

Early Drama

Borough and guild accounts frequently mention entertainers—actors, mimes, minstrels, bear baiters. If we discount payments in Shrewsbury in 1447/8 to the mimes of lords Stafford and Arundel, the first reference to drama there seems to be the '*ludum et demonstracionem*' (play and demonstration) on the martyrs Felicia and Sabina in Whitsun Week, 1516, for which those taking part received ten shillings, together with a further three shillingsworth of refreshments (wine, wafers and fruit). Ludlow soon follows, in 1530/1, with 'Item spend on my lady princes[s's] players, xijd. Item have them in reward iij d. iiijd.'. Bridgnorth's first record is the sum of 20 pence paid 'to the players' in 1551/2.

Such actors (as with the singers in chapter 10) are often identified as being from the companies of various royal and noble personages—king, queen, prince, princess, the earls of Essex, Leicester and Worcester, Lords Arundel, Chandos, Stafford and Strange (the celebrated actor, Edward Alleyne, was in Shrewsbury with Strange's company in 1592/3), the Lord President of the Council of the Marches, The Lord Privy Seal, and many others. No doubt the burden of supporting these companies was lessened when they went on tour, and the accounts are full of entries such as this, at Shrewsbury in 1527/8:

> *dato interlusoribus domini Regis, xs. Et in vino expendito super dictos interlusores & ballivos & compares suos ultra ijs. ijd. colectos, viijs.* (given to the players of the lord King, 10s. And in wine spent on the said players & bailiffs and their colleagues in addition to the 2s. 2d. collected, 8s.).

Perhaps more humble performers made up the troupes recorded as coming from towns such as Wrexham—in Shrewsbury in 1540/1—and from Shrewsbury itself, where for performing in May 1549/50 Walter Taylor and others were paid 3s. 4d. and given the same sum again for shoes. The church-wardens' accounts at Worfield saw payments to players on several occasions,

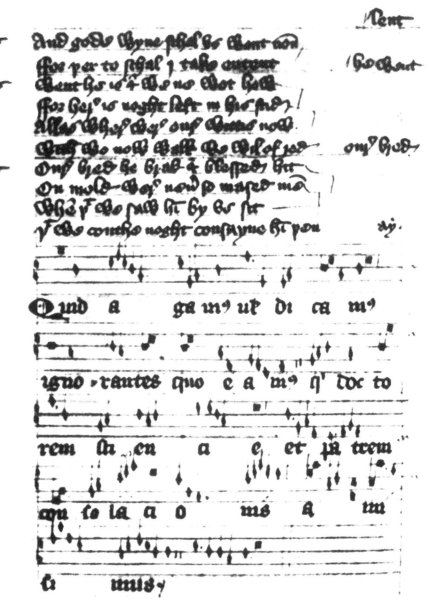

Part of a manuscript of an early play, with music,
preserved at Shrewsbury School

including to those from Claverley in 1588/9. Almost a century earlier, in 1401, various men from Whitchurch performed an interlude (dramatic show) at Blake Mere on the feast of St. Stephen (26 December), and in the same place the household accounts of John Talbot, Lord Strange, record payment of 3s. 4d, the time-honoured sum of a third of a pound, to '*ij hominibus de Salopia ludentibus quoddam interludium coram domina die Epiphanie*' (two men of Shrewsbury playing a certain interlude in the presence of the lady on the day of Epiphany). All that remains of the manor house where the actors played is now just a low mound on the south shore of Blake Mere, a mile north-west of Whitchurch.

Details of the plays and of times of performance are sparse. At Ludlow 'the players whiche played the enterlude in the Castell' received 16d. in 1553/4. The Queen's Players performed one November in the Guildhall (1559/60) and 'Robin Whod' was given 10s. in 1566/7. For ease of recall the actor is remembered by the name of the character he plays; but at Bridgnorth in 1588/9 2s.6d. was paid to 'them which plaied Robin Hood', so the reference here seems to be to the play.

Back in Ludlow, 10s. was given in 1566/7 on 'the xxix[th] of may to the chylderne which did play in the castell', and in 1568/9 6s. 8d. 'in Rewarde to the scollmaster of lemster [Leominster] Comynge to thys towne and pleynge with his scollers before us and certen of our brethren at my lady townsendes'. Children and 'scollers' also featured in Shrewsbury as well as professional performers like 'my lorde prinsys pleares' who appeared 'on sonday after seint Bartlamow day' (28 August 1541) and 'my Lord Wyllbyes playarys' who acted at 'the Gullet' (1560/1). The latter place remained in favour 20 years later:

> Inprimis to my Lord Staffordes Players, x s. ...
> Inprimis spent by them and the vj men in the company of the Right Honorable the yerle of Lesters men And master heyghe sheryffes dowghter in the gullett, vj s. viij d. (1581/2).

One performance is listed in St. Chad's churchyard (1540/1), another 'notable stadge play ... in the heye streete in Shrewsbury in the aple market place there by the Earle of Essexe man openly and freely' (17 July 1584). The following day the actors turned out to fight a fire on St. John's Hill, and were rewarded for doing so by the bailiffs. The apple (or green) market was an open space in front of the Booth Hall (pulled down in 1784), part of which is now called the Square. The actors would probably have erected a platform, using barrels and boards. Spectators, numbering several hundreds, would have stood to watch the play. There is unfortunately no record of what they saw.

The most favoured time for plays in Shrewsbury seems to have been Whitsun. As early as 1525/6 the bailiffs spent over £10 on 'Saynt Kateryn is play', with a further sum for materials including moss (2d.), wigs and false

Apple Market, Shrewsbury

beards, a dozen each of silver, gold, 'synaper & grene' paper, gold foil, six dozen bells, camphor, salt petre and four pounds of gunpowder. In 1552/3 they paid Lord Russell's actors 5s. 6d, spent 3s. 8d. '*die lune in Le Whitsun wiick post visum lusum*' (a farrago of Latin, French and English, meaning on Monday in Whitsun week after seeing the play), and then paid for costumes and a picture of Robin Hood. To the total for all this, £2 3s., was added the further sum of 13s. for wine for the performers.

In May 1556 the Mercers', Ironmongers' and Goldsmiths' Company provided financial support for 'the furnyture & charge of a playe at Whitsontyde ... to be played in the gwarell behynde the walles'. This was 'the playe of St. Julian the Apostate ... called Anot & Magot'. The Quarrell, according to Augustus Hare, was the site behind the former walls laid out in 1719 as the quarry, and later the site of a public baths. The poet, Thomas Churchyard, wrote of the Quarrell in *The Worthiness of Wales* (1587):

> There is a ground, newe made Theator wise,
> Both deepe and hye, in goodlie auncient guise:
> Where well may sit, ten thousand men at ease,
> And yet the one, the other not: displease.
>
> A space belowe, to bayt both Bull and Beare,
> For Players too, great roume and place at will.
> And in the same, a Cocke pit wondrous feare [fair],
> Besides where men, may wrastle in their fill.

In 1560/1 another subject is mentioned, 'Mr. Ashton's first playe upon the passion of Christe'. Thomas Ashton, appointed head of Shrewsbury Free School in 1561, remained in post for a decade, by which time there were 266 boys, half from the town and half from elsewhere. (In 1564 the future poet, Philip Sydney, was admitted to the school, together with his cousins, Fulke Greville and James Harrison). Ashton was clearly a skilled and enthusiastic producer of plays.

> ... the master baylyffes shall confer with mr assheton to know the charges to set forth a play at wytsontyde next [May 1564]
> *Et solutum Magistro ashton in regardo ad Lusum apud Le Whitson wicke ultra pecunias datas per confratres, xxv li. xiiij s.* (And the usual to Master Ashton for the play at Whitson week in addition to the sums given by colleagues, £25 14s. (1564/5)
> Item payd to Mr assheton toward his wages, xxix s. viij d. (1565-6)

There was a belief in Shrewsbury (but see chapter 7) that in the last year mentioned, 'Queen Elizabeth made progress as far as Covintry intending for Salop to see Mr. Astons play, but it was ended'. In 1567/8 Ashton's remuneration was £23 14s. 8d. Taylor noted in his history of the town:

> at whytsoontyd was a notable stage playe playeed in shrosberie in a place there cally[d] the quarrell which lastid all the holly dayes unto the which cam graete number of people of noblemen and others which was praysed greatlye and the chyffe auctor therof was one master Astoon beinge the

Misericord at Ludlow Church which may depict a scene in a mystery play, with a grotesque harridan and attendants

head scolemaster of the free scoole there a godly and lernyd man who
toocke marvelous greate paynes therin.

In 1569 Ashton again delivered a Whitsun play, but this seems to have been
the last. However, in 1577/8 one of the regulations of the school stipulated that
'every Thursday the schollars of the highest forme before they go to play shall
for exercise declame and play oon acte of a Comedy'.

Drama soon came to be less favourably viewed. A town order in
Shrewsbury of October 1594 stated 'that there shall not be hereafter any
interludes or playes made within this towne or liberties uppon anye soundaye,
or in the night-tyme'. For good measure it added: 'Neyther shall there be any
playinge at foot-ball, or at hiltes, or wastrells, or beare baytinge, within the
walles of this towne'.

A series of cases came before church courts. Walter Burry was charged at
Church Stretton in 1589 with 'setting forth playes and enterludes on the Sabothe
daye'. Again 'uppon the Saboth daie' at Michaelmas in 1606 at Wellington,
William Eyton of the Star Inn, John or Thomas Wildblood, Pugh, a tailor and
servant to John Wildblood, and Walter Clarke, caused offence by acting 'a
stage play'. The outcome is unknown, but Richard Clee of Tenbury, together
with Thomas Whatmore, Thomas and John Turner, John Farmer and William
Norgrove of Cleobury, and Humfrey Evans of Hopton Wafers, had a similar
charge dismissed in 1613 after pleading that the 'companie plaied at Cleburie on
a munday, and at Neene on a Tuesday, and not upon the saboth day'.

In the same year John Gardner stood accused of 'plainge of an enterlude
uppon the saboth daie' at Diddlebury. He appeared in Ludlow Church and
confessed that 'he withe his Companie plaied likewise at lidbury northe
uppon a Saboath daie'. He was required to do three days' penance, one each
in his own church, at Lydbury and at Ludlow. He failed to comply, and was
excommunicated. The rest of the actors and some of the spectators were also
ordered to do penance.

Richard Bishop of Clee Staunton (Stoke St. Milborough) doubly trans-
gressed in 1615. On the Sunday (25 June) after Midsummer Day he danced
'a greate parte of the said daie uppon Stokes Green' with his wife, Francisca,
and he attended 'a stage playe at Stokes gorst upon the saboth daie [20 or 25
August] about St. Barthelomewe', and there 'committed greate assaultes and
divers misdemeanors by reason whereof much bludd was shed: And then most
wickedlie blashephemed the name of god'.

Meanwhile, plays continued, subject to restrictions. The queen's players
made their last recorded visit to Shrewsbury in 1614/5, and those of the king
to Ludlow in 1633/4. Drama was eclipsed during the Civil War, and when
it resumed afterwards the gulf between popular and cultivated drama had
widened.

Folk Plays

By what appears to be a curious survival, plays continued until the mid-19th century in parts of Shropshire and Montgomery in some ways as they had been before the Civil War. A couple of farm waggons drawn up before a public house provided a stage. The actors, local men and boys (even in the case of women's parts, as in Shakespeare's day) entered from the pub and returned to it, where they were regaled with cakes and ale, their only remuneration. Except in the play's finale, no more than two actors were normally on stage together. One person acting as chairman, prompter and call boy sat in full view on the stage with his book. Spectators came from miles around, with up to 1,000 present on some occasions. Performances of up to three hours in duration were followed by fiddling and dancing, in which the audience could join.

Plays were put on during the parish wakes at Church Stoke in May, Shelve in July and Chirbury in October. Other venues were at Church Stretton and its neighbourhood, including the inn at All Stretton and the Sun at Little Stretton; Hyssington; Rorrington (Halliwell Wakes); Shawbury Wakes (August); Westbury Wakes (February); West Felton and Worthen. Others may have gone unrecorded.

The plays favoured included *Prince Musidorus*, *St. George and the Fiery Dragon*, *Valentine and Orson*, *Dr. Forster* (Faustus) and *The Rigs of the Times*, all of which were in print in various forms in the late 17th century or earlier. Full texts were kept only by the chairman-prompter, and from his book each actor copied his own part. It was customary for a man to burn his book—shades of Prospero—when he got married, thus saying farewell to the drinking (and perhaps sexual opportunities) which attended performances. As a result, no full text has survived, though some actors remembered sections. A blacksmith who as a boy of 14 played the heroine in *Prince Musidorus*—perhaps the most popular of all the plays—summarised the plot for Offley Wakeman:

> The heroine (name forgotten) [Amadine] being lost in a wood is attacked by a bear (represented by a man named Whettal dressed in a shaggy skin), and rescued by Prince Musidorus who after a terrific contest slays the bear with his sword. ... the Prince thereupon fell in love with, and eventually married, the heroine...

In *St. George* a monster made of wood was worked from the side by a long pole, its fiery breath supplied by a gunpowder squib. 'In the last scene there was a great fight, the dragon rearing up on its hind legs, but in the end St. George struck off its head with his sword, to the great amusement of the spectators'. At Little Stretton St. George was on horseback, and the dragon all in green. *Dr. Forster* seems to have been considered unlucky, as *Macbeth* is with modern actors. Bad weather plagued performances, and if the actors reached the point where the devil entered they invariably had the feeling that 'there was always one too many on stage', and were relieved when they reached the end.

According to Wakeman a fool or jester featured in all of the plays, making 'all manner of megrims', and 'going on his his manoeuvres all the time'. His dress included bells at the knees, a paper mask, and a cap with the ears raised, made of a hare skin or a stuffed squirrel. A prologue included lines such as 'We are all actors young, that never acted before, / But we will do our best, and the best can do no more'; or:

> Good morrow, gentlemen, every one,
> From half an hour to three score and ten.
> We've come here today some pastime for to show,
> But how we shall behave indeed I do not know.

The action was interspersed with songs. For example, in *Musidorus*, after the death of the bear:

> Down in yonder pleasant valley where the shepherd slew the bear,
> There I'll sit me down and tarry till the coming of my dear.
> He's my prize above all others since he slew the mighty bear.

A song always came at the end of the play. This is from *Valentine and Orson*:

> Our play is all over and all's at an end,
> I hope there's none of you that we did offend.
> If we have offended you right sorry we are,
> It was not our intention when we did come here.
>
> We came here today for the good of the house;
> They've well entertained us at great charge and cost.
> I hope there's each of you sixpence will spend,
> Because they are willing to make us amend.
>
> I may be contented and tarry till night,
> The moon and the stars will serve you for light;
> Likewise your own sweetheart at home you will send,
> And every one ought to take care of his friend.
>
> As for those bakers pray take them in thought,
> I have here today got choice of cake bought
> For all you young lovers to pick, choose, and buy,
> And call for some liquor, perhaps you are dry.

> All you here that has a wife,
> Prize her as dear as your own life,
> And in your wives take great delight,
> So now I wish you all goodnight.

The only dialogue of any substance to have survived is thanks to the memory of a man from Hyssington Marsh, aged 87 in 1884, who had played both Death and the Miser in *The Rigs of the Time*, and could remember both parts:

> *Death*
> Oh wealthy man with great possession here,
> Amounting to some thousand pounds a year,
> Take notice thou must die this very day,
> And quick must kiss thy bags and come away.

> *Miser*
> I can't nor won't believe thou art proud Death,
> Here come today to stop my vital breath,
> Whilst I in perfect good health do remain
> Free from diseases, sorrow, grief, and pain;
> No heavy heart nor fainting fits have I,
> And dost thou say that I am now drawing nigh
> The latter minute? Sure it cannot be!
> Depart, proud Death, thou art not come for me.

> *Death*
> Yes, yes, I am; for did you never know
> The tender grass and sweetest flowers that blow,
> Grow up one minute, and the next cut down?
> And so are men of fame and high renown.
> Now let me tell you - when my warrant's sealed,
> The sweetest beauty that this earth doth yield,
> At my approach doth turn as pale as lead:
> It's me that lays them on their dying bed.
> I cure the dropsy, fidgets, stone, and gout,
> And when my wasting fever flies about,
> I strike the man - perhaps say overnight -
> He scarcely lives to see the morning light.

> *Miser*
> Oh hold your hand and be not so severe,
> I have a hopeful son and daughter dear;
> All that I beg for is to let me live
> That I may them in lawful marriage give.

They are but young - when I'm laid in the grave
They will be wronged, I fear, of all they have.
Although on me you will no pity take,
Oh spare me for my little infants' sake.

Death
Oh, if such vain excuses e'er would do,
It would be well for mortals to go through,
And every one then something quick would find,
Something to say, why they should stay behind.
But see, I've held you in a long dispute;
Now after all, here is a sharp salute. (*strikes him*)
And I will end thy pain, and days, and years,
And cause thine eyes to flow with dying tears. (*exit Death*)

Miser
To my last chamber let me be conveyed.
Farewell, false world, for thou hast me betrayed.
Oh, had I never wronged the fatherless,
Nor moaning [? mourning] widows when in their distress!
Would I had ne'er been guilty of this sin!
Would I have never known what gold had been!
I little thought that Death would call so soon,
Now I must leave you all this afternoon!
Put not your trust in anything that's here,
For you don't know how soon 't will disappear
Into the chamber of the darksome grave.
Oh, how uncertain is the life we have!
Farewell, farewell, I ne'er shall see you more,
Now I must part with all this precious store;
My precious friend to whom I've been a slave,
Will not come down with me into the grave. (*dies*)

In fact, this sequence is a condensed version of a lengthy ballad in dialogue form, 'The Midnight Messenger; or, A Sudden Call from an Earthly Glory to the Cold Grave' first published in the 17th century.

The descriptions of the plays and their performers, together with the examples of songs and dialogue, inexorably bring to mind the 'rude mechanicals' in Shakespeare's *Midsummer Night's Dream*. It would surely be interesting to try to stage a revival of one of these productions, complete with farm waggons by a village inn, and followed by fiddling and dancing. Dialogue would have to be reconstituted, but this would not be too difficult: there are prose narratives extant which would supply the basic material, and some models for the dialogues, such as that between Death and the Miser, would show the way.

Christmas Mummers (1852)

Revivals have already been staged of the mumming plays which have much in common with the 'stage' variety. They had would-be heroic combat, a fool, extravagant costume, men only as actors, an opening and closing song, and a dialogue strongly reminiscent of that of the other form of traditional play.

Very few sightings of mumming plays have been reported in Shropshire, as it happens. There are references to Clunbury in the early 19th century, and to Edgmond (at the wakes) in 1884, but the only text to have been recorded comes from Newport, where the play was last performed, apparently, at Christmas in 1890. Charlotte Burne had a copy written down for her by Elijah Simpson, a Newport chimney sweep. The characters are Open-the-Door, Singuy [? Sir Guy of Warwick], King George, Noble Soldier, Little Doctor, Billy Belzebub, Little Jack Dout.

> *Open-the-Door*
> I open the door as I walk in,
> To ask your favour for to win,
> Whether I rise or stand or fall,
> I do my duty to please you all.
> But room, brave gallant, room!
> And give me room to rise.
> I come to show you pretty sport

This merry Christmas time.
Acting well or acting vain,
It is the grandest act on any stage.
But room, brave gallants, room I do require!
Enter in, Singuy, and show thy face like fire!

Singuy (enters)
Here I am, Singuy! Singuy is my name!
From English ground I sprang and came.
I search the nations round and round,
And if I find King George I give ten thousand pound!
King George he stands right at the door, he swears he will come in.
With his bright sword and buckler by his side he swears he'll
pierce my skin
Although I think he is a cowardly dog, I am afraid he is not stout,
He swears he will have his revenge before he goes out.

Open-the-Door
King George is here ready at hand.
I'll fetch him at thy command.
If you can't believe me what I say,
Step in King George and show the way!

King George
I am in search of an enemy, and if I find him this sword shall end his life.

Singuy
Pierce me then, thou vile and treacherous dog!

King George
Have I found thee? I pierce my sword in style: I'll crop thy wings,
thou shalt not fly, this sword shall end thy life!
(They move round each other, striking their swords one
against the other)

Open-the-Door
Stir up the fire and make a light
To see this awful battle by night.

Singuy
Enter in that noble soldier bold,
Before King George he strikes me cold.
I see him coming,
I'm afraid it's too late!
Spare me a few minutes, consider my hard fate!
(Singuy leans on his sword as if wounded)

King George
Where is this man before me stands?
I'll cut him down with sword in hand!

Open-the-Door
Enter in Noble Soldier!
(Soldier rushes forward and strikes up King George's sword;
the wounded Singuy retires from between them)
Soldier
Forbear, forbear, King George! Look down with pity on him,
and use him as thyself. Thou shalt not wrong him!

King George
Who bist thou? a soldier?

Soldier
A soldier? yes, a noble soldier bold, and Slasher is my name.
With my bright sword and buckler by my side I hope to win this game.
And if this game should do me good
I'll first draw sword and then thy blood.

King George
How hasher, now slasher? how canst thou talk so hot
When there's one in this room thou little thinks thou'st got?
That will hash thee and slash thee as I told thee once before,
And I always gain the championship wherever I do go!

Soldier
'How hasher, how slasher, how canst thou talk so hot?'
When my arms are made of iron, my body's made of steel,
My head is made of beaten brass, no man can make me feel!

King George
Stand off, thou swaggering dog, dos'n't thou know
I am the great and valiant George, the conquering hero?
Who slew the fiery dragon and brought him down to slaughter,
And by that means I gained the king of Egypt's daughter.
And dragon is my enemy. I'll quickly end thy life.
I'll crop thy wings, thou shalt not fly, this sword shall end thy life.
(They fight, clashing swords as before)

Open-the-Door
Strike up, King George, it must be so,
The horriblest battle that ever was know,
The clock struck one, the hour is gone,
It is time this horrid battle had adone! *(Soldier falls prostrate)*

Open-the-Door
King George, King George, what hast thou done?
Thou hast killed and slain my only son!
My only son, my only heir!
Can't you see him bleeding there?

King George
His wounds are mortal, call for a doctor!

Open-the-Door
I'll give five pounds for a doctor!

King George
Never a doctor come yet! I'll give ten pounds for one!

Open-the-Door
Enter in, Little Doctor!

Doctor
Rut, tut, tut: here comes a doctor, and a doctor so good,
And with my hand I'll quench his blood.
I carry ills and pills to cure all diseases.
Ladies and gentlemen, take my word just as you pleases.
I can cure the itch, the pitch, the palsy and the gout;
If there is nineteen old diseases I can fetch twenty out.

Open-the-Door
How far have you travelled, noble doctor?

Doctor
As far as from the fireplace to the bread-and-cheese cupboard.

Open-the-Door
No further?

Doctor
Oh yes, over England, Ireland, Scotland, France, Germany and Spain,
And all the parts that thou canst name.

Open-the-Door
What's the finest cure thou hast ever done, noble doctor?

Doctor
I once rode ten miles one morning before I had my breakfast,
to cure an old lady with the pimly-pam, that couldn't sneeze.
I gave her one of my small pills that did her good. She could

either sing a song or smoke a pipe or eat her breakfast as well
as any old man the next morning.

Open-the-Door
Try thy skill, noble doctor.

Doctor (stooping over Soldier)
Cup, Jack! take one my my nip-naps,
Put it down thy tip-taps,
And since thou hast been slain,
Rise up and fight King George again

Soldier (rising)
O horrible! O terrible! The like was never seen!
A man knocked out of seven senses into seventeen,
Out of seventeen into seven score,
The like was never seen here nor yet done before!

Doctor
Ladies and gentlemen, you see I have brought this man safe and sound,
As well as any man on English ground.
I have healed his wounds, I have searched his blood,
I have give him one of my small pills and it has done him good.

Soldier
How much is your demand, noble doctor?

Doctor
Ten pounds, but since thou hast been slain, I'll take five.

Soldier (attacking King George)
My sword is indebted to thy blood, and I'll still have my revenge!

King George
Have it then!
(Clashing of swords as before)

Open-the-Door (strikes up the swords)
Put up them swords and be at rest,
For peace and quietness is the best!
Enter in Old Belzebub!

Belzebub
Here, here, here comes one that never come yet!
With a big head and a little wit.
Although my wit is so small,

I think I've enough to please you all.
Ah, ah, ah, how funny! *(indicating his garments of shreds and patches)*
All these fine things and no money!
My name is old Billy Belzebub,
And on my left shoulder I carry a club,
And in my right hand a dripping pan,
So I think myself a jolly old man!

(sings)

I am a jovial tinker and have been all my life, So now I think it's time— to seek a fresh-young wife. And then with a friend we'll a merry life spend, which I never did yet, I vow—with my pink-a-tink-tink and a sup more drink, I'll make your old kettles cry sound, sound, sound, I'll — make your old kettles cry sound.

They drawed me to the barracks, they drawed me up and down,
They draw me to the barracks, and put my poor legs in pound,
But now with a friend I'll a merry life spend, *etc.*

My jacket's all pitches and patches, and on it I give a sly look,
My trousers all stitches and statches, wouldn't quite suit or lord
or a duke,
But it's pitches and patches I wear till I can get better or new;
I take this wide world as I find it, brave boys, if I'm ragged and true,
True, true, brave boys, if I'm ragged I'm true.

Open-the-Door
Enter in, little Jack Dout! Jack Dout
Here comes little Jack Dout, *(sweeps)*
And with my brush I'll sweep you all out!
It's money I want and money I crave,
Or else I'll sweep you all into your grave.
Now, ladies and gentlemen, you that are able,

Put your hands in your pockets and remember the ladle,
For when I am dead and in my grave,
No more of the ladle I shall crave!
(The party stand in a semi-circle, linking their little fingers together,
and sing)

We wish you a merry Christmas, also a New Year,
A pantry full of good roast beef, and barrels full of beer!
(Jack Dout presents the ladle for contributions)

CHAPTER 12

Calendar Customs

A sense of civic or religious obligation, the urge to secure and retain one's balance in a precarious world, the desire to seize opportunities for diversion, such were some of the factors underlying seasonal observances and calendar customs. Now, the third of these predominates, with commercial and secular considerations playing a major part, even on occasions such as Christmas.

Traditional events have increasingly been replaced by organised activities such as, say, the Ludlow festival, which, admirable though it is, caters more for the spectator than the participator, with the impact of high culture rather than popular kermesse. The heart of traditional custom still beats in Shropshire, though, thanks to the vigorous and determined support which sustains events such as Arbor Day at Aston-on-Clun or the Olympic Games at Much Wenlock. Furthermore, there is a palpable feeling abroad that some of the colourful seasonal happenings of yesteryear are ripe for revival. St. George's Day junketings, lifting at Easter, bound-beating in the summer, wassailing at Christmas and the New Year, for example, may already be taking place once more, albeit with changes, additions and re-interpretations to suit new times.

Shrovetide

A survey conducted in 2003 revealed that 83% of those interviewed would be cooking pancakes on Shrove Tuesday. It is perhaps a century since some churches rang a pancake bell signalling, among other things, that apprentices could down tools for the rest of the day. At Shrewsbury a bell continued to be rung until the 1970s, though by then the apprentices' holiday had long since gone. Shrove Tuesday is the last day before Lent, which can begin, depending on the date of Easter, on any Wednesday between 3 February and 9 March.

Children's play on Shrove Tuesday with whips and tops, though fondly remembered by some, is now long superseded, a casualty of increased road traffic. Other activities have vanished because of too much support, rather than too little, such as the annual tug o' war at Ludlow. Burne quotes a man who remembered in 1826 'being dragged into the crowd and remaining fully ten minutes borne on the shoulders of others, his feet never touching the ground'. The contest involved pulling a rope with a red wooden ball at one end, a blue at the other, which the mayor dropped from a window in the Market House to the waiting crowd. Members of the Broad Street ward attempted to pull the rope down Mill Street and dip the red ball in the Teme, while those from Corve Street tried to drag the blue end to the Bull Ring (which would seem to have been a much shorter distance). The best of three pulls determined the winners.

The contest ended in 1851, but Rev. James Davies witnessed earlier occasions:

The annual tug-o-war between The Black Bull and The Feathers

> It was the custom for the Mayor and Corporation every Shrove Tuesday to provide a rope three inches in thickness and 36 yards in length, and to give it out from one of the windows of the market place as the clock struck four, when a large body of the inhabitants, divided into two parties, according to the wards or the streets of the borough, commenced a vehement struggle to force the rope towards their respective goals. The meed of victory and the cessation of pulling took place as soon as one or other party succeeded in pulling the rope beyond its prescribed limits. This arduous and frequently dangerous contest I myself have several times witnessed as a boy from the windows of the building whence the rope was thrown. ... No explanation of the custom has, so far as I am aware, ever been authoritatively given, though it seems to be symbolical of some famous faction fight, or struggle between two contending parties in time past. It used to be said that the Corporation knew the inner meaning of the custom. If they did, they kept it to themselves in a spirit of profoundest wisdom, or that which passed for it, mystery. Perhaps the corporative wisdom shone brightest when it decided on abolishing a custom fraught with little less than rough horse-play, a good deal of beer-swilling, many bloody noses, and not seldom a broken limb!

The contest, later revived, still takes place each year between the habitués of two Ludlow public houses (see illustration).

Just as disorderly, no doubt, were the scenes at the Shrovetide cat whipping at Albrighton, some three miles north of Shrewsbury. Equally, the activity may have been mythical, a joke, formerly depicted on the village inn's sign, with the words: 'The finest pastime under the sun / Is whipping the cat at Albrighton'. In the 17th century 'to whip the cat' meant to be drunk; and Grose's *Dictionary of the Vulgar Tongue* (1811) contains this entry:

CAT WHIPPING, or WHIPPING THE CAT

A trick often practised on ignorant country fellows, vain of their strength, by laying a wager with them that they may be pulled through a pond by a cat. The bet being made, a rope is fixed round the waist of the party to be catted, and the end thrown across the pond, to which the cat is also fastened by a packthread, and three or four sturdy fellows are appointed to lead and whip the cat; these on a signal given, seize the end of the cord, and pretending to whip the cat, haul the astonished booby through the water. - To whip the cat, is also a term among tailors for working jobs at private houses, as practised in the country.

At Norton-in-Hales the 'brading' (see chapter 1) of men and boys who worked on Shrove Tuesday was undoubtedly vigorous; so, too, was (until 1854) the noisy church clipping at Wellington, where boys marched round with a tin trumpet band, making as much noise as they could.

Simnels

The fourth Sunday in Lent came in the 17th century to be known as Mothering Sunday. Grown up children who lived away travelled to visit their mother, and the family enjoyed a modest feast. Veal, followed by rice pudding, was a favoured menu according to Augustus Hare. The occasion was also called Refection Sunday. Among other delicacies were those mentioned in Robert Herrick's poem: 'I'le to thee a simnell bring / Gainst thou go'st a mothering'. According to *Chambers's Book of Days* (1863) simnels 'are raised cakes, the crust of which is made of fine flower and water, with sufficient saffron to give it a deep yellow colour, and the interior is filled with the materials of a very rich alum-cake, with plenty of candied peel, and other good things. They are made up very stiff, tied up in a cloth, and boiled for several hours, after which they are brushed over with egg, and then baked'. The writer goes on to speculate that the name came from a baker, father to Lambert Simnel, 'the well known pretender in the reign of Henry VII'—though in fact it derives from the Latin, *simila*, a kind of fine flour. He or she continues:

There is another story current in Shropshire, which is much more picturesque, and which we tell as nearly as possible in the words in which it was related to us. Long ago there lived an honest old couple,

Simnel Cakes

boasting the names of Simon and Nelly, but their surnames are not known. It was their custom at Easter to gather their children about them, and thus meet once a year under the old homestead. The fasting season of Lent was just ending, but they still had some of the unleavened dough which had been from time to time converted into bread during the forty days. Nelly was a careful woman, and it grieved her to waste anything, so she suggested that they should use the remains of the Lenten dough for the basis of a cake to regale the assembled family. Simon readily agreed to the proposal, and readily reminded his partner that there were still some remains of their Christmas plum pudding hoarded up in the cupboard, and that this might form the interior, and be an agreeable surprise to the young people when they had made their way through the less tasty crust. So far, all things went on harmoniously; but when the cake was made, a subject of violent discord arose, Sim insisting that it should be boiled, while Nell no less obstinately contended that it should be baked. The dispute ran from words to blows, for Nell, not choosing to let her province in the household be thus interfered with, jumped up, and threw the stool she was sitting on at Sim, who on his part seized a besom, and applied it with right good will to the head and shoulders of his spouse. She now seized the broom, and the battle became so warm, that it might have had a very serious result, had not Nell proposed as a compromise that the cake should be boiled first, and afterwards baked. This Sim acceded to, for her had no wish for further acquaintance with the heavy end of the broom. Accordingly, the big pot was set on the fire, and the stool broken up and thrown on to boil it, whilst the besom and broom furnished fuel for the oven. Some eggs, which had been broken in the scuffle, were used to coat the outside of the pudding when boiled, which gave it the shining gloss it possesses as a cake. This new and remarkable production in the art of confectionery became known by the name of the cake of Simon and Nelly, but soon only the first half of each name was alone preserved and joined together, and it has ever since been known as the cake of Sim-Nel, or Simnel.

Perhaps the eating of simnels moved to Easter as Mothering Sunday declined. This had largely disappeared by the 1930s, but after the Second World War manufacturers started producing greetings cards for the occasion, possibly influenced by the American Mother's Day (instituted in 1913, and celebrated on the second Sunday in May). Family reunions for meals once more became part of the celebratory ritual.

Eastertide

Palm Sunday is a week before Easter, which in turn is the Sunday following the first full moon after the vernal equinox, and therefore falls between 21 March and 25 April. In 1884 a woman from Castle Pulverbatch described for Burne the 'annual picnic' held on Pontesford Hill on Palm Sunday. Every household was occupied beforehand in baking cakes and packing up kettles and crockery ready for 'going a-palming'. The first to gather a 'palm' in the shape of a spray from the haunted yew tree on the hill would have good luck for the ensuing year, providing the trophy were carefully stored. The rather raffish wake on the hill—games, dancing, drinking—had as its object the search for the Golden Arrow, though people were notoriously unclear as to what this entailed. The arrow, apparently, had been lost in times long past by some great personage. If it were found a great estate (possibly Condover) would be restored to its rightful heir (possibly Edric the Wild); alternatively, a curse would be undone. One ryder made finding the arrow more or less impossible because it claimed that only a maiden under 20, the seventh daughter of a seventh son, could succeed, and then only at midnight on Palm Sunday. Mary Webb seized on the story as part of the background for *The Golden Arrow* (1916), her first novel, which was planned when she was living at Weston-super-Mare.

The Palm Sunday custom continued in attenuated form until the 1950s, but then faded away. The tentative and unlikely suggestion advanced by C.H. Hartshorne in *Salopia Antiqua* (1841) that the wake commemorated a battle

Pontesford Hill

fought at Pontesbury in 661 has subsequently—and unaccountably—been repeated as factual by some recent commentators.

Until the 1860s, when the well was drained, it was the custom on Good Friday to dip one's hand in the water, deemed good for weak eyes, of St. Margaret's Well at Wellington. Much more recently, comfortably into the 20th century, the congregation of Lords Hill Baptist Church met at Snailbeach in the afternoon and perambulated the area, pausing to sing hymns to the accompaniment of a brass band.

Until the 1930s, most places of work closed on Good Friday. People traditionally spent the time in their gardens, and this was considered a good time for planting potatoes. Formerly, bread baked on this day (see chapter 7) was believed to have curative properties. Many Shrewsbury families trekked to Haughmond Hill, following the canal tow path to Uffington. Children played and picnicked on the hill until the Second World War ended the custom.

On Easter Sunday at Ford, five miles from Shrewsbury, until the 1880s at least one man got up before dawn to climb a hill 'to see the sun dance'. Villagers collectively did the same thing round the Wrekin until the end of the 19th century. Later the climb became simply a recreational occasion. Ellis Peters recalled: 'The thing to do was to have tea or ice-cream at the Wrekin Cottage, half-way up, where at that time there were swingboats as an additional attraction, and then complete the climb to squeeze through the chink of the crowning rocks known as the Needle's Eye'.

Burne has pointed out a possible analogy between the fancied dancing or leaping of the sun on Easter Day and the lifting or heaving ceremony on Easter Monday and Tuesday, though the latter took place in parts of England and Wales well away from the Wrekin, as well as in Shropshire. On Easter Monday the men heaved the women, who reciprocated on Easter Tuesday. The lifting was done (three times) in a chair carried round for the purpose, decorated with evergreens, flowers and ribbons. Victims' feet were sprinked with drops of water from a bunch of flowers. The lifting party expected a kiss and, especially when men were heaved, some money or a forfeit. '"Yer cap or yer money", was the demand of the pit-girls, under these circumstances', wrote Burne.

Not everyone was happy to be heaved. As early as 1548/9 Taylor noted: 'This yeare & the tuesday after Ester hollydays ij yo'nge men of Salop [Shrewsbury] whose names were Esmonde Reynolds & Robart Clarke were smoothered under the castell hill hiding themselves from mayds the hill falling part thereof upon them'. In 1799 a Mr. Thomas Loggan wrote:

> I was sitting alone last Easter Tuesday, at breakfast, at the Talbot at Shrewsbury, when I was surprised by the entrance of the female servants of the house handing in an arm-chair, lined with white, and decorated with ribbons and favours of different colours. I asked them what they

wanted. The answer was, they came to *heave* me; it was the custom of the place on that morning, and they hoped I would take a seat in their chair. It was impossible not to comply with a request very modestly made, and to a set of nymphs in their best apparel, and several of them under twenty. I wished to see all the ceremony, and seated myself accordingly. The group then lifted me from the ground, turned the chair about, and I had the felicity of a salute from each. I told them I supposed there was a fee due upon the occasion and was answered in the affirmative; and, having satisfied the damsels in this respect, they withdrew to heave others.

Charles Hulbert in his *History and Description of Shropshire* (1837) gave an account of the rather genteel version of lifting which he witnessed at Acton Reynald Hall, where the owner at the time was Sir Andrew Vincent Corbet:

a chair was introduced into the room in which we were sitting, handsomely adorned with ribbons, flowers and etc., followed by all the female servants of the family, who with smiles of cheerful modesty requested the honour of lifting us; the highly distinguished owner of the mansion had previously honoured the group with his compliance,

When William Hone reprinted Mr. Loggan's account of heaving in 1826
he commissioned this illustration from Thomas Williams

then who with the smallest degree of good nature could refuse ... we were each three times raised above our level to the innocent diversion of all parties.

Others reacted differently. A Wesleyan minister, Joseph Whitehead, newly appointed to Oswestry in 1842, heard of this 'singular practice', judged it 'a relic of popery', and walked 'a mile round part of the town in a circuitous path' to escape it. Burne wrote:

> Not many years ago, young women in the colliery district found it neces-
> sary to stay indoors on Easter Monday. A maid-servant of the late vicar of
> Ketley, within the last ten years, was incautiously sent to the post-office
> on Easter Monday, and was so beset by heaving parties in the street, that
> her master, who fortunately became aware of her plight, was obliged to
> go and rescue her from their hands. But even in the collieries, where
> it has lingered longest, heaving is said to be very much on the decline,
> and elsewhere in the county it is, as a general public custom, dead. The
> remembrance of it is still fresh, however, and servants in country places
> frequently heave their fellow servants by way of 'a bit o' fun'.

However, in the 1990s a woman remembered as a small girl the heaving at Wellington, and had been given confirmatory details by her mother. A further custom she recalled was that of nailing a hot cross bun to the door to keep ill luck from the house.

Bannering

The perambulation of parish boundaries (see also chapter 5), known in Shropshire as bannering, took place at Rogationtide (the three days preceding Ascension day) or on Ascension Day itself (the sixth Thursday after Easter). On Ascension Day a party of boys and officials (churchwardens, beadle, sexton) set off from each of the five parishes which made up the borough of Shrewsbury. The boys blew penny trumpets and carried long sticks with bunches of flowers attached. The sticks doubled as weapons when the parties of rival parishes happened to meet. 'I believe the discontinuance of the custom', wrote Burne, 'is due to the serious nature of the fights, when the "rough" population had begun to join the bannering parties, tempted by the refreshments, which of course held an important place in the day's proceedings'. In 1838 the St. Chad's party finished the day with 'a sumptuous cold collation' at the house of W. Jones of Shelton, after which 50 boys managed to squeeze into the hollow of the famous Shelton Oak (see chapter 4). Such actions were no doubt thought to impress the memory of boundaries on the boys' minds.

Processions in the 'franchise' of Much Wenlock, which comprised 18 parishes, came to an end in the 1770s. They took place on Ascension Day or in Whitsun week. The party involved, known as the 'Boys' Bailiff', consisted of 'a man who wore a haircloth gown and was called the bailiff, a recorder, justices, town clerk, sheriff, treasurer, crier, and other municipal officers'. They were on horseback, as were boys armed with wooden swords. In its final years the cavalcade did not go round the boundaries but called at 'all the gentlemen's houses, where they were regaled with meat, drink and money'. At the end of the day the party assembled at the Guildhall, where the town clerk read out the 'charter', of which only one couplet seems to have survived:

> We go from Beckbury and Badger to Stoke on the Clee,
> To Monk Hopton, Round Aston, and so return we.

At Ludlow 'Processioning Day' on the eve of Ascension Day involved the town's schoolboys and a clergyman. From the church they carried birch boughs, with pauses for bible readings, to Corve Bridge, then eastwards to the Weeping Cross and back along the Teme to Ludford Bridge. There, the possession of a decorated birch bough fastened to the parapet was furiously disputed by the boys of different schools. The day ended with plum buns at the Guildhall. The boys particularly enjoyed the fight, and also the scramble over walls and through houses bisected by the boundary.

Bannering retained its appeal on Clee Hill until late in the 19th century. The newly-created parish of Cleeton St. Mary inaugurated its boundaries in 1879 (see also chapter 5), and a lively procession there was described by Thomas Powell in the *Shropshire Star* in 1885. Almost a century later some parishes (not on the Clee)—for example, Mucklestone, near Market Drayton—revived the custom in modified form. Processions previously followed boundaries precisely where they happened to be; latterly they have walked and assembled at adjacent points which happened to be accessible.

Ludford Bridge in 1905, on the route of Ludlow's 'Processioning Day'

May

On 2 May in 1593 one Thomas Jones of Longdon-on-Tern was taken up as a rogue or vagabond for 'synginge of may songes abrode the contrey'. He seems to have been both energetic and well received. With a pavior from Alscot, Richard Golborne, and his wife,

> on Saturday night last he was ... singinge at Uckington, donington, yenton, leighton & from thence on the next morninge he went over the water to Cressege & upon Sonday they dyned at harley, & from thence to wiggwigge, from thense to belserdyne, from thence to sheynton, & so that night backe again to Cressage upon Sonday night to Coone & from thense to harnage & from thens back againe to Cressage & there staide untill the eveninge on monday, & then they went to the Iron fornaces ...

and so it continues.

The Ludlow town accounts show money spent on gunpowder for 'pastyme' on May Day as early as 1577. The people objected to the curtailment of traditional pleasures for the sake of doctrinaire religion, and in the following century the redoubtable Lady Brilliana Harley of Brampton Bryan complained that 'at Louwdlow they seel [set] up a May Pole and a thinge like a hd [head] upon it ... and shot at it in derishion of Round heads' (letter of 4 June 1642).

According to Burne, maypoles were still being set up in Ludlow in her time, as in a number of other places including Child's Ercall, Colebatch (near Bishop's Castle) and Edgmond. Grinshill, like Wem, had a permanent maypole until some time in the 19th century. At Ashford Carbonel villagers fought strongly for their Maypole Field on several occasions. The owner of the land in question, Samuel Downes, agreed in 1762 to allow the children of the parish to play there two days a year. The field gradually became a recreation ground for people of all ages, at all times. In the 1840s farmers tried to restrict access. Some 30 years later the then owner, Miss Mary Ann Hall, took to court some of the villagers who had obstructed her men's attempts to take a crop of hay from the field. The news that her case failed led to the publication in *Punch* on 27 November 1875 of this poem:

> The men of Ashford Carbonel they doughtily declared,
> That where their Maypole had been raised, that pole should still be reared;
> But the Lady of the Manor and her myrmidons of Law
> Took counsel with a view to strike those villagers with awe.
>
> Is it in England's favoured land, on turf by Britons trod,
> Where 'proputty's' a fetish, and the landlord is a god,
> That resistance to the sacred rights of owners of the soil
> Is found among its rustics and its humble sons of toil?

ASHFORD CARBONEL

SHROPSHIRE.

The Daily Telegraph and Mr. Punch.

NOTICE IS HEREBY GIVEN,

That the plucky boys of Ashford intend to celebrate on

NEW YEAR'S DAY

The decision given in their favour by the High Court of Justice, in establishing to them the right to use the

MAY-POLE FIELD

AS A VILLAGE GREEN.

The Pole, which is generally understood to be reared in the merry month of May, will, on this occasion, be gaily painted and surmounted by a handsome flag, around which the triumphant Villagers will dance, rejoicing that the Parishioners have a Recreation Ground for ever. There will be a

BONFIRE

AND A DISPLAY OF FIREWORKS,

If funds will permit, and Cider and good old Shropshire Ale will be given away on the ground.

Contributions in aid of the Rejoicings from all interested in securing recreation ground to the people of England will be thankfully received by JOHN WATKINS, Ashford Carbonel, Ludlow, one of the defendants in the late action.

Alas! e'en so; the times have changed; LORD DARNLEY knows it well:
And she learns it too, the Lady high of Ashford-Carbonell;
While, sadder still, Law's powers refuse an owner to support -
And the great High Court of Justice backs the Ludlow County Court!

So the Parish beats the Lady, for the big-wigged Barons found
That reserving here and there a space for recreation-ground
Was a 'reasonable' practice, and that 'proputty's' tight clutch
Must be relaxed, nor landlords play the Ahab overmuch.

Hard lines for injured owners! Ay! But tenure of earth's soil
Must be viewed with other eyes than robbers' swag or warriors' spoil;
From 'Custom immemorial' as clear a right may flow
As any Norman WILLIAM or Eighth HARRY could bestow.

If 'proputty' were but compelled to render back in full
All it has cribbed from 'common-land', how long a face 'twould pull!
How many a Lord-of-Manors would have to tithe his hoards,
And make bonfires of his fences and his threatening trespass-boards!

O Lady of the Manor fair of Ashford-Carbonell,
Though you lose that longed-for acre, and pay legal costs as well,
What think you is the usufruct: of one of many fields
To the pleasure which the village-green to landless hundreds yields?

Madam, when next that Maypole's reared in its accustomed place,
To play the Lady Bountiful, with a British Matron's grace,
Were worthier of your Sex and State than waging stubborn fight
With a plucky Shropshire parish for a more than doubtful right.

Phyllis Ray, Ashford's historian, adds: 'It is ironic that, after this resounding victory, the importance of the Maypole Field has gradually diminished. ... At the beginning of the Second World War, the field of which it formed part was ploughed up, and it is still arable land. It was recently [1998] agreed that part of the relevant area be exchanged with a similar area by the church, to provide badly needed car parking space, The small part which remains uncultivated ... has been taken over by the village school, fenced off, and developed as a nature reserve'.

When adults gave up May customs, children sometimes took over. Until at least 1960, in parts of Shrewsbury, including Ditherington and Monkmoor, children made maypoles consisting of a pram wheel decorated with red, white and blue crepe paper and streamers, and set on the top of a broomstick so that it could revolve. The May queen sat on a stool and held the pole while other girls danced round and sang:

Round about the maypole merrily we go,
Singing hip-a-cherry, dancing as we go.
All the happy children upon the village green
Sitting in the sunshine, hurrah for the queen!

I'm the queen, don't you see?
I have come from a far country.
If you wait a little while
I will dance the maypole style.

Three cheers for the red, white and blue,
Three cheers for the red, white and blue.
The army, the navy and the air force,
Three cheers for the red, white and blue.

Rule Britannia, Britannia rules the waves,
Britons never, never shall be slaves.

After the performance money was collected from nearby houses. Michael Rix, who observed the custom, expressed the hope that it would long continue. It is not known to what extent his wish was fulfilled.

The May wakes on the Wrekin (see also chapter 9) attracted very large crowds both to the various attractions and to the annual combat between countrymen and colliers for ritual possession of the summit. There is no precise record as to when these wakes came to and end. In 1826 'W.P.' of Wellington wrote in William Hone's *Every-day Book*:

> It has been usual for the people of this neighbourhood to assemble on the Wrekin-hill, on the Sunday after Mayday, and the three successive Sundays, to drink a health 'to all friends round the Wrekin'; but, as on this annual festival, various scenes of drunkenness and other licentiousness were frequently exhibited, its celebration has, of late, been very properly discouraged by the magistracy, and is going deservedly to decay.

The correspondent fails to mention the deliberate campaign by new landowners to close down the wakes. Despite this, Burne notes that 'great numbers of holiday-makers ascend the Wrekin on "Wrekin May Sunday" even now'. Other May Fairs continue to the present day (see chapters 8 and 9).

Oak Apple or Royal Oak Day (29 May) was instituted by Act of Parliament to commemorate Charles II's entry into London on his birthday in 1660, and it alludes to the episode of the tree at Boscobel (see chapter 4). In Shropshire the occasion used to be called Oak-ball Day and also Nettling Day, since nettles could be applied to the legs of any boy not sporting a sprig of oak—at Market

Drayton, for example, and until the late 19th century at Oswestry Grammar School. At Wem until the mid-1970s the headmaster's chair at Sir Thomas Adams Grammar School was decorated with oak apples and greenery on the morning of 29 May. Until a similar time men and boys at Weston Rhyn wore sprigs of oak in their hats on the day. At Whitchurch they pinned oak apples to their clothing. This applied to both boys and girls at Baschurch until well into the 20th century—as indeed it did, according to the Opies, to a broad belt of the country running from Shrewsbury to the Wash. In other places, Empire Day (24 May) assumed great importance, perhaps because children were given a half-holiday, which they anticipated by singing (as at Ludlow):

> Empire Day, Empire Day,
> If you don't give us a holiday we will all run away.

At Plealey, near Pontesbury, the children even had a maypole on the day. Elsewhere they had sports, such as sack, egg and spoon, wheelbarrow and three-legged races, followed by tea. In Shrewsbury children from all the schools marched to the Quarry for patriotic songs and a service before being given the rest of the day off.

To return to 29 May, one notable Shropshire event, held on the nearest Sunday to it, is the Arbor Tree ceremony at Aston-on-Clun. Strangely enough, the first recorded mention of the decoration of the tree with flags dates only from 1912, with J.E. Auden's account, even though local tradition suggests that it goes back to the marriage on 29 May 1786 of a local squire, John Marston, and Mary Carter, in the neighbouring parish of Sibdon Carwood. After the ceremony the wedding carriage stopped at the parish boundary, Long Meadow End, and, after the horses were taken out, was pulled by enthusiastic local men to Marston's house, Oaker. When on the way the party paused to admire the tree, which had been decked with flags for the occasion, the bride felt moved to give money to support the perpetuation of the custom. Much of this is unverifiable, but John Box of Ironbridge has established that the wedding took place as described, and that the couple indeed lived at Oaker.

Like many calendar customs the Arbor Tree ceremony and associated events have varied over the years. Local brides were presented with rooted cuttings from the tree (a black poplar) for a period in the 1950s. Pageants, maypole and morris dancing were also held, dropped, then (in the 1970s) revived. 'The pageant has now become a successful annual event', wrote Box in 2003, '... and has expanded to include a fete and associated celebrations'. The pessimistic view expressed by Michael Rix in 1960 that the custom was 'in danger of dying out' has proved to be wrong, thanks to the efforts made by the local people and the attention accorded by the wider world. Fringe beliefs connected with pagan tree spirits and Celtic goddesses have surfaced, whacky but harmless.

Feasts and Wakes

Shropshire's summer was predominantly a time for work, with sheep shearing and hay harvesting to be done, though the conclusion of each was duly celebrated (see chapter 8). Time would also be found for 'club days', when the friendly societies which provided sickness benefits and the like before the advent of the welfare state (and sometimes after it) celebrated with an annual procession and feast. The Baschurch Ladies' Club, founded in 1802 as The Baschurch Female Friendly Society, held its anniversary walk as nearly as possible to 24 June. Members walked in procession to the parish church, carrying flower-decked wands (as in bannering) which were set up to form an arch by the door. After a special service the members marched away to a meal at Mrs. Dawson's tearoom. Wands and flowers were judged, and prizes awarded. The men's club held a similar parade, following a large banner. The associated fair's attractions included swingboats and coconut shies. The ladies' club continued in existence until 1975.

Members of the Oddfellows' Club at Clee Hill marched behind a brass band to Knowbury. After dinner in their club room at the Crown Inn they enjoyed sports on the field, and more music. Many similar events would have taken place up and down the county. In mid-July the Much Wenlock Olympic Games still take place (see chapter 9), and in 2003 Queen Elizabeth II attended. Summer festivals now range from walking (Bishop's Castle) to story telling (Much Wenlock), folk (Shrewsbury) and classical (Ludlow) music. There are carnivals at Shrewsbury and Wem. Ellesmere holds a regatta and Oswestry a show, the latter for the 118th time in 2003. The biggest event of the summer, though, is probably 'the Show' itself, Shrewsbury's flower show (see chapter 9).

Many village events formerly took place in October, when agricultural work became less pressing than in the busy days of harvest. On the first Sunday in October, for example, wakes were held at Pulverbatch, Leighton-under-the-Wrekin and Shifnal's Pain's Lane. A full calendar of such occasions in Shropshire would be lengthy.

Soul-cakes and Bonfires

Hallowe'en (31 October) is the eve of All Saints' Day (1 November), which is followed by All Souls' Day. Of the last occasion, John Aubrey wrote in the late 17th century:

> 'In Salop, &c: *die omnium Animarum* there is sett on the Board a high heap of Soule-Cakes, lyeing one upon another like the picture of the Sew-Bread in the old Bibles. They are about the bigness of twopenny-cakes, and every visitant that day takes one; and there is an old Rhythm or saying,
>
> A Soule-cake, a Soule-cake,
> Have mercy on all Christen Soules for a Soule-cake.
> This custom is continued to this time.

Sew bread, otherwise called shew (or show) bread, was the 12 loaves placed every sabbath before the altar, and eaten later in the week by priests. Soul cakes were round or oval, flat, and made of light dough, sweetened and spiced. Some 200 years after Aubrey, Burne could cite versions of the 'rhythm' or chant from Baschurch, Berrington, Edgmond, Ellesmere, Hodnet, Kinnerley, Market Drayton, Newport, Oswestry, Pulverbatch, Rodington, Wellington, Welshampton, West Felton and Whittington. She considered Market Drayton's 'the purest and oldest':

> Soul, soul, for a soul cake!
> I pray, good missis, a soul cake!
> An apple or pear, a plum or a cherry,
> Any good thing to make us merry.
> One for Peter, two for Paul,
> Three for him who made us all.
> Up with the kettle and down with the pan,
> Give us good alms and we'll be gone.

A perhaps earlier tradition preferred to ask for ale, as in the souling song taken down by Georgina Jackson in 1863 from William Porter of Edgmond:

> The streets they are gotten dark, dirty and cold,
> We are come a-souling, this night we'll make bold.
> We are come a-souling as well doth appear,
> And all that we soul for is ale and strong beer.
>
> Abroad in your meadows, alone in your streets,
> If this be a good house we shall have some relief.
> If this be a good house, as well doth appear,
> And all that we soul for is ale and strong beer.
>
> Look out for your cellar key, your cellar key, good dame,
> By walking and talking you shall get a good name.
> By walking and talking we've got very dry,
> So I hope my good missis will not us deny.

Go down into your cellar and there you shall find
Both ale, beer and brandy and the best of all wine
And when you are drawing don't let your heart fail,
But bring us one jug of your bonny brown ale.

I pray, my good missis, don't tarry to spin.
Look for a jug to draw some drink in,
And when you have got it oh then you shall see,
And when we have drunk it, how merry we'll be.

In 1909 Rev. E.A. Godson of Clive published the words he had heard sung by children calling from door to door:

Soul, soul for an apple or two.
Got no apples, pears will do.
Up with the kettle and down with the pan,
Give me an apple and I'll be gone.
One for Peter, two for Paul,
Three for him that made us all.
Apple or pear, plum or cherry,
Any good thing for to make us merry.
Merry I am and merry I be,
Please give an apple away to me.

Phyllis Crawford pointed out in 1938 that at Wem 'the "souling cake" has died away, but the children still knock at the doors every November 2nd, crying "Please I've come a-souling"'. In the same year Lilian Hayward observed that in villages near Oswestry, including West Felton and Llynclys children still went round: 'The soul cakes are, I believe, no longer made, but nuts, sweets and apples are put ready for them'. Some 20 years later the Opies noted that souling continued among 'children living in rural parts of Cheshire, with Shropshire, and along the adjoining Staffordshire border'.

An Act of Parliament of 1606 ordered that the anniversary of 5 November be commemorated by church services. By some 15 to 25 years later the occasion had become Bonfire Night. At Ludlow in the 18th and early 19th centuries a big communal fire was lit on Whitecliff Hill, outside the town, and fireworks added to the festivities. In the 1880s, wrote Burne:

At an appointed hour in the evening a procession of men and boys walking two and two, and carrying lighted torches, starts from the Bridge Inn at the bottom of Corve Street, headed by a drum-and-fife band playing some lively tune (such as 'Shrewsbury Quarry'), and marches through the Bull Ring in the centre of the town, over Ludford Bridge up to Whitcliff Hill outside the town, the appointed site of the bonfire. The

'Guy', with a pipe in his mouth and a turnip lantern in his hand, is borne in a chair by four men in the midst of the procession, and duly burnt on the bonfire. If any well-known person in the place should happen to have excited the enmity of the populace, his effigy is substituted for, or added to that of Guy Fawkes.

In a different account the tune played was 'The Rogues' March'.

Until the late 20th century people at Wem remembered gangs of youths who had gone out not only with their guys but with burning tar barrels. Their horse-play sometimes led to court appearances, but 'if anyone got into trouble', wrote Iris Woodward, 'there were always plenty of sympathisers to pay the fine'.

Christmas

In Tudor times 12 strikes (bushels) of corn for bread making were given to the parishioners of Shifnal each year on the eve (10 November) of St. Andrew's Day—the church there is dedicated to St. Mary and St. Andrew. Under Elizabeth this was reduced by half, and called Pardon Bread. Nevertheless, it helped the poor to prepare for winter.

On St. Thomas's Day (21 December) many Shropshire farmers provided a sack of corn, known as the Wheat Dole, for distribution among the needy. The farmers' wives and daughters gave it out, a pint or a quart at a time. At Clun a measure of wheat was given for the people and one of barley for their pig. Unfortunately, wrote Veronica Thackeray,

Christmas Festivities in 1852

over the years the generosity of the Clun farmers was so abused that the custom became a sort of marathon favouring the able-bodied poor, who would scamper from farm to farm getting hand-outs at each, while the more frail among them could only stagger to one farmhouse. Aware of this trying state of affairs, the farmers eventually joined together in sending all the 'wheat dole' to Clun Town Hall, where it was distributed fairly.

Edward Brayne, who died at Oswestry in 1902, aged 84, remembered how the women and children went round 'begging corn on St. Thomas's Day'. In some parishes payments were made by the overseers of the poor. At Hope Bowdler the sum of one shilling was devoted to this purpose on 'St. Thomsday' in 1760. In the early 19th century the vicar distributed bread to the value of 12s.

Holly and mistletoe from many areas, including Shropshire, are auctioned each year at Tenbury Wells, Worcestershire, on the four Tuesdays between mid-November and mid-December

together with up to 10s. in cash. Various names were given to the custom—Thomasing (Church Stretton, Pulverbatch, Much Wenlock), couranting (Abdon), gooding (Eardington), clogging (Clun) or clog-fair day (also Clun).

Until perhaps 1900 a yule log, previously prepared, was taken in on Christmas Eve. The log, known as a Christmas bron or brund (brand), of oak, holly, or crab, was bored twice through the middle, and the flames which came through the holes were called Christmas candles. The lighting was always an occasion for merriment, and 'journey's end meant a convivial drinking of ale, served in huge tankards'. The brand would burn through the 12 days of Christmas. At Vesson's Farm at Habberley flagstones can reportedly be still seen which were broken when horses dragged the brand in, in 1895. The mistletoe bough, also taken in at Christmas Eve, would be kept for 12 months until it was burned and replaced by its successor.

In Welsh-speaking areas congregations met in churches and chapels at five or six on Christmas morning and sang carols until daybreak. The ceremony, known as *plygain*, still lingers in parts of the county. Christmas Day was 'rung in' by the bell ringers in some churches. At Myddle in Richard Gough's time 'in the afternoon after divine service, and when the minister was gone out of the church', it was the custom that 'the clerk should sing a Christmas carol'. More recently—and until the 1950s—children before Christmas in Shrewsbury and district sang from house to house:

> The road is very dirty, my shoes are very clean [? thin],
> I've got a little pocket to put a penny in.
> If you haven't got a penny a ha'penny will do,
> If you haven't got a ha'penny a mince pie will do,
> If you haven't got a mince pie a drink of wine will do,
> If you haven't got a drink of wine, God bless you.

The tower at Myddle Church

A century earlier, at Hope Bowdler, adult carol singers sometimes became involved in fights with rival parties, such as those from Cardington. Like the soul cakers they preferred offerings of beer. It was a point of honour to drink all that was offered, and on one occasion, to avoid the shame of declining the men of Hope Bowdler took with them as an insurance a villager known from his great capacity as 'George the Bottle'.

Even when children were singing, references to ale might remain, as in these words, recited by Henry Bould at Donnington Wood in 1911 to Cecil Sharp, 'as sung by children in those parts':

> The cock sat up in the yew tree,
> The hen came chittering by.
> I wish you a merry Christmas
> And a good fat pig in the stye.
> A jug of ale and a good pork pie,
> For the carol singers is very dry.

Two years earlier, Godson reported from Clive:

I wish you a merry Christmas and a happy New Year,
A pocket full of money and a cellar full of beer.
A good fat pig to last you all the year,
A lump of cake and a bowl of beer,
Christmas comes but once a year.

As for the carols themselves, Lilian Hayward noted that the traditional repertoire, as opposed to items learnt in school, was still 'occasionally heard' in 1938. She mentions 'Dives and Lazarus', and quotes from another carol:

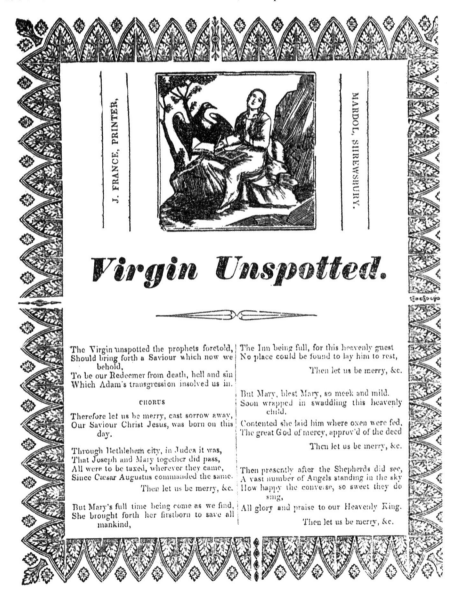

J. FRANCE, PRINTER,

MARDOL, SHREWSBURY.

Virgin Unspotted.

The Virgin unspotted the prophets foretold,
Should bring forth a Saviour which now we behold,
To be our Redeemer from death, hell and sin
Which Adam's transgression insolved us in.

CHORUS

Therefore let us be merry, cast sorrow away,
Our Saviour Christ Jesus, was born on this day.

Through Bethlehem city, in Judea it was,
That Joseph and Mary together did pass,
All were to be taxed, wherever they came,
Since Cæsar Augustus commanded the same.

Then let us be merry, &c.

But Mary's full time being come as we find,
She brought forth her firstborn to save all mankind,

The Inn being full, for this heavenly guest
No place could be found to lay him to rest,

Then let us be merry, &c.

But Mary, blest Mary, so meek and mild.
Soon wrapped in swaddling this heavenly child.
Contented she laid him where oxen were fed,
The great God of mercy, approv'd of the deed

Then let us be merry, &c.

Then presently after the Shepherds did see,
A vast number of Angels standing in the sky
How happy the converse, so sweet they do sing,
All glory and praise to our Heavenly King.

Then let us be merry, &c.

> Oh, it's under the leaves, and the leaves have light
> Where we saw maiden of heaven,
> Oh, the warden of them be Mary mild
> Was our king's mother of heaven.

Both these were among the ten carols taken down by Cecil Sharp in Shropshire during several visits in 1911 and 1923. The remainder were 'Awake, awake', 'God rest you merry', 'The Little Room', 'The Man that lives', 'On Christmas Night', 'The Truth sent from above', 'When Jesus Christ had lived' and 'The Virgin Unspotted'.

In the 19th century the oral tradition which carried these carols was supplemented, so far as the texts were concerned (though not the tunes), by sheets issued among others by John France of Mardol, Shrewsbury, printer, stationer

and toy dealer, in business from 1827 until about 1840. Among extant sheets with France's imprint are 'Away, Dark Thoughts', 'The Carnal and the Crane', 'God's Dear Son', 'Herald Angels', 'Mirth Inclined', 'Righteous Joseph', 'Star of Bethlehem', 'The Truth sent from above' and 'The Virgin Unspotted'.

'Under the leaves of life' appeared with the title of 'The Seven Virgins' in *A Good Christmas Box*, a collection published by G. Walters in Dudley in 1847. Fred Hamer recorded it from May Bradley (for whom, see also chapter 10) of Ludlow, and she can be heard singing it on the cassette, *The Leaves of Life*, issued by the English Folk Song and Dance Society in 1989.

It's all under the leaves and the leaves of life, where I saw maidens seven, And it's one of those was Mary mild, Was our King's mother from heaven.

Then I asked them what they were looking for,
All under the leaves of life,
I am looking for sweet Jesus Christ,
To be our heavenly guide.

Go you down, go you down to yonder town,
As far as you can see,
And there you will find sweet Jesus Christ,
With his body nailed to a tree

Dear mother, dear mother, do not weep for me,
Your weeping does me harm;
But John may be a comfort to you
When I am dead and gone.

There's a rose and a rose, a genteel rose,
The charm that grows so green,
God will give us grace in every mortal place
For to pray to our heavenly queen.

The text from Dudley makes matters rather clearer:

May Bradley

313

THE

SEVEN VIRGINS.

All under the leaves, and the leaves of life,
  I met with virgins seven,
And one of them was Mary mild,
  Our Lord's mother in heaven.
O what are you seeking you seven pretty maids,
  All under the leaves of life ;
We're seeking for no leaves, Thomas,
  But for a friend of thine ;
We're seeking for sweet Jesus Christ,
  To be our heavenly guide.
Go down, go down to yonder town,
  And sit in the gallery,
And there you'll see sweet Jesus Christ,
  Nailed to a yew tree.
And down they went to yonder town,
  As fast as foot could fall,
And many a bitter and grievous tear,
  From the ladies' eyes did fall.
O peace, mother, O peace, mother,
  Your weeping doth me grieve.
I must suffer this he said ;
  For Adam and for Eve,
O how can I my weeping leave,
  Or my sorrows undergo,
Whilst I do see my own son die,
  When Sons I have no more ?
O mother, take you John Evangelist,
  To be your favourite son,
And he will comfort you sometimes,
  Mother, as I have done.
O come then John Evangelist,
  Thou'rt welcome unto me,
But more welcome my own dear son,
  Which I nursed upon my knee.

Then he laid his head on his right shoulder,
  Seeing death it struck him nigh,
The Holy Ghost be with your soul,
  I die, mother, I die.
O the rose, the gentle rose,
  And the fennel that grows in the Spring,
And God give us grace in every place,
  To pray for Victoria our Queen.
Furthermore for our enemies all,
  Our prayers they are so strong,
Amen, good Lord, your charity is,
  The ending of my song.

Boxing Day

Reminiscing in the last years of the 20th century, Women's Institute members from Madeley recalled the 'usual parties of carol singers' up to Christmas, and afterwards 'the wassailers, black faces and cap in hand'. One woman from New Dale spoke of 'morris dancers':

> They would be youths out of the village, ten or a dozen of them, and they used to dress up in their mothers' dresses and their mothers' hats and black their faces. They would each have a broom stake, and they would dance around singing:
>> Somebody's in the house of Dinah,
>> Somebody's in the house I know.
>> Somebody's in the house of Dinah,
>> Playing on the old banjo.

Alf Jenkins had similar memories from Clee Hill:

> Having blacked their skin and donned very colourful clothes they [men] made a very early start and visited every public house in the locality. One member played a row of tin whistles and another played bone clappers. These were usually made from ribs. There would be a melodeon and probably a banjo. The group sang, danced, changed shirts and drank great quantities too.

Rix, still on Boxing Day, heard boys at Bridgnorth in the mid-20th century singing, with actions, 'This old man, he played one'. The boys went from Low to High Town. 'Their cheeks are blacked with soot, their jackets turned inside out and decorated with coloured cloth. Each carries a broomstick and they work in couples. They sing the ten verses of the song through, hitting each other's staves in mock single-stick fashion and collect money from onlookers. The performance only lasts till noon'.

The context of such practices was the poor Christmases experienced by some children in the past. 'Our Christmas', said Arthur Lane (see above) 'we'd be having an apple tied to a string at the top, and then we'd be trying to see which could bite him, with our hands fastened behind us. That was our sports. There was not much preparations. Oh, the plum pudding, the mince pies and that, we always had our share of those'.

The New Year

John Noake, the letter writer of 1855 (see chapter 7), recording the belief that it was unlucky 'to have a female come into your house [first] on New Year's morning', added: 'So generally does this absurdity prevail, that in many towns young lads "make a good thing of it" by selling their services to go round and enter the houses first that morning'. Some 30 years on, Charlotte Burne listed numerous further examples. In the 1950s the Opies noted that a boy of about 10 banged on a door at Pontesbury and recited:

> Happy New Year! happy New Year!
> I've come to wish you a happy New Year.
> I've got a little pocket and it is very thin,
> Please give me a penny to put: some money in.
> If you haven't got a penny a halfpenny will do,
> If you haven't got a halfpenny, well God bless you.

A decade later in the Clun Valley Michael Rix found small boys still going 'gifting':

> On New Year's Day as early as possible they visit outlying farms and cottages to recite versions of the poem,
>> The cock sat up in the yew tree,
>> The hen came chuckling by.
>> Please give us some pudding or a mince pie.
>> We wish you a merry Christmas and a cellar full of beer,
>> A good fat pig in the sty to last you all the year.
>> Please to give us a New Year's gift.
> The first boy to reach the house got silver (a sixpence), all later comers coppers.

Until within living memory at Rushbury people turned out of their houses to hear the new year rung in at St. Peter's Church, after which the choir sang from the top of the tower Martin Luther's hymn, 'Lord Jesus Christ', beginning 'Give heed, my heart, lift up thine eyes', and ending 'While angels sing with pious mirth / A glad new year to all the earth'. Arthur Lewis (1876-1961), recorded in 1952 by Peter Kennedy, was born at All Stretton. After working at wheelwrighting 'beyond Birmingham', then at Pulverbatch and Acton Scott, he moved to Hope Bowdler in 1913 when he married Sarah Croxton from the family of blacksmiths mentioned in earlier chapters. He sang:

Kind mas-ter and mis-tress may God bless all here By your leave we are come to sing in the New Year. The old one is — en - ding and bids us a — dieu, And we are com - men - ded to wel - come the new.

It is better to do so than it is to do worse,
To go to some ale house to swear and to curse.
There is none that will condemn us, we need not to fear,
And we hope God will send you a happy New Year.

We don't sing for money, nor none we deserve;
We've other employment or else we should starve,
For cold is the season and the bells they do ring,
And that is the reason that's caused us to sing.

There's no better enjoyment can be upon earth
Than friends met together in God's civil mirth,
For hymning and singing is everywhere,
And we hope God will send you a happy New Year.

Please you, master and mistress, or else we'll sing none,
Or perhaps we may be wanted when thus we are gone;
But although by some people disdained may be,
Perhaps they are more uncivil than we.

Kind master and mistress, now we must depart.
We hope God will protect you, asleep and awake,
And all that belongs to you that's everywhere,
And we hope God will send you a happy New Year.
And now if you please, ma'am, we'll taste of your beer.
(Spoken) Happy New Year! Happy New Year!

The singer explained:

> This is an old carol from the Hope Bowdlers near Church Stretton in the
> county of Salop. After we finished ringing the bells - old year out and
> new year in - we used to go down to the square [at Church Stretton] and
> sing this old carol. We generally met in the square - all the bell ringers.
> Off down to the town, take the handbells to play round the pubs. Stop
> there till ten then ring till midnight. Always brought a pitcher o' beer up
> with us. 'Ad a good 'ow-de-do in the belfry. Then all the Christmas week
> we used to go round the different places, several villages round about,
> and always get plenty o' summat to drink and plenty o' summat to eat,
> like. Come to the New Year's Eve, then off to the town again - so much
> beer and playing the bells, and back up into the village and ring the bells
> till midnight, then down to the square and sing the old carol, then back
> up into the belfry - a drop more beer and a bit o' bread and cheese, a few
> mince pies, and stop there till mornin', some of us. Some never went
> home at all, all the week.

Arthur Lewis's copy of the 'old carol' (preserved by a former neighbour, Peter Morgan) was written out, probably in the 1860s, by his wife's

317

aunt, Catharine Croxton. Arthur sang in the Hope Bowdler church choir for over 45 years and was a bell ringer for 20. He also played the fife. 'Many were the local tales he could relate, spiced with Shropshire dialect', wrote his obituarist in a local paper.

Cledwyn Hughes reported that in his village on the Shropshire-Montgomery border on the eve (5 January) of Epiphany people went round and drank a toast at each of seven holly trees. Farm hands

Rare picture of he singer, Arthur Lewis

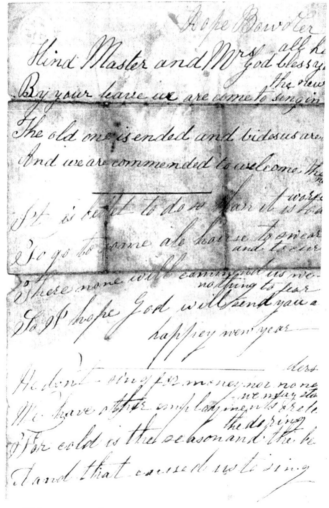

This page and opposite: a family song manuscript

pleaching hedges all over Britain left such trees untouched, possibly from a belief that Christ's cross was made of holly—though the more usual notion preferred elder (see chapter 7).

By Candlemas Eve (1 February), very late by modern standards, all Christmas greenery had to be down in houses, or there would be a death in the family before the following Christmas. This belief was particularly strong in the Clee Hills. Sometimes when holly and ivy came down they were replaced by bowls of Candlemas Bells—snowdrops.

Wright and Lones noted that 'A Shropshire custom was the "purification" of the house, on or about Candlemas day, by placing within it a bunch of snowdrops or Christ's flowers; this was called "the white purification"'. According to a traditional couplet, 'The snowdrop in purest white array / First rears her head on Candlemas Day', yet increasingly mild winters have produced 'the fair maids of February' in January. Broad beans were traditionally planted on Candlemas Day, and cattle on farms given ivy to eat. So continued the year's cycle.

Welcome Yule
Welcome be thou Mary mild,
Welcome be thou and thy child.
Welcome thee who art our shield,
Welcome yule for ever and ay.

Welcome be ye Steven and John,
Welcome children everyone.
Welcome, Thomas, martyr, all one,
Welcome yule for ever and ay.

Welcome be thou good new year,
Welcome be twelve days together,
Welcome be ye all that be here,
Welcome yule for every and ay.

Welcome be ye lord and lady,
Welcome be ye all this company.
For yule's love make merry,
Welcome yule for ever and ay.

Bibliography

Anon, 'Charms' [MS. from Clun], *Folk-Lore*, 7 (1896), 202-4

Armstrong, Edward, *The Folklore of Birds* (1970)

Ashman, Gordon (1935-2003) 'Custom in Conflict: the Morris Dance in the
    Shrewsbury and Ironbridge Area of Shropshire', in *Traditional Dance*,
        ed. T. Buckland, vol. 5/6 (1988), 135-158

    'With One Bound They Were Free: From the Cotswolds to the Welsh Border
        in One Stride', *Lore and Language*, 6, pt 2 (1987), 105-116

    (ed.), *The Ironbridge Hornpipe. A Shropshire Tune Collection from John
        Moore's Manuscripts* (Blyth, 1991)

    and Bennett, Gillian, 'Charlotte Sophia Burne: Shropshire Folklorist',
        Folklore, 111, no. 1 (2000), 1-21, and 112, no.1 (2001), 95-106

Aubrey, John, *Remaines of Gentilisme and Judaisme*, in *Three Prose Works*, ed. J.
    Buchanan-Brown (Fontwell, 1972)

Auchmuty, S.F.F., *The History of the Parish of Cleobury Mortimer* (Cleobury
    Mortimer, 1996; orig. Hereford, 1911)

Audelay, John, *The Poems of John Audelay*, ed. J.O. Halliwell (1844)

Auden, John Ernest, *Shropshire* (nd [1912])

Bailey, Brian J., *Portrait of Shropshire* (1981)

Barratt, Alick and Fiona, *Clungunford. 950 Years of a Rural Community* (2002)

Baxter, Richard, *Reliquiae Baxterianae* (1696)

Bilbey, David, *Church Stretton. A Shropshire Town and its People* (Chichester, 1985)

Bird, A.J., 'History and Legend', *Shropshire Magazine*, 5, no. 2 (June 1954), 28

Bond, W.G., *The Wanderings of Charles I and his Army in the Midlands*
    (Birmingham, 1935)

Bord, Janet and Colin, *The Secret Country* (1976)

Box, John, 'Dressing of the Arbor Tree', *Folklore*, 114 (2003), 13-28

Bracher, Terry, and Emmett, Roger, *Shropshire in the Civil War* (Shrewsbury, 2000)

Bradley, A.G., *The Romance of Wales* (1929)

Brewster, Waldegrave, MS. Logbook, Middleton-in-Chirbury, 1877–1901, Shropshire
    Records and Research Centre, P 187/E/2/1

Briggs, Katharine M., *A Dictionary of British Folk-tales*, (4 vols, 1970–1)

    A Dictionary of Fairies (Harmondsworth, 1977)

    and Tongue, Ruth L. (eds.), *Folktales of England* (1965)

Brown, I.J., *The Mines of Shropshire* (Stafford, 1976)

    'Shropshire Tragedies. A Collection of Old Ballads commemorating
        Industrial Tragedies', *Shropshire Mining Club Journal* (Dec. 1977)

Bryan, W.T., *Circles, Cairns and Axes. A Prehistoric Landscape around Corndon Hill* (np, nd)

    Ghost Stories for a Winter Fireside (np, nd)

    The Roaring Bull of Bagbury. A Legend and its Story (np, nd)

Burne, Charlotte S. (1850–1923), 'The Collection of English Folk-lore', *Folklore*, 1 (1890), 313-330

    The Handbook of Folklore (1914)

    (ed.), *Shropshire Folk-Lore: A Sheaf of Gleanings, edited by Charlotte Sophia Burne from the Collections of Georgina F. Jackson* (2 vols, East Ardsley, 1973; orig. London, Shrewsbury and Chester, in three parts, 1883-6)

    'Souling, Clementing and Catterning: Three November Customs in the Western Midlands', *Folklore*, 25 (1914), 285-99

Burritt, Elihu, *Walks in the Black Country and its Green Borderland* (Kineton, 1976; orig. London, 1868)

Butterworth, George (coll.), *The Ploughboy's Glory. A selection of hitherto unpublished folk songs*, ed. M. Dawney (1977)

Byford-Jones, Wilfred [Quaestor], *Both Sides of the Severn* (Birmingham, nd)

    Midland Murders, Hauntings and Characters (Birmingham, nd)

    Severn Valley Stories (Wellington, 1967)

Cameron, David Kerr, *The English Fair* (Stroud, 1998)

Carlton, Charles, *Going to the Wars. The Experience of the English Civil Wars, 1638–1651* (1992)

Cawte, E.C., 'The Morris Dance in Herefordshire, Shropshire and Worcestershire', *Journal of the English Folk Dance and Song Society*, 9, no. 4 (Dec. 1963), 197-212

    Helm, Alex, and Peacock, N., *English Ritual Drama. A Geographical Index* (1967)

Chambers, E.K., *The Elizabethan Stage* (4 vols, Oxford, 1923)

    The English Folk-Play (Oxford, 1933)

Chambers, R. (ed.), *The Books of Days. A Miscellany of Popular Antiquities* (2 vols, London and Edinburgh, nd [1863])

Cholmondeley, Mary, *Under One Roof: A Family Record* (1918)

Christian, Roy, *Old English Customs* (Newton Abbot, 1972)

Cobbett, William, *Rural Rides*, ed. G. Woodcock (Harmondsworth, 1967; orig. London, 1830)

Coles, Gladys Mary, *Mary Webb* (Bridgend, 1990)

Collinson, Patrick, 'The Shearmen's Tree and the Preacher: the Strange Death of Merry England in Shrewsbury and Beyond', in Patrick Collinson and John Craig (eds.), *The Reformation in English Towns, 1500-1640* (Basingstoke, 1998)

Cooper, Quentin, and Sullivan, Paul, *Maypoles, Martyrs & Mayhem* (1994)

Courcy-Parry, C.N. de [Dalesman], *Here Lies My Story* (1964)

Cranage, D.H.S, *An Architectural Account of the Churches of Shropshire* (3 vols, Wellington, 1900-07)

Crawford, Phyllis, *In England Still* (Bristol, 1938)

Dakers, Alan, *Fordritshope. History of a Shropshire Parish* (Church Stretton, 1986)

Darling, E. Moore, *Seeing Shropshire* (Shrewsbury, 1937)

Davies, Brenda, and Williams, Jocelyn, *Llanfair-Waterdine. A Parish Remembered* (Llanfair Waterdine, 1988; orig. *Llanfair-Waterdine, a Portrait of a Parish*, Llanfair Waterdine, 1988)

Davies, James, 'Old Herefordshire Customs', *Transactions of the Woolhope Society* (1877-80), 22-30

Davies, J.H., *A Bibliography of Welsh Ballads Printed in the Eighteenth Century* (1911)

Davies, Owen, *Cunning-Folk. Popular Magic in English History* (2003) 'Healing Charms in Use in England and Wales, 1700-1950', *Folklore*, 107 (1996), 19-32

Davies, Peter (born 1928), *Mare's Milk and Wild Honey - A Shropshire Boyhood* [at Little Ness] (1987)

Davies, R.R., *The Revolt of Owain Glyn Dŵr* (Oxford, 1997; orig. 1995)

Davis, John, *Cleobury Mortimer. The Parish in Pictures* (Cleobury Mortimer, 1989)

Davis, Norman (ed.), *Non-Cycle Plays and Fragments* [including from Shrewsbury] (1970)

Doel, Fran and Geoff, *The Green Man in Britain* (Stroud, 2001)

Defoe, Daniel, *A Tour through the Whole Island of Great Britain* (Harmondsworth, 1971; orig. 1724-6)

Drayton, Michael, *Poly-olbion*, vol. 4 of *The Works of Michael Drayton*, ed. J. William Hebel (Oxford, 1933; orig. 1613 and 1622)

Dukes, Thomas Farmer, *Antiquities of Shropshire* (Shrewsbury, 1844)

Elderwick, David, *The Lord of Burghley and Sarah Hoggins* (np, 1982)

Errington, C.J.R., *et al*, *A Short History of Moreton Corbet Castle and Church* (np, nd)

Evans, Simon (1895-1940), *A Simon Evans Anthology* (Kidderminster, 1981) *At Abdon Burf: More Tales from Shropshire* (1932) *Round about the Crooked Steeple: a Shropshire Harvest* (1931) *Shropshire Days and Shropshire Ways* (1938)

Eyton, R.W., *Antiquities of Shropshire* (12 vols, London and Shifnal, 1854-60)

Farmer, David Hugh, *The Oxford Dictionary of Saints* (Oxford, 1987)

Fewtrell, John, 'Parochial History of Llanymynech', *Montgomeryshire Collections*, 10 (1877), 379-96; 11 (1878), 179-232; 12 (1879), 109-166 and 361-412; 13 (1880), 125-160 and 389-416; and 14 (1881), 71-80.

Field, John, *English Field Names* (Stroud, 1989)

Fox, Adam, *Oral and Literate Culture in England, 1500-1700* (Oxford, 2000)

Foxall, H.D.G, *Shropshire Field-Names* (Shrewsbury, 1980)

Friar, Stephen, *A Companion to the English Parish Church* (Stroud, 1996)

Gandy, Ida, *An Idler on the Shropshire Borders* (Shrewsbury, 1970)

Gardiner, Joyce, 'In a Shropshire Village' [Bucknell], *The Countryman*, 71, no. 1 (autumn 1968), 108-117

Gaskell, Catherine Milnes, 'Old Wenlock and its Folklore', *The Nineteenth Century* (1894), 259-267

Gibbons, Gavin, *Welsh Border from the Wirral to the Wye* (nd)

Godson, E.A., 'Children's Rhymes and Games', *Caradoc and Severn Valley Field Club Transactions*, 5 (1909-12), 1-7

Gough, Richard (1634-1723), *Human Nature Displayed in the History of Myddle* [also known as *Antiquities and Memoirs of the Parish of Myddle, County of Salop*], with an introduction by W.G. Hoskins (Fontwell, 1968; orig. written 1700-1706; first published completely in 1875)

Greenoak, Francesca, *All the Birds of the Air* (Harmondsworth, 1981)

Grice, Frederick, *Folk Tales of the West Midlands* (1952)

Grigson, Geoffrey, *The Englishman's Flora* (St. Albans, 1975)

Grinsell, Leslie V., 'Hangman's Stones', *Folklore*, 96, pt 2 (1985), 217-222

Groome, Francis Hindes (1851-1902), *In Gipsy Tents* (Edinburgh, 1880)

Gwalter, Mechain [Peter Davies (1761-1849)], *History of Llansilin* (1795)

Hamer, Fred (coll.), *Garners Gay. English Folk Songs* (1967)
    (coll.), *Green Groves. More English Folk Songs* (1973)

Hancock, C.V., *East and West of Severn* (Faber, 1956)

Hare, Augustus J.C., *Shropshire* (1898)

Hartshorne, C.H., *Salopia Antiqua* (1841)

Harvey, Sally P., *A Short Guide to St. Peter's, Diddlebury* (np, nd)

Haye, W., 'Folklore and Tradition', *Shropshire Magazine*, 5, no. 2 (June 1954), 29-30

Hayward, L[ilian] H., 'Shropshire Folklore Today and Yesterday', *Folklore*, 49 (1938), 223-243
    'When "charms" cured our ills', *Shropshire Magazine*, 2, no.2 (June 1951), 23

Henken, Elissa R., *National Redeemer. Owain Glyndŵr in Welsh Tradition* (Cardiff, 1996)

Herring, Maisie, *Shropshire* (1949)

Higham, H.J., *King Arthur. Mythmaking and History* (2002)

Hill, Robin, and Stamper, Paul, *The Working Countryside, 1862-1945* (Shrewsbury, 1993)

Hodges, Geoffrey, *Owain Glyn Dŵr and the War of Independence on the Welsh Borders* (Logaston, 1995)

Hole, Christina, *British Folk Customs* (1976)

Holloway, John (ed.), *The Oxford Book of Local Verses* (Oxford, 1987)

Holt, J.C., *Robin Hood* (1982)

Hone, William (ed.), *The Every-Day Book* (2 vols, 1826-7)

Hope, Robert Charles, *The Legendary Lore of the Holy Wells of England* (1893)

Horner, Heather, 'Frederick Charles Jordan (1922-2002)', *Folk Music Journal*, 8, no. 4 (2004), 559-60

Housman, A.E., *A Shropshire Lad* (1896)

Hughes, Cledwyn, *The House in the Cornfield* (1957)

Hughes, Jean, *A Light-hearted Look at Our Shropshire History* (2nd ed, Shrewsbury, nd)
    Shropshire Folklore, Ghosts and Witchcraft (Shrewsbury, 1977)

Inwards, Richard, *Weather Lore* (1893)

Jackson, Georgina F. (1824-95), *Shropshire Word-Book* (Shrewsbury, 1982; orig. London, Shrewsbury and Chester, 1879)

James, R.B., *Whitchurch. A Short History* (Whitchurch, 1979)

Jenkins, A.E, *Titterstone Clee Hills - Everyday Life, Industrial History and Dialect* (Orleton, 1982)

Jones, Dave, *The Roots of Welsh Border Morris* (Putley, 1995; orig. 1988)

Jones, John B., *Offa's Dyke Path* (1976)

Jones, Lavender M., 'The Gentlemen Locks', *English Dance and Song*, 26, no.4 (Aug. 1964), 84-5

'The Shropshire Morris Dance', *English Dance and Song*, 18, no.5 (1954), 167-9

Jones, P. Thoresby, *Welsh Border Country* (3rd ed, 1949; orig.1938)

Karlin, Daniel, 'It isn't believing' [in ghosts], *Times Literary Supplement* (14 June 2002), 36

Keenan, Siobhan, *Travelling Players in Shakespeare's England* (Basingstoke, 2002)

Kightly, Charles, *Folk Heroes of Britain* (1982)

Country Voices (1984)

Kissack, Keith, *The River Severn* (Lavenham, 1982)

Klein, Peter, *A Guide to St. Peter's Church, Stanton Lacy* (Stanton Lacy, 1989)

A Guide to Stoke St. Milborough Parish Church (Stoke St. Milborough, 1992)

The Misericords and Choir Stalls of Ludlow Parish Church (Ludlow, 1986)

The Temptation and Downfall of the Vicar of Stanton Lacy (Ludlow, 1005)

Lean, V.S., *Collectanea* (2 vols, 1902-3)

Leather, E.M., with a note by T.W. Thompson, 'Collecting Folk-melodies from Gypsies in Herefordshire', *Journal of the Gypsy Lore Society*, 3rd. ser, 4, pt 2 (1925), 59-73

The Folk-Lore of Herefordshire (East Ardsley, 1970; orig. Hereford and London, 1912)

'Scraps of English Folklore: Shropshire', *Folklore*, 25 (1914), 372

Lias, Anthony, *Place Names of the Welsh Borderlands* (Ludlow, 1991)

McCarthy, Christine, 'Ghost Stories of Shropshire', in D.J. Brierley (ed.), *Shropshire* (Gloucester, 1988)

Mee, Arthur, *Shropshire* (1939)

Mendham, Geoffrey, 'Encounters with the Morris Dance in Shropshire', *English Dance and Song*, 18, no.3 (1953), 100

Menefee, S.P., *Wives for Sale* (Oxford, 1981)

Millward, Roy, and Robinson, Adrian, *The Middle Severn Valley* (1971)

Moore, John C., *The Welsh Marches* (1933)

Morgan, Richard, *Welsh Place Names in Shropshire* (Cardiff, 1997)

Morris, Rosie, 'The "Innocent and Touching Custom" of Maidens' Garlands: a Field Report', *Folklore*, 114 no.3 (2003), 355-88

Morton, Andrew, *The Trees of Shropshire. Myth, Fact and Legend* (Shrewsbury, 1986)

Mulroy, Betty, *Carving by Candlelight. A History of Middleton Church* (Worthen, 1988)

Negus, Tim, 'Medieval Foliate Heads: A Photographic Study', *Folklore*, 114 (2003), 247-70

Nicolle, Dorothy, *Shropshire Walks with Ghost and Legends* (Wilmslow, 2003)

Nimrod [C.J. Apperley], *Memoirs of the Life of the Late John Mytton, Esq.* (1906; orig. 1835)

Noake, John, 'Superstitions of Worcestershire [and Shropshire]', *Gentleman's Magazine*, 41, pt 2 (1855), 384-6

Ollard, Richard, *The Escape of Charles II after the Battle of Worcester* (1966)

O'Neil, B.H. St. J., 'Excavations at Titterstone Clee Hill Camp, Shropshire', *Archaeologia Cambrensis*, 89 (1934), 83-111

Opie, Iona and Peter, *The Lore and Language of Schoolchildren* (Frogmore, 1977; orig. Oxford, 1959)

Opie, Iona, and Tatem, Moira (eds.), *A Dictionary of Superstitions* (Oxford, 1989)

Otter, Laurens, 'Notes towards a Survey of Shropshire Holy Wells' (5 parts, 1985-8, internet http://www.bath.ac.uk/lispring)

Palmer, Roy, *Britain's Living Folklore* (Newton Abbot, 1991; repr. Felinfach, 1995)
    The Folklore of Radnorshire (Logaston, 2001)
    'A Happy Man, A Hard Life - The Story of Arthur Lane (1884-1975)', *Oral History*, 8, no. 2 (autumn 1980), 30-35
    Herefordshire Folklore (Logaston 2002)
    'Thomas Percy', in *The Oxford Dictionary of National Biography* (Oxford, 2004)

Peel, J.H.B., *Portrait of the Severn* (1968)

[Peele, E.C, and Clease, R.S. (eds.)], *Shropshire Parish Documents* (Shrewsbury, nd)

Peele, Michael, *Old Shrewsbury Show* (Shrewsbury, 1980; orig.1934)

Perry, J., 'Carrying Garlands at Funerals', *The Antiquary*, 3 (3 May 1873), 207-210

Peskin, Charles F., 'Memories of Old Coalbrookdale', *Transactions of the Caradoc and Severn Valley Field Club*, 11, no. 3 (1941), 217-8

Peters, Ellis [Edith Pargeter], *Ellis Peters' Shropshire* (1992)

Pevsner, Nikolaus, *The Buildings of England: Shropshire* (1958)

Philip, Neil, *Victorian Village Life* (Tydbury, 1993)

Phillips, G., and Keatman, M., *King Arthur. The True Story* (1993)

Prentice, Rob, *A History of Newport* (Chichester, 1986)

Preshous, Janet, *Bishop's Castle Well-remembered* (2nd ed., 1995)

Price, Derek (born 1928), *Up and Down the Patches. A Shropshire Boyhood* (Dereham, 1997)

Price, P.E., 'The decline and fall of the old Shrewsbury show', *West Midlands Studies*, 11 (1978), 29-33

Purton, W., 'The Clee Forest and the Clees', *Transactions of the Severn Valley Naturalists' Field Club: A Selection of the Papers* (Wellington, 1872), pp. 7-13

Quaestor: *see* Byford-Jones

Ralphs, Geoffrey, 'What the miner's daughter saw', *Shropshire Magazine*, 15, no. 8 (Aug. 1963), 37

Randall, John (1810-1910), *The Severn Valley* (Madeley, 1882; orig. London, 1862)

Raven, Michael, *Land of Lost Content* (Market Drayton, 1999)
    A Shropshire Gazetteer (Market Drayton, 1989)
    Song of the Fox (Market Drayton, 1997)

Ray, Phyllis M., *Ashford Carbonel. A Peculiar Parish. A Brief History* (Ashford Carbonel, 1998)

Richardson, John, *The Local Historian's Encyclopedia* (New Barnet, 1974)

Rix, M[ichael] M., 'More Shropshire Folklore', *Folklore*, 71 (1960), 184-7

Roberts, Michael, '"Waiting upon Chance": English Hiring Fairs and their Meanings from the 14th to the 20th Century', *Journal of Historical Sociology*, 1, no.2 (1988), 120-160

Roger, Alexander, 'Roger Ward's Shrewsbury Stock: An Inventory of 1585'. *The Library*, 5th Ser., 13 (1958), 247-68

Rogers, Nicholas, *Halloween from Pagan Ritual to Party Night* (New York, 2002)

Rossington, Eileen, *St. Michael and All Angels' Lydbury North: A Visitor's Guide* (Lydbury North, 1999)

Roud, Steve, *The Penguin Guide to the Superstitions of Britain and Ireland* (2003)
        The English Year (2006)

Samuel, Raphael (ed.), *Miners, Quarrymen and Saltworkers* (1977)

Sandford, Jeremy, *Songs from the Roadside. 100 Years of Gypsy Music* (Clun, 1995)

Sandys, William, *Christmastide: its History, Festivities and Carols* (nd [1852])

Saville, Malcolm, and O'Hanlon, Mark, *The Silent Hills of Shropshire* (Worcester, 1998)

Seymour, John, *The Countryside Explained* (1977)

Sharp, Cecil, *Cecil Sharp's Collection of English Folk Songs*, ed. M. Karpeles (2 vols, 1974)

Shropshire Federation of Women's Institutes, *Shropshire within Living Memory* (Newbury and Shrewsbury, 1992)

Simpson, Jacqueline, *The Folklore of the Welsh Border* (1976)
        and Roud, Steve, *A Dictionary of English Folklore* (Oxford, 2000)

Somerset, J. Allen B. (ed.), *Records of Early English Drama: Shropshire* (2 vols, Toronto, Buffalo and London, 1994)

Spraggs, Gillian, *Outlaws & Highwaymen. The Cult of the Robber in England from the Middle Ages to the Nineteenth Century* (2001)

Stephens, Meic (comp. and ed.), *The Oxford Companion to the Literature of Wales* (Oxford, 1986)

Strange, Alf (born 1925), *Me Dad's the Village Blacksmith* [at Welsh Frankton] (Denbigh, 1983)

T., J., 'The Loppington Bear', *Salopian Shreds and Patches*, 7 (7 Jan. 1885), 16

Taylor, 'Dr. Taylor's History', ed. W.A. Leighton, *Transactions of the Shropshire Archaeological and Natural History Society* (1880)

Thackeray, Veronica, *Tales from the Welsh March* (Malvern, 1992)
        This Enchanted Land (Malvern, 2000)
        Wandering in Wales and the Borderland (Malvern, 1995)

Thistleton Dyer, T.F., *The Folk-lore of Plants* (1889)

Thomas, Keith, *Religion and the Decline of Magic* (Harmondsworth, 1973)

Thompson, T.W.: *see under* Leather, E.M.

Thursby-Pelham, A., 'The Berrington Love Feast', *Transactions of Shropshire Historical and Archaeological Society*, ser. 2, 7 (1895), 203-6

Timmins, H.T., *Nooks and Corners of Shropshire* (1899)

Tinsley, A.B., *With Horse and Cart and Friend. Memories of a Salop Farm Boy* (Church Stretton, nd)

Trinder, Barrie, *'The Most Extraordinary District in the World'. Ironbridge and Coalbrookdale* (London and Chichester, 1977)
        Barges and Bargemen, A Social History of the Upper Severn Navigation, 1660-1900 (Chichester, 2005)
        and Cox, Nancy, *Miners and Mariners of the Severn Gorge* (Chichester, 2000)

Tyack, G.S., *Lore and Legend of the English Church* (1899)

Vale, Edmund, *Shropshire* (1949)

Vickery, Roy, *A Dictionary of Plant Lore* (Oxford, 1995)

Waite, Vincent, *Shropshire Hill Country* (1970)

Wakeman, Offley, 'Rustic Stage Plays in Shropshire', *Transactions of the Shropshire Archaeological Society*, 1st ser, 7 (1884), 383-8

Ward, Colin, *Cotters and Squatters* (Nottingham, 2002)

Warde, R.C., 'Shropshire Superstitions', in [W.J. Thoms, ed.,] *Choice Notes from 'Notes and Queries'* (1859), p. 57

Warner, Ann, *Newport, Shropshire - Past and Present* (Newport, 1983)

Waters, Brian, S*evern Stream* (1949)

Watkin, Isaac, *History of Llanyblodwel* (Oswestry, 1905)

Watkins, Alfred, *The Old Straight Track* (1925)

Weale, Magdalene, *Through the Highlands of Shropshire on Horseback* (1935)

Webb, Mary, *The Golden Arrow* (1916)
> *Gone to Earth* (1917)
> *Precious Bane* (1924)
> *Seven for a Secret* (1922)

West, J.M., *Shrewsbury* [School] (1937)

Westwood, Jennifer, *Albion. A Guide to Legendary Britain* (1987) and Simpson, Jacqueline, *The Lore of the Land* (2005)

White, K.G., 'The Legend of Satpeley Hill', *The Countryman* 38:1 (1953), 116-117

White, Walter, *All Round the Wrekin* (1860)

Williams, Tim, 'Customs and Folklore' in *Aspects of Shropshire* (Shrewsbury, 1994), 56-62

Windsor, George R., *Handbook of Church Stretton* (1885)

Wood, John, *Quietest under the Sun. Footways on Severnside Hills* (1944)

Woodward, Iris, *The Story of Wem* (Wem, 1996; orig. 1952)

Wright, A.R., and Lones, T.E., *British Calendar Customs: England* (3 vols, London and Glasgow, 1936-40)

Wright, Thomas (1810-77), 'On the Local Legends of Shropshire', *Collectanea Archaeologica*, 1, pt 1 (1862), 50-66

Records and Tapes

Crowther, Dennis, *Reminiscences of Titterstone Clee* [poems], audio-cassette (1991)

Jenkins, Alf, with Dennis Crowther, *'Up the Lane and back Again'. Memories of Bygone Days around Titterstone Clee*, videocassette (2000)

Jordan, Fred, *In Course of Time* [songs], audio-cassette (English Folk Dance and Song Society, VWML 006, 1991)
> *Songs of a Shropshire Farm Worker*, LP record (Topic Records, 12T150, 1966)
> *A Shropshire Lad: English Folk Songs*, double CD records (Veteran, VTD 148 CD, 2003)
> *When the Frost is on the Pumpkin*, LP record (Topic Records, 12TS233, 1974)

Kirkpatrick, John, and Harris, Sue, *A Really High Class Band*, LP record (Topic, 12TS295, 1976)

Life and Times, *Shropshire Iron*, LP record (Fellside Recordings, FE 071, 1989)

Various artists, *The Leaves of Life. The field recordings of Fred Hamer* [including May Bradley], audio-cassette (English Folk Dance and Song Society, VWML 003, 1989)

Index

Abdon 44, 264, 309
Abingdon, John 97
acting companies 274-9
Acton Burnell 65, 71, 92, 103, 115, 161, 273
    parliament at 74
Acton Reynald Hall 297
Acton Scott 34, 35, 90, 103
Adderley 34
Adeney 39
Adley, Mary 95
Aelnoth, son of Edric the Wild 88
Aethelbald, king of Mercia 4
Alaric, King 55-6
Alarme for Sinners, An 120, *120*
Alberbury 33, 78, 79, 89, 100
Albrighton 33, 41, 88, 117, 220, 241, 271, 293
Aldrich, Dr. Henry 37-8
All Saints' Day 305
All Souls' Day 305-7
All Stretton 27, *28*, 216
Alveley 3, *3*, 80, *80*, 91
    Three Horseshoes Inn 80
Anchor Inn, nr. Kerry 190, 215
Arthur, King 70-1
Ascension Day 66, 105, 118, 176, 217, 298
Ashford Carbonel 35, 90, 91, 96, *102*, 266, 300-2
Ashman, Gordon 109, 238-9, 241, 265
Ashton, Thomas 278, 279
Astley Abbotts 88, 102, 115, *115*, 264
Aston Munslow 246
Aston-on-Clun 51, 266
    Arbor Tree Ceremony 304
    Kangaroo Inn 240
Atcham 33, 71, 88, 103
    Mytton & Mermaid Inn 135, *135*
Aubrey, John 305, 306
Audelay/Audley, John 230
Auden, J.E. 39, 219, 304
Audley, Lord 77
    Cross 77, *77*
Avoncroft Museum, Worcs. 209

Babes in the Wood 34
Babbinswood, nr. Whittington 34
Bachelor's Buttons 151
Badger Hall 128
Bagbury, bull of 124
Bagford, John 172
Ball, William 201
ballads 29, 156, 176, 193-4, 252, 253, 254, 255-60, 213-4, *214*, 230, 243, 265, 283
    printers 253-60
    Titles:
        'An English lady ... Welsh Plough-boy' 256-7

'Country Hirings' 176-7
'Death and the Lady' 257, *257*, *258*
'George Barnwell' 253
'John Hobbs' 156-7, *157*
'Lamentation ... J. Newton ..., The' 258, *259*
'Loppington Bear, The' 252
'Midnight Messenger ..., The' 283
'Shropshire Wakes' 265
'bannering' 118-21
bargemen 49-50, 206, 211, 213, 236, 237
barges 48
Barnefield, Richard 93
Baschurch 66, 89, 105, 146, 171, 273, 304, 306
    Ladies' Club 305
Batley, Richard 250
Battlefield 77, 103
Baugh, William, ballad printer 257
Baxter, Richard 253, 262, 264
Bayston Hill *xi*, 57, 124
bear baiting 34, 205-6, 277, 279
Beard, Eustace 97
beating the parish bounds 2, 118-21, 298-9
Bebb, Mary 145
Beckbury 35
    Lower Hall 129
Bedlam 38, 98
Beeches, the (east of Montgomery) 8, 217
Beelzebub, Kynaston's horse 23
Beguildy, Wizard 162
Bell, Alan 230
bells 58, 59, 80, 102-7, 120, 130, 143, 184, 291, 310, 317
Benbow, Admiral John 254, *255*, 260
Bennett, Jane 250
Benthall 97, 195, 268
Berrington 33, 110, 111, 118, 306
Berth Pool 58-9
Betjeman, John 51
Bettws-y-Crwyn 5-6, 30, 32, 64, 113, *172*, 190, 218
Bewdley, Worcs 53
Bewick, Thomas *209*
Bird, Colin 42-46, *43*, 159, 180
Bishop's Castle 3, 17, 30, 33, 35, 46, 91, 167, *173*, 178, 180, *181*, 185, 215, 220, 221, 237, 240, 266, 305
Bitterley 33, 35, 38, 38, 97-8, 138, 262
    Court 80
black dog, ghostly 124
Blackmere 55, 236
Blake Mere, nr. Whitchurch 276
Blakeway, Maria 237
Bleddyn of Gwynedd 72
Blore Heath 77
Blount, family 124-6, *125*, *126*

Sir George 125
Bog Mine 191
Bolas Magna 109
Bolas Villa *182*, 183
Bomere Pool 56-8, *57*
Boscobel 81, 82, *82*, 83, 303
    Royal Oak 83
Botfield, Beriah, MP 6
boundaries 1-5
    of Mercia 176
Bowton 146
bow-hauliers 48-50, *49*
Box, John 304
Boxing Day 175, 267, 269, 315
Brading Stone 7
Bradley/Smith, May 244, 246, 313, *313*
brass bands 238
    Little Billy Martin's 238
Breidden Hills 1, 6, *6*, 23, *24*, 41, 50, 69, 74, 78
Brewster, Waldegrave 8, 11, 12, 42, *111*, 113, *114*, 151, 160, 161, 171
Brider/Symonds, Margery 2653
Bridgeman, Sir John 95
Bridgnorth 18, 20, *20*, 34, 41, 42, *47*, 48, 50, 87, 103, 104, 156, 168, 176, 205, 209, 220, 233, 261-2, 266, 274, 276, 305, 315
    Cann Hall 126
    Castle 18, *18*
    Crown Inn 209
    Hermitage, The 18, 20, *20*
    Thmas Percy's House 230
Broke, Sir Robert *92*, 93
Bromdon 266
Bromfield 17, 34, *34*, 35
Brookes, Dr. William Penny 147, 203, *203*
Broseley 49, 141, 183, 208, 211, 220, 244, 264, 266, 267
    The Lawns 199
Brown, Rev. G.O. 122
Brown Clee 1-2, *2*
Bruyère, Marion de la 67-8
Bucknell 2, 89, 90, 143, *185*
Buildwas 51, 52, 79, 142
    Abbey 19, 74
bull baiting 203, *205*, 206-8, 216, 277
buried treasure 16-7
Burford 33, 94, 113, *114*
Burne, Charlotte *xi-xiii*, xii, 3-4, 17, 23, 64, 73, 78, 79, 131, 137, 154, 155, 167, 168, 175, 176, 181, 186, 191, 206, 210, 216, 243, 244, 256, 257, 266, 284, 291, 295, 296, 298, 300, 303, 306, 308, 316
Burnell, Hugh 74
'burning the mawkin' 164
Bury Walls 70
Butler, Albert Thomas 63
Butter Cross, Alveley 3, *3*
Butterworth, George 244

Buttery 39
Byford-Jones, Wilfred 79, 88, 119, 127, 128, 133, 136, 229

Cadman, Robert 95, **95**
Caer Caradoc, Chapel Lawn 69
    nr. Knighton 2, 26, *26*
    Stretton Hills 28, 69
Caer Ogryfan 70
'caking' 96
Calverhall, John 233
Calverhill 41
Camden, William 70, 75
Cameron, David Kerr 204
Candlemas Eve (1 Feb) & Day 319
Cantlin Stone 5-6, *5*, 190
Cantlin, William 5-6
Capel, Lord 83
Caratacus 69
Cardeston 108, 109
Cardington 71, 99, 104, 132, 244, 310
Careless, Major Richard 81
carol singing 109, 244, 255, 257, 310-4
    'Herald Angels' 312
    'Under the leaves of life'/'The Seven Virgins' 313, 314
    'Virgin Unspotted' 311, 312, 313
Carreg-y-Big, Selattyn 3
Carr, Rev. E. Donald 187-8
Carregofa 21
Carter, 'Wisdom Tom' and Martha *166*
'cat whipping' 293
Caus Castle 153
Caynham 34
Cecil, Henry, Lord Burghley 182-3
Cefn-y-Castell 69
Challenger, Jon, wait 234
Chapel Lawn 3
Charles I 80, 126
    II 27, 80-81, 88, 208, 303
charmers 161-7
charms 165-6
Chelmarsh 33, 34, 102, 140
    Stern's Cottage 140
Cherrington 39
Cheswardine 33, 34, 105
Chetwynd, nr. Newport 80, 126-7, 218
Child's Ercall 59, 300
Chipnall 34
Chirbury 64, 151, 171, 280
    Priory 30, 86
Cholmondeley, Mary 108, 122, 272
    Rev. 122, 272
Christmas 96, 101, 109, 128, 173, 175, 197, 231, 234, 242, 263, 265, 266, 267, 268, 284, 285, 290, 291, 294, 308-15, *308*
church bands 106-9
Church Preen 2, 90

Church Pulverbatch 40, 89, 105, 218, 220, 295, 305, 306, 309, 279, 280, 309
Church Stoke 280
Church Stretton 21, 27, 33, 91, 98-9, 103, 105, 114, 137, 162, *166*, 170, 176, *180*, 187, 216, 218, 220
Churchman, William 99
Churchyard, Thomas 4, 277
Churm, Jane 139-40, *139*
Churton 40
cider *185*, 191-2
Civil War, the 68, 79-84, 94, 133, 134, 279, 280
Clarke, Richard 172
Claverley 34, 90, *92*, 93, *93*, 116, *116*, 117, *117*, 119, 172, *206*, 276
Clayton, Ralph 120
Clee 38
Clee Hill 41, 120, 141, 147, 150, 153, 161, 170, 174, 191, 192, 195-8, *196*, *197*, *198*, 222-3, 238, 240, 266, 267, 272, 299, 315, 319
    Oddfellows' Club 305
Clee St. Margaret *2*, 33, 34, 264
Cleeton 119
    St. Mary 299
Cleobury Mortimer 25, 33, 41, 65, *65*, 105, 220, 279
    North 262
'clipping' 117
Clive family 129
    Robert 83
Clive 19, 307, 310-1
Clog-fair day 309
'clogging' 309
Clun 32, 33, 36, 37, *37*, 39, 45, 90, 94, 103, 108, 150, 162, 165, 176, 190, 220, 221, 238, 240, 308, 309
    Castle 18, 19
    Valley 268, 316
Clunbury 34, 39, 148, 284
    Chapel Farm 143
Clungunford 39, 41, 118
Clungunus 103
Clunton 39
Clydach 39
Coalbrookdale 50, 52, 141, 156, 191, *199*, 201, 266, 277
Cobbett, William 218
cockfighting 50, 167, 203, 208-10, *209*, 277
Coke, Sir Edward 152
Cold Hatton 190
Cold Weston 121
Colebatch 238, 300
'Colebrook Dale' 198-9
Colemere 58, *58*, 79
Combermere Abbey, nr. Whitchurch 140
Come Merry Inn 50
Condover 35, 57, 103, 105, 132, 178, *236*, 295
    Hall 131-2, *131*
Cook, Ann 98-9

Cookson, Judy 155
Copper Hole, Hope Bowdler 137
coracles 24, 50-3, *51*, *52*
    racing *51*, 53
Corbet, Richard 93
    Robert 153
    Thomas 153
    Sir Vincent 19, 145-6
Corfham Castle 67
corn dollies 185
Corndon Hill 8, 9, *9*
Cornes, Ethel 152, *153*
Corneywall, Edmond 94
Corpus Christi, feast of 222, 233
Corve, River 60, *61*, 65
Cosford, RAF museum 139
Cothercott 40
Cotton, John, ballad printer 255
Cound 33, 110, 116
'couranting' 309
Courcy-Parry, Charles de 215-6
Court of pie-powder 220
Coxall Knoll 69
Crab Wakes 218
Craven Arms *190*, *219*, 220, 221
    Fair 180
Crawford, Phyllis 307
Crawl Meadow 34, *34*, 35
Cressage 28, 33, 273, 300
Cromwell, Oliver 58, 79, 80
Crosemere 59
Crowther, Dennis 25, 196, 272
crwth/Crowther 235
'crying the mare' 186
Cuckoo's Cup, Wrekin 14
cuckoo, hearing the 192
Culmington 34, 104
Cunde, Joan 250
cunning folk (see charmers)
curfew bells 105-6
'cutting the gonder's neck off' 185
Cynddylan, King of Powys 16-17, 59, 71

Dafydd ap Gruffyd 74
dancing, (see also morris) 35, 261-273
    broom dance 272
    step dancing 272
Darling, E.M. 37, 121
Davies, Rev. James 292
    Joan 145
    John 163-5
    Thomas (es) 95, 98
Dawkin, Rowland 99
Dawley 33, 57, 192, 194, 266, 273-4
    Oaves 37
    The Swan 135
Defoe, Daniel 55
'deodand', law of 104

Devil 4, 8, 15-6, 33, 40, 71, 89, 90, 91, 95, 132, 142-5, 160, 171, 281
Devil's Causeway 71, *71*
Devil's Chair, Stiperstones 15-6, *15*, 142-3, 147
dialect 41-6, 170, 229
'Dick Spot the conjurer' 166-7
Dickens, Charles 102
Diddlebury 41, 64, 89, 279
Dilke, Charles 102
Din Gwrygon, the Wrekin 71
Dinan, Joce de 67
Ditton Priors 33, 141
Donington 88
Donnington Wood 194, 310
Douglas's Leap, Haughmond Hill 76
Downes, Samuel 300
dragons 17, 33
Drayton, Michael 4
drovers 189-91
druids 88
Ducarel, James
Duckett, Sarah 137
ducking stool *154*, 155
Dudleston Heath 38
Dudley 313
Duff, Fanny 244
Durston, Thomas, ballad printer 255

Eardington 138, 209, 309
Eardiston, Pradoe Park 130
Earl's Hill 16
earnest money 180
Easter 232, 291, 294, 295-8
    'Love Feast' 118
Easthope 89, 90, 91, 110, 130, *130*, 239
Eaton 103
Eaton Constantine 262
Eaton Mascott 111
Eaton-under-Haywood 33, 34, 35
Eddowes, Joshua, ballad printer 255-6, *256*
Edgmond 34, 39, 42, 105, 117, 127, 128, 184, 300, 306
Edgton 103
Edith, Queen 86
Ednop, nr. Mainstone 245
Edric the Wild 57, 72-3, 88, 124
Edward II, as prince 235
Edwards, William, ballad printer 235
eel weirs *53*
Ellesmere 23, 32, 34, 40, 54-5, *54*, 99, 103, 107, 121, 152, 175, 208, 220, 257, 305, 306
Ellis, Mrs. 54, 55
    Jeremiah *173*
    Thomas 133-4
Empire Day 304
Ercall Hill *xi*, *xii*, 13, 15
Ethelbert of East Anglia 5
Ethelward, brother of King Athelstan 20

Evan, David Syr 145
Evans, Simon 25, 32-3, *32*, 243
Evelith Mill 80
exorcism 124-6
Eyton 109

fairies 8, 91, 140-1, *142*, 150
fairs 204, 218-22, *221*, 245
    hiring/mop 175-7, 179-80, *181*, 221
Farlow 33, 210, 262
'Farmer's Boy, The' (poem) 44-5
    (song) 245-6, 247
farmwork 177-86
    harvest 184-7
    haymaking 183-4
    shearing 181-2, *182*
Farquhar, George *xii*
feasts 305
fitz Warin, Fulk 78, 79
Fitzwarine, Romance of 15
fives 92
Fletcher, John 95
Flounder, Benjamin 3, 7
Flounder's Folly 3
Flowering Sunday 117
foot-ale 192
Ford 33, 34, 296
Foulkes, Robert 120, *120*
fox hunting 211-6
France, John, ballad printer 257, 312-3
Frodesley 109
funerals 91, 106, 172, 173, 174

Gandy, Ira 84, 144, 152, 163, 218, 221
Garmston, Will 130
Gaskell, Catherine 116, 146, 147, 155, 176
Gatacre, Francis & Elizabeth 93, *93*
Gay, John 115
Gerald of Wales 71
ghosts 84, 123, 124, 126-41, 178, 215
giants 9, 13, 15, 16, *16*, 17, 21, 70, 71, 115
Giant's Cave, Stapeley Hill 21
'gifting' 316
Giles, Benjamin 97
Gittin, Edward 97
Glyndŵr, Owain 74-7
Glyndŵr's Oak 76
Goblin Hole, nr. Myddle 20
Gobowen 27, 122
Goddard, Dr. 169
Godson, Rev. E.A. 307, 310
Golden Arrow, The 16, 295
Good Friday 160, 296
'gooding' 309
Gospel Oaks 119-20
Gough, Richard 20, 21, 29, 77, 84, 121, 133, 166, 169, 171, 172, 217, 251, 271, 310
Granville Colliery, nr. Oakengates 191

Great Bolas 182-3
green man 113-4, *114*
Greenteeth, Jenny 55
Greete 145, 212, 262
    Court, nr. Ludlow 80
Grinshill 266, 300
Groome, T.H. 141, 144, 242
Guto'r Glyn 29
Guy Fawkes Night 307-8
Gwên 72
Gwendol-Wrekin ap Shenkin ap Mynnyddmawr 13
gypsies 243

Habberley 237, 309
hagoday 110
Halfpenny, Mrs. 244
Hall, Mary Ann 300
Halliwell Wakes 217, 280
Hallowe'en 151-2, 171, 305
Hamer, Fred 313
Hanwood 115
Hardwick Hall, Welsh Frankton 24, 215
Hare, Augustus 8, 23, 35, 36, 57, 77, 98, 106, 115,
    124, 127, 143, 150, 161, 186, 277, 293
Harley 266
Harley, Lady Brilliana 300
Harrow 265
Hartshorne, Charles 4, 10, 295
Harvest Home 186-7
Hatton, Francis 152
Haughmond 41
    Abbey 19, 230
    (Aymon) Hill 26, 68, 76, 296
Hawkstone (park) 15, 70, 186
Hayward, Lillian 129, 132, 141, 148, 150, 161, 162,
    170, 171, 187, 307, 311
Hazler Gate, Hope Bowdler 137
Hazlitt, William 273
Heath 264
heaving ceremonies 296-8, *297*
Hengist 72
herbal remedies 161, 163, 170
    foxglove/digitalis 170
hermits 20
Herring, Maisie 1, 21, 111, 201, 218, 268, 273, 274
Heynes, Richard 94, 133
Hick, Francis 98
High Ercall 19, 82, 120, 244
Highley 273
Hinstock 33
histriones 231, 232
Hoar Stones, Clunbury Hill 3
hob 33
Hodnet 33, 108, 122, 152, 189, 220, 266, 272, 306
    Bear Inn 145
Hoggins, Sally/Sarah 182-3
Holdgate 114, *115*
    Castle 18

Holmyard, Paul 19, 145-6
Homer 266
Hope Bagot 64, *64*, 90, 97, 104, 130, 140, *140*
    Bowdler 63, 97, 103, 107, 137, 176, 309,
        310, 316, 317, 318
Hopesay 1, 10-3, 152, 262
Hopton Castle 84, *84*, 133
    Cangeford 121
    Court, Hopton Wafers 138
Hopton Wafers 138, 279
Horderley 8
Hordley 33
Horsehay, nr. Wellington 201, 274
horseshoes, reversing direction of 27, 76, 77
Hotspur, Harry 75, 76
Housman, A.E. 39, 70, 220, 244
Howard, Sir Robert 152
Hughes, Cledwyn 104, 119, 172, 176, 181, 210,
    318
Hughley 138
Huglith 40
Hulbert, Charles 297

Ice Ages 48
Ightfield 143-4
illegitimacy 150
Ippikin's Rock, Wenlock Edge 136-7
Ireland, Samuel 50
iron industry 198-202
Ironbridge 50, 51, *200*, 201, 266

Jack o'the Weald Moors 167
Jackfield 49, 50
Jackson, Georgina *xii*, 40, 42, 53, 218, 252, 253, 306
Jagger, Arthur 39
James II 27, 169
Jasper, Cecil 128
Jenkin, Richard 251
Jenkins, Alf 41, 161, 174, 195, 197, 221, 272, 315
Joan of Navarre, 2nd wife of Henry IV 27, 77
John, King 78, 79
Jones, Dave 269
    Lavender 268
    Mary 155
    P. Thoresby 121
    Thomas 300
    William 99
Jordan, Fred 229, 246-7, *247*, 249
Jukes, Thomas 251
    Vincent 251-2

Kemberton Pit, Madeley 183-4
Kempton, nr. Clun 218
Kenley 89
Ketley 161, 193, 208, 266, 267, 298
Kettlemere 55
Kinaston, Rev. 121
Kinlet 86, 89. 92, 124-6, *125*, *126*, 167, 262

Kinnerley 32, 34, 64, 306
Knevett, Lord 131-2
Knockin 23, 30, 133-4
Knott, Edward 97
Knowbury 136, 305
Kynaston, family 77
    Humphrey 21-4, 27, 78
    Humphrey's Cave 23
    John 75
Kyndrytha 5

Ladies in Grey/White 128
Lady Oak, Cressage 28, 28
Lady's (ies') Walk 54
Lancett, Mrs. 96
Lane, Arthur 178-80, 178, 187, 244-6, 245, 247,
    249, 272, 315
Langton, Ray & Bev 270
Laud, Archbishop 118
Lawley, The 2
Lea/Lee, Sir Richard 118
Lea Stone, nr. Bishop's Castle 8
Lee Bridge 210
Leebotwood 89, 103
Leighton 33, 109, 305
Leighton Monument 99
    Sir William 132-3
Leintwardine, Herefs. 53
Leland, John xi, 36, 60
Lewis, Arthur 244, 316, 317, 318, 318
Leyte, Molly de 147-8
Lhuyd, Edward 9
    Humphrey 55, 69
Light, Thomas, conjuror 167
Lilleshall 41, 86, 244
    Abbey 19, 19
Linley 113
Lisle, Arnold de 67-8
Little Dawley 194
    Nell 102
    Ness 7, 16-7, 34, 66, 115
    Stretton 27, 216, 244
    Wenlock 35, 147, 237, 262
    Wrekin 13
Llanbrook 31, 160, 163
Llanedric, Clun 72
Llanfair Waterdine xiii, 31, 31, 32, 108, 160, 180,
    190, 218
    Black, Tithe or Morris Barn 242, 271, 271
Llansilin 74, 250, 273
Llanyblodwel 4, 29, 30-1, 30, 88, 106, 107, 108-9,
    108, 110, 110, 112, 113, 144-5, 163, 173, 216
Llanymynech 30, 64, 191, 220
    Hill 15, 17, 21, 141
Llynclys 55-6, 55, 307
Llywelyn the Great 78
'Lob' xii
Lock, family 240-3, 247, 271

    Charlie 242
    Esmerelda 242
    Ezekiel 240, 241
    Gipsy 242-3
    Herbert 242
    James 241, 271
    John 240-1, 243
    Polin 240, 243
Lockley, Mr. 244
Lodge Pit, Donnington Wood 194
Loggan, Thomas 296-7, 297
Long Mynd 31, 34, 72, 73, 74, 142, 187, 188, 190,
    242
Longdon-on-Tern 250, 300
Longford Hall 19
Longnor 103, 140
Longville-in-the-Dale 134
Loppington 205, 206, 252
Loughton 90, 90
luck, ill 158-9, 160, 298
    good 159, 160
Ludford 64, 65, 90, 119
    House 20
    Huck's Barn 253, 254
Ludlow 16, 20, 30, 41, 65, 83, 95, 103, 112, 113,
    118-9, 120, 136, 155, 176, 190, 192, 205,
    206, 208, 208, 220, 221, 231, 234, 236,
    251, 253, 263, 266, 274, 276, 278, 279,
    291-2, 300, 304, 307-8
    Boiling Well 64-5
    Bull Inn 20, 135, 237
    Castle 67-8, 67, 84, 120, 161
    Fair 180
    Palmers' Guild 65
    Processioning Day 299
    Tolsey 208, 220
    tug o'war 292, 292
Lurkenhope 26, 263
Lutwyche, Sir Edward 129
Lydbury North 5, 72, 73, 87, 87, 88, 266, 279
    Red House Farm 210, 210
Lycett, J. 258
Lyth Hill 18

Madeley 37, 80, 148, 152, 206, 217, 266, 267, 273,
    315
    Wood 266
magpies and luck 159-60
Maid of the Green Forest 55-6
maiden's garlands 114-5, 115
Mainstone 2, 5, 94, 107, 145
    boulder at 7, 7
Major's Leap, Wenlock Edge 83
Malpas, John, of Kinlet 167
Map, Walter 72
mark stones 2, 3
Market Drayton 91, 175, 188, 217, 219, 220, 303-4,
    306

Four Alls 136
marriage 149, 151-4
Marshall, Richard, abbot of Shrewsbury Abbey 135
Mary, Queen, 1st wife of Henry IV 27
Masefield, John *xi*
Maserfield, battle of 26, 59
May Day 271, 300-3
Mechain, Gwalter 30
Meddins, William, curate 250
Meer Oak 2
Melverley 6, 7, 32, 34, 37, 89, 89, 109
Mendham, Geoffrey 268
Meole Brace 34
Merewald, King 62
mermaids 59, 113, *113*, 135
Middleton-in-Chirbury 8, *10*, *11*, *111*, 113, *114*, 160, 171, 189
Middleton Scriven 104
Midsummer Day 117
Milwood, Sarah 253
miners 9, 73, 140, 141, 191-5, 206, 211, 213, 217, 258, 265, 266, 303
    coal 192-5
    lead 191
    reluctance to work on Mondays 192
mining, accidents 193-4, 258
Minsterley 33, 73, 109, 115, 191
minstrels 231, 232, 233, 235, 236, 237, 263, 274
    Ethiopian 267
miracles 61, 62, 63, 86, 88
misericords *112*, 113, *278*
mistletoe 309
Mitchell's Fold 8-13, *9*, 66, 134
    Tenement 8, 9
Moat Hall Colliery 193
Moat House Colliery, nr. Longden 192
'Molly' dancers 269, *269*
Monarch's Way 82
Monaughty Poeth 32
Montford 33, 34, 250
    Bridge 7, 22, *22*, 74
Montgomery, Adelisa de 86
Moody, Tom 213-5, *214*
Moore, Francis 168
    John 109, 238, 239, 240
More 34
More, Samuel, of Linley 83, 84
Moreton Corbet 19, 93, *93*, 106, 153
    Say 109, 129, 135, 145-6
Morgan, family, ballad writers 193-4, 258
    Nanny 146-7
Morris, Richard, 'Dick Spot the conjurer' 166-7
morris dancing 263-71, *267*, *269*, *270*, 304, 315
    Ironmen 269, 271
    Merrydale Mixed Cotswold Morris 271
    Much Wenlock Morris *267*, *269*
    Severn Gilders 271
    Shrewsbury Arcadian Morris 266

Shrewsbury Morris 270-1
    Bull & Pump Morris 270
    Shrewsbury Lasses 270
    Shropshire Bedlams 271
    South Shropshire Morris men 271
    Westwood 268
Morville 34, 106
Moseley Hall, Staffs. 81
Moseley, Cyril 269, *269*
Mount St. Gilbert 15
Much Wenlock 62, 63, *63*, 79, 105, 113, 119, 155, 156, 169, 176, 185, 203-4, *203*, *204*, 210, 266, 267, 268, 298-9, 305, 309
    St. Owen's Well 66, *66*
Mucklestone, nr. Market Drayton 77, 299
mumming plays 284-90, *290*
Munslow 99, 205, 264
    Swan Inn 79
Munslow, John 116
Murrell, Hilda 68, *68*
music 35
    'Ironbridge Hornpipe, The' 238, 239
    'Morning Star' 241
    'Rakes of Shrewsbury' 239
    'Shropshire Quick Step' 239
    'Three Jolly Sheepskins' 241, 271, 272
musicians 229-252, *235*, 262-3
Myddle 34, 121, 171, 251, 252, 271, 310, *310*
    Castle 21, *22*
    Hill 172
Myndtown 262
mystery plays *278*
Mytton, Mad Jack 135, 204, 212-3, *213*, 215
    Thomas 68

Needles' Eye, The, Stiperstones 14
    Wrekin 14, *14*, 15, 296
Neen Savage 262
    Sollars 33
Neenton 148
Nesscliffe 22, 23, 27, 78
    Three Pigeons Inn 23, 78
New Invention 27
New Year 215, 290, 315-9
Newcastle 152, 217, 240
Newport 34, 64, *83*, 104, 105, 118, 175, 220, 221, 241, 244, 266, 284, 306
    Shakespeare Inn 229
nicknames 41-2, 310
Noakes, John 158, 315
Norbury 90, 103, 117
Norton and Shaw 118
Norton-in-Hales 7, 33, 216, 217, 293
Nott, William 97-8

Oak Apple Day (29 May) 303-4
Oakengates 41, 192, 203, 206, 208, 217, 218, 225
Oakley, family 87-8

oaks, as markers 2
Offa, King 4
Offa, of Angel 4
Offa's Dyke 1, 3-5, *4-5*
Ogof's Hole 21, *21*, 56
'Olympian games', Much Wenlock 203-4, 227, 305
Onibury 35, 266
Oswestry *xiii*, 3, 4, 23, 26, 29, 30, 32, 41, 42, 56,
        59, 70, 74, 75, 80, 83, 103, 155, 176,
        220, 230, 255, 266, 298, 304, 305, 306
    Coach & Dogs tearooms *235*
Oteley Hall 128, *128*
    White Lady of 128
Owd Scriven *110*, 111
Owen, Thomas 145
    Wilfred 230
    a lawyer 131-2

pagan sites 88
Palm Sunday 16, 66, 90, 117, 295
Pant 197
Parks, William 99
Parr, Robert 102
        Thomas (old) 100-2, *100*, 116
            cottage *101*
Pearce, Isabella 163
penance 116-7, 152, 264, 279
Penda, King 26, 59
Penderel, Richard 80
    William & Joan 81
Pengwern 4, 17, 71
Pennell, William 251
Pepys, Samuel 81
Percy, Thomas 229-30
    house *230*
Perkins, Samuel 96
'permanenting' 151-2
Peters, Ellis 201, 296
Petsey, Stoke-upon-Tern 133, *133*
Phillips, Hannah 115
Philpott, Edward 239, *239*, 240
Pigott, Madame 127-8
    Thomas 127
    Walter 127
pipe & tabor 236-7, *236*, 262
Pitchford 64
Pitt, Humphrey 229-30
Pitts, John, ballad printer 258
place names 25, 26-30, 71, 76, 130, 183, 190
Plaish 71
    Hall 132
Platt Bridge 77
plays 261, 273-90
    Dr. Forster 280
    mummers' 284-90, *284*
    mystery *278*
    Prince Musidorus 280, 281
    Rigs of Time, The 282-3

St. George and the Fiery Dragon 280
Two Disciples going to Emmaus, The 274, 275
Valentine and Orson 281-2
Plealy, nr. Pontesbury 304
Plowden, family 87-8
plygain 310
Pontesbury 33, 41, 162, 237, 262, 304, 316
Pontesford 41
    Hill 16, 295, *295*
    Wakes 16
Pool Quay 50
Porth-y-Waun 197
    Cooper's Quarry 195
    Limekiln Inn 195
Pradoe Park, nr. Eardiston 130
Preece, William 20
Prees 32, 33, 141, 273
    Hawk and Buckle Inn 79
    High Heath 167
Preston Boats 53
Preston-on-the-Weald Moors 53
Price, Samson 244
    Stephen 152, *153*
pride/prejudice 36-7
Pritchard, Rev. 130
Prolley Moor 148
Prys, Stafford 255
Puck 33
pudding bell 106
Pulestone, Sir Roger de *83*
Pulpit Rock 18
Pump Action, ceilidh band 271

quacks 168-70
quarrymen 174, 191, 195-8, 267, 269
Quatford 20, 29, 34, 86, *87*
guilds (see under Shrewsbury)
quoiting 263

Randall, John 192
Rampaigne, John de 79
Ratlinghope 41
    Horseshoe Inn 220
Raven, Michael 15, 117, 118, 129, 130, 139, 190,
        209, 230
Raven's Bowl, Wrekin 14
Ray, Phyllis 302
recreation 34
Red Castle, Hawkstone Park 15, 70, 77
'Red Moll' *xiii*, 155
Redlake, River 26
remedies 160-1
    ague and fever 165
    bleeding 165
    drawing a thorn 166
    rheumatism 161
    royal touch, the 169
    scalds and burns 165

scrofula 169-70
strains and sprains 165-6
toothache 153
warts 162
Rhiwallon of Powys 72
Rhyd-y-Groes 71, 72
Rhydderch, John, ballad printer 255
Richard's Castle 34
'riding the stang' 154
Rix, Michael 303, 304, 315, 316
Robin Hood's Butts 16
Rodington 34, 208, 306
Rodney, Admiral Lord 6-7
Rodney's Pillar 1, 6-7, *6*, *101*
Rogationtide 118, 298
Rogers, family, of Ironbridge 51-2
    Eustace 52, *52*
    Harry 52
    Tom 51
Rogers, John, ballad printer 255
Roman Bath, nr. Plaish 71
Rorrington 54, 66, 151, 217, 280
Rushbury 35, 116, 117, 316
Ruyton-XI-Towns 23, 66, 220

St. Alkmund 86
St. Andrew's Day, eve of (10 Nov) 308
St. Calixtus 88
St. Eatha 88
St. Ethelfleda 85
St. George's 195, *195*
St. Melangell 110
St. Milburga 60-3, *62*
    grave 62, 63
St. Milburga's Well 63, *63*
St. Oswald 59
St. Oswald's Well 59-60, *59*
St. Swithin's Day 189
St. Thomas's Day (21 Dec) 308, 309
St. Winifred 60, *60*, 86
St. Wistan 86
Salter, John, ballad printer 255
sanctuary, claiming 110
Scapula, Ostorius 69
Scudamore, Phillip 75
Selattyn 3, 4, 5, 27, 32, 33, 72, 81, 90
Seven Whistlers 74, 171, 192
Severn, River *xi*, *xii*, 3, 7, 14, 15, 18, 20, 22, 24, 30,
    32, 37, 38, 41, 47-53, *47*, 71, 95, 103, 115,
    135, 213
Seward, Ann 198
Seymour, John 244
Sharp, Cecil 240, 241, 244, 310, 312
'sharpshins' 36
Skakehead, Egwin 88
Shakespeare 75, 93, 95, 115, 280, 283
Shavington 41
Shaw, John 250

Shawbury 280
sheila-na-gig 114, *115*
Sheinton, nr. Much Wenlock 250, 251
Shelton Oak 75-6, *75*, 298
Shelve 280
Sherrifhales 166
Sherwood, William 251
Shifnal 33, 35, 95, 105, 220, 230, 266, 305, 308
Shipton Hall 129, *129*
Shomere 58
Shrawardine 41, 115
    Castle 83
Shrawley 20
shrew's bridle 155
Shrewsbury *xii*, 2, 3, 4, 13, 20, 22, 27, 28, 29, *29*,
    30, 32, 34, 35, 36, 37, 40, 41, 47, 48, *49*,
    50, 60, 68, 71, 72, 74, 75, 80, 86, 95,
    104, 105, 132, 134-5, 143, 145, 155, 166,
    169, 176, 187, 190, 204, 205, 208, 209,
    218, 220, 222-8, 231, 232, 233, 234,
    235, 236, 237, 250, 253, 254, 255, *255*,
    256, 257, 258, 263, 266, 267, 274, 275,
    276, *277*, 278, 279, 291, 296, 298, 302,
    304, 310
    Abbey 20, 47, 132
    Abbey Foregate 40, 217
    Admiral Benbow Inn *254*
    Bakers Row 35
    Barge Inn, Mountfields 213
    battle of 26-27, 75
    Cardellan 36
    Castle 18, 71
    Cornchepynge 35
    Corvisors Row 35
    Ditherington 302
    Dogpole 35
    English Bridge 213
    Frankwell 35, 236
    guilds 224, 232, 274, 277
        Glovers 265
        Shearmen 223, 232, 233
    Kingsland 224, *225*, 227
    Lion Inn 131, *131*, 213
    Mardol 35
    Merival 36
    Monkmoor 302
    Murivance 35-6
    Quarry, the 227, 277, 304
    St. Chad's 89, 107, 276, 298
    St. Mary's 254, 263
    School 132, *225*, 227, 274, 275, 278, 279
    Sextry 36
    Shete Place 36
    Show (Flower), the 176, 204, 222-8, *222-7*, 305
    Tomboldesham 36
    Weeping Cross, the 223
    Wyle Cop 35, 36
Shropshire Militia 257

Shrovetide 291-3
    Tuesday 8, 291-3
Silvington 147
simnels 293-308, *294*
sin-eating 172
Skyborry 32, 144-5
Smallman, Major Thomas 82
Smethcott 104
Smith, Mrs. Esther, née Whatton/Wharton 244
    Hubert 242
Smout, Becky 147
    Charles 176
Snailbeach 296
snowdrops 319-20
songs 229-30
    'The Farmer's Boy' 245-6
    'Outlandish Knight'/'Six Pretty Maids' 247-9
    souling song 306-7
    'True Salopian Hunting Song, A' 211-2
    'When the Frost is on the Pumpkin' 249-50
Springwell Pit, Little Dawley 194
Stanley, Sir Thomas 93-4
Stanton, villages of 38-9
    Lacy 60, *61*, 89, *92*, 94, 98, 120, 133, 236,
        237, 263
    Long 29, 63, 108, 110, 262, 263
Stanton-upon-Hine-Heath 33
Stapeley Hill 24
Stenton, Francis, wait 234
Stiperstones 8, 9, 14, 15-6, 30, 72, 73, 124, 142-3
Stirchley 33
Stoke St. Milborough 61, *62*, 86, *86*, 92, 119, 264,
    279
Stoke-upon-Tern 33, 90, 152
    Petsey 133, *133*
Stokesay 33, 39, 96, 99, 100, 103, 108, 109, 262
    Castle 17-18, *18*
stone circles 8-13
Stow 42, *44*, 69, 159, 262, 263
Strange, Alf 150, 161, 174, 184, 215
    Joseph 215
Stretton Hills 2, 124
Stretton Westwood 266
Stubbes, Philip 208
    Squire of Beckbury 212
Styche Hall, Moreton Say 129
superstitions 149-68, 171-4
    birth 150
    christening 150
    courtship 151-4
    death 171-4
    luck 158-60
    marriage 151-4
    working practices 160
Sutton 33, 223
Sutton Maddock 33
Swainson, Charles 160
Swift, Jonathan 28

Swyney, Mrs. 155, 185
Sydney, Phlip 278

Talbot, John, conjuror 166
Tallis, William 129
Tarlton, Richard *236*
Taylor, Dr. 208, 223, 278, 296
Telford 96, 124
Teme, River *xiii*, 30, 39, 47, *48*, 65, 69, 144, 292,
    299
Tenbury, Worcs. 279, *309*
Tennant, Enoch 197-8
tennis 263
Thackeray, Veronica 84, 124, 135, 215, 308
Thomas, Edward *xii*
    William 100
'thomasing' 209
Tibberton 39
Timmins, H.T. 8, 36, 114, 218
'tin-panning' 154
tithes 120-1
Titterstone Clee 2, 119, *196*
    Cottage, Bitterley 138, *138*
    Wake 193, 217
Todley Tom 167-8
Tomkys, Rev. 223
Tong 102, 104, 105, 113, 117, 118, 129-30
    Castle 72
treasure, buried (*see* buried treasure)
Trewern 32
Trial, The 199
trowmen 49-50
trows 48
Tudor, Henry 68
Tudur, Edwin 96
Tugford 35, *107*, 108, 109, 114, *115*
tunnels 18-20
Turpin, Dick 27, 79
Tyack, Rev. G.S. 117, 150
Tyn-y-Rhos Hall, Weston Rhyn 138

Uffington 33
United Hunt, the 215
Uppington 90
Upton Cressett 18, 104
    Magna 29, 104

Vale, Edmund 67, 141, 143
Vardy, George 142-3
Vaughan, Sir William 82
Vaughan Williams, Ralph 244
Viam, John 131-2
Villa, The 18
Villiers, Sir John 152
Vyrnwy, River 7, 21, 30, 32, 37, 47, 50, 74, 89

Waidson, James, ballad printer 256
  Mary 256
  R. 256, 257
waits 231, *232*, 233, 234
Wake Sunday 8
wakes 204, 206, 216-7, 280, 284, 295, 303, 305
Walcot, family 87-8
wall paintings 116, *116*
Walton, nr. High Ercall 167
Ward, Roger 254-5
warlocks 91, 143
wassailers 291, 315
Waters, Brian 50, 53, 209, 211
Watkin, Isaac 56, 109
Watkins, Alfred 3
Wat's Dyke 4
Wattleborough 153
Wattlesbury 221
Weale, Magdalene 96, 124, 163, 220, 242
weather lore 188-9
Webb, Sir Aston 113
  Mary *xiii*, xiii, 16, 56, 160, 162, 172, 187,
    208, 295
  Matthew 51
Wellington 13, 64, 109, 117, 170, 175, 221, 225,
    250, 279, 293, 298, 306
  St. Margaret's Well 296
wells 30, 48, 59-66, 71, 86, 189, 296
Welsh, language, names 2, 7, 8, 21, 25, 26, 27, 29-
    32, 42, 50, 59, 71
  printers 255
  relations with 74-7
Welsh Frankton 24, 150, 183, 215
Welshampton 306
Wem 33, 37, 38, 42, 64, 83, 103, 105, 107, 109,
    135-6, 139-40, *139*, *140*, 154, 172, 173,
    175, 176, 210, 221, 253, 273, 300, 304,
    308
  Ranters 37
Wenlock Edge 7, 17, 48, 83, 136-7
  Priory 19, 63, *63*, 130, *143*
Wenlock, Reece, conjuror 166
Wentnor 34, 96
West Felton 32, 33, 35, 280, 306, 307
Westbury 33, 34, 97, 221, 262, 263, 280
Weston Lullingfields 183
Weston Rhyn 304
  Tyn-y-Rhos Hall 138
Westwood, nr. Wenlock 146-7
Whethill 217
Whetstones, the, Corndon Hill 8
Whirlstone, the 8
Whitchurch 30, 34, 76, 86, 103, 267, 175, 221, 266,
    276, 304
Whitcot Keysett, stone at 5
White Ladies Priory 80, 81
Whitehead, Joseph 298
Whiteladies, nr. Tong 80, 129-30

Whiting, Mrs. 244
Whitsburn Hill 8
Whitsun 263, 264, 266, 276, 277, 278, 279, 299
Whittington 30, 90, 306
  Castle 78, *78*, 79
Whixall 252
Widerley 40
wife-selling 155-7
Wiggins (a miller) 138
Wild Edric (see Edric the Wild)
  Humphrey (see Kynaston, Humphrey)
  Hunt 63-4
Wilderhope Manor *82*, 83
Wilkinson, John ('Iron Mad') 199-201
Willey 199, 265
  Hall 213, 215
William, The 50
William I, King 72, 73
Williams, Hywel 25
  Tim 46, 168
  William, ballad printer 255
wimberry picking 8, 187-8, *188*, 240, 242
Wingfield, John 40
Wistanstow 33, 86, 104, 110
Withering, William 170
witches/craft 9, 12, 91, 123, 124, 143, 145-8, 159,
    167, 168, 241
  defences against 148
wizards 130, 162, 163, 166, 167
Woden 59
Wollaston 100
Wood, the (farmhouse) 136
Wood, Henry 251
Woolstaston 33, 41
Woolston 60, 86
Woore 191
Wordy 32
Worfield 33, 34, 35, 89-90, *90*, 152, 231, 275
Worthen 35, 95, 280
Wrekin, The *xi-xii*, xi, *xiv*, *1*, 2, 13-5, *13*, 30, 41,
    64, 71, 147, 181, 296, 303
  Bladder Stone 14, 15
  Heaven Gate 114
  Hell Gate 14
  Needle's Eye 14, *14*, 15
  Raven's Bowl / Cuckoo's Cup 14
  Wakes 217, 218
Wrexham 275
Wright, Thomas 10, 17, 35, 57, 58, 141
Wrockwardine 33, 148
Wroxeter 13, 15, 17, 70, *70*, 71, 102, *106*, 109
W.T., conjuror 168

Yardington 168
yew trees 90-1, *90*, *91*, 161
yule log 309
Yr Hên Ddinas, Old Oswestry 70

Other Shropshire titles from Logaston Press

Shropshire Almshouses *by* Sylvia Watts

This book considers the nearly 40 surviving almshouses in the county, founded between the 12th and 20th centuries. Their history is often intriguing: the personalities of the founders, the sometimes diminished enthusiasm of his or her descendants when faced with repair bills, the greater or lesser efforts of Trustees to manage the buildings down the decades, the degree of social control to which the residents were subjected, and the ways which those residents found to evade the rules and regulations.

144 pages with 50 colour and 15 black and white illustrations
Paperback £12.95   (ISBN 978 1906663 31 5)

The Story of Shrewsbury *by* Mary de Saulles

Shrewsbury has a rich history, having been a frontier town and a centre of England's thriving medieval woollen industry sited on a major trading river. Wealth was also brought to the town as a result of the abbey becoming a centre for pilgrimage. The abbey was also the early industrial hub of the city, and the venue for two early parliaments. In the Georgian period the town began to exert its influence as the county town, where the gentry came to spend their leisure time at the various entertainments. But not all was gentility, for the river encouraged the establishment of industries, from noxious tanyards in the medieval period, to equally troublesome leadworks and noisy cloth and spinning enterprises. With the coming of the railways, suburbs grew and the economy diversified. After the Second World War, the town's rich architectural heritage was threatened by redevelopment.

272 pages with 120 colour and 100 black and white illustrations
Paperback   £15   (ISBN 978 1906663 68 1)

Severn *by* Richard Hayman

The Severn is one of Britain's great rivers. It was on an island in the Severn in 1016 that Cnut and Edmund settled their competing claims to the throne of England, and it was at the Severn that the English formally recognised Llywelyn ap Gruffudd as the Prince of Wales. From the Iron Age to the Second World War, regimes have built fortresses and other defences to ensure their control over the Severn and, throughout the Civil Wars, Royalists and Parliamentarians fought bitterly for possession of it. Three of Britain's finest bridges were built over the Severn – the medieval Welsh Bridge in Shrewsbury, the 18th-century Iron Bridge and the modern Severn Bridge. Along the riverbank are also the smaller details of history, the redundant slipways, stone quays, canal interchanges, mills and warehouses, all of which are remnants of once vibrant riverside industry. The Severn is also one of the few British rivers big enough to have engendered its own culture.

272 pages with over 120 colour and 20 black and white illustrations
Paperback   £15   (ISBN 978 1906663 66 7)